Trajectories of Empire

Trajectories of Empire

Transhispanic Reflections on the African Diaspora

Edited by
JEROME C. BRANCHE

VANDERBILT UNIVERSITY PRESS
Nashville, Tennessee

Copyright 2022 Vanderbilt University Press
All rights reserved
First printing 2022

Cover image: Jean Baptiste Debret, "Marchand de Fleurs, a la Porte d'Une Eglise," *Voyage Pittoresque et Historique au Bresil (Paris, 1834–39)*, vol. 3, plate 6, p. 125 (top).

Library of Congress Cataloging-in-Publication Data
Names: Branche, Jerome, editor.
Title: Trajectories of empire : transhispanic reflections on the African diaspora / edited by Jerome Branche.
Description: Nashville, Tennessee : Vanderbilt University Press, [2022] | Includes bibliographical references and index.
Identifiers: LCCN 2022000550 (print) | LCCN 2022000551 (ebook) | ISBN 9780826504593 (paperback) | ISBN 9780826504609 (hardcover) | ISBN 9780826504616 (epub) | ISBN 9780826504623 (pdf)
Subjects: LCSH: Black people—Iberian Peninsula—History. | Black people—Iberian Peninsula—Social conditions. | Black people—Latin America—History. | Black people—Latin America—Social conditions. | African diaspora. | Iberian Peninsula—Race relations—History. | Latin America—Race relations—History.
Classification: LCC DP53.B45 T73 2022 (print) | LCC DP53.B45 (ebook) | DDC 305.896046—dc23/eng/20220328
LC record available at https://lccn.loc.gov/2022000550
LC ebook record available at https://lccn.loc.gov/2022000551

Contents

Acknowledgments vii

Introduction 1
Jerome C. Branche

PART I. THE IBERIAN SCENARIO

1. Tracing the "Fragmentary Facts" of a Foundational Slave Voyage 11
   Elizabeth R. Wright

2. *Christianos nigros*: Afro-Iberian Confraternities' Social and Cultural Roles 29
   Miguel A. Valerio

3. In Search of the Black Swordsman: Race and Martial Arts Discourse in Early Modern Iberia 46
   Manuel Olmedo Gobante

4. On Enslaving and Impalement: The "Life" and Death of Chicaba, Black Woman Saint in Empire 79
   Jerome C. Branche

PART II. CONTINUING EXPANSIONISM AND THE CIRCUM-ATLANTIC

5. Facing the Enslaved: Explorations for a Transatlantic Archive 103
   Agnes Lugo-Ortiz

6. A Postcard from Wakanda to the King of Spain: The Portrait of the *Mulatos de Esmeraldas* (1599) 142
   Baltasar Fra-Molinero

7. A Transhistorical and Translocal View of the Luso-Brazilian Imperial/Colonial World through the Poetry of Gregório de Matos (1636–1695) to Domingos Caldas Barbosa (1740–1800) 161
   Lúcia Helena Costigan

8. Silences and the Corporeal: The Enslaved Body in (Historical) Pain 191
   Cassia Roth

PART III. AFRO-LATIN AMERICA:
BLACK MARGINALITY IN THE NEW CENTURY

9. Racial Dynamics and Tensions in Twenty-First Century
   Post-Revolutionary Cuba   215
   Alberto Abreu

10. *Senzalas e Quilombos Modernos*: Evoking the Legacy of Slavery
    in Brazilian Hip Hop   245
    Eliseo Jacob

11. Honoring the Bones beneath Us: Conjuring Black Heritage
    in the Performances of "Intervenções Urbanas" in the Gamboa
    Neighborhood, Rio de Janeiro   265
    Maria Andrea dos Santos Soares

Contributors   283
Index   289

Acknowledgments

I'd like to express my sincerest thanks to my colleagues who contributed chapters toward the realization of this volume. Thanks as well to the named and unnamed production team at Vanderbilt University Press: to Zachary Gresham, the acquisitions editor, to Joell Smith-Borne, the managing production editor, and especially to the copyeditor, Laura Fry, for her painstaking and meticulous copyediting. Here at Pitt, a debt of gratitude is owed to the European Studies Center for its support of the project during the recent Year of Global Europe, and to the Faculty Research and Scholarship Program of the Graduate Studies Office, as well, for underwriting the project.

Introduction

JEROME C. BRANCHE

The present volume follows a roughly historical trajectory and visits representative sites of the African diaspora within what used to be the Ibero-American empire in order to highlight some of the experiences and realities of Africans and their descendants in Spain and Portugal and in their former colonies in the Americas. Its basic objective is to explore salient issues in imperial domination, accommodation, race/ing, and resistance, in relation to these experiences, that have largely escaped the attention of traditional, discipline-bound scholarship. The varying contributions, made in the spirit of interdisciplinary "dialogue" among the chapter writers, representing history, visual culture, anthropology, cultural studies, as well as traditional literary analysis, will hopefully allow our readers a greater appreciation of the workings of empire as these workings filter through the operationality of church and state, through the canonical premises of art, literature, science, language, and everyday life, and through the way they shaped the experience/s of Afro-diasporans in the Ibero-Atlantic world over time and space.[1] We have accordingly made a historico-spatial division that speaks to the fifteenth-century beginnings of the phenomenon as it manifests itself in Iberian maritime expansionism and the ensuing settlement of Africans in the Iberian Peninsula, exploring thereby their integration into Spanish and Portuguese society, both within and outside of bondage. After that, we turn our attention to the centuries-long (colonial) interim in Latin America, and then finally to the question of Black marginality in the twentieth and twenty-first centuries, where we offer two paradigmatic examples of Cuba and Brazil as independent republics in order to provide a sense of what Black cultural critique and the Black condition is like in these postcolonial states in the face of the ever-present Eurocentric premise.

Trajectories of Empire also stresses that although African American Studies, and the wider-reaching field of Africana Studies, have both earned themselves curricular and institutional recognition over the past few decades, it is significant that the anti-Black ethic that is central to modernity in its imperial register, and which these teaching and research enterprises pursue, is also a key feature of Iberian colonialism and is largely lacking in these areas of study, particularly bearing in mind the epistemologies of power and control that characterize both the Spanish and the Portuguese as the first of the modern global empires. We recognize, similarly, that even the fields of Latin American and Ibero-American studies, evocative as they are of the Black diaspora, particularly through slavery and contract labor in the colonial and postcolonial scenarios and through the ideologies of social stratification and their racial analogues over time, lack a diachronic and synchronic account of these themes' effects on Black subjectivity and the Black historical presence, hence our focus on them here. We acknowledge, of course, our own space limitations in this volume, as there is much more that might be said on our topic in relation to both our general premise and its applicability to such other locations as Panama, Colombia, or Mexico. We are confident, however, that the reflections contained herein provide fruitful points of departure for further inquiry, given the time and place coordinates we follow, as well as the topic's breadth.

Our initial chapters, which cover the meaning and significance of the first shipload of captive Africans to Portugal in 1444 (Elizabeth Wright); the contemporaneous establishment of Black brotherhoods in the Peninsula (Miguel Valerio); the involvement of these early "Afro-Iberians," also as freed individuals, in the socially ascendant activity of fencing (Manuel Olmedo); or their curious incorporation into the Church (Jerome C. Branche), all have this historical trajectory as their objective. So, too, does our attention to the Afro-accented Portuguese language in two Brazilian poets of the seventeenth and eighteenth centuries, Gregorio de Matos and Domingos Caldos Barbosa (Helena Costigan), and, in the genre of portrait painting of the period, to the personae of the marginal Black subjects (Agnes Lugo-Ortiz). In this latter regard, the political significance of the famous 1599 portrait of *Los mulatos de Esmeraldas* stands out for its implicit challenge to the imperial iconography and its racialist counterpoints (Baltasar Fra-Molinero). By the nineteenth century, with the onset of scientific racism proper, the benign dismissal of the humanity of Black female patients in Brazilian medical discourse, which too often put their lives in danger (Cassia Roth), complemented the region's endorsement of the European-derived "racial contract," starkly illustrated in subsequent immigration policies that sought to increase the White demographic both in Brazil and in the Spanish-speaking republics. We anticipate, also, that our readers will be able to connect the dots across the historical and geographical maps, as evidence of the old (imperial) racial dictum persists in evolved formats more than a century after purportedly enlightened precepts underwrote both emancipation in its moment and the politico-ideological profiles of independent statehood in Spanish and Portuguese America, thereby forcing Black and other racialized subalterns into a multilateral defense of their rights to a dignified selfhood, as evinced in our final chapters on contemporary Cuba and Brazil.

The first section, The Iberian Scenario, starts with Elizabeth Wright's chapter, "Tracing the 'Fragmentary Facts' of a Foundational Slave Voyage." Here the author revisits the arrival of the first Portuguese cargo of sub-Saharan captives, 235 in number, and discusses Gomes Eanes da Zurara's transhistorical role in his chronicling of the larger event pertaining to the "discovery and conquest" of Africa.[2] With Wright we witness particular rhetorical turns and emphases of imperial discourse that would repeat themselves over time and help form the triumphalist template of *crônicas* and travel writing that would evolve into their own genre. Important among these texts of empire would be the writers' apologia for Euro-Christian supremacy and the evangelical project, seen in this case through Zurara's emphasis on the young male African, who would turn out to be a "devout auxiliary" in a Franciscan convent, and his simultaneous dismissal of the inevitable trauma of the other captives in describing their purportedly happy and untroubled cultural assimilation into Portuguese society. In Chapter 2, Miguel Valerio's "*Christianos nigros*: Afro-Iberian Confraternities' Social and Cultural Roles" highlights the function of these associations of mutual assistance for formerly enslaved Africans and Afrodescendants, both in the Iberian Peninsula and in colonial Latin America, and makes the important point that their early establishment in the middle of the fifteenth century (1455) predated the ubiquitous cultural marker of the first transatlantic Columbus voyage (1492), even as the tradition of solidarity and social and cultural recuperation they established would color the wider processes of syncretism and transculturation in the Americas for centuries to come.

Manuel Olmedo's Chapter 3, "In Search of the Black Swordsman: Race and Martial Arts Discourse in Early Modern Iberia," offers a rare glimpse of Afro-Hispanics' deployment of the few available legal precepts governing racialized identity within the imperial order, in which an affirmation of ethnic Blackness on the part of the Alba-Medrano clan (their Wolof lineage), would distinguish them from the even more socially suspect *moriscos* in Spain, whose association with Islam still linked them with earlier moments of rebellion at the turn of the century (1499–1501), and again in 1568–1570. This was seen in the infamous Alpujarra uprisings, as the country aggressively moved from centuries of religious and cultural diversity toward Catholic uniformity. The 1600 lawsuit filed by the Alba-Medranos in 1600, to have themselves officially deemed Black/Christian vis-à-vis the *morisco* ethnic community, aimed primarily to protect their aspirations to social orthodoxy and insiderness—particularly since it guaranteed their right to bear arms, the art of swordsmanship itself being a link to gainful employment—as well as to respectability and upward social mobility. The chapter offers a specific instance of a member of a Black confraternity responding to a case of "racial profiling" and asserting his right to carry a sword and to the prestige associated with the art of fencing. Significantly, the discussion allows us to see an affirmative dimension in the real-world experience of the Afro-Spanish in contrast to the limiting negative stereotypes to be found in Golden Age writing.

(Dominant) Catholicism, in its evangelical register this time, is again the topic of Chapter 4, with Branche's discussion of the controlling hand of the amanuensis, Father Miguel de Paniagua, in the fashioning of the *Exemplary Life of the Venerable Mother Teresa Juliana de Santo Domingo* (1752), according to the structure and precepts of the hagiographic genre. The chapter, "On Enslaving and Impalement: The 'Life' and Death of Chicaba, Black Woman Saint in Empire," reviews the life story of the nine-year-old captive Chicaba, who passes from seventeen years of slavery in the home of the Marquis of Mancera to a further four decades of service at La Penitencia convent at Salamanca. The chapter proposes that any hypothetical agency and autonomy of the persona of Chicaba is buried under the rhetoric of suffering and Christlike sacrifice that ostensibly defines the lives of saints and their corresponding hagiographies. It also proposes that the autobiography helps establish the narrative superstructure of colonialism and racism by celebrating slavery in Europe over freedom in Africa and by having the subject disavow her family and her cultural past while overlooking the material and symbolic violence of her captors, supposedly in the name of "evangelization."

If Chicaba's, or the Venerable Mother Teresa's, story represents the voice of evangelical and imperial "success" writ large even as it enhances the writerly persona of De Paniagua, the amanuensis, it turns out that the imperial portraiture conventions of the circum-Atlantic in the period covering the sixteenth to the nineteenth centuries would reprise the paradigm of subjection for empire's African captives. Agnes Lugo-Ortiz begins the second section, "Continuing Expansionism and the Circum-Atlantic," in Chapter 5, "Facing the Enslaved: Explorations for a Transatlantic Archive." She examines the development of what she calls a "metaphysics of the subject, by which the enslaved of the colonies" become the Other in front of whom "the essentiality of the European 'One' is established." Lugo-Ortiz goes on to trace a visual economy across time in which Black faces would appear mainly as a function of enhancement of the primary White personae or of dominant White civilization, whether in the conventions of courtly portraiture or in the subsequent daguerreotype photos of Black heads and profiles that physiognomy and phrenology used to underwrite the scientific racism of the eighteen-hundreds. Her analysis offers a striking documentary contrast to the overly reproduced image of the laboring body of the enslaved, with which the visual archive is saturated, to focus on the *face*, for what it tells us of the intentionality of dominant representational practice, which, even as it apprehends the enslaved as visage, simultaneously inscribes his or her ontological unimportance vis-à-vis those White subjects whose presence creates the contrast.

In this broad panorama, Juan de Pareja, biracial slave to Spanish painter Diego Velázquez, would famously insert himself into the archive, not as dishonorable social subaltern, following established custom, but as a dignified and *Christian* gentleman, in his famous *The Calling of Saint Matthew* (1661). In a similar instance of visual counternarration, Baltasar Fra-Molinero's Chapter 6, "A Postcard from Wakanda to the King of Spain: The Portrait of the *Mulatos de Esmeraldas* (1599)," discusses the 1599 painting by Ecuadoran painter Andrés Sánchez Gallque of three armed and richly clothed Black leaders from the Esmeraldas Maroon province, allowing us to appreciate not only the commanding centrality of their personae but, just as importantly, their spears, emblems of their autonomy and political agency. He proposes that the fact that the subjects' imposing presence continues to be so easily communicated hundreds of years later to two young Black visitors at Madrid's Museo de América, to the degree that they immediately associate them with the invincibility of the fictional Wakanda of the recent Hollywood blockbuster *Black Panther* (2018), speaks to the Afrofuturistic potentiality of the piece and to the horizon of liberation. In this colonial-era portrait by an Indigenous painter, the other subaltern personae silently perform a counterdiscursive role to the sustained inferiority that the dominant tradition would wish to naturalize.

In Chapter 7, "A Transhistorical and Translocal View of the Luso-Brazilian Imperial/Colonial World through the Poetry of Gregório de Matos (1636–1695) to Domingos Caldas Barbosa (1740–1800)," Lúcia Costigan allows us to see, in the case of the former, a *mazombo* or "local White" from Salvador da Bahia and, in the case of the latter, a *mulato* from Rio de Janeiro, the effect of race on their creative work and on its contemporary and subsequent critical reception. We thereby appreciate, via De Matos, that being "White, but not quite," per Homi Bhabha, carries with it a penalty for the Brazilian in seventeenth-century Portugal, particularly given his penchant for satire and for infusing his lyric with the Tupi and African resonances of his Brazilian vernacular.[3] The censorship of his writerly persona and of his work, even in Brazil, by the guardians of Portuguese (imperial) linguistic and canonical purity would persist until the second half of the twentieth century. Not dissimilarly, in 1770s Coimbra the biracial *carioca* native, Caldas Barbosa, absent the support of his Portuguese father, is forced by circumstance to become an itinerant singer and to peddle his native *lundus* and *modinhas* for their exotic value at the Portuguese court, disturbing its placidity but introducing a tropical content that would enrich it, as has so often been the case when the marginal Afro-descendant culture meets the metropolitan.

Cassia Roth's Chapter 8, "Silences and the Corporeal: The Enslaved Body in (Historical) Pain," trains a critical lens on the clinical reports that document medical (gynecological, obstetric) practice in the eighteen hundreds in order to highlight the differential treatment received by Afro-Brazilian women in childbirth, vis-à-vis their Eurodescendant counterparts, and the effect of this treatment on the former. To the extent that physicians disregard the personhood of the enslaved women entrusted to their care, Roth argues, or seem impervious to their pain in their clinical practice, they formalize and authorize the notion of their subhumanity. Roth therefore exhorts fellow researchers today to read between the lines of these medical reports and to practice a "corporeal reading" that might appropriately acknowledge the visceral and imaginary impact of the medical archive and thereby accord these subjects the racial justice historically denied them. Her intervention is a most timely one, given the once-in-a-century pandemic that descended upon us in 2020 and the much commented upon COVID-19 vaccine hesitancy among African Americans, given the increasing awareness of past crimes perpetrated against Black bodies in the name of medical science.

In Chapter 9, the first chapter that addresses the contemporary section, "Afro-Latin America: Black Marginality in the New Century," Alberto Abreu, writing on the "Racial Dynamics and Tensions in Twenty-First Century Post-Revolutionary Cuba," reminds us of the perceived threat of Blacks as fellow citizens of a hypothetical post-slavery republic, as documented in Cuban nineteenth-century historiography in the wake of the Haitian Revolution. Between the alarmist and negrophobic narrative of the slave-owning classes of the eighteen-hundreds and the guarded inclusion of the Revolution in the second half of the twentieth century, Abreu sees a politics of discourse that has translated, in its most optimistic registers, into the folklorization of African cultural premises. In highlighting the "unfinished" nature of the Cuban Revolution, he also points to a vigorous counter-narrative by Afro-Cuban voices, which have occupied available contemporary digital platforms and have gained in stridency after their more tentative beginnings at the start of the revolution in the 1960s. Eliseo Jacob's Chapter 10, "*Senzalas e Quilombos Modernos*: Evoking the Legacy of Slavery in Brazilian Hip Hop," also focuses on the fate of Afro-Brazilians facing the extended fallout of slavery. His chapter signals, importantly, the role of hip-hop artists in keeping the wider public aware of the antihuman menace of the carceral state and its genocidal implications for Brazil's Black and poor mestizo populations, reprising such slavery-era tropes as the Big House and the Slave Quarters (*Casa grande e senzala*), the quilombo/favela geography of historical disadvantage and marginalization, and the obfuscation created by Freyrean notions of racial democracy in Brazil. Finally, Maria Andrea dos Santos Soares's Chapter 11, "Honoring the Bones beneath Us: Conjuring Black Heritage in the Performances of 'Intervenções Urbanas' in the Gamboa Neighborhood, Rio de Janeiro," complements Jacob's essay in its focus on the transgenerational, ongoing marginalization and commodification of Afro-Brazilian culture. Her essay focuses on the recent rediscovery of the Valongo wharf in Rio, where slave ships docked historically to unload their cargo, its repeated "burial" and repurposing by the authorities, its recent recognition by both an astute White commercial class and the representatives of the Black Movement, and the ensuing contest between the two over its value, whether as cultural heritage for the Black community or as marketable motifs for the White-dominated tourist industry. The essay, for its focus on the (unearthed) bones of the captives who made the

Middle Passage but who did not quite make it into colonialism's production machinery, may nonetheless be seen as marking the end of the journey that the African body was made to travel from the slave trade's somber beginnings in 1444, as explored by Elizabeth Wright at the beginning of the book. They constitute a telling sign of Empire's sustained politics as it pertains to the Africans it engaged and conscripted and a fitting material counterpoint to its narratives of evangelism.

Our intention in these essays, then, is to continue to tell the long story of the diaspora, with attention to the imperial project responsible for the greatest number of uprooted Africans, and to look beyond the easy rhetorics of enlightenment and emancipation in the Iberian and Ibero-American colonial world, of mestizaje and racial democracy in the period of the new republics, or more latterly of their purportedly multiculturalist inclusion. Our aim is to show not only the big picture of imperially originated racialized power but also the ongoing challenges faced by Afrodescendant citizens both on the Iberian Peninsula and here in the Americas, as these have persisted, and to argue for its focused study, particularly given its wide geographical expanse and its historical extension. If we paint with a broad brush, it is because the geography and the longevity of Empire demands it, and it is our hope that the chapters, in the individual "disciplinary" or interdisciplinary foci, provoke further inquiry into this vastly rich but still insufficiently studied area.

NOTES

1. The chapters derive from presentations and the ensuing conversations that took place on April 4–6, 2019, at the symposium "Empire and its Aftermath: Transhispanic Dialogues on Diaspora" at the University of Pittsburgh.
2. Gomes Eanes Da Zurara, *The Chronicle of the Discovery and Conquest of Guinea*, vol. 1, trans. C. R. Beazley and E. Prestage (New York: Hakluyt Society and Burt Franklin, 2010).
3. Homi Bhabha, *The Location of Culture* (New York: Routledge, 1994), 86.

PART I

THE IBERIAN SCENARIO

CHAPTER I

Tracing the "Fragmentary Facts" of a Foundational Slave Voyage

ELIZABETH R. WRIGHT

The spark of inspiration for my reflections on diaspora comes from Arturo Schomburg (1874–1938), the prominent historian and bibliophile of the Harlem Renaissance. In 1926, he traveled from New York to Spain in search of archival documents, books, and oral history that would cast more light on Afro-Hispanic artists, intellectuals, and artisans. This fact-finding trip culminated in decades of research and reflection on Blacks in the Hispanic world that began in Schomburg's native Puerto Rico and continued in New York City.[1] His first port of call in Spain was Seville, where he asked those he met a seemingly simple question, whose vague and contradictory responses still resonate: had they known any Blacks in their city? An antiquarian book dealer told the New York visitor he had encountered "a few during his boyhood but these had gone to their fathers' home."[2] Schomburg was perplexed. Hadn't Washington Irving in the previous century encountered numerous Afro-descendant *Sevillanos*? Confronted with an utter lack of awareness of the contributions of Blacks in Seville from its time as Spain's gateway to the Atlantic world, the New York bibliophile concluded that "the judgement of history has closed its case and posterity has reduced to dust the fragmentary facts which might justify our belief."[3] This metaphor for the fragility of historical memory—archival records and material traces float away as countless dust particles—is still apt.

A testament to this abiding problem comes at the conclusion of Alessandro Stella's indispensable study of slavery from 2000, which focuses on Cadiz in the later part of the early modern era. In a section titled "À la recherche des Africains disparus," Stella puzzles at the disjuncture between the extensive presence of enslaved and free Blacks in Andalusia in the early modern era and the almost complete lack of awareness about this history.[4] This problem remains, as attested to in Tamar Herzog's article of 2012, "How Did Early Modern Slaves in Spain Disappear?" Pondering the lack of awareness of diasporic Black Africans in Spain, Herzog notes that the debates about Spanish citizenship that engendered the 1812 Constitution of Cádiz pivoted on the assumption that individuals of African descent lived in the Spanish New World, not peninsular Spain. This blind spot where Black Africans in Spain are concerned is significant, given that the Constitution of Cádiz is the charter that reconstituted the Spanish Monarchy as a modern, constitutional state.[5] Today, there is a new urgency driving research about the impact of Black and Afro-descendant Spaniards at the dawn of early modernity, since a linchpin of ascendant white-Nationalist, anti-immigrant political parties— in Spain, as elsewhere—is the myth of an ethnically homogenous past, construed as a golden age of imperial grandeur.

A testament to the task at hand for scholars of empire building in early modern Iberia is the statistical summary provided by the indispensable *Slave Voyages* database. One of the great scholarly collaborations of all time, Slavevoyages.org, at latest consultation, documents 34,476 slaving expeditions from 1501 to 1875, with 10,665,568 men, women, and children loaded in chains onto slave ships.[6] But by 1501, slave voyages from the west coast of Africa to port cities of Portugal and Spain had been underway for over half a century. From the statistical precision of the table's 10,665,568, we arrive at fifty-plus years in which uncounted, now-forgotten multitudes—impossible to tally much less name, trace, and honor—were brutally seized from their homes in the greater Senegambia region, herded in chains to its ports, packed into rickety galleons, and carried to a distant peninsula. There, those who survived a perilous sea journey were sold into slavery with scant hope of freedom and return to their homelands. In consequence, three to four generations of Blacks and Afro-descendant Iberians enriched the nascent Portuguese and Spanish maritime empires: uncounted thousands toiled in households, stables, and shipping docks; many banded together to form confraternities for mutual comfort and protection; quite a few litigated for basic human rights; others cultivated skills in the visual and dramatic arts.[7] It is unlikely that social historians will be able to piece together more accurate statistical documentation of the first Atlantic slave voyages (ca. 1444–1500), since the first ones recorded unfolded as the personal ventures of a succession of royal sponsors from Portugal's Avis dynasty; therefore, whatever account books slave traders maintained became the property of a succession of royal households, not state papers preserved in a royal chancery. The more detailed documents that would have been required after Portugal's Casa da Guinea emerged to govern Atlantic commerce (ca. 1500) were lost in the fires after the Lisbon earthquake of 1755. Spanish slave voyages, in like manner, were not systematically documented until the founding of Seville's Casa de Contratación in 1503. This gap in statistical documentation has important implications for ideas of nationhood and imperial grandeur at the pivotal moment when the monarchies of Spain and Portugal emerged from relative isolation at the margins of Western Europe to become the first two seafaring empires of the modern world. Nonetheless, narrative accounts of the beginnings of the Atlantic slave trade reveal much about when and how it took shape.

In the pages ahead, I follow the chronicle of the first 235 men, women, and children who were captured in West Africa and brought to Iberia, tracing memories of their fate from eye-witness account to imperial chronicle and, finally, to fictional parody. The slave voyage in question transpired in the spring and summer of 1444. Though it began and ended in Lagos, Portugal, it would, in time, become a touchstone for the imperial imaginary of Spaniards, as well. We unfortunately will never know the names of the first 235 victims of the Atlantic slave trade. We do, however, know a bit about their captor, who bore a sonorous name reminiscent of the Arthurian legends of the Round Table.

A Knight Turned Human Trafficker

In the spring of 1444, Lançarote da Ilha (Lancelot of the Isle), a court squire turned tax collector, mounted an expedition of six galleons. He and his crew raided communities on the coast of West Africa, seizing any defenseless residents they found. In August, the galleons docked in the squire's home city of Lagos in southern Portugal, bearing 235 men, women, and children in chains. His men marched the captives off the ships and divided them into lots, after which the squire supervised an ad hoc slave auction, using the framework of a *partilha*, or partition of war spoils.

What we can piece together about this foundational slave voyage is found in the vivid account prepared by Gomes Eanes de Zurara, the *Crónica dos feitos notáveis que se passaram na conquista de Guiné* (Chronicle of the Notable Deeds that Transpired in the Conquest of Guinea). Zurara (ca. 1405–1474) wrote as an officially sanctioned chronicler for Portugal's Avis dynasty, drawing on both his own firsthand observations of events that transpired in Lagos as well as the now-lost travel account of Afonso de Cerveira.[8]

While many key details are missing, Zurara's account of the 1444 slave voyage offers what little we know the first individuals of the Atlantic slave diaspora. In his telling, the expedition leader presents his African captives to his royal patron as *Mouros*:

> E agora estes Mouros, peo grande tempo que andamos no mar, assim pelo nojo que deveis considerar que terão em seus corações, vendo-se fora da terra da sua natureza e postos em cativeiro, sem havendo algum conhecimento de qual será sua fim; d'ai a usança que não hão de andar em navios; por tudo isto veem assaz mal corregidos e doentes.
>
> *And now these Moors, because of the long sea journey and the heartsickness you can well imagine they have on being captives so far from home, unaccustomed to long sea journeys, without the least inkling of their ultimate fates. For all these reasons, they arrive in poor condition and ill.*[9]

The captives are physically ill but also spiritually troubled by heartsickness, described as *nojo*, from the Latin *nauseum*. This speech attributed to the squire recognizes that the malady results from having been transported to a faraway, unknown land ("vendo-se fora da terra da sua natureza e postos em cativeiro, sem havendo algum conhecimento de qual será sua fim"). We have a passing recognition of African subjectivities, even though Lançarote collapses the diverse ethnicities under the imprecise ethnonym of *Mouros*, a simplification Josiah Blackmore has analyzed.[10] Indeed, Zurara's account of the raids in previous chapters make it clear that the people he captured and brought to Portugal included lighter-skinned Berbers kidnapped from coastal communities, as well as Black Africans, likely from Wolof communities of the Senegambia region. Having brought them by force to Portugal, the knight takes note of their misery. As the speech continues, Lançarote's solution to the *nojo* is not restitution and return but an improvised slave market:

> Pelo qual me parece que será bem que de manhã os mandeis tirar das caravelas, e levar áquele campo que está alem da porta da vila, e farão deles cinco partes, segundo o costume, e seja vossa mercê chegardes aí e escolher uma das partes, qual mais vos prouver.

> *For these reasons, I recommend you order that tomorrow they be unloaded from the caravels and taken to the field just beyond the city gate, where we could divide the five traditional lots, from which your grace could take your pick.*[11]

Early the next morning, the captives are marched off the ship and to a field, where an ad hoc slave auction transpires.

The chapter (24) concludes with Prince Henry ordering the "best" captives from his royal fifth be given to the church. At this point, Zurara shifts forward in time. Through a temporal sleight-of-hand, the 235 captives fade to the background while Zurara tells how one young captive later became a devout auxiliary in a Franciscan convent:

> Pero primeiramente que se em aquilo outra cousa fizesse, levaram em oferta o melhor daqueles Mouros á igreja daquele lugar, e outro pequeno, que depois foi frade de S. Francisco, enviaram a S. Vicente do Cabo, onde sempre viveu como catolico Cristão, sem havendo conhecimento nem sentimento doutra lei senão daquela santa e verdadeira em que todolos Cristãoes esperamos nossa salvação.

> *So before anything else they took an offering of the best of those Mouros to a local church, and another boy—who later became a Franciscan—was taken to São Vicente do Cabo where he always lived as a Catholic Christian without knowledge of any other law save the holy and true faith in which all Christians place our hope of salvation.*[12]

The passage abstracts and allegorizes 235 traumatized individuals into one devout convent auxiliary, who embodies a convert's Catholic faith. In the oldest surviving textual witness, the disjuncture between past and present leaves a textual trace. In the margin, we find the figure 235. This data point migrates in subsequent manuscript versions and in the eventual print editions—including the Prestage and Beasley translation into English—as editors transpose the head count written in the margin, rendering it as the culminating statement of Zurara's chapter. Unless one goes to the

Paris manuscript or the León Bourdon translation into French, this revealing textual manifestation of the moral incongruity between a Christian apologia in the narrative passage and a bare-facts accounting of human trafficking in the margin is folded into the apologetic narrative.[13] With incomplete surviving information about the Zurara manuscript's composition, we have no way of knowing whether this accounting for the exact number of individuals sold into slavery was the work of the chronicler himself or another hand.

Zurara's next chapter (25) remains focused on the site of the dividing of the captives into lots (*partilha*). In an emotional invocation, the chronicler asks what the dire fate inflicted on the captured Africans portends for his own soul:

> E te rogo que as minhas lagrimas não sejam dano da minha consciencia, que nem por sua lei daquestes, mas a sua humanidade constrange a minha que chore piedosamente o seu padecimento. E se as brutas animalias, com seu bestial sentir, por um natural instinto conhecem os danos de suas semelhantes, que queres que faça esta minha humanal natureza, vendo assim ante os meus olhos aquesta miseravel companha, lembrando-me de que são da geração dos filhos de Adão!

> *And I beseech you: that my tears not become a stain on my conscience, for it is not their law but their humanity that incites my human feeling to piously weep for their suffering. And if untamed animals, with their savage feelings, recognize damage to their fellow beings by some instinct, what could you expect of my human nature, seeing before my eyes this miserable group, reminding me they are fellow children of Adam.*[14]

In this somewhat tortured casuistry, the chronicler fears that the uncontrollable impulse to weep for fellow "children of Adam" who are about to be sold into slavery could leave a lasting blemish on his conscience. In other words, would the captives' tears haunt him permanently? This anguished invocation anticipates how observers and beneficiaries of the nascent Atlantic slave trade would find themselves morally adrift between its two irreconcilable poles, of Christian virtue and economic gain. Above, the chronicler acknowledges, however fleetingly, that something is wrong with the commercial enterprise on display. But as the passage continues, Zurara renders himself the victim.

Returning from his anguished aside back to the ad hoc slave market, Zurara recollects the tears, wails, struggle, and violence he witnessed as families were torn apart. Some mothers cradled infants in their arms to prevent their separation, others charged or jumped to rescue children seized by Portuguese mariners: "Os filhos, que viam os padres na outra, alevantavam-se rijamente e se iam-se para eles; as madres apertavam ous outros filhos nos braços e lançavam-se com eles de bruços, recebendo feridas, com pouca piedade de suas carnes, por lhe não serem tirados" (The children, who saw their fathers in another [lot] decisively broke away to join them; the mothers held other children firmly in their arms and threw themselves to the ground with them, suffering injuries, taking little pity on their own injured flesh, in an effort to spare them from seizure).[15]

As the chronicler moves on from here, a rare picture of an emerging laboring class comes into focus, yielding an implicit contrast between *jornaleiros* assembled on the one hand, and, on the other, the elites who were poised to profit from the new kind of slave voyage, whether courtiers-turned-mariners who led the expedition, members of the prince's retinue who were given a share of profits or slaves, or convents who were granted slaves. Zurara thus describes how day laborers of Lagos and neighboring villages—who had rushed to the port to celebrate the return of the sailors and catch a glimpse of their cargo—became agitated at the sight of these men, women, and children's suffering: "Porque alem do trabalho que tinham com os cativos, o campo era todo cheio de gente, assim do lugar como das aldeas e comarcas de arredor, os quaes leixavam em aquele dia folgar suas mãos, em que estava a fôrça de seu ganho, somente por ver aquela novidade" (For in addition to the difficulties they [the mariners/slave traders] had with the captives, the field was full of people—from the town and neighboring villages and counties—who that day took a break from their manual labors that were their sole sustenance, drawn by the force of that novelty alone).[16] The assembled laborers become agitated. In Zurara's telling, some cry, others argue, and the prince and his men begin to fear a riot: "E com estas cousa que viam, uns chorando, outros departindo, faziam tamanho alvoroço, que poinham em turvação os governadores daquela partilha" (And on seeing this spectacle, some weeping, others arguing, they created a great tumult which unsettled the commanders directing that partition [of spoils]).[17]

With the city's laborers on the verge of a riot, Prince Henry appears atop his horse in the company of his courtly retinue: "O Infante era ali em cima de um poderoso cavalo, acompanhado de suas gentes repartindo suas mercês" (The Prince was there atop a powerful steed, flanked by his men, dispersing his largesse).[18] Royal liberality in the form of prizes (*mercês*) alternates with violent coercion. (A reader who has been among revelers or demonstrators at the moment a band of police mounted on horseback arrives with orders to disperse them can conceive of the menacing sense of the prince on horse dispensing "his largesse"). On that August day in Lagos, however angered or agitated by the cruelty in view, the day laborers who traveled on foot or by mule might have thought twice about resisting when set upon by the prince and his retinue towering atop horses. Others, given some kind of *mercê*, might have been enticed into silence or active cooperation with the market.

Already, scholars have long drawn attention to the foundational importance of this scene. Jerome Branche ponders the empire-building gesture of the prince on horseback, noting how a brief recognition of fellow humans shifts to an emphasis on the workings of fate and on the "compensatory value of Euro-Christian culture for the captives." Josiah Blackmore, in turn, contemplates the unstable construction of racial hierarchy in the chronicler's depiction of the captives' skin color.[19] For my part, I propose we reflect still more on the moral implications of this scene. In particular, the authorial intrusion that interrupts the narrative flow bears special attention for how it yields a momentary glimpse of an Iberian Black Atlantic taking shape before the chronicler's eyes: "E eu que esta história ajuntei em este volume, vi na via de Lagos moços e moças, filhos e netos daquestes, nados em esta terra, tão bons e tão verdadeiros Cristãos como se descenderam do começo da lei de Cristo, por geração, daqeles que primeiro foram bautisados" (And I myself, who gathered this history into this volume, saw in the city of Lagos the sons and daughters and grandchildren of these [captives], born in this land and such virtuous and sincere Christians as the very first baptized Christians).[20] Zurara momentarily shifts here from the anguished description of the partitioning of captives to an anticipation of Lagos as a new kind of Atlantic trade metropolis, where the children and grandchildren of the captives sold into slavery on that August morning in 1444 have blended into the city. Moreover, the royal librarian accords the captives' progeny the highest marker of Iberian political virtue as "old Christians" and, in so doing, incorporates them into the general population of city dwellers. This recognition is, to be sure, a partial and fleeting one: Zurara confers subjectivity and citizenship to the extent that the children and grandchildren of the first captives practice Christianity in visible, even performative ways.

Missing from Zurara's emotional account of the first recorded slave auction of the Atlantic slave trade are the firsthand recollections from the 235 men, women, and children marched off the galleons and divided into lots. There is no sign in the chronicle that the keeper of the royal library sought the kinds of information that would have acknowledged the captives had agency. Zurara neither discusses the language differences between the Portuguese and their captives and among the 235 captives nor explains the work of translators in this scene, though elsewhere in his chronicle we find passages where the Portuguese take captives for the express purpose of training them to translate. As concerns the suffering of the African captives, the chronicler confers sounds and sights, but no signification. Mothers lunge for children seized from their arms ("alevantavam-se . . . iam-se") or throw themselves to the ground ("lançavam-se"). The chronicler records wails and sad songs but makes no effort at the kind of translation, found in the earlier chapters, that recounts the African raids themselves, with the intrigues surrounding translation given their due. Here, on the day of the *partilha* in Lagos, signification belongs to the Europeans alone. Thus, the mortified day laborers of Lagos are depicted as arguing ("departindo"). But what did the 235 individuals say, see, and feel? Zurara consoled himself upon recalling the horrific scene for his chronicle by looking ahead to the long service of one of the younger captives in a Franciscan convent. But one would so much like to recover that voice of a boy, already weary from a sea journey, when he was suddenly torn from his mother or father.

An idea of what might have transpired comes from the angry recollection of another boy who was torn from the only family he had known and sold in a violent and degrading spectacle: "Men and women, young and old, married and single, moral and intellectual beings, in open contempt of their humanity, leveled at a blow with horses, sheep, horned cattle and swine!! . . . Personality swallowed in the sordid idea of property! Manhood lost in chattlehood!"[21] These recollections from Frederick Douglass draw emotional force from his focalization on the perspective of an innocent child of eight who abruptly discovers the violent ritual of a slave auction. The August morning in Lagos would have brought over two hundred variations on this violence of the individual facing social death. Douglass's *My Bondage and My Freedom* of 1855 astutely contrasts the devout Christianity of the slave masters of Eastern Maryland with their depraved, uncharitable treatment of fellow men, women, and children. Zurara's aside—begging for God's forgiveness—resides in the same discursive space where economic practice corrupts Christian virtue. But in contrast to Douglass's dual subjectivity, where the child as victim transforms into the adult as agent and orator, Zurara's authorial intrusion claims emotional impact through his own sense of moral innocence.

As Zurara's chronicle moves on from the account of the slave auction, it also records the cultural change that the new business of slave trafficking engenders. He notes, in particular, that popular murmurings against the high costs of Prince Henry's Atlantic expeditions go silent once residents of Lagos see the houses of mariners filling with enslaved men and women ("vendo as casas dos outros cheas de servos e servas.")[22] As merchants like Lançarote and his men reap profit from slave trafficking and begin to live like aristocrats, the residents of Lagos who had complained about taxes levied for ocean-bound voyages become Prince Henry's enthusiastic proponents. The ruler they denounced as spendthrift is now hailed as an Alexander the Great for Portugal's new maritime empire. Zurara, as commissioned royal chronicler, provides his own endorsement of the African slave trade as part of as an imperial *gesta*, labeling his history an account of "grandes feitos principalmente nos começos" (great gests, especially at their foundation),[23] invoking Livy's *History of Rome from Its Foundations*.

Notwithstanding this lofty rhetoric in positioning his own chronicle at the pinnacle of Portuguese imperial historiography, Zurara's chronicle attained limited circulation in the century ahead and then disappeared from view for almost two hundred years. In the early sixteenth century, manuscript copies reached Madrid and Munich but remained the purview of a select few. The ornate copy made for Zurara's Avis patron was copied at least twice, archived in Portugal's Torre do Tombo, moved abroad, archived again, and forgotten, until its rediscovery in the Bibliothèque Nationale de Paris at the beginning of the nineteenth century.[24]

During the mid-sixteenth century, as the narratives of Portuguese empire building gained wider circulation through printed editions of chronicles, the fame and influence as a "Portuguese Livy" would accrue to Joaõ de Barros (1496–1570). His *Decada primeira da Asia: Dos feitos que os portugueses fezerão no descobrimento e conquista dos mares e terras do Oriente* (ca. 1549; The First Decade of Asia: On the Deeds of the Portuguese in the Discovery and Conquest of the Lands of the East) attained wide print dissemination in multiple editions. As the second part of the title suggests, Barros's narration of the first slave raids and auctions is enveloped in the resolutely epic-heroic narration of the "discovery and conquest of the seas and lands of the East." Under this rubric, Barros's *Decada primeira*, drawing on Zurara, recounts the foundational voyage of the Atlantic slave trade under the stewardship of Lançarote da Ilha. Like Zurara before him, Barros recounts how murmurs against Prince Henry's costly enterprises give way to ever louder praises: "Acrescentava tambem neste louuor, verem que aquelles que seguião esta carreira se engrossauam em substancia com os retornos et escravos que trazião daquellas partes" (Praise grew louder as well, seeing how those who undertook these voyages accumulated notable wealth from the traded goods and slaves they brought back from those lands).[25] But Barros otherwise pares the Zurara narrative of human trafficking down to a skeletal outline, thereby underreporting the extent to which the nascent Atlantic slave trade powered imperial expansion. In contrast to the dramatic account of the slave auction organized after the expedition docked in Lagos, Barros reduces the return by Lançarote to Portugal and his ensuing slave auction to one sentence: "E porque os mantimentos com os muitos captivos lhe começarão desfaecer, tornara-se pera o Reyno, onde o capitão Lançarote foi recebido com tanta honra do Infante que per sua pessoa o armou cavalleiro com acrescentamento de mais nobreza" (And because the provisions began to run out because of the many captives, they returned to the Realm, where captain Lancelot was received with such honor that the Prince himself knighted him.)[26]

For the many readers who had access to the print editions of the Barros *Decada primeira da Asia* but did not have a court insider's access to one of the small number of Zurara manuscripts, the foundational narrative of the Atlantic slave trade was deceptively streamlined and suggestively literary: a squire with a name out of the Arthurian legends mounts an expedition to raid and trade in West Africa; he returns to his hometown bearing captives, reaps bounteous profits, and wins courtly honors. Erased from this concise account are the 235 captives sold into slavery by Lançarote and his men. Nor does the reader learn of the rumblings of outraged Lagos *jornaleiros* who watched those captives being torn from their family members and sold into slavery. Rather, one squire gains knighthood and great profits.

João de Barros's closing summation of the pivotal chapter would have profound historiographical consequences, which still inform how these first slave voyages of the Atlantic slave trade are construed within a more laudatory history of exploration and discovery. Thus, after recounting Lançarote's *acrescentamento*, Barros concludes by noting that Prince Henry redoubles his focus on the enterprise that would bring the most benefit:

"era em *aquelle descobrimento*, por ser cousa, que ele plantara, et criara com tanta industria, e despesa" (and it was *that discovery*, for being something he had planned and financed with great skill and expense).[27] In the grammatical and contextual logic of the expedition's narrative, *aquelle descobrimento* would be the revelation of a new route for human trafficking. After all, in chapter 8 of the Barros *Decada primeira*, there are no other spoils displayed and distributed in exchange for royal prizes from the Lançarote voyage than the captives whose enslavement yield *acrescentamento*. But the *discovery* narrative would be the triumphalist, epic, and proto-scientific notion of the charting and exploration of previously unknown lands. In fact, Peter Russell emphasizes Barros's importance in canonizing Prince Henry in proto-scientific terms with the sobriquet of *the Navigator*.[28]

Beyond Portugal, the Barros chronicle of vertiginous upward mobility—with its silence on the suffering of the first victims of the Atlantic slave trade—would attain wide influence. In chapter 29 of *Don Quijote*, part 1 (1605), Miguel de Cervantes parodies the chronicle of Lançarote's upward mobility through slave trading in the absurd reverie in which Sancho Panza imagines himself a slave trader. Inspired by his encounter with the Princess of Micomicón—the witty Dorotea in disguise—Don Quijote's squire plots his path to riches as a merchant who returns from a distant land with a boat laden with *vasallos negros*: "¿Habrá más que cargar con ellos y traerlos a España, donde los podré vender, y adonde me los pagarán de contado, de cuyo dinero podré comprar algún título o algún oficio con que vivir descansado todos los días de mi vida?" (What else would I need to do but load and transport them to Spain, where I could sell them, and be paid on the spot, with money I could use to buy some title or office, with which I would live with ease for the rest of my life?).[29]

Sancho's plan for wealth and ennoblement echoes that of the enigmatic Lançarote da Ilha as recalled in Barros's chronicle: a squire organizes a slave-trading expedition, returns home, holds a slave auction where his master receives the requisite royal fifth, at which point the courtier-turned-slave trader is knighted and positioned for even greater wealth. Contemplating this passage, Baltasar Fra-Molinero notes how Cervantes transposes the mythical Ethiopia evoked in the chivalric fiction *Tirant lo Blanc* to an early modern Ethiopia construed in Sancho's imagination as a "land of slaves." He also draws attention to how Sancho's reverie is a silent one: the normally talkative squire does not tell his master about his scheme for getting rich. For his part, Augustin Redondo shows how Sancho's leap of imagination—in which Micomicón signifies a land of Blacks—follows from Cervantes's engagement with European travel literature from John Mandeville to writings by Iberian missionaries. As well, Redondo explores how Sancho's profit-conjuring monologue adapts the literary trope of an imagined buying and selling, a fantasy best known through the story of the hapless milkmaid who counts the profits she will generate from her one pail, only to distractedly spill it.[30] Building on these two classic studies of Sancho as slave trader, we must also take note of the uncanny echoes of João de Barros's account of Lançarote's wealth and ennoblement, which Cervantes would likely have known from the edition published in Lisbon in 1552 by the print shop of Germão Galharde.[31]

A paradox emerges in the trail of history writing. As royal chroniclers organize the dispersed, disorderly papers of the late fifteenth century into a coherent narrative of empire building, they overlook the records of one population most affected by its violence. Barros describes how he composed his *Decada primeira* by piecing together and giving order to the Zurara history, drawing attention to the arduous labors involved: "Não foi pequeno o trabalho que tivemos em ajuntar cousas derramadas, e per papeis rotos e fora da ordem que elle Gomezeanes levou no processo deste descobrimento" (It was no small labor we had in collating scattered things, and through damaged or disordered papers in which Gomes Eanes [de Zurara] left behind about this discovery).[32] Barros probably refers to a lost textual witness by Afonso de Cerveira that Zurara drew on for the firsthand account of African expeditions. But in the gathering together and ordering of scattered papers from Zurara and his enigmatic predecessor, Cerveira, Barros passed over or set aside a few essential folios, in which Zurara recalls the heart-rending sound of parents weeping or the sight of mothers falling prostrate as their children are sold as slaves. This strategic ordering of a messy stack of documents would have profound ethical and historical consequences for the public conception of European empire building and the nascent Atlantic slave trade. Cervantes parodies the get-rich-quick schemes of slave traffickers but does not allude to the suffering of those kidnapped in Africa and loaded onto ships. His satirical eye is trained on the lowborn, illiterate merchants gaining social advancement.

A few readers and observers did note the depraved and immoral new mode of human trafficking that troubled Zurara's conscience. Most prominently, Bartolomé de las Casas retraced the Portuguese empire building as recounted in the *Decada primeira*, which he called the *Historia portuguesa*.

The Dominican's own monumental *Historia de Indias* prepared in the mid-sixteenth century retraces the steps of Barros and, before him, Zurara. As is well known, Las Casas, once an advocate of enslaving Black Africans to alleviate the oppression of Amerindians, ultimately condemned the Atlantic slave trade.³³ An eloquent testimony to this change of heart is his analysis of the Lançarote expedition of 1444. Chapter 24 of his *Historia de Indias* follows Barros in noting the *acrecentamiento* and ennoblement of the expedition leader, stating that Lançarote "fue recibido del infante con tanta honra, que por su misma persona lo armó caballero y le acrecentó en mucha honra" (was received by the Infante with such honor, that he himself performed the knighthood ceremony and enriched him with many honors).³⁴ But from here, the Dominican incorporates details found only in Zurara's more expansive account. On the young boy given as a slave to the Franciscan convent—whose life of devotion consoled Zurara—Las Casas quotes Ecclesiastes: "No aprueba Dios los dones de los que, con pecados y daños de sus prójimos, ofrecen a Dios sacrificio de lo robado y mal ganado" (God does not welcome those gifts wrought through sin and harm to fellow humans, where the sacrifice offered God comes from that which was stolen or ill gotten).³⁵ Similarly, in response to Zurara's celebration of the many captives-turned-slaves who became devout Christians, the Dominican ironizes:

> ¿Tenían o podían tener a la fe y cristiana religión, para convertirse a ella, los que así lloraban y se dolían y alzaban las manos y ojos al cielo, viéndose así, contra ley natural y toda razón de hombres, privados de su libertad y mujeres e hijos, patria y reposo?
>
> *Did or could they harbor faith and Christian tenets, when to be converted to it they were made to weep, suffer, raise their hands and eyes to the sky, upon seeing themselves, against laws of nature and human reason, thus deprived of freedom, wives and children, homelands and refuge?*³⁶

That is, are conversions made in the context of violent enslavement efficacious or merely cynical farces? Las Casas, bringing this narrative sequence to a close, suggests Zurara and the Portuguese prince he chronicled were "whitewashing and sterilizing" violence, tyranny, and theft with "divine grace and mercy" ("enjabona o alcohola con la misericordia y bondad de Dios").³⁷

But the Dominican's denunciation of the growing Atlantic slave trade, rooted in a meticulous textual analysis of his Portuguese sources, circulated only in manuscript until the mid-nineteenth century. The vast majority of Las Casas's readers for three centuries would only access this denunciation as diffused in the fiercely polemical rhetoric of his *Brevísima relación de la destruición de las Indias* (1552), which shed his *Historia*'s scholarly review of evidence for the rhetorical vehemence of a bitter, high-stakes dispute. But it is the Las Casas of the *Historia de Indias* that brings us closer to an accurate account of empire building, its scientific and navigational feats, and its atrocious violence. It features the Dominican's arresting descriptions of the navigational feats of the Portuguese and Spanish empire builders who dared to sail south of Cape Bojador in West Africa. But it also presents a firm denunciation of how these intrepid explorers transformed into thieves, kidnappers, and murderers.

Yet even Las Casas's unsparing, experienced voice stopped short of proposing the abolition of the Atlantic slave trade. As Antonio Domínguez Ortiz noted in his seminal article of 1952: "Ante todo, debemos expresar sinceramente un sentimiento de decepción por el hecho de que en ninguno de ellos [Las Casas, Tomás Mercado et al.] se formule una condena tajante, incondicional, del principio mismo de tan odiosa institución, contraria a la dignidad humana y al espíritu evangélico" (First off, we must express frankly our sense of disappointment due to the fact that none of them expressed a complete and unconditional rejection of an institution so odious, contrary to human dignity, and the spirit of the Gospels).[38] While much remains to be done to fully address this overarching question of why moral censure of the first Atlantic slave voyages did not foment full-fledged abolitionism, we must also continue to attend, like Arturo Schomburg, to the vibrant new society that took shape in early modern Iberia. That is, what kinds of cities, confraternities, and cultural practices emerged with the young men and women, sons, daughters, and grandchildren descended from and following the first 235 captives brought to Lagos?

When, in 1926, Schomburg concluded that his search for Blacks in Spain would remain in the realm of fragmentary facts, he was all too prescient in providing the still apt metaphor for the search for the first Black Atlantic in early modern Iberia. Indeed, the editorial practices and teleologies of national literary traditions, from Barros's *Decadas*, first published in 1552, to works by recent editors, require we unpack the orderly *discovery* narratives to return to the original *papeis rotos e fora da ordem*, wherever they may be found. As is clear to readers of Zurara, Barros, and Las Casas, many of these accounts are found at the nexus where the monarchies of Portugal and Spain collaborated, competed, and collided. A succession of kings, courtiers, and upwardly mobile adventurers imagined and then carried out plans for trade and conquest overseas, deeds long celebrated in lengthy accounts of notable deeds and the discoveries of distant lands. Far less attention has been paid to the sons, daughters, granddaughters, and grandsons of the kidnapped Africans whose sale and forced labor financed many subsequent voyages. Their stories remain, as they did in 1926, in the realm of fragmentary facts still awaiting our sustained attention.

NOTES

1. Schomburg's scholarly practice is attested to in his papers, which are preserved in the New York Public Library's Schomburg Center for Research in Black Culture and are also available on microfilm (see *The Arthur A. Schomburg Papers*, Microfilm, University Publications of America, 1991).
2. Arthur A. Schomburg, "Negroes in Sevilla," *Opportunity* 6 (March 1928): 70–71, 93.
3. Ibid., 93.
4. Alessandro Stella, *Histoires d'esclaves dans la péninsule Ibérique* (Paris: École des Hautes Études en Sciences Sociales, 2000), 178–83.
5. See Tamar Herzog, "How Did Early Modern Slaves in Spain Disappear? The Antecedents," *Republic of Letters: A Journal for the Study of Knowledge, Politics, and the Arts* 3, no. 1 (2012): 1–7. On the Constitution of Cádiz, see Herzog's *Defining Nations: Immigrants and Citizens in Early Modern Spain and Spanish America* (New Haven, CT: Yale University Press, 2003), 43–45; Antonio Feros, *Speaking of Spain: The Evolution of Race and Nation in the Hispanic World* (Cambridge: Harvard University Press, 2017), 233.
6. "*Slave Voyages* summary statistics," Slavevoyages.org, accessed December 17, 2019, www.slavevoyages.org/voyage/database#tables.
7. For a broad overview and bibliography of the presence of Blacks in Renaissance Europe, see José Ramos Tinhorão, *Os negros em Portugal: Uma presença silenciosa* (Lisbon: Editorial Caminho, 1988); Kate Lowe, "The Lives of African Slaves and People of African Descent in Renaissance Europe," in *Revealing the African Presence in Renaissance Europe*, ed. J. Spicer (Baltimore, MD: Walters Art Museum, 2012), 13–33. Studies of specific realms where Black and Afro-descendant individuals made notable contributions include painting and martial arts. See, respectively, Carmen Fracchia, *'Black but Human': Slavery and Visual Art in Habsburg Spain, 1480–1700* (Oxford: Oxford University Press, 2019); Manuel Olmedo Gobante, "'El mucho número que hay dellos': *El valiente negro en Flandes* y los esgrimistas afrohispanos de *Grandezas de la espada*," *Bulletin of the Comediantes* 70, no. 2 (2018): 67–91.

8. On Zurara's life, see Peter Russell, *Prince Henry 'The Navigator': A Life* (New Haven, CT: Yale University Press, 2000), 5.
9. Gomes Eanes da Zurara, *Cronica do descobrimento e conquista da Guiné*, ed. J. de Bragança (Porto: Livraria Civilização, 1937), 148. In the interest of legibility for the greatest number of readers, and given my analysis does not hinge on philological intricacies, I cite Zurara using Bragança's modernized Portuguese orthography, noting the chapter and page numbers that will allow readers to consult other textual witnesses. The editor follows the oldest surviving textual witness (the manuscript preserved in the Bibliothèque Nationale de France [catalogued under Portugais 41]; a digitization of a black-and-white microfilm is available at gallica.bnf.fr/ark:/12148/btv1b10032760d/f4.item. Translations from Portuguese and Spanish texts to English are mine unless otherwise specified.
10. Josiah Blackmore, *Moorings: Portuguese Expansion and the Writing of Africa* (Minneapolis: University of Minnesota Press, 2009), 1–32.
11. Gomes Eanes da Zurara, *Cronica do descobrimento e conquista da Guiné*, 148.
12. Ibid.
13. The original margin annotation appears in manuscript "Portugais 41" of the Bibliothèque Nationale de France (fol. 48r); and in Gomes Eanes da Zurara, *Chronique de Guinée*, trans. L. Bourdon and R. Ricard (France: Editions Chandeigne [1960] 2011), 149. Editions that incorporate the margin gloss into the chapter's narrative include Gomez Eanes de Zurara, *Crónica dos feitos notáveis que se passaram na conquista de Guiné por mandado do Infante D. Henrique*, ed. T. de Sousa Soares (Lisbon: Academia Portuguesa de História, 1978), 106; Gomez Eanes de Zurara, *Crónica dos feitos de Guiné*, vol. 2 (Lisbon: Agência Geral das Colónias, 1949), 149; and Gomez Eanes de Zurara, *The Chronicle of the Discovery and Conquest of Guinea*, vol. 1, trans. C. R. Beazley and E. Prestage (New York: Hakluyt Society and Burt Franklin, 2010), 80.
14. Gomes Eanes da Zurara, *Cronica do descobrimento e conquista da Guiné*, 152.
15. Ibid., 154.
16. Ibid.
17. Ibid.
18. Ibid.
19. See Jerome C. Branche, *Colonialism and Race in Luso-Hispanic Literature* (Columbia: University of Missouri Press, 2006), 41; Blackmore, *Moorings*, 27–29.
20. Gomes Eanes da Zurara, *Cronica do descobrimento e conquista da Guiné*, 155.
21. Frederick Douglass, *My Bondage and My Freedom*, ed. D. W. Blight (New Haven, CT: Yale University Press, [1855] 2014), 142–43.
22. Gomes Eanes da Zurara, *Cronica do descobrimento e conquista da Guiné*, 119.
23. Ibid., 117.
24. On the circulation of manuscript versions of the Zurara chronicle and its rediscovery in the nineteenth century, see Gomez Eanes de Zurara, *Crónica dos feitos notáveis que se passaram na conquista de Guiné por mandado do Infante D. Henrique*, vol. 1, ed. T. de Sousa Soares (Lisbon: Academia Portuguesa de História, 1978), 363–69.

25. João de Barros, *Decada primeira da Asia: Dos feitos que os portugueses fezerão no descobrimento e conquista dos mares e terras do Oriente*, book 1, ch. 8 (Lisbon: Jorge Rodriguez, 1628), fol. 15v.
26. Ibid., fol. 16v.
27. Ibid. (my emphasis).
28. Peter Russell, *Prince Henry 'The Navigator': A Life* (reprint, Granada: Editorial Comares), 6.
29. Miguel de Cervantes, *El ingenioso hidalgo Don Quijote de la Mancha*, ed. L. A. Murillo (Barcelona: Castalia, 2010), 366.
30. See Baltasar Fra-Molinero, "Sancho Panza y la esclavización de los negros," *Afro-Hispanic Review* 12, no. 2 (1994): 25–31; Augustín Redondo, "Burlas y veras: La princesa Micomicona y Sancho negrero (*Don Quijote*, I, 29)," *Edad de Oro* 15 (1996): 125–40.
31. The *princeps* appeared as João de Barros, *Asia de Joam de Barros: Dos feitos que os portugueses fizeram no descobrimento [et] conquista dos mares [et] terras do Oriente* (Lisbon: Germão Galharde, 1552); a facsimile edition is available from (Lisbon: Imprensa Nacional–Casa da Moeda, 1988). A digitized version is available through the *Internet Archive* (archive.org/details/asia00barr), see frame 32 (fol. 12r).
32. João de Barros, *Decada primeira da Asia*, book 2, ch. 1, fol. 32r.
33. Rolena Adorno, *The Polemics of Possession in Spanish American Narrative* (New Haven, CT: Yale University Press, 2007), 11.
34. Bartolomé de Las Casas, *Historia de las Indias*, vol. 1, ed. A. Millares Carlo and L. Hanke (Mexico: Fondo de Cultura Económica, 1951), 130.
35. Ibid.
36. Ibid.,133.
37. Ibid., 134.
38. Antonio Domínguez Ortiz, *La esclavitud en Castilla en la Edad Moderna y otros estudios de marginados* (Granada: Editorial Comares, 2003), 39.

CHAPTER 2

Christianos nigros

Afro-Iberian Confraternities' Social and Cultural Roles

MIGUEL A. VALERIO

On March 20, 1455, a group of free Blacks from the parish church of Sanct Jaume (St. James the Great, d. 44 CE, patron saint of Spain) in Barcelona received royal permission from John II of Navarre to establish a confraternity, or lay Catholic brotherhood:

> Nos Iohannes etc. caritatis zelus et ingens devocio quos nec sine cordis puritate vigere comprehendimus in vos *christianos nigros* libertate donatos et qui in civitae Barchinone habitatis instituendi seu faciendi confratriam inter vos et alios christianos ex gente vestra nigra libertate donatos et qui in futurum ipsa libertate donabuntur sub invocacione et ecclesia parrochiali Jacobi.
>
> *We John etc. understand that you, freed Black Christians residing in the city of Barcelona, moved by the zeal for charity and devotion that emanates from pure hearts, seek to establish among yourselves and other freed Blacks, and other Blacks who will be freed in the future, a confraternity under the invocation and in the parish church of St. James.*[1]

This is the oldest surviving founding charter of a Black confraternity in the Iberian world, but Sanct Jaume was not the first Black sodality in the Iberian Mediterranean. Toward the end of the fourteenth century, Seville's archbishop, Gonzalo Mena Roelas (r. 1393–1401), founded a confraternity for infirm Blacks.² As Karen B. Graubart has proposed, these Blacks may have been West Africans enslaved in the Iberian Peninsula through the trans-Saharan slave trade (eighth through fifteenth centuries).³ However, Afro-Sevillanos—the Iberian-born descendants of these West Africans—would eventually take control of the confraternity and make it their own. In the 1460s, moreover, Afro-Iberians in Lisbon would be admitted to that city's Rosary brotherhoods.⁴ Finally, in Valencia, in 1472, Afro-Iberians followed the example of St. Jaume and founded their own confraternity.⁵

These confraternities speak to the Black presence in late medieval Iberia. While Sub-Saharan Africans have been present in the Iberian Peninsula since ancient times, the modern wave began arriving in the late medieval period through the trans-Saharan slave trade. According to the historian Leo Garofalo, there were 35,000 Afrodescendants in the peninsula by 1492.⁶ This population would continue to grow with the Atlantic trade, which brought enslaved Africans into not only the Americas, but also Europe, especially the Iberian Peninsula. Lisbon, Seville, Valencia, and Barcelona became the Peninsula's main slave ports, as well as sites of the region's largest concentration of Afrodescendants. It was in these cities that a free Black population, and with this population Black confraternities, began to surface.⁷

"Caritatis zelus": *Afro-Iberian Confraternities' Social Roles*

As John II of Navarre states in his decree, Afro-Iberians who founded brotherhoods were "moved by [a] zeal for charity and devotion." St. Jaume's charter articulates what this charity and devotion looked like in terms that would be found in every Black sodality's statutes:

> Item que dels diners del acapte o de la caxa de la confraria sia dita una missa per anima de cascun defunt de la dita confraria lo dia de la sua mort o lo dia que diran les misses de aquell en aquella esglesia on aquell tal cors jaura a la qual missa sien presents tots auqells qui esser hi poram et los prohomens de la dita confraria hi demanaran.
>
> Item sia ordinacio de la confraria que si algun confrare o confraressa vendra a pobressa o fretura per malaties o perdues o en altra qualsevol manera que los prohomens de la dita confraria e caxa segons llur bon vijares a aquell o aquella la dita fretura sostendra axi en provisio de son menjar com

en necessitats de metges et de medecines com en totes alters coses a ell o a ella necesaries.

Item que si algun confrare morra lo qual sia pobre a conexença dels dits prohomens que dels diners de la dita caxa sien pagades messions de la dita sepulture a coneguda de aquells prohomens.

Money should be taken from the confraternity's money box for a mass for the soul of every deceased member on the anniversary of his/her death or on the day on which the church celebrates the mass of the dead. This mass should be attended by all the members who can and those who are asked by the confraternity's board.

It shall be a statute of this confraternity that if any member falls into poverty through illness or loss of goods or any other manner, the board shall provide for their sustenance, medicine, or any other need.

If any member who is known to be poor by the board dies, his burial mass shall be paid from the confraternity's money box.[8]

These three stipulations encapsulate Afro-Iberian confraternities' main raison d'être as well as the principal social roles they fulfilled. Together, they stress the communal identity Africans valued. The first provision reveals how Afrodescendants may have adapted ancestor worship in the diaspora. Within a Christian framework, Afro-Iberians could continue worshipping their ancestors through suffrage for the souls of deceased confraternity members, a perfectly acceptable Christian practice. Since ancestor worship required communal participation, all members of the confraternity were required to attend suffrage masses. The second provision stresses this communal identity. In a world where their lives were precarious, Afro-Iberians used confraternities to sustain kinship networks and, through those networks, build a safety net for all. The third provision, more than any other, underscores the importance Afro-Iberians, like medieval Christians, placed on proper burial, and it emphasizes how Afro-Iberians responded to their diasporic precarity.

In the Iberian Peninsula, deceased African slaves' corpses were abandoned in "dung heaps" and fields on cities' outskirts. In 1515, for example, King Manuel I of Portugal expressed his shock at the way slaves' corpses were being treated in Lisbon:

Nos somos certificado que os escravos que falleçam nesa cidade, asy ds tractadores de Guinee, como outros, nam ssam bem soterados, como devem, nos lugares omde sa llamçados, e que sse llaçam sobre a teerra en tal maneira que fiqua descubertos, ou de todo ssobre a terra sem cousa allguma delles se cobryr, e que os caees os comeem; e que a maior parte destes escravos se llaça no monturo . . . e asy tambem em outros llugares pellas herdades dhy darredor.

> *We are informed that slaves who die in this city, brought from Guinea, like others, are not buried very well as they should be; their bodies are thrown on the fields in such a manner that they are discovered, in many cases uncovered so that the dogs eat them; a great many of these slaves are thrown in dung heaps . . . or in the fields of nearby farms.*[9]

This was not only an affront to the king, who was worried about public hygiene, but also to Afro-Iberians themselves, who saw it as a desecration of the dead person's body and, more importantly, spirit. This accorded with the significance West and Central African societies place on the corpse, and many of these followed such norms as washing the body, wrapping it in cloth, or watching over it at a sitting wake.[10] Afro-Iberian confraternities took it upon themselves to correct this wrong and became so preoccupied with proper burial, setting aside funds for the burial of members and destitute Blacks, that in the 1970s Patricia Mulvey suggested that they emerged as a form of death insurance.[11] However, while proper burial was a central concern for Afro-Iberian confraternities, their social and cultural functions were more comprehensive.

Through confraternities, moreover, Afro-Iberians could honor Black saints, which were initially promoted by the Church and eventually embraced by Black brotherhoods as their own.[12] Saints and biblical figures like the Queen of Sheba; the Black magus Balthazar (or sometimes Caspar); Iphigenia, a legendary first-century Aksumite (Ethiopian) princess said to have been converted to Christianity by the Apostle Matthew; and another sixth-century Aksumite royal convert, Kaleb of Axum, inscribed Blacks in the story of salvation from antiquity and allowed Afrodescendants to make claims to Old Christian blood.[13] For the Church, more contemporary saints like St. Nicholas of Mount Calvary (c. 1246–1305), a supposed mulatto, and the sixteenth-century Afro-Sicilian lay Franciscan friars St. Benedict the Moor (1526–1589) and Anthony of Carthage (d. 1549) served as models of the kind of piety they wished to instill in Blacks (see Figures 2.1 and 2.2).

FIGURE 2.1. Left to right: Our Lady of the Rosary, St. Martin de Porres, St. Benedict the Moor in the Church of Our Lady of the Rosary, Ouro Preto, Minas Gerais, Brazil, eighteenth to twentieth centuries. Photo by author, June 2016.

FIGURE 2.2. Left to right: St. Anthony of Carthage, St. Iphigenia of Ethiopia, St. Helena, in the Church of Our Lady of the Rosary, Ouro Preto, Minas Gerais, Brazil, eighteenth to twentieth centuries. Photo by author, June 2016.

With their King and Queen:
Afro-Iberian Confraternities' Cultural Practices

Afro-Iberian confraternal life was not limited to the important social roles outlined in St. Jaume's charter. These confraternities also fulfilled important cultural roles. As we know, slave societies were marked by practices that gave the enslaved a release valve so as to prevent rebellion, or as a Sevillian alderman put it in the seventeenth century, so that they would "work with greater joy and better bear their captivity."[14] While William Phillips holds that the Iberian Peninsula was never a slave society because its slave population never reached twelve percent of the total population, it was precisely within slavery that the practice apparently began.[15] According to the same Sevillian alderman, "in Seville, Blacks have been treated with great benignity since the time of King Henry III of Castile—that is, the fourteenth century—being allowed to gather for their dances and fiestas on holidays."[16] Yet, while seen from the European perspective as a means to prevent resistance, as they did with confraternities, Afro-Iberians took advantage of this freedom to build community and give form to their culture through festive practices.[17] Confraternities were instrumental in the development of this festive culture, which was truly Afro-Iberian, for it mixed African festive practices with European ones. From the earliest days of the African diaspora in the Iberian world, confraternities were identified as the sites of Afro-Iberians' festive life. A particular performance that became associated with Afro-Iberian confraternities was the election and coronation of kings and queens.

According to Isidro Moreno, Blacks in Seville may have elected kings and queens as early as the 1470s, when a certain Juan de Valladolid, known as the "Black Count," was the magistrate of the city's Black population.[18] In the nineteenth century, the Portuguese historian José Ribeiro Guimarães wrote that the first recorded instance of this performance in Lisbon took place in 1484.[19] While we cannot confirm that these performances actually took place, this performance certainly became common practice among Afro-Iberian confraternities. For example, the 1565 charter of Lisbon's Black Rosary confraternity called for the election of "principe, reys, duque, condes, marquezes, cardeal & quaes quer outras dignidades" (kings and queens, princes and princesses, dukes and duchesses, counts and countesses, marquises and marchionesses, cardinals, and other dignitaries).[20] Moreover, the French historian Didier Lahon cites an undated election by a Black confraternity from the city of Vila Viçosa, Évora, Portugal, indicating that it took place before 1639.[21]

The Dominican order, which had been founded in the thirteenth century to teach Catholic doctrine to Europe's plebeian population, in particular promoted Afro-Iberian confraternities.[22] Thus, Our Lady of the Rosary, patroness of the Dominican order, became the patroness of many Afro-Iberian confraternities (see Figure 2.3). Thus, her feast day, October 7 or the nearest Sunday, became Afro-Iberian confraternities' most festive occasion. It was on this day that Afro-Iberian confraternities usually elected their kings and queens in the Lusophone world, while they did so on the feast of the Epiphany (January 6) in the Hispanic world.

On Friday, October 6, 1730, Lisbon's weekly satirical *Folheto de ambas Lisboas* (Pamphlet of Both Lisbons) made fun of this performance by a Black Rosary confraternity in the Alfama district scheduled for the upcoming Sunday. While the pamphlet is laden with racist satire, written in *fala de negros* (Black speech), it still outlines the form this performance took. First, in its parody of the kind of announcements confraternities made inviting other Afrodescendants to the celebration, the pamphlet reveals how Afro-Iberians built communal networks through their festive culture. The satirized invitation reads:

> Seoro compadra Re Mina Zambiampum tatè: sabe vozo, que nossos fessa sà Domingo, e que vozo hade vir fazer os forgamenta: oya vussè naõ falta vussè comprada, que as may Zoana os fia dos pay Maulicia, e dos may Zozefa sa biscondeça dos taraya: nos procissaõ vozo cantar o Zaramangoè, e traze vussè nos fofa que os pay Zozè nos fezo os cutambala, cuzambala cuyè nunas minueta; agora se vozo vem zangana se naõ vem zangana vussè homo Zambiampum tatè muitos anos.

> *The Lord be with you, brother, King of Mina. You know that our feast is on Sunday, and that you should come celebrate with us. Make sure you don't miss it, brother, because sister Susana and the daughter of brother Mauricio will be there, and sister Josefa's daughter is the viscountess. You will sing the Zaramangoè and dance the fofa in the procession. Brother José prepared the music to accompany the dancing. Now, if you come great, and if you don't, also. May God keep you many years, brother.*[23]

Not only does the satirized invitation bear witness to Afro-Iberians' kinship networks, it also mentions Afro-Iberian dances, such as the *Zaramangoè* and the *fofa*, that were known by their names at the time even among non-Black Iberians.[24] Finally, in its mockery of the music that accompanied such occasions, the pamphlet attests to the kind of cultural mixing that characterized Afro-Iberians' festive culture: "No adro estava hum rancho de instrumentos, com huma bizarra dissonancia; porque estavaõ tres marimbas, quatro pifanos, duas rebecas do peditorio, mais de trezentos berimbaus, pandeiros, congos, e cangáz, instrumentos de que uzaõ" (There were myriad instruments in the churchyard, with a bizarre dissonance; because there were three marimbas, four piccolos, two fiddles, more than three hundred berimbaus, tambourines, African drums, the instruments they use).[25] Even if we were to question the pamphlet's verisimilitude, as we should, other sources highlight this kind of cultural mixing. And as we will see below, the performance of kings and queens itself was the product of this cultural syncretism.

Afro-Iberian confraternities performed with their king and queen when Iberian cities celebrated major religious as well as secular occasions. For example, when, on May 27, 1731, the northern Portugal city of Braga celebrated the feast of Corpus Christi, one of Catholicism's most solemn feast days, the festivities held in the city's streets included, among seventeen total performances, a *bayle dos negros*, or "Black dance" (see Figure 2.3). This was a dance in the early modern sense, that is, a quasi-theatrical performance similar to what we see in Carnival today. According to the celebration's program, *Breve extracto*: "Logo em nono lugar, virà a Fulia Preta, formada com nova composiçaõ, e agradavel musica, e por serem nella destrissimas as Figuras, formaõ hum vistoso, e alegre bayle" (Then in ninth place, will come the Black company, with a new composition, and pleasing music, and their ceremonial figures being most talented, they will perform an elegant and jovial dance).[26]

The dance troupe was to be composed of a king, queen, "six Black men," "four Black women," "two dwarfs," "and musicians [and] instruments from the same naçaõ," or "nation," as Black groups were known in Iberia. Like the other performers in the festival, and in accord with baroque custom, the Black troupe was to travel in a sumptuous carriage ("vistoso Carro, ou Carroça"). According to the *Breve extracto*:

> Formarse-ha hum vistoso Carro, ou Carroça, pela qual hiraõ puxando dous Leões, no frontespicio, do Carro se veraõ duas Aguais, e no fim se levantarà huma gruta, dentro da qual hiraõ sentados Rey, Rainha, sobre a gruta se

BAYLE DOS NEGROS.

Rey. Rainha.
Seis negros. Quatro negras.
Dois Titeres. Acompanhamento,
e Muſicos inſtrumentos da meſma naçaõ.

ORMARSE-HA hum viſtozo Carro, ou Carroça, pela qual hiraõ puxando dous Leões, no frontefpicio, do Carro ſe veraõ duas Aguias, e no fim ſe levantarà huma gruta, dentro da qual hiràõ ſentados Rey, Rainha, ſobre a gruta ſe verà hum pavilhaõ, ou guardaſol de penas, o qual ſuſtentarà hum Negro veſtido à Ethiopeza, hiraõ cobrindo à ſuperficie deſte Carro variedades de paſſaros, como Araras, Papagayos, como tambem Bugios; ſobre os Leoens hiraõ os Titeres, & finalmente ſe ſatisfarà tudo à propriedade da Naçaõ.

BAYLE.

Introdu. Toro os pleto q̃ ha em Blaga
     N   aos feſſa vem com plimor,
           que sà huns feſſa que alegia
           plo ſer feſſa do Sior.
               Vaya vaya ri ſorſa,
               que os blanco paſma
               ver que toca os pletio,
               e as neglas baya.
Rey. Ah reſtos grutas!
Rainha. Ah reſtos mattos.
Negros. Vozo que manda?
Rey.Ray. Que oy toro os pleto ri Angora
           faſſa feſſa, canta, y toca.
Negros. Toro os pletio ſiolo
           que he teu Vaſſáro
           baya, canta, toca, y ſarta,
           que he ſeu regáro,

Titer. E voſo pletia canta,
         vozo faça cabriola,
         e vozo ſiolo Monarca,
         manda que eſtos neglos toca.
Rey.Rai. Si ſi ſi ſi ſi,
           plo que os blanco oya,
           que ri Angora os pleto
           cantar ſabe os ſorta.
Todos a 4. Si ſi ſi ſi ſi, &c.   *Volta.*
             Vem decendo.
Rey.Rai. Quello al Pan glaciozo
           ſazer huns dança
           Vozo negloblıozo   (ta
           huns baya, outro toca, vozo cã-
Tir. 1. Ea ſiòro Rey
         vozo me mandà
         plo que eu ſa ſeus ſervo

FIGURE 2.3. "Bayle dos negros," *Breve extracto*, Coimbra, Colegio das Artes da Companhia de Jesu, 1731. © Biblioteca Nacional de Portugal, Lisbon, Portugal.

verà hum pavilhaõ, ou guardasol de penas, o qual sustentarà un Negro vestido à Ethiopeza, hiraõ cobrindo à superficie deste Carro variedades de passaros, como Araras, Papagays, como tambem Bugios; sobre os Leoens hiraõ os Titeres, & finalmente se satisfarà tudo à propiedade da Naçaõ.

There will be an elegant carriage drawn by two lions, there will be two eagles in the front of the carriage, and on the back there will be a cave, inside which will travel the king and queen. On top of the cave there will be a parasol held by a Black person dressed in African custom. There will be many birds on top of the carriage, such as macaw, parrot, as well as monkeys. The dwarfs will ride on the lions, and finally everything will be done according to their custom.[27]

While this performance, on the one hand, displayed the kind of exoticism that delighted European audiences, on the other hand, it accentuated this practice's syncretic nature. While the event's non-Black organizers had a big part in shaping the *bayle de negros*, from the exotic exuberance of the float to the dialogue in *fala de negros*, the Black performers also had a significant role. The non-Black organizers designed the sumptuous float and wrote the dialogue, yet the performance itself was the Blacks' doing, as evidenced by the directive, "everything will be done according to their custom." This performance underscores the kind of intergroup negotiations that went into planning public acts with Afro-Iberian performers, through which Afro-Iberians also created opportunities for future negotiations. They could remind city and church authorities of their contribution to public festivities and, on that basis, demand certain privileges or accommodations.

As we have seen, the confraternities' practice of electing kings and queens emerged in tandem with the organizations themselves. Art historian Cécile Fromont explains how these performances mixed African and European elements: in the Iberian Peninsula, Afro-Iberians added ceremonial royalty to an African dance that, in the Christian Kongo, where the Portuguese arrived in 1482, celebrated the Kongo's conversion to Christianity. Confraternities were a perfect site for this performance, which carried Christian undertones from its African origin.[28] Fromont, however, neither asks nor seeks to answer why Afro-Iberians added ceremonial royalty to this dance. While some scholars may be tempted to make the argument that this performance imitated or parodied European pageantry in a carnivalesque fashion, a la Rabelais, the Brazilian historian Marina Mello e Souza has argued that it instead imitated the pageantry of the king of

Kongo. This hypothesis is borne out by the fact that in Africa the dance was normally performed on royal occasions before the monarchs.[29] Thus, a possible answer to why Afro-Iberians added ceremonial royalty to the original African dance is that they sought to hold on to some semblance of sovereignty in the diaspora. Confraternities, in fact, offered Afro-Iberians some degree of sovereignty, as they allowed them to have some power over their fate, fulfilling in this fashion important social and cultural functions.

While Afro-Iberians have appeared in the secondary literature on early modern Spain and Portugal, the scholarship has mainly focused on their literary and artistic representations in the Renaissance and baroque period.[30] Thus, Afro-Iberians have only appeared as "ghosts" in extant research. Particularly, the scholarship has focused on how Afro-Iberians were represented as caricatures; the use of blackface in baroque theater is one example. Meanwhile, the confraternity practices discussed above point to Afro-Iberians of flesh and blood, men and women who sought freedom and established these confraternities to form community, care for each other, and develop "creole" or hybrid Afro-Christian festive traditions.

From the Old to the New World

As Moreno and others have argued, Afro-Iberian confraternities established a precedent that was followed in the diaspora. Indeed, Blacks in Lima, Peru, had established a confraternity by 1549, eleven years after the Spanish city's founding. The founders of this confraternity must have been Afro-Iberians, many of whom had participated in the "conquest" of the Americas.[31] And if Afro-Iberians had established a confraternity in Lima so soon after their arrival, it is likely that the same model was followed in Mexico City.

In fact, in 1538 the Dominicans (who had arrived in Mexico in 1516) founded a Rosary confraternity, and according to Nicole von Germeten, "it was open to all."[32] Indeed, the confraternity's charter does not bar membership on the basis of race.[33] Moreover, given the Dominicans' sponsorship of Black sodalities in the Iberian Peninsula, it is likely that they admitted Blacks to the brotherhood. Thus, Afro-Iberians in Mexico City at the time may have joined this confraternity. This is suggested by the fact that in 1539 a group of Blacks appeared "with their king and queen" in Mexico City's commemoration of the Truce of Nice (1538).[34]

Black confraternities' social and cultural role would be far more important in the Americas, which would be home to the world's largest slave societies. While in the Iberian Peninsula Black confraternities were made up of free(d) Blacks, in the Americas they expanded to include enslaved Afrodescendants. This was especially true of cities such as Mexico City and Lima, where enslaved Afrodescendants were commonly hired out as *jornaleros* (day laborers) who could retain a portion of their earnings. This allowed enslaved Afrodescendants to afford confraternity fees and gain access to the benefits they provided.

As in the Iberian Peninsula, performing burial rites was an important social role Black sodalities fulfilled in the Americas, for just as in the Iberian Peninsula, slave owners and other colonizers neglected their Christian responsibility to properly bury deceased Afrodescendants. As Manuel I had done in 1515, the Jesuit missionary Alonso de Sandoval (Seville 1576–Cartagena de Indias 1652) complained about this neglect in his treatise on Africans, titled *Naturaleza, policia sagrada i profana, costumbres i ritos, disciplina i catechismo evangelico de todos etiopes* (1627), better known by its 1647 edition, *De instauranda Aethiopum salute*:

> Pues ya si el negro se muere, el amo enterrarlo ha. No tiene esso remedio (no hablo de los que mueren en las armazones) sino es que pidan para su entierro limosna sus parintes, contribuyan todos los de su casta, pongase para ello una mesa junto al cuerpo muerto: echese derrama, dando aviso a su cofradia, deonde no, ay está el cementerio, aunque sea muy ladino, y muy antiguo en casa.

> *After arriving here [in Cartagena de Indias], slaves will not be buried unless their relatives provide money to pay for their burial. People from their caste [group] will collect donations and bring the money together over the dead body. They also depend on their brotherhoods to bury them, even if they are very ladino [Hispanized] and have lived many years in the same house.*[35]

As Sandoval notes, even American-born Creoles relied on confraternities for burial. Indeed, as in the Iberian Peninsula, confraternity membership functioned as a form of death insurance for its members, for in the Americas, confraternities of every social and ethnoracial makeup were the sole providers of burial services.[36]

Colonial Afro-Latin Americans also relied on confraternities for medical care. In Lima, where Afro-Limeños were excluded from the city's "hospitals" reserved for Spaniards and the native population, two Black sodalities founded two hospitals for Blacks outside the city walls, across the Rímac River, where the Black population lived.[37] One of the hospitals, called San Lázaro, was designed to care for enslaved Afro-Limeños; the other, San Bartolomé, cared for free(d) Afro-Limeños. In Mexico City, a group of mulattos tried to start a hospital in 1568, "because those in the city only serve[d] Spaniards and Indians."[38] Although the Council of the Indies gave them permission to do so, ordering city officials to grant them the land, the viceroy, Martín Enríquez, instructed the Council to revoke its permission.[39] The viceroy feared that Black confraternities would be sites of Black rebellion. Nonetheless, the Afro-Mexican brotherhood of La Concepción was able to care for infirm Blacks in the city's hospital for *Naturales* (natives), founded by Hernán Cortes in 1519.

As Viceroy Enríquez's reluctance to allow Afro-Mexicans to establish a hospital for fear that they may use it to subvert colonial rule shows, colonial authorities did not want to allow Black confraternities because they did not want to see Blacks gathering in large numbers. As Irving A. Leonard noted in the 1950s, this fear corresponded to a colonial neurosis that Blacks were always plotting against colonial rule.[40] Even Church officials tried to stop Black sodalities. In this respect, the Church not only tried to control popular devotion, as it was constantly attempting with the Spanish population, but it also saw Africans as neophytes, or new converts, who were still prone to engaging in non-Catholic rituals. For their part, city officials saw Black confraternities as sites of drunkenness and criminal activity such as theft.[41]

Notwithstanding, Black confraternities also served as the principal sites of colonial Afro-Latin Americans' festive customs and regularly participated in colonial public festivals. These practices underscore how Afrodescendants continued the confraternal traditions inaugurated by Afro-Iberians in the late medieval period. From the sixteenth to the nineteenth centuries, Black brotherhoods carried out their social and cultural activities on both sides of the Atlantic, demarking a cultural space where Black bodies and cultural practices circulated with a high degree of frequency. A traveler could witness essentially the same confraternal practices in Buenos Aires, Lima, Rio de Janeiro, Salvador, Cartagena de Indias, Panama, Mexico, Havana, Lisbon, Seville, and Madrid, to name the principal cities of the Iberian Atlantic. And although I know of no research that has been done on Black confraternal practices in the Spanish Philippines, it is possible that the same is also true of the Pacific. This is a question that merits investigation and perhaps even the next stage of Afro-diasporic studies.

Why Black Confraternities Disappeared

Black sodalities did not disappear with the age of liberalism or abolition. In Brazil, in fact, they remain a large part of many Afro-Brazilian communities. In Cuba they morphed into *sociedades de negros* (Black societies), known as *cabildos* today. In Mexico, although their number had dwindled, they were ultimately outlawed by the liberal reforms of the 1850s, which dissolved all religious institutions within the national territory. What remains a mystery, or has not yet been studied, is how they disappeared in the Iberian Peninsula—except for the *Negritos* of Seville—and in places like the River Plate region, where they were active at the beginning of the nineteenth century but were all gone by the end of it. We do not know what happened in the rest of the Iberian Peninsula, as not enough research has been dedicated to the phenomenon, yet, ironically, the rise of liberalism in Spain saw the erasure of Afro-Hispanics from the national imaginary. In South America, we know that in Argentina and Uruguay they morphed into Black dance troupes, known for their Carnival performances, which led to their gradual secularization until they became fully secular social clubs of an intellectual hue, promoting Black civil rights. In Peru, as in Seville, those that did not disappear were taken over by non-Black groups.[42]

NOTES

1. Ordenanzas de la cofradía de los cristianos negros de Barcelona, March 20, 1455, R. 3298, f. 3r, Archivo General de la Corona de Aragón (hereafter AGCA), Barcelona, Spain (emphasis added). All translations are mine unless otherwise noted.
2. Carmen Fracchia, *'Black but Human': Slavery and the Visual Arts in Hapsburg Spain, 1480–1700* (Oxford: Oxford University Press, 2019), 48–55; see also Isidro Moreno, *La antigua hermandad de los negros de Sevilla: Etnicidad, poder y sociedad en 600 años de historia* (Seville: University of Seville, 1997), 23–56.
3. Karen B. Graubart, "'So color de una cofradía': Catholic Confraternities and the Development of Afro-Peruvian Ethnicities in Early Colonial Peru," *Slavery and Abolition* 33, no. 1 (2012): 46–48.
4. Jorge Fonseca, *Religião e liberdade: Os negros nas irmandades e confrarias portuguesas (séculos XV à XIX)* (Lisbon: Humus, 2016), 23–37.
5. Fundación de la cofradía de los negros libertos de la ciudad de Valencia, 1472, R. 3512, ff. 217–18, AGCA.
6. Leo Garofalo, "The Shape of the Diaspora: The Movement of Afro-Iberians to Colonial Spanish America," in *Africans to Spanish America: Expanding the Diaspora*, ed. S. K.

Bryant, R. S. O'Toole, and B. Vinson III (Urbana-Champaign: University of Illinois Press, 2012), 28. On slavery in the Iberian Peninsula, see William D. Philips, *Slavery in Medieval and Early Modern Iberia* (Philadelphia: University of Pennsylvania Press, 2014); Alastair Corston de Custance Maxwell Saunders, *Social History of Black Slaves and Freedmen in Portugal, 1441–1555* (Cambridge: Cambridge University Press, 2010).

7. For a somewhat comprehensive list of Afro-Iberian confraternities, see Patricia Ann Mulvey, "The Black Lay Brotherhoods of Colonial Brazil: A History" (PhD diss., City University of New York, 1976), 283–85.

8. Ordenanzas de la cofradía de los cristianos negros de Barcelona, f. 3v. See also Reglas de la cofradía de Nuestra Señora de los Ángeles, Institución Colombina, 1558, Sección Justicia, Serie Hermandades y Cofradías: 94, Seville, Spain, Fondo Archivo Arzobispal.

9. Para a cidade sobre o poço hi es lançarem os escravos, 1515, Provimento da saude, 1, f. 51, Archivo Nacional da Torre Tombo, Lisbon, Portugal.

10. See J. Omosade Awolalu, *Yoruba Beliefs and Sacrificial Rites* (London: Longman, 1979), 53–68.

11. Ibid.

12. See Larissa Brewer-García, "Hierarchy and Holiness in the Earliest Colonial Black Hagiographies: Alonso De Sandoval and His Sources," *William and Mary Quarterly* 76, no. 3 (2019): 477–508; Erin K. Rowe, *Black Saints in Early Modern Global Catholicism* (Cambridge: Cambridge University Press, 2019); Rowe, "Visualizing Black Sanctity in Early Modern Spanish Polychrome Sculpture," in *Envisioning Others: Race, Color, and the Visual in Iberia and Latin America*, ed. P. A. Patton (Leiden: Brill, 2016), 51–82; Rowe, "After Death Her Face Turned White: Blackness, Whiteness, and Sanctity in the Early Modern Hispanic World," *American Historical Review* 121, no. 3 (2016): 726–54.

13. See Chloe Ireton, "'They Are Blacks of the Caste of Black Christians': Old Christian Black Blood in the Sixteenth and Early Seventeenth-Century Iberian Atlantic," *Hispanic American Historical Review* 97, no. 4 (2017): 579–612.

14. Diego Ortiz de Zuñiga, *Anales eclesiásticos y seculares de la muy noble y muy leal ciudad de Sevilla que contienen sus más principales memorias desde el año de 1246 hasta el de 1671* (Madrid: Royal Printing Office, 1677), 374.

15. William D. Philips, *Slavery in Medieval and Early Modern Iberia* (Philadelphia: University of Pennsylvania Press, 2014), 10–11.

16. Ortiz de Zuñiga, *Anales eclesiásticos y seculares*, 374.

17. See Michael D. Bristol, *Carnival and Theater: Plebian Culture and the Structure of Authority in Renaissance England* (New York: Methuen, 1985), 27; James C. Scott, *Domination and the Arts of Resistance: Hidden Transcripts* (New Haven, CT: Yale University Press, 1990), 183–201; Peter Stallybrass and Allon White, *The Politics and Poetics of Transgression* (Ithaca: Cornell University Press, 1986), 13–14.

18. Isidoro Moreno, "Plurietnicidad, fiestas y poder: Cofradías y fiestas andaluzas de negros como modelo para la América colonial," in *El mundo festivo en España y América*, ed. A. Garrido Aranda (Córdoba: Universidad de Córdoba, 2005), 169–88.

19. José Ribeiro Guimarães, *Summario de varia historia. Narrativas, lendas, biographias, descripcões de templos e monumentos, estadisticas, costumes, civis, politicos e religiosos de outras eras*, vol. 5 (Lisbon: Rolland and Semoind, 1872), 148.
20. Compromisso da irmandade de Nossa Senhora do Rosário dos homens pretos, 1565, MS 151, ff. 9v–10r, National Library of Portugal, Lisbon, Portugal.
21. Didier Lahon, "Esclavage, confréries noires, sainteté noire et pureté de sang au Portugal (XVIème–XVIIIème siècles)," *Lusitana Sacra* 2, no. 15 (2003): 41–42.
22. See Elizabeth W. Kiddy, "*Congados, Calunga, Candombe*: Our Lady of the Rosary in Minas Gerais, Brazil," *Luso-Brazilian Review* 37, no. 1 (2000): 47–61.
23. *Folheto de ambas Lisboas*, 1730, no. 7, f. 4, Oficina de Música, Lisbon.
24. See Tania Alkmim, "Falas e cores: Um estudo sobre o português de negros e escravos no Brasil do século XIX," in *História da língua nacional*, ed. L. do Carmo and I. Stolze Lima (Rio de Janeiro: Casa de Rui Barbosa, 2008), 247–51; José Ramos Tinhorão, *Os negros em Portugal: Uma presença silenciosa* (Lisbon: Caminho, 1988) 201–5; MarcellaTrambaioli, "Apuntes sobre el guineo o baile de negros: Tipologías y funciones dramáticas," in *Memoria de la palabra. Actas del VI Congreso de la Asociación Internacional Siglo de Oro*, ed. M. L. Lobato and F. Domínguez Matito (Madrid: Iberoamericana, 2004), 1773–83.
25. *Folheto de ambas Lisboas*, no. 7, f. 3.
26. Anonymous, *Breve extracto do augustissimo triunfo, que a augusta Braga prepara em obsequio do Santissimo Sancramento* (Coimbra: Colegio das Artes da Companhia de Jesu, 1731), f. 2.
27. Ibid.
28. Cécile Fromont, "Dancing for the King of Congo from Early Modern Central Africa to Slavery-Era Brazil," *Colonial Latin American Review* 22, no. 2, (2013): 184–208.
29. Mariana de Mello e Souza, *Reis negros no Brasil escravista: Historia da festa de coroaçõ de rei congo* (Belo Horizonte: Universidade Federal de Minas Gerais, 2002), 85–95.
30. Fracchia, *'Black but Human'*; Baltasar Fra-Molinero, *La imagen de los negros en el teatro del Siglo de Oro* (Madrid: Siglo XXI, 1996); Nicholas R. Jones, *Staging habla de negros: Radical Performances of the African Diaspora in Early Modern Spain* (University Park: Pennsylvania State University, 2019).
31. Moreno, "Plurietnicidad, fiestas y poder." See Graubart, "'So color de una cofradía'"; Matthew Restall, "Black Conquistadors: Armed Africans in Early Spanish America," *The Americas* 57, no. 2 (2000): 171–205.
32. Nicole von Germeten, *Black Blood Brothers: Confraternities and Social Mobility for Afro-Mexicans* (Gainesville: University Press of Florida, 2006), 22.
33. "Reglas de la cofradía del Rosario (1538)," in *Juan Bautista Méndez, Crónica de la provincial de Santiago de México de la Orden de Predicadores, (1521–1564)*, ed. J. A. Fernández (Mexico City: Porrua, 1993), 80–81.
34. Bernal Díaz del Castillo, *Historia verdadera de la conquista de la Nueva España (manuscrito "Guatemala")*, ed. J. A. Barbón Rodríguez (Mexico City: Colegio de México/UNAM, [c. 1550] 2005), 753–60. See Miguel A. Valerio, "A Mexican *Sangamento*? The First Afro-Christian Performance in the Americas," in *Afro-Catholic Festivals in*

the Americas: Performance, Representation, and the Making of Black Atlantic Tradition, ed. C. Fromont (University Park: Pennsylvania State University Press, 2019), 59–74.
35. Alonso de Sandoval, *Un tratado sobre la esclavitud*, ed. E. Vila Vilar (Madrid: Alianza, 1987), 238. Translation from Sandoval, *Treatise on Slavery*, trans. N. von Germeten (Indianapolis: Hackett, 2008), 70–71 (my brackets). See also Margaret M. Olsen, *Slavery and Salvation in Colonial Cartagena de Indias* (Gainesville: University Press of Florida, 2004).
36. See João José Reis, *Death Is a Festival: Funeral Rites and Rebellion in Nineteenth-Century Brazil*, trans. H. Sabrina Gledhill (Chapel Hill: University of North Carolina Press, 2003).
37. See José Ramón Jouve Martín, *The Black Doctors of Colonial Lima: Science, Race, and Writing in Colonial and Early Republican Peru* (Montreal: McGill-Queen's University Press, 2014), 10–14; Nancy E. van Deusen, "The 'Alienated' Body: Slaves and Castas in the Hospital de San Bartolomé in Lima, 1680 to 1700," *The Americas* 56, no. 1 (1999): 1–30.
38. Memorial de vecinos mulatos de la Nueva España, March 5, 1568, Archivo General de Indias (hereafter AGI), México, 98.
39. "Real cédula a la Audiencia y a el arzobispo de México para que, en la solicitud de los mulatos de Nueva España, hijos de negros e indias o de españoles y negras, que piden licencia y ayuda para hacer un hospital donde sean curados y fundarlo junto a la iglesia de San Hipólito, en unos solares al lado de la ermita de los Mártires, les proporcionen sitio en dichos solares sin perjuicio de tercero y el favor y ayuda necesarios," AGI, México, 1089:5, ff. 260 (November 4, 1568); "Real cédula a Martín Enríquez, virrey de Nueva España, y a la Audiencia de México para que provean lo que convenga en la solicitud de los mulatos de México que piden un sitio, con estancias y propios, para fundar un hospital, pues los que hay en México son para españoles o para los indios," AGI, México, 1089:5, ff. 347v–348v (June 2, 1569); "Real cédula al virrey de Nueva España y presidente de la Audiencia de México para que informen sobre la solicitud de los mulatos de Nueva España que piden ayuda para la fundación y edificación de un hospital," AGI, México, 1090:6, f. 180 (November 3, 1570); Carta del virrey Martín Enríquez, AGI, México, 19:82, f. 1v. (April 28, 1572).
40. Irving A. Leonard, *Baroque Times in Old Mexico* (Ann Arbor: University of Michigan Press, 1959), 19–20. See also Jean-Pierre Tardieu, *Resistencia de los negros en el virreinao de México (siglos XVI–XVII)* (Frankfurt: Vervuert, 2017), 213–25.
41. See Graubart, "'So color de una cofradía.'"
42. Julia Costilla, "Una práctica negra que ha ganado a los blancos: Símbolo, historia y devotos en el culto al Señor de los Milagros de Lima (siglos XIX–XXI)," *Anthropológica* 34, no. 36 (2016): 149–76.

CHAPTER 3

In Search of the Black Swordsman

Race and Martial Arts Discourse in Early Modern Iberia

MANUEL OLMEDO GOBANTE

It was the year 1600. On January 3, the Alba-Medrano family filed a peculiar lawsuit at the town hall of Úbeda, Spain.[1] They demanded to be officially recognized as Blacks. Their complaint was that they were wrongly identified as Moriscos, that is to say, as the descendants of Spain's Muslim population that was forcibly converted to Christianity in the early sixteenth century. The Alba-Medranos were included in the registry of Moriscos because of the neighborhood in which they lived and because they were *atezados*; that is, they had dark skin. They claimed that their inclusion in the registry had been unlawful because, in reality, they were Wolof people (*negros jolofos*), an ethnic group from modern-day Mauritania, Senegal, and Gambia.[2] Thus, they demanded to be recognized as such and removed from the registry of Moriscos. In order to succeed, the Alba-Medrano family had to prove their identity as Blacks. To do this, they adduced the legal record of Luis Alba, a relative who had allegedly fought against the Moriscos in the Alpujarra wars.

Luis Alba had filed many lawsuits against civil authorities in the cities of Écija and Jaén more than ten years before the Alba-Medranos' case. He complained, for example, that he had been wrongly compelled to attend Mass in a Morisco church, when he was actually a member of an Afro-

Iberian confraternity called Cofradía de la Misericordia. Luis also complained, on multiple occasions, that law enforcement authorities in both Écija and Jaén used to "bother" and arrest him for carrying a sword. In modern-day terms, he was being racially profiled. After years of litigation, Luis Alba won every case. He was allowed to attend his confraternity and obtained a license to carry swords, a permit that, in theory, he should not need, because the prohibition against owning swords applied only to Moriscos, who were under permanent suspicion after the Rebellion of the Alpujarras.[3] In any case, ten years later, the sword that Luis Alba fought to keep became a key element in the Alba-Medranos' litigation.

Stories like that of the Alba-Medranos show that, more than mere weapons, swords functioned as ethnic markers capable of mediating racial difference. This was due to the strong influence of martial arts culture on many aspects of early modern society, including class, gender, and race relations. Martial arts have been understood as a form of violence management. The question of who is allowed to control or exert violence is key to the organization of a society. For this reason, throughout world history, oppressed groups have striven to engage in martial arts to confront oppression in both a symbolic and a literal way.[4]

This chapter demonstrates how, as the most popular martial art in early modern Iberia, swordplay offered people of African descent the opportunity to improve their lives. The social impact of the institution of fencing, combined with the prestige granted by martial art discourses, enabled them not only to ameliorate their socioeconomic position in a slave-owning society, but also to oppose stereotyping and discrimination. Moreover, sword culture, in all its manifestations, played a crucial role in how Blackness was understood in the period. In order to substantiate these claims, we will explore the practices and discourses of early modern fencing, in search of Black swordsmen.[5] In part one, we will examine their presence in Iberian society by providing an overview of the early modern fencing world. In part two, we will discuss their textual representations both in martial art treatises and in literature. Studying the intersections between race and martial arts explains the strong Black Iberian participation in early modern martial arts, warns us against the unintentional biases with which we may read Spanish Golden Age literature, and provides the sociocultural context that allowed people like the Alba-Medranos to pursue an Afro-Hispanic identity.

Black Swordsmen in the Early Modern World of Fencing

Fencing is the art of fighting with swords following certain sociability codes and safety measures. In contrast with the traditional image of fencing as a chivalric exercise, in the early modern world it was indeed an everyday urban phenomenon. People of all social strata paid to attend fencing schools, which were located in all sorts of public venues, such as town squares and private houses, for example. On feast days, municipalities or, on occasion, fencing masters themselves organized fencing games (*juegos de esgrima*), massive fencing competitions where both professional swordsmen and the general public fought under the supervision of a sword master.[6] For safety reasons, sharp weapons were not allowed, so rebated swords (*espadas negras*) were used instead. Unlike other sports of the period—such as jousts, bullfights, or games of canes—the *juego de esgrima* was fully open to the entire adult male population. In theory, noblemen and commoners, rich and poor alike competed under the same conditions with literally the same swords. One cannot overstate the popularity of the *juego de esgrima* in early modern Spain. Many idioms now alive in the Spanish language also come directly from the everyday practices of the *juego de esgrima*, such as *saltar a la palestra* (to make a public appearance; Real Academia Española, "palestra") and others that are less used but still found in dictionaries, such as *echar el bastón* or *meter el montante* (to conciliate two parties; Real Academia Española, "Bastón" and "Montante").[7]

Fencing was also a large social institution. Swordsmen were organized in a complex hierarchy that ranged from beginning students and bachelors to provosts and masters. The highest rank was the headmaster and examiner (*maestro examinador mayor*), whose duty was to oversee a structure of professional examinations and licenses (*cartas de examen*) known as the Spanish system. In theory, the headmaster could exercise his jurisdiction in all the Iberian kingdoms and its colonies, making the Spanish system one of the few institutions of imperial transatlantic proportions.[8]

Beyond being a popular sporting event and a social institution, fencing's status as a martial art means that it should be regarded as a self-defense system with strong sociocultural and philosophical implications. As a form of embodied knowledge, martial arts often are corporeal expressions of gender, religious, or ethnic identities.[9] The transmission of fencing, as a martial art, required textual mediators. Swordplay was taught face to face, but also through a wide variety of "technical" or "pragmatic literature," from short notes on fencing techniques—*tretas en nota*—to full-fledged treatises.[10] Hundreds of books on swordplay were published in early modern Iberia. Also called "fight books"—or *libros de esgrima*, in the Spanish context—these martial arts treatises constitute an inestimable source for reconstructing not only the practice of early modern fencing but also the ideas on martial arts of the period.[11]

Literature in all its forms—drama, poetry, and prose— also played a significant role in the representation, mediation, and mediatization of fencing.[12] The same way that twentieth century audiences learned about kung fu or karate from cinema and TV, early modern people learned about fencing from chivalric literature and action drama. In turn, swordsmen adapted their practice according to the expectations created by these martial arts discourses.[13]

One school of fencing was particularly successful in early modern Iberia: the Verdadera Destreza (literally "True Fencing"), founded by Jerónimo Sánchez de Carranza in the second half of the sixteenth century. Verdadera Destreza became practically hegemonic in most of the empire after Luis Pacheco de Narváez, a self-proclaimed follower of Carranza's art, emerged as the Spanish headmaster in 1624. Iberian treatises on Verdadera Destreza were still being written and published as late as 1805.[14]

Years before Carranza and Narváez's fencing was declared official in the Iberian Peninsula, Verdadera Destreza had already become a global movement, internationally called "Spanish fencing."[15] According to Ordóñez de Ceballos's travel accounts, the "fencing of Carranza" was known by almost every Spanish and Portuguese sailor in an expedition and was once practiced "somewhere on the coast of Cochinchina" (in modern-day Vietnam) in 1592, ten years after the publication of the first fencing treatise on Verdadera Destreza.[16]

Spanish fencing can also be found in England at the end of the sixteenth century. Aside from the uncertain references in Shakespeare's *Romeo and Juliet* and *Hamlet*, Verdadera Destreza was alluded to on many occasions by other Elizabethan dramatists such as Ben Jonson, Francis Beaumont, John Fletcher, and Philip Massinger.[17] English sword master George Silver describes the Spanish "perfect ward" (*ángulo recto*) in his fencing treatise of 1599: "This is the manner of Spanish fight. They stand as brave as they can with their bodies straight upright, narrow spaced, with their feet continually moving, as if they were in a dance, holding forth their arms and rapiers very straight against the face or bodies of their enemies."[18]

FIGURE 3.1. Views of the University of Leiden / *Delineatio Ludi Publici Gladiatorii* (1610). Courtesy of the British Museum, number 1875,0814.740.

By this date, Verdadera Destreza was practiced and taught regularly in Mexico City, as shown in master Sancho Ibáñez de Agurto's license of 1603.[19] It also spread throughout Europe. In the Dutch Netherlands, Willem Swanenburgh's engraving of a fencing school at the University of Leiden shows a number of swordsmen practicing recognizable techniques of Verdadera Destreza, such as the aforementioned *ángulo recto* and the *atajo* (see Figure 3.1).[20] As we see below, a geometrical diagram drawn on the ground of said fencing school also manifests Carranza's art.

Beyond being a style of fencing, Verdadera Destreza was also a philosophical and cultural movement. The main characteristic of its martial art discourse is the distinction between two kinds of fencing, one "vulgar," "common," or "ordinary" and the other "true" (*verdadera*) and based in science, theology, and reason. According to *diestros verdaderos* (the truly skilled), their fencing was true because it drew heavily on disciplines such as medicine, ethics, astronomy, natural philosophy, and especially geometry.[21] For this reason, they argued, (true) fencing was as a liberal art.

Claiming the dignity of the liberal arts was not *flatus vocis*. Since Antiquity, social stratification and even slavery have been justified with the distinction between the liberal (those belonging to the free) as opposed to the mechanical, servile, or vulgar arts of the commoners.[22] In early modern Spain, being recognized as a liberal artist offered many advantages, from an increase in social status to substantial tax exemptions. The claims of Verdadera Destreza can be understood in light of other workers who attempted to legitimize their professions with the liberal arts discourse.[23] The best-known case is that of the Spanish painters, the celebrated Diego Velázquez, for example, who strove to classify painting as a liberal art in the seventeenth century.[24]

Scholars have interpreted Verdadera Destreza as a reactionary, elitist discourse. According to Mary Theresa Dill Curtis, Carranza's art was "an exclusionary practice" intended "to reform and promote Spanish swordplay as a necessary and noble elite activity."[25] This is partially true. Carranza devoted hundreds of pages to berating the "ignorant plebs" (*vulgo ignorante*) in his *Filosofía de las armas*.[26] He also lamented that fencing had ceased to be the chivalric art that it, supposedly, once was. The characters of this dialogue state that even miners—who have the lowest profession literally and figuratively—are quitting their jobs and training in fencing to make a living: "Los cavadores han dejado de cavar por darse a enseñar armas, que es más fácil."[27] Indeed, as we have seen, fencing had become extremely popular, both as martial art and as profession.

In order to differentiate themselves, Carranza and his followers elevated fencing to the category of liberal art, constituting a discipline "reservada para hombres nobles y sabios" (reserved for noble and wise men). Lettered men, according to him, have the same right as the nobility to practice fencing. Furthermore, he claimed that "los hombres, aunque sean grandes, muy poco voto tienen en lo que no saben" (men, even if they are noble, have very little say on what they don't know).[28] Thus, in its socio-historical context, Verdadera Destreza can be understood as a revolutionary martial art. Its purpose never was in making swordplay noble again but rather the opposite. In the end, its discourse allowed more people to access the cultural capital of chivalry and offered some fencers the opportunity for upward mobility. Unsurprisingly, most of the diestros verdaderos were lowborn people. Some, like Carranza, experienced a spectacular social advancement chiefly due to their martial arts careers. Consequently, the liberating promises of Verdadera Destreza may have resonated well with those who were most disadvantaged in early modern Spain: the enslaved and freemen of African descent.[29]

Almost certainly, there were diestros verdaderos of African descent. The most remarkable example may be master Francisco Hernández, a mulatto sword master who founded the fencing school of Sevilla, one of the most important lineages of sixteenth-century martial art masters. Even though we lack information about master Hernández, we know that one of his direct disciples was Méndez de Carmona, author of three treatises on Verdadera Destreza and defender of the Sevillian school (known as *carrancistas*) against the ascendance of Pacheco de Narváez as headmaster.[30] Méndez Carmona allegedly taught fencing to master Francisco de Añasco, who was remembered long after his death as the champion of the Sevillian school.[31] In turn, Añasco instructed Baltasar de los Reyes, mentor to Juan Ignacio de la Muñecas Marmontaño. Curiously enough, we only know about master Hernández's race as a chance occurrence. Had it not been for a passing comment by Pacheco Narváez, we would not know that the long tradition of the *carrancistas* started with a mulatto sword master.[32] This warns us against assuming the Whiteness of any particular historical fencer.

Regardless of their adhesion to Verdadera Destreza, the historical record is full of examples of Afro-Hispanic swordsmen, as demonstrated by the first modern scholars who studied fencing in Iberia: Sousa Viterbo (1897) and Gestoso y Pérez (1911).[33] The former, shocked by "the large number of people of color" in fencing, found several Black and mulatto sword players in early modern Portugal, such as Jorge Fernandes, a mulatto master from Setubal; master Francisco da Fonseca, a Black freeman from Africa who owned a fencing school in Lisbon; and Roque, a skillful enslaved Black who attended master Henrique's school.[34] Gestoso Pérez provided information on master Vella, a fencer married to a Sevillian mulatto woman in 1556, as well as on master Juan Dominguez, a mulatto swordsman who lived in Seville in the first half of the seventeenth century.[35] Another mulatto swordsman from Seville died during a fencing tournament in 1573.[36] Recent historians have provided more examples of Black Luso-Hispanic fencers, such as Master Pedro, who taught swordplay in the Azores around 1580.[37]

In other words, Iberia was not an exception within its European context, where a great number of Black Africans and people of African descent practiced fencing on a regular basis. According to Kate Lowe: "Black Africans were also skilled at swordplay of various sports and were often allowed to continue working or encouraged to work in this area, so that Africans were often associated with displays of swordsmanship" (33).

While Lowe acknowledges that "martial skills would have found favour in Renaissance Europe, where it was believed that a gentleman should possess the 'manly' virtues manifested by skill at arms" (32), she suggests that Black people's high participation in the world of fencing was both a cause and an effect of their systematic oppression and marginalization:

> Yet allowing that people of African descent were good at certain physical activities also led to a negative stereotype, as they were prized for their physical rather than their intellectual or human qualities. Pursuits involving intellectual skills are, on the contrary, only very infrequently mentioned in connection with Black Africans.... Their pigeonholing in occupations related to physical prowess and entertainment, resulted not only in their exclusion from much of mainstream European life, but also in their denigration. (41)

However, it may be misleading to count fencing among "other pastimes involving physical prowess (or enhanced physicality)" (34). Contrary to what we may believe today, swordsmen of the time did not see fencing as a brutish exercise or even as an athletic activity. For instance, according to Headmaster Pacheco de Narváez, swordplay does not involve bodily qualities like strength or speed but rather intelligence, along with other mental faculties such as wit, memory, prudence, and courage.[38] Thus, it is hard to understand how being proficient in swordplay would result in further downward mobility in a slave-owning society, especially if we consider that, as we have previously seen, few institutions were more "mainstream" than fencing in early modern Iberia.

In any case, Afro-Hispanics were definitely not "encouraged to work" in fencing, as Lowe states.[39] Quite the opposite, efforts were systematically made to prohibit Black people and other racialized minorities from engaging in fencing in any manner. For example, since 1478, two out of the nine provisions stated in the headmaster's diploma served this purpose (titles five and six, according to Guilmaín Alonso).[40] By virtue of this document, the headmaster had to report any "Moor, Black, Jew, or slave who dares to teach [fencing] ... whether in public or in private." Moreover, the headmaster had to penalize with a large fine any master who taught fencing to any of these minorities.[41]

Masters often vowed not to teach minorities at their examination ceremonies, although some skipped this part for unspecified reasons. For example, Master Cristóbal Martínez swore not to "teach the aforementioned profession to any Moor or Jew" (que no mostraría el dicho oficio a moro ni judío) in 1523, without mentioning Black people. Master Diego de Bernal's license (carta de examen) of 1526 went further by not mentioning any kind of restriction, since he was authorized "to teach anybody who wanted to learn" and "to set a stand or open a shop and instruct whoever he wants in said arts" (mostrar a las personas que lo quisieren aprender . . . Poner plaza e tienda de mostrar las dichas artes a quien quisiere).[42] Master Fernando de Algarbe's 1528 license, granted by Diego de Bernal, states that he swore not to "teach fencing to any Moor, Jew, neither to any slave White or Black" (mostrar la esgrima a ningún moro, ni judío, ni esclavo blanco ni negro),[43] possibly implying that Black freemen would be allowed to learn under his supervision. However, most of the licenses—e.g., Martín de Vargas's carta of 1660— prohibited masters from teaching Black people, regardless of whether they were enslaved.[44]

Moorish people and Moriscos had been banned not only from fencing but also from owning and carrying swords since 1405.[45] The same applied to enslaved people of all kinds, both in Iberia and in its colonies. As an exception, some were allowed to carry swords only when working as bodyguards, something that had been relatively common since the Middle Ages.[46] For example, the prior of Peru and his officials were regularly escorted by two "armed slaves" beginning in 1613. Black freemen could, in theory, carry a sword in early modern Iberia.[47] However, as we have seen with the Alba-Medrano case, in practice this was not always so.

In reality, Afro-Hispanics faced great difficulties not only in carrying swords but even handling rebated weapons in fencing games. For example, a 1570 legal petition demanded the prohibition of "slaves and mulattos" from carrying arms and entering juegos de esgrima in Córdoba. A year later, the Courts of Madrid voted on a bill in which again "slaves and mulattos" were banned from carrying swords and even accessing fencing academies, with penalties for those masters who allowed them.[48] Even though the king overturned the petitions of 1570 and 1571, Black people continued facing discrimination in the world of fencing.[49] An eighteenth-century manuscript on how to behave in the fencing classroom still had to denounce the exclusion of Black fencers from the juego de esgrima: "No kind of person—even if they are Black men or slaves—should be prevented from entering public fencing games. Because they are contests of skills, not of lineages."[50]

To recapitulate, despite a fierce opposition and even attempts to legislate against it, many Afro-Hispanics did participate in fencing, and some actually became sword masters. The question arises: if fencing was a denigrating pastime, as Lowe suggests, why did so many strive to take an active part in it?[51] As we have seen, teaching swordplay was a high-demand profession that could improve their economic conditions substantially. Moreover, the institution of fencing—both the local social spaces and the aforementioned Spanish system—may have allowed for collective spaces of resistance to oppression, similar to the *nación de negros* that emerged from the Black confraternities.[52] From this perspective, the early modern Afro-Hispanic engagement with fencing can be considered as one chapter in the long history of the martial arts communities of the African diaspora.[53]

However, engaging in martial arts meant more than having a profession and socializing in certain spaces. In addition to not being allowed to own and utilize swords, enslaved Blacks shared one other prohibition with Jews and Moriscos: none of them could legally own people. As Baltasar Fra-Molinero explains, the rationale for this may have been that slavery was essential in the very definition of freedom. Following Angela Davis's application of Hegel's master and slave dialectic, Fra-Molinero argues that a free self-consciousness can only be attained from the "negative point of reference" of the slave-Other by the "negation" of Black people.[54] The application of Hegel's metaphor to the actual history of slavery has met criticism, mainly because, as Fanon famously objected, the enslaved Black does not seek his liberation in his work but "wants to be like his master."[55] In this context, the sword—even the rebated simulation of a sword—could be a *positive* point of reference for freedom, as the Wólofs from Úbeda seem to confirm. This implies replicating and appropriating the martial art discourse of the dominant class, as Fanon predicted.

However, martial arts discourse is not a static collection of ideas but the result of a series of negotiations. Thus, the strong participation of Afro-Hispanics in the world of fencing may have also contributed to the development of the ideas on race and the logics of liberation in martial arts discourses such as that of Verdadera Destreza. An examination of the presence of Black fencers in the textual mediators of early modern fencing—both functional treatises and literary works—may confirm that martial arts discourses offered Afro-Hispanics a set of strategies to define and pursue both freedom and a sense of identity, or at least to contest stereotyping and discrimination.

Black Swordsmen in Early Modern Martial Arts Discourse

To contextualize the role played by the sword in the Alba-Medrano litigation, it is helpful to understand how extensively Black swordsmen were represented positively in early modern martial arts discourse. Fencing treatises offer a good starting point, since many of them feature Black Africans. The earliest example may be *Alte Armatur und Ringkunst*, a 1459 manuscript by German master Talhoffer. This *Fechtbuch* features illustrations of two Black men, each fencing with polearms against a White opponent (see Figures 3.2 and 3.3).[56] Although Talhoffer's Black fencers are represented as a clear minority—they account for only two of over a hundred drawings—they are depicted wearing high-status clothing and on an equal basis with their White counterparts. Nothing here signals the racial discrimination they faced in and outside the world of fencing.

The same applies to the Black swordsmen drawn by Jörg Breu the Younger for the three manuscripts of *De arte athletica*, a series of fight books commissioned by Paulus Hector Mair in the mid-sixteenth century. One has been noted by Lowe: a Black fighter who fences with a sickle in the Bayerische Staatsbibliothek version (see Figure 3.4).[57] This sickle fencer is "extravagantly dressed" and wears golden earrings. The fact that he is the only Black fencer in the entire codex made Lowe posit that the image may refer to a real person.[58] However, he is not the only Black fencer of *De arte athletica*. In another manuscript kept now at the Sächsische Landesbibliothek in Dresden, we find another, this time fencing with the rapier and also wearing a similar—but not identical—earring (see Figure 3.5).[59]

Three more Black swordsmen are found in the version that resides at the Österreichische Nationalbibliothek. The first fights with a rapier and wears an ostentatious purple and yellow garment. The second fences with rapier and dagger and also wears a conspicuous earring.[60] The third fights with rapier and buckler, is barefoot, and wears much humbler clothes—though not humbler than his opponent's (see Figures 3.6, 3.7, and 3.8).[61] Lastly, a recently rediscovered fight book by Joachim Meyer offers yet another example of a visibly Afro-descendant fencer, depicted in luxurious garments (see Figure 3.9).[62]

The eight Black swordsmen featured in these fight books are portrayed as grave, neat, and proud martial artists. This confirms that martial arts discourse offered some Black fencers the opportunity to challenge the stereotypes typically associated with Black Africans in early modern Europe.

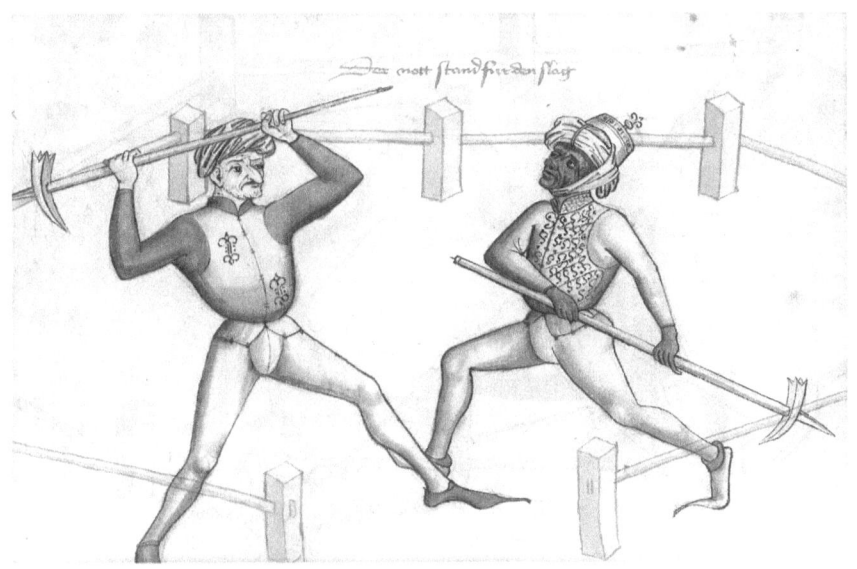

FIGURE 3.2. *Alte Armature und Ringkunst* (Talhoffer 1459, 73r).
Courtesy of the Royal Danish Library. Thott 290, 73r.

FIGURE 3.3. *Alte Armature und Ringkunst* (Talhoffer 1459, 74v).
Courtesy of the Royal Danish Library, Thott 290, 74v.

FIGURE 3.4. *De Arte Athletica*. Ms. Cod.icon.393. Courtesy of the Bavarian State Library, Bayerische Staatsbibliothek München, BSB Cod.icon. 393, 1, fol. 227r.

FIGURE 3.5. *De Arte Athletica. Ms. Dresd.* C.94 Courtesy of the Saxon State and University Library Dresden, SLUB Dresden / Digital Collections / Mscr. Dresd. C.94, 141r.

FIGURE 3.6. *De Arte Athletica*. Ms. Cod. 10826. Courtesy of the Austrian National Library, Österrreichische Nationalbibliothek, Ms. Cod. 10826, 122v.

FIGURE 3.7. *De Arte Athletica*. Ms. Cod. 10826. Courtesy of the Austrian National Library, Österrerchische Nationalbibliothek, Ms. Cod. 10826, 126r.

FIGURE 3.8. *De Arte Athletica*. Ms. Cod. 10826. Courtesy of the Austrian National Library, Österreichische Nationalbibliothek, Ms. Cod. 10826, 143r.

FIGURE 3.9. Joachim Meyer's *Fechtbuch gefertigt für Johann Pfalzagraf bei Rhein*. Courtesy of the National Museum of Bavaria, Bayerisches Nationalmuseum Ms. Bibl. 2465, 58v.

Our next example substantiates that this can be extrapolated to the Iberian context.

In a previous article, I provided information regarding a notable reference to Black swordsmen in the first work by Luis Pacheco de Narváez—the aforementioned master of Verdadera Destreza who argued that swordplay was an intellectual activity.[63] In a three-page digression within his *Grandezas de la espada* (1600), Narváez claims that every swordsman should be cautious about a "great number" of Black fencers, for many of them have the "virtue of courage," and many others are so skillful that they "should be envied by many Whites."[64]

Black swordsmen, Narváez says, pose the additional challenge of being hard to read. A number of pages before, Narváez explains that—as Galenic medicine used to teach—everybody fights according to their predominant humor: cholera, blood, phlegm, or melancholy.[65] As the master explains, good fencers are supposed to tell their opponent's temperament through the art of physiognomy, that is, by interpreting physical traits such as skin tone or hair type. The additional challenge, according to Narváez, is that Black people conceal their true colors, because they "hide" their true skin tone under a "veil of black."[66] In order to overcome this "obstacle," Narváez recommends paying attention to their personality, since their mental and behavioral traits will always betray their prevalent humor. Consequently, the master provides what can be considered the first scientific typology of Black Africans, a taxonomy that divides Black swordsmen into four categories: the melancholic Black, the phlegmatic Black, the sanguine Black, and the choleric Black.

According to Narváez, one should be especially cautious about the Black choleric. Cholera was thought to be influenced by planet Mars, which in turn ruled over war and warriors (hence the word "martial"). Unsurprisingly, choleric or martial Black swordsmen are the most suited for fencing. In order to identify them, the master provides a long list of positive qualities. A set of five characteristics can be extracted from said description: courage, gravity, pride and social intelligence, neatness, and articulateness.[67] Needless to say, these are extremely positive qualities that were typically associated with nobility at the time. More importantly, as we will see next, they contrast with our current understanding of early modern ideas on race.

Scholars such as Lowe have long studied the pervasiveness of stereotypes and negative representations of Blacks in early modern Europe. Fra-Molinero convincingly argues that literature played a crucial role in this, by fixing a stable "image" of the literary Black based on two comical features: childishness and poor speech. Santos Morillo continues this research line by positing a list of seven traits that define the characterization of Black men and women in sixteenth-century Spanish literature: quarrelsomeness, childishness, melomania, lust, presumptuousness, brutishness, and ignorance of God.[68] Very little attention has been paid, in contrast, to positive representations of early modern Afro-Hispanics.

Narváez's classification, however, yields a heterogeneous image of Black people, one that perpetuates some stereotypes often associated with them but that also acknowledges mental and moral virtues in a great number.[69] In sum, *Grandezas de la espada* challenges our current understanding of the ideas on race in early modern Iberia, exactly in the period and location where racism was supposedly invented.[70] Nonetheless, we need to determine whether Narváez's martial arts discourse is representative of the period, or rather just a rare exception. For this purpose, it is necessary to re-examine early modern Spanish literature in search of Black swordsmen.

We find our earliest example in *La pícara Justina*, a picaresque novel published a few years after Narváez's treatise. At the beginning of the second *número* of chapter 4, the protagonist, Justina, mentions a Black fencer who was praised at a *juego de esgrima* for being extremely skillful in playing the case of rapiers (*dos espadas*) and the great sword (*montante*).[71] Even though the allusion is quite short, nothing in the text conveys a negative view of the character. Quite the opposite: on one hand, being able to fight using two swords was regarded as a great achievement. According to Pacheco de Narváez, Spanish master Pedro Torre supposedly invented the skill.[72] Since then, many authors of fencing treatises have discussed this combination—e.g., Giacomo di Grassi, Domingo Luis Godinho, and Pedro Heredia. Lope de Vega mentions the double-sword fencers (*diestros de dos espadas*) as a metaphor for his unmatched writing virtuosity.[73] On the other hand, the *montante* was considered an "honorable weapon" (*arma de ventaja*) for being the symbol of the fencing master.[74] For this reason, being proficient in its use can be interpreted as a positive trait. Moreover, even though Justina regards fencing as a low-class profession, she also holds it in very high esteem. Right after mentioning said Black fencer, she recalls the tragic end of her former lover, who was also a sword master.[75]

We find a more developed Black swordsman in another picaresque novel, in this case by Francisco Quevedo. At the beginning of the second book of *El Buscón* (often translated as *The Swindler*), the protagonist meets two fencers. One is a mad aficionado fascinated by the teachings of Verdadera Destreza. The other is a mulatto sword master who defeats the former and makes him look ridiculous. Traditionally, critics have interpreted the mulatto swordsman as a grotesque, comical figure, either seeing him as a supposed embodiment of "vulgar fencing"—that is, the social pejorative coined by Carranza—or as a "worthless being."[76] In this sense, the mulatto would be an echo of the enslaved Black who reveals the truth about the emperor's new clothes in Don Juan Manuel's famous *exiemplo*.[77]

There are some reasons to interpret Quevedo's mulatto fencer in this manner. His description is openly comical: his fierce posture is compared to that of a heraldic eagle (*aguila imperial*), the scar that crosses his face is referred to as the Sign of the Cross (*signum crucis*), and his profuse beard and mustache are likened to the swept guards of a rapier and a dagger (*barba de ganchos, con unos bigotes de guardamano*).[78] In addition, the mulatto master fails to understand the geometrical jargon of the mad *diestro verdadero*. Nonetheless, these interpretations may be affected by our literary expectations. The mulatto fencer does not conform to any of the aforementioned stereotypes. His comical description is not particularly denigrating, especially if compared to almost every other character in *El Buscón*. His misunderstandings are not due to ignorance or stupidity but mostly to the nonsensical nature of the madman's language, as pointed out throughout the chapter. It is also worth noting that the mulatto swordsman has taken the masters exam and holds a license (*Yo soy examinado y traigo la carta*),[79] which means not only that he is not enslaved but also that he is in a relatively comfortable position since he could afford the costs of the examination and has a job to support himself. Accordingly, nobody in the novel questions that he is the best fencer.

This is not the only instance in which Quevedo writes about Black or mulatto swordsmen in his *jácaras*.[80] In "jácara 3," a prostitute named Perala mentions that her new pimp is a left-handed mulatto who works as a deputy. The allusions to his left-handedness as well as his "swept-hilt beard" (*barba y bigotes de ganchos*) point to the possibility that Perala's husband may be an accomplished fencer. Mari Pizorra, the prostitute who sings the "jácara 11," mentions she married a "notorious" mulatto from Ronda, without explaining the nature of his fame. Much more developed is Jerónimo, a respected mulatto that appears at the end of "jácara 13."[81] Likened to legendary medieval hero Bernardo del Carpio, Jerónimo is able to stop a tavern fight between Ganchoso and Andrés just by drawing his sword and saying a few sentences. By appeasing the two drunken ruffians, Jerónimo demonstrates that he is an articulate and respected swordsman, with no trace of negative stereotyping.

To recapitulate, López de Úbeza's and Quevedo's Black swordsmen call into question our current understanding of the literary function of Blacks in early modern Spain. However, they are secondary and thus little-developed characters. Attention should be paid, thus, to fencing protagonists of African descent.

In his little-known dissertation of 1934, Manrique Cabrera analyzes an extensive corpus of early modern plays and posits the literary type of the "Black hero."[82] He defines this as a main character of African descent who is characterized by five traits, namely, elevated style (62–66), courage (66–69), platonic conception of love (69–73), honor and aspiration to nobility (73–76), and preoccupations with fame, royalty, and religion (76–79). Surprisingly, despite not having read Narváez's treatise, Manrique Cabrera's portrait of the Black hero closely resembles that of the Black choleric of *Grandezas de la espada*. For example, the elevated tone of the former coincides with the articulateness and good pronunciation of the latter. The Black choleric's pride and networking skills, in turn, correspond to the Black hero's aspirations to nobility. These similarities can only be explained by recognizing a martial arts discourse that underlies all of these texts.

According to Manrique Cabrera, Black heroes fall into five "groups" or categories: the Black rebel, the Black person who prospers, the Black king or courtier, the Black deceiver, and the White in blackface (79–80). Although this classification has a number of flaws —some categories are ad hoc or arbitrary, some cases could be cross listed, etc.— and does not reflect the relation that the different types of Black heroes have with fencing and other martial arts, it will serve, in the following paragraphs, as a point of departure for our search for the early modern literary Black swordsman.

There are only two extant examples of Manrique Cabrera's second type, that is, of Black protagonists that prosper. Both have been studied as *exceptional* cases in which a "humble" Afro-Hispanic protagonist achieves social recognition through his effort in one of the two pillars of the Spanish imperial ideology: the arms and letters. Diego Jiménez de Enciso's *Juan Latino* fictionalizes the life of the famous Afro-Hispanic humanist of the same name.[83] *El valiente negro en Flandes* by Andrés de Claramonte tells the story of Juan de Mérida, an enslaved Black whose fencing skills and heroic military career enable him to defeat the Dutch, become a knight, and even marry his former owner at the end of the play. As argued in Olmedo Gobante, Claramonte's Black hero is an accomplished swordsman who shares every single trait with Narváez's choleric Black.[84]

The last three types have been notably less studied. Manrique Cabrera provides a list of Black kings and courtiers that has not to date been analyzed as a whole.[85] The Black deceiver corresponds to the tradition started with Francisco de la Torres's *La confesión con el demonio*, a play in honor of Saint Vicent Ferrer in which a Black main character tricks and abuses the saint's sister.[86] More critical attention has been paid to the last type, or the "fake Black," since it was a very common trope in early modern theater.[87] Although the courage of most of these characters is emphasized throughout their respective plays—especially in the case of Torres's Teucapel—no particular martial arts skills are attributed to them.

However, Manrique Cabrera's first type, the Black rebel, does engage in martial arts in a more distinct way. The scholar's category alludes to those protagonists of African descent who fight against slavery at any particular point of the plot. The best-known example of this type is arguably Lope de Vega's *El santo negro Rosambuco*, chronologically the first of several early modern plays that fictionalize the story of Saint Benedict the Moor.[88] Critics have studied the protagonist, Rosambuco, chiefly as a "submissive Black" by focusing on his conversion to Christianity at the end of Act 1. The transformation of Rosambuco, from fierce pirate to subservient saint, has been seen, at the same time, as a negation of his Blackness and the affirmation of his natural condition as a slave.[89] Very little has been said, one the other hand, about Rosambuco's characterization prior to his conversion, that is, the positive qualities that would eventually lead him to sanctity.

Unlike the historic Saint Benedict, who was likely born into slavery, Rosambuco was born free.[90] Enslaved in his childhood, Rosambuco regained freedom thanks to his martial skills. From his first words at the very beginning of the play onward, his dexterity with the sword is evident. From the point of view of characterization, the story of Rosambuco does not differ much from other hagiographies, such as Cervantes's *El Rufián dichoso*, in which an accomplished fencer follows a pacific path to sanctity.

Filipo, the rebel protagonist of *El prodigio de Etiopia* (The wonder of Ethiopia)—a play traditionally attributed to Lope de Vega—has been interpreted in a similar way. Loosely based on the life of Saint Moses the Black, his story is that of an Ethiopian who, despite being enslaved at the beginning of the play, turns into a bandit, becomes king, and redeems himself in the final scenes.[91] Filipo is characterized by an unstoppable drive to ascend socially: "Mi inclinación voy siguiendo, / trepar, ir a cosas altas" (I follow my inclination to great things),[92] an ambition he shares with Narváez's Black choleric fencer and Manrique Cabrera's Black hero. For this reason, Filipo is ironically called "negro grave" (noble Black),[93] the exact same adjective used by Narváez to describe his type. Unsurprisingly, Filipo proves to be an outstanding martial artist. So much so that he comes up with the invention of gunpowder many centuries before its discovery. He is also a remarkable fencer, capable of keeping at bay four bandits simultaneously and defeating his former owner, Alejandro, on several occasions throughout the play. Filipo even stands his ground against the Devil himself in a fight equated to the biblical story of Jacob and the angel, as related in the book of Genesis 32:22–32.

Rosambuco and Filipo are not the only Black rebels in Lope de Vega's work. As Sánchez Jiménez has studied, the playwright offers a very positive image of other Black warriors—as well as Black people in general—in *cantos* four and seven of his *Dragontea*, an epic poem written around the same time as *El prodigio de Etiopia*. Like Rosambuco and Filipo, the Maroons from Santiago del Príncipe are Black rebels who once escaped slavery to eventually fight against the enemies of the Spanish Empire. In general terms, they are systematically described as brave people (*valientes*), a quality that also is frequently attributed to the aforementioned rebels. As with Filipo, they also are portrayed as experts in firearms.[94]

Not all the heroes of Santiago del Príncipe are anonymous. There are some particular individuals who also receive a rather positive description in Lope de Vega's epic poem, like Pedro Yalonga, for example, a historical enslaved Black who defended the Spanish interests against Francis Drake.[95] According to the poet, Yalonga seemed European "in his deeds and words."[96] This corresponds to the articulateness of Narváez's Black swordsmen, who can speak Spanish with clear pronunciation and rich vocabulary even when recently enslaved and imported from Africa.[97] King Luis de Mazambique, the leader of the Maroons of Santiago del Príncipe, is represented as a "brave" elder and compared to Spartan lawgiver Lycurgus.

Even though Luis's vivid depiction has been interpreted as "mildly comical," his portrait still challenges the most common stereotypes of Black people in Spanish literature, as Manrique Cabrera pointed out. For Sánchez Jiménez, the representation of the Maroons as an ambiguous force at the limits of the empire plays a significant role in Lope de Vega's self-fashioning as a lowborn writer who aspired to upward mobility.[98] A further comparison among Lope de Vega's Black rebels could allow for a better understanding of the writer's ideas on race, merit, and martiality.

Although Lope de Vega's Maroons have been considered an "exception," and much more research on the matter is required, the truth is that Maroons also appear—relatively free of stereotypes—in other epics of the time.[99] For example, the Maroon leaders of *Armas Antárticas*—an epic poem by Juan de Miramontes y Zuázola—are described as "barbarian," "imprudent," and "chimeric" people but also are ascribed many positive qualities that contrast with the stereotyping of the period. The voice given to these Maroons has been interpreted as a clear testimony against slavery, or at least as a justification of rebellion on the Maroons' part.[100]

The rebellious words of Miramontes's Maroons sprang from the pen of a White author, and yet they do not differ greatly from discourses proffered by historical Maroons. A well-known example is that of King Miguel de Buría, the escaped enslaved Black who led an insurrection against the Spanish and reigned as a rebel king in modern-day Venezuela. According to fray Pedro Simón, Miguel once harangued his people, claiming that their natural freedom, usurped by the Spanish tyranny, was founded in their ability to fight with "bravery and spirit" (ánimo y brío).[101] King Miguel's address resonates with martial arts discourses of the same time. For example, Jerónimo Sánchez de Carranza, the aforementioned founder of the Verdadera Destreza, argued for enslaved people's right to legitimately wound or even kill their masters in self-defense.[102] According to Carranza, the right of self-protection—which is the moral foundation of Verdadera Destreza—is granted by natural law and overrides slavery, which is supported by the law of nations and not by nature, as Aristotle states.[103]

The stories of these Maroons, made public by innumerable official reports and chronicles dating from the early sixteenth century, could have not passed unnoticed in early modern Iberian culture despite the apparent reluctance in the Peninsula to discuss the topic.[104] Combined with fictional tales of brave Black heroes, these stories—historical or not—could have spurred the imagination of more than one Afro-Hispanic, contributing to the formation of a particular martial arts discourse on race in the early modern period.

Conclusions

For many decades, scholars have agreed that "the literary treatment of Blacks was inevitably comical" in early modern Iberia.[105] Even for Manrique Cabrera, who coined the term "Black hero" and provided so many examples of this literary type, the Black buffoon was still "the true core of 'Blackness' in Spanish literature." Every single deviance from this norm has been deemed uninteresting or "exceptional."[106] Even when examining positive Black figures, scholars have interpreted them as rhetorical mechanisms to reinforce racism. As Fra-Molinero argued, representing Black people in an unrealistic positive way means to further denigrate them as a collective, since there is an implicit—or otherwise—contrast with a comical image of Blacks that is presumed by default.[107] Fra-Molinero's theory of "racism by reduction" has been generally well received, although it, too, has caused discontent among some critics who consider it overly generalizing.[108] However, it remains critically unchallenged thus far.

The purpose of this chapter has not been to contradict this line of interpretation but to contribute to it with three points that should be taken into consideration: First, the sheer number of exceptions invites us to reconsider the paradigm from which we study early modern ideas on race in literature.[109] I have examined more than twenty-five cases of Black Africans who are not portrayed as natural slaves, evil beings, or stupid buffoons. The chief commonality among these characters—fictional or not—is their relation with martial arts: most, if not all of them, are either professional fencers or at least accomplished swordsmen. Moreover, many share a very specific set of traits. So much so that two scholars separated by centuries, Pacheco Narváez and Manrique Cabrera, came to a very similar typology of the Black swordsmen.

Second, not all Blacks were portrayed as a negation of either their humanity or their Blackness in early modern literature. There is only one substantial difference between Manrique Cabrera's heroic Black and Narváez's choleric Black. For the former, the traits that characterize a Black hero are those that allow them to "overcome" their Blackness, making them somehow less Black as they approach the White reference.[110] Fra-Molinero and others have studied this phenomenon thoroughly. For Narváez, however, the Black cholerics' features make them superior to many Whites without negating their identity as Afro-descendants. We have also seen this in literary works in which Black swordsmen and warriors are portrayed in a dignified, un-Whitened manner.

Third and last, attention has to be paid to the role that real-life Black people played—as part of the public or in any other way—in the production, distribution, and consumption of early modern culture, as recent studies are starting to consider.[111] As we have seen, Black Africans and their descendants left an indelible mark on the history of Hispanic fencing, despite many attempts to negate their participation and legacy in Iberia. By examining the Afro-Hispanic presence both in the world of fencing and in its martial arts discourse, we get a much deeper appreciation of many literary works that, despite having much in common, have been regarded as isolated exceptions.

Contrary to what we used to think, martial arts practices and discourses offered some Afro-Hispanics a wide set of strategies to ameliorate their social condition, as well as to contest stereotyping and discrimination. Such discourses and practices also had a strong influence on people's ideas on race in Iberia. With massive tournaments being performed in the streets regularly, hundreds of treatises being published, sword masters being celebrities in their time, and theatrical works featuring swordplay as a matter of usual practice, the world of fencing presented itself as a social space to be conquered, as confirmed by the fierce opposition that Black people faced. The social heterogeneity of said institution, combined with the revolutionary discourses on race by schools such as Verdadera Destreza, intersected with the proliferation of literary textual mediators that featured Black heroes as protagonists. The result was an epistemic framework that made possible the idea of a dignified Afro-Hispanic identity.

In 1600, the same year that Narváez published his typology of Black swordsmen, the Alba-Medrano family demanded being officially recognized as Blacks.[112] They succeeded. On April 19, the Alba-Medranos were declared "legitimate descendants of Black men from Wolof" and were afforded the right to carry swords explicitly. The sentence had serious consequences. Nine years later, Spanish King Philip III ordered the massive expulsion of Moriscos from Iberia. Thanks to their successful complaint, the Alba-Medranos most probably escaped the calamity.[113]

Luis Alba could not have foreseen the Moriscos' expulsion. In fact, it is impossible to know his reasons for insisting with such persistence on carrying swords. However, it is certain that he followed—and probably also contributed to—a martial arts discourse that was at the root of his ideas on class and race. By capitalizing said discourse, Luis Alba had the opportunity to factually resist oppression and regain his individual rights. Moreover, because he fought for his arms, his descendants, the Alba-Medranos, acquired full citizenship as Afro-Hispanics.[114] Their swords made them free, and also made them Black.

NOTES

1. The case of the Alba-Medranos rests in the Archivo Municipal de Úbeda (leg. 109.1) and was first found by Pedro Andrés Porras Arboledas, "Los moriscos en el archivo municipal de Úbeda," *Etudes d'Histoire Morisque* 23 (2003): 317–27. I thank Javier Irigoyen García for informing me of it.
2. Felipe Andrés Roa Contreras, "Negros musulmanes, esclavos y libres en la América Colonial: Cofradía de Jolofos de Lima correspondiente de la nación de los Jolofos" (PhD diss., Universidad de Chile, 2010), 30–35.
3. Enrique Soria Mesa, "Una gran familia. Las élites moriscas del reino de Granada," *Estudis* 35 (2009): 9–35.
4. Raúl Sánchez García and Dale C. Spencer, "Introduction: Carnal Ethnography as Path to Embodied Knowledge," in *Fighting Scholars: Habitus and Ethnographies of Martial Arts and Combat Sports*, ed. Sánchez García and Spencer (London: Anthem Press, 2013), 2. The best-known example of a martial art as social and political resistance may be capoeira, which was famously developed by Black enslaved people on Brazilian plantations. See Matthias Röhrig Assunção, *Capoeira: The History of an Afro-Brazilian Martial Art* (New York: Routledge, 2004). Similar narratives of origin are shared by a great number of martial arts, including Chinese taijiquan, Philippine arnis, and Okinawan karate.
5. The approach to martial arts discourse—in addition to the study of its practice—as an essential part of martial arts studies is one of the most prominent innovations in said field. This paradigm defines martial arts as a phenomenon in which physical practices are intertwined with embodied knowledges that include experiences, ideas, myths, and narratives. See Sixt Wetzler, "Myths of the Martial Arts," *JOMEC Journal* 5 (2014): n.p.; Douglas S. Farrer and John Whalen-Bridge, "Introduction: Martial Arts, Transnationalism, and Embodied Knowledge," in *Martial Arts as Embodied Knowledge: Asian Traditions in a Transnational World*, ed. Farrer and Whalen-Bridge (Albany: State University of New York Press, 2011), 1–28; Sánchez García and Spencer, "Introduction: Carnal Ethnography," 1–6; Paul Bowman, *Martial Arts Studies: Disrupting Disciplinary Boundaries* (London: Rowman and Littlefield International, 2015), 7; Christopher S. Goto-Jones, *The Virtual Ninja Manifesto: Gamic Orientalism*

and the Digital Dojo (London: Rowman and Littlefield International, 2016); and Tim Trausch, "Martial Arts as Embodied, Discursive and Aesthetic Practice," in *The Martial Arts Studies Reader*, ed. P. Bowman (London: Rowman and Littlefield International, 2018), 188.

6. See Manuel Olmedo Gobante, "Del frente a la palestra: Esgrima y ejército en la carrera autorial de Jerónimo Sánchez de Carranza," in *Vidas en armas*, ed. A. Castellano López and A. J. Sáez (Huelva: Universidad de Huelva, 2019), 104; Miguel González Ancín and Otis Towns, "Las nueve reglas de la espada de dos manos, y la práctica de la esgrima en Zaragoza hacia 1526," *Gladius. Estudios sobre armas antiguas, arte militar y vida cultural en oriente y occidente* 37 (2017): 157, 160, 200; David Nievas Muñoz, "La esgrima y el mundo de la espada en la España Moderna" (master's thesis, Universidad de Granada, 2012), 94–99.

7. The quarterstaff (*bastón*) and the Iberian great sword (*montante*) were typically used by fencing masters to conduct the *juego de esgrima*. The idiom *echar el bastón* was in common use in early modern dictionaries. See Sebastián Covarrubias Orozco, *Tesoro de la lengua castellana, o española* (Madrid: Luis Sánchez, 1611), entry: "bastón."

8. For the approach to martial arts as institutions, see Bowman, *Martial Arts Studies*, 6–7. For information on the swordsman hierarchy, see Miguel González Ancín and Otis Towns, "Las nueve reglas de la espada de dos manos," 159–60; for more on the Spanish system, see Sydney Anglo, *The Martial Arts of Renaissance Europe* (New Haven, CT: Yale University Press, 2000), 9; Juan Guilmaín Alonso, "'La espada es el fundamento de todos los escudos.' La esgrima hispalense en el Quinientos," in *In medio orbe (II). Personajes y avatares de la I Vuelta al Mundo*, ed. M. J. Parodi Álvarez (Sevilla: Junta de Andalucía, 2017), 138.

9. See Paul Bowman, "The Definition of Martial Arts Studies," *Martial Arts Studies* 3 (2017): 6–23; Sánchez García and Spencer, "Introduction: Carnal Ethnography," 8–12.

10. Daniel Jaquet, "Martial Arts by the Book: Late Medieval and Early Modern European Martial Arts," in *The Martial Arts Studies Reader*, ed. P. Bowman (London: Rowman and Littlefield International, 2018), 42; Olmedo Gobante, "Del frente a la palestra," 104–5.

11. See Manuel Valle Ortiz, *Nueva bibliografía de la antigua esgrima y destreza de las armas* (Santiago de Compostela: AGEA / Edizer, 2012), 387–90; Jaquet, "Martial Arts by the Book," 41–43; Enrique de Leguina, *Libros de esgrima, españoles y portugueses* (Madrid: Los Huérfanos, 1891).

12. For concepts such as "mediatization" applied to martial arts, see Paul Bowman, *Beyond Bruce Lee: Chasing the Dragon through Film* (New York: Wallflower Press, 2013), 7–8.

13. See Jaquet, "Martial Arts by the Book," 41; Gary J. Krug, "At the Feet of the Master: Three Stages in the Appropriation of Okinawan Karate into Anglo-American Culture," *Cultural Studies—Critical Methodologies* 1, no. 4 (2001): 398. Also see Bowman, *Beyond Bruce Lee*, 10; Bowman, *Martial Arts Studies*, 7.

14. Juan I. Laguna Fernández, "Luis Pacheco de Narváez: Unos comentarios a la vida y escritos del campeón de la corte literaria barroca de Felipe III y Felipe IV, y su supuesta

relación con el *Tribunal de la justa venganza* contra Francisco de Quevedo," *Lemir* 20 (2016): 252. For one such early nineteenth-century treatise, see Manuel Antonio de Brea, *Principios universales y reglas generales de la Verdadera Destreza del espadín según la doctrina mixta de francesa, italiana y española* (Madrid: Imprenta Real, 1805).

15. Manuel Valle Ortiz, "The Destreza Verdadera: A Global Phenomenon," in *Late Medieval and Early Modern Fight Books: Transmission and Tradition of Martial Arts in Europe (14th-17th Centuries)*, ed. D. Jaquet, K. Verelst, and T. Dawson (Leiden: Brill, 2016), 324–53.

16. Pedro Ordóñez Ceballos, *Viaje del mundo*, ed. I. B. Anzoategui (Buenos Aires: Espasa / Calpe, [1614] 1947), 164.

17. See Adolph L. Soens, "Tybalt's Spanish Fencing in Romeo and Juliet," *Shakespeare Quarterly* 20, no. 2 (1969): 121–27; Craig Turner and Tony Soper, *Methods and Practice of Elizabethan Swordplay* (Carbondale: Southern Illinois University Press, 1990), 6; Pedro Javier Romero Cambra, "Massinger and Carranza: A Note on Fencing and Points of Honour in Sixteenth- and Seventeenth-Century Drama," *Notes and Queries* 54, no. 4 (2007): 392–93; Steward Hawley, "The Italian, Spanish, and English Fencing Schools in Shakespeare's England," *Quidditas* 30 (2009): 108–18; Mary Theresa Dill Curtis, "Legitimizing Discourses: A Vindication of Swordplay through Letters in *The Philosophy of Arms*" (PhD diss., University of California-Davis, 2012), 310–18.

18. I quote from the 1599 princeps: George Silver, *Paradoxes of Defense* (London: Edward Blount, 1599), 14–15, modernizing the spelling.

19. Ibáñez de Agurto's license rests in Archivo Nacional General de la Nación, Indiferente virreinal. Acta de indiferente de guerra, *Otorgamiento del título de maestro de armas en la Nueva España*, México, May 5, 1603. I thank master Juan Guilmáin Alonso for informing me of it. Also see Alejandra Vargas Gracia, "La esgrima histórica en la Ciudad de México, una práctica cultural emergente en nuestros días," paper presented at the forty-ninth *Encuentro Nacional de Estudiantes de Historia*, Saltillo, Coahuila, October 24–28, 2016.

20. For Willem Swanenburgh's engraving, see Sydney Anglo, *The Martial Arts of Renaissance Europe*, 14–15, 82. Also see Luis Pacheco de Narváez, *Libro de las grandezas de la espada en que se declaran muchos secretos del que compuso el comendador Jerónimo de Carranza. En el cual cada uno se podrá licionar y deprender a solas, sin tener necesidad de Maestro que le enseñe* (Madrid: Herederos de Juan Íñiguez de Lequerica, 1600), 77r, 272r.

21. Jerónimo Sánchez Carranza, *Libro de Jerónimo de Carranza, natural de Sevilla, que trata de la filosofía de las armas y de su destreza y de la agresión y defensión cristiana* (Sanlúcar de Barrameda: Casa del autor, 1582), 148r.

22. Ernst Robert Curtius, *European Literature and the Latin Middle Ages* (Princeton, NJ: Princeton University Press, [1953] 2013), 36–37.

23. Manuel Ángel Candelas Colodrón, "La Silva 'El pincel' de Quevedo: La teoría pictórica y la alabanza de pintores al servicio del dogma contrarreformista," *Bulletin hispanique* 98, no.1 (1996): 86. Also see Rodrigo Cacho Casal, "Quevedo y la filología de autor: Edición de la silva 'El pincel,'" *Criticón* 114 (2012): 26; Felix K. E. Schmelzer, "La esgrima como ciencia matemática: El caso curioso de Luis Pacheco de Narváez," *Hipogrifo* 4, no. 2 (2016): 340–41.

24. Juan Antonio Díez-Monsalve Giménez and Susana Fernández de Miguel, "Documentos inéditos sobre el famoso pleito de los pintores: El largo camino recorrido por los artistas del siglo XVII para el reconocimiento de su arte como liberal," *Archivo Español de Arte* 83, no. 330 (2010): 149–58. Also see Adrián J. Sáez, *El ingenio del arte: La pintura en la poesía de Quevedo* (Madrid: Visor libros, 2015), 113–31.
25. Dill Curtis, "Legitimizing Discourses," 197–98.
26. Sánchez Carranza, "Prólogo al Duque," *Libro de Jerónimo de Carranza*. For the recurrent theme of *vulgo ignorante*—a common trope since antiquity—see Américo Castro, *El pensamiento de Cervantes* (Barcelona: Editorial Crítica, [1925] 1987); Alberto Porqueras Mayo, *Temas y formas de la literatura española* (Madrid: Gredos, 1972).
27. Sánchez Carranza, *Libro de Jerónimo de Carranza*, 101r. I quote from my forthcoming critical edition.
28. Ibid., 64r, 75r. Also, in a separate instance, he defines Verdadera Destreza as "doctrina para letrados y hombres graves" (a discipline for learned and noble men). Ibid., 133v.
29. Olmedo Gobante, "Del frente a la palestra"; Olmedo Gobante, "'El mucho número que hay dellos': *El valiente negro en Flandes* y los esgrimistas afrohispanos de *Grandezas de la espada*," *Bulletin of the Comediantes* 70, no. 2 (2018): 74.
30. Enrique de Leguina, *Bibliografía e historia de la esgrima española* (Madrid: Fortanet, 1904), 37; Laguna Fernández, "Luis Pacheco de Narváez," 248. Also see Valle Ortiz, *Nueva bibliografía de la antigua esgrima y destreza de las armas*, 165.
31. Juan Ignacio de las Muñecas Marmontaño, *Panegírico a Don Francisco de Añasco*, ed. E. de Leguina (Sevilla: Imprenta de E. Rasco, [c.1675] 1887); Nicolás Tamariz, *Cartilla y luz en la verdadera destreza* (Sevilla: Herederos de Tomás López de Haro, 1696), 65.
32. Juan Fernando Pizarro, *Apología de D. Luis Pacheco de Narváez* (n.p.: [Trujillo?],[1623?]), 9v. Also see Valle Ortiz, *Nueva bibliografía de la antigua esgrima y destreza de las armas*, 165.
33. Francisco Marqués de Sousa Viterbo, *A Esgrima em Portugal. Subsidios para a sua historia* (Lisboa: Typographia Universal, Imprenta da Casa Real, 1897); José de Gestoso y Pérez, *Esgrimidores sevillanos. Documentos inéditos para su historia* (Madrid: Revista de archivos, bibliotecas y museos, 1911).
34. Francisco Marqués de Sousa Viterbo, *A Esgrima em Portugal*, 20–27.
35. José de Gestoso y Pérez, *Esgrimidores sevillanos*, 15.
36. Archivo Histórico Provincial de Sevilla (AHPSe), Protocolos notariales, legajo 10731, f. 569, pieza 2. I thank Manuel F. Fernández Chaves and Juan Guilmaín Alonso for informing me of it.
37. Kate Lowe, "The Stereotyping of Black Africans in Renaissance Europe," in *Black Africans in Renaissance Europe*, ed. T. Foster Earle and K. Lowe (Cambridge: Cambridge University Press, 2005), 33.
38. Luis Pacheco de Narváez, *Libro de las grandezas de la espada en que se declaran muchos secretos del que compuso el comendador Jerónimo de Carranza*, 247r, 12r–22r.
39. Lowe, "The Stereotyping of Black Africans in Renaissance Europe," 33.
40. Juan Guilmaín Alonso, "'La espada es el fundamento de todos los escudos,'" 137.
41. Domingo Ruiz de Vallejo, *Título de maestro en la filosofía y destreza de las armas, para en todos los reinos y señoríos de su Majestad. Por Domingo Ruiz de Vallejo, maestro del Rey*

nuestro señor, 4r, quoted in Francisco Saucedo Morales, "Jerónimo Sánchez Carranza y la escuela española de esgrima" (PhD diss., Universidad Politécnica de Madrid, 1997), 254.

42. José de Gestoso y Pérez, *Esgrimidores sevillanos*, 8, 10. For a close examination of early modern sword masters' licenses (*cartas de examen*), see Juan Guilmaín Alonso, "'La espada es el fundamento de todos los escudos.'"

43. Guilmaín Alonso, "'La espada es el fundamento de todos los escudos,'" 137.

44. Ruiz de Vallejo, *Título de maestro en la filosofía y destreza de las armas*.

45. Miguel Fernando Gómez Vozmediano, *Mudéjares y moriscos en el Campo de Calatrava: Reductos de convivencia, tiempos de intolerancia: siglos xv–xvii* (Ciudad Real: Área de Cultura, Diputación Provincial, 2000), 14. Exceptions were made, as studied by Max Deardorff, "¿Quién es morisco? Desde cristiano nuevo a cristiano viejo de moros: Categorías de diferenciación en el Reino de Granada (siglo XVI)," *Forum historiae iuris*, December 20, 2018, doi.org/10.26032/fhi-2018-004.

46. See Rafael Martínez del Peral Fortón, *Las armas blancas en España e Indias: Ordenamiento jurídico* (Madrid: Mapfre, 1992), 113; Debra Blumenthal, *Enemies and Familiars: Slavery and Mastery in Fifteenth-Century Valencia* (Ithaca: Cornell University Press, 2009), 158–69.

47. See Encarnación Rodríguez Vicente, *El tribunal del consulado de Lima en la primera mitad del siglo xvii* (Madrid: Ediciones Cultura Hispánica, 1960), 77. The situation was very different in the colonies of the Iberian empire. In Peru, for example, Black people were systematically punished for carrying swords or even knives, regardless of their legal status. See Pedro León Portocarrero, *Descripción del virreinato del Perú*, ed. E. Huarag Álvarez (Lima: Universidad Ricardo Palma, 2009), 26. I thank Miguel Martínez for this information.

48. Cortes de Castilla, *Actas de las Cortes de Castilla*, vol. 3 (Madrid: Imprenta Nacional, 1853), 86, quoted in Pablo Moya Montes, "La esgrima vulgar en los siglos XV y XVI" (master's thesis, Universidad de Cantabria, 2017), 55, 402–3.

49. Moya Montes, "La esgrima vulgar en los siglos XV y XVI," 55.

50. Anonymous, *Diálogo Maestro discípulo* (Oviedo, 1724), quoted in J. Girona Durán, *Obligaciones del maestro y el discípulo en las artes marciales antiguas europeas* (Sociedad de Esgrima Española de St. Louis), www.spanishsword.org/es/documentos/obligaciones; and Moya Montes, "La esgrima vulgar en los siglos XV y XVI," 56.

51. Lowe, "The Stereotyping of Black Africans in Renaissance Europe," 41.

52. See Carmen Fracchia, "Picturing the Afro-Hispanic Struggle for Freedom in Early Modern Spain," in *Post/Colonialism and the Pursuit of Freedom in the Black Atlantic*, ed. Jerome C. Branche (New York: Routledge, 2018), 43; Fracchia, *'Black but Human': Slavery and Visual Arts in Hapsburg Spain, 1480–1700* (Oxford: Oxford University Press, 2019).

53. Thomas J. Desch Obi, *Fighting for Honor: The History of African Martial Art Traditions in the Atlantic World* (Columbia: University of South Carolina Press, 2008).

54. Baltasar Fra-Molinero, "Los negros como figura de negación y diferencia en el teatro barroco," *Hipogrifo* 2, no. 2 (2014): 20, 16.

55. Frantz Fanon, *Black Skin, White Masks*, trans. R. Philcox (New York: Grove Press, [1952] 2007), 195.

56. Hans Talhoffer, *Alte Armatur und Ringkunst*, Manuscript, Royal Danish Library, 1459, MS Thott 290, 2° folio, 73v, 74v.
57. See Lowe, "The Stereotyping of Black Africans in Renaissance Europe," 33–34. Talhoffer, *Alte Armatur und Ringkunst*; Paulus Hector Mair, *De arte athletica I*, mid-sixteenth century. Bayerische StaatsBibliothek BSB Cod.icon. 393, vol. 1. Augsburg.
58. Kate Lowe, "The Black Diaspora in Europe in the Fifteenth and Sixteenth Centuries, with Special Reference to German-Speaking Areas," in *Germany and the Black Diaspora: Points of Contact: 1250–1914*, ed. M. Honeck, M. Klimke, and A. Kuhlmann (New York: Berghahn Books, 2013), 50.
59. Paulus Hector Mair, *Fecht-, Ring- und Turnierbuch (De arte athletica)*. 1550. SLUB Dresden Mscr.Dresd.C.94, 141r. Augsburg; also see Moya Montes, "La esgrima vulgar en los siglos XV y XVI," 1; Ben Miller, "The Greatest African American and Afro-American Martial Artists in History," *Out of This Century* (blog), March 25, 2014, outofthiscentury.wordpress.com/category/bizarre-and-unusual.
60. Paulus Hector Mair, *Fechtbuch (De arte athletica)*, Österreichische Nationalbibliothek, Ms. Cod.10826, 122v, 126r. Augsburg.
61. Mair, *Fechtbuch*, 143r.
62. Oliver Dupuis, "A New Manuscript of Joachim Meyer (1561)," *Acta Periodica Duellatorum* 9, no. 1 (2021): 1–14, doi:10.36950/apd-2021-004; Joachim Meyer, *Fechtbuch*, dated 1561, Bayerisches Nationalmuseum, Ms. Bibl. 2465.
63. Olmedo Gobante, "'El mucho número que hay dellos,'" 67–91.
64. Luis Pacheco de Narváez, *Libro de las grandezas de la espada en que se declaran muchos secretos del que compuso el comendador Jerónimo de Carranza*, 259v.
65. For an introduction to the concept of Galenic complexion and its role in the categorization of individual natures, see Valentin Groebner, "Complexio/Complexion: Categorizing Individual Natures, 1250–1600," in *The Moral Authority of Nature*, ed. L. Daston and F. Vidal (Chicago: University of Chicago Press, 2004), 361–83.
66. Luis Pacheco de Narváez, *Libro de las grandezas de la espada en que se declaran muchos secretos del que compuso el comendador Jerónimo de Carranza*, 259v.
67. Olmedo Gobante, "'El mucho número que hay dellos,'" 77–82.
68. See Lowe, "The Stereotyping of Black Africans in Renaissance Europe"; Baltasar Fra-Molinero, *La imagen de los negros en el teatro del Siglo de Oro* (Madrid: Siglo veintiuno, 1995), 20–22; Antonio Santos Morillo, "Caracterización del negro en la literatura española del xvi," *Lemir* 15 (2011): 28, respectively.
69. Olmedo Gobante, "'El mucho número que hay dellos,'" 82.
70. Tamar Herzog, "Beyond Race: Exclusion in Early Modern Spain and Spanish America," in *Race and Blood in the Iberian World*, ed. M. S. Hering Torres, M. E. Martínez, and D. Nirenberg (Berlin: Lit Verlag, 2012), 151–53.
71. Francisco López de Úbeda, *Libro de entretenimiento de la pícara Justina*, ed. E. Suárez Figaredo (n.p.: [1605] 2005), 226. Retrieved from users.pfw.edu/jehle/cervante/othertxts/Suarez_Figaredo_PicaraJustina.pdf
72. Luis Pacheco de Narváez, *Nueva ciencia y filosofía de la destreza de las armas, su teórica y práctica, que dejó escrita don Luis Pacheco de Narváez* (Madrid: Melchor Sánchez, 1672), 499–515.

73. Giacomo di Grassi, *Ragione di adoprar sicuramente l'arme si da offesa come da difesa, con un trattato dell'inganno, e con un modo di essercitarsi da se stesso, per acquistare forza, giudicio, e presteza* (Venice: Giordano Ziletti, 1570), 85; Lope de Vega y Carpio, *La Vega del Parnaso*, vol. 2, ed. F. B. Pedraza Jiménez and P. Conde Parrado (Almagro: Universidad de Castilla - La Mancha, 2015), 62. I thank Antonio Sánchez Jiménez for pointing this out.
74. For *arma de ventaja*, see Sebastián Covarrubias Orozco, *Tesoro de la lengua castellana, o española*, 554v; Ton Puey, "An Overview of the Iberian Montante," *HROARR*, July 31, 2015, hroarr.com/article/an-overview-of-the-iberian-montante.
75. Manuel Olmedo Gobante, "'Más locos que diestros': El diestro loco y la locura de la destreza del Siglo de Oro," in *Enfermedad y literatura: Entre inspiración y desequilibrio*, ed. C. López Lorenzo and J. Botteron (Kassel: Reichenberger, 2020), 35.
76. Aurelio Valladares Reguero, "La sátira quevedesca contra Luis Pacheco de Narváez," *Epos: Revista de filología* 17 (2001): 179; Stefano De Merich, "Un testo picaresco del 1582: Il Diálogo de la falsa destreza di Jerónimo de Carranza," *Rivista di filologia e letterature ispaniche* 7 (2004): 67.
77. Valladares Reguero, "La sátira quevedesca contra Luis Pacheco de Narváez," 179.
78. Francisco de Quevedo y Villegas, *La vida del buscón*, ed. F. Cabo Aseguinolaza (Madrid: Real Academia Española, 2011), 61.
79. Ibid.
80. *Jácaras*, or pimp poetry, are baroque songs that represent pimps (*jaques*) in a heroic manner. It may be considered the early modern counterpart of pimp rap. For the close relation between swordsmanship and Quevedo's pimps, see Frederick A. De Armas and Manuel Olmedo Gobante, "De espadas y de cañas: Esgrima y astrología en las jácaras de Quevedo," *La Perinola* 23 (2019): 215–30.
81. "Jácaras 3, 11, and 13" in Francisco de Quevedo y Villegas, *Poesía original completa*, ed. J. Manuel Blecua (Barcelona: Planeta, 1996), 1127, Bl.851, v.25; 1159, Bl.859, v.61; 1164, Bl.861, vv.93–104, respectively.
82. Francisco Manrique Cabrera, *El negro en la literatura española*, ed. J. F. de Cabrera and L. de Arrigoitia (San Juan: Fundación F. Manrique Cabrera, [1934] 1992), 61, 79. The following have also studied the figure of the Black hero, using different terminology and narrowing Manrique Cabrera's corpus down to their respective scholarly interests: Enrique Martínez López, *Tablero de ajedrez: Imágenes del negro heroico en la comedia española y en la literatura e iconografía sacra del Brasil esclavista* (Lisboa: Centre Culturel Calcouste Gulbenkian, 1998); Baltasar Fra-Molinero, *La imagen de los negros en el teatro del Siglo de Oro*; John Beusterien, "La discriminación contra los Afro-Hispanos en una obra teatral del siglo xvii: Una escena grotesca de *La confesión con el demonio* de Francisco de la Torre y Sevil," *Hispania Felix* 7 (2016): 97–118.
83. Baltasar Fra-Molinero, *La imagen de los negros en el teatro del Siglo de Oro*, 125–62; also in Fra-Molinero, "Los negros como figura de negación y diferencia en el teatro barroco," 7–29.
84. There are several literary works that feature the protagonist of *El valiente negro en Flandes*, including a sequel to the play. See Olmedo Gobante, "'El mucho número que hay dellos,'" 69, 77–82.
85. Francisco Manrique Cabrera, *El negro en la literatura española*, 85–86.

86. See David Gitlitz, "La angustia vital de ser negro, tema de un drama de Fernando de Zárate," *Segismundo* 11 (1975): 65–85; Michael D. McGaha, "Entre el 'Noble Moor' y el 'Negro Perro Moro': *Otelo* y *Las misas de San Vicente Ferrer*," in *Vidas paralelas: El teatro español y el teatro isabelino, 1580–1680*, ed. A. K. Stoll (London: Tamesis, 1993), 37–44; Harm Den Boer, "¿Católico Zárate, judío Muley? Nueva lectura de *Las misas de San Vicente Ferrer*," in *Antonio Enríquez Gómez. Un poeta entre santos y judaizantes*, ed. J. I. Díez Fernández and C. Wilke (Kassel: Reichenberger, 2015), 15–34; John Beusterien, "La discriminación contra los Afro-Hispanos en una obra teatral del siglo xvii: Una escena grotesca de *La confesión con el demonio* de Francisco de la Torre y Sevil," *Hispania Felix* 7 (2016): 97–118.
87. Moses E. Panford, "La negra por el honor: Una aproximación postcolonial," in *Locos, figurones y quijotes en el teatro del Siglo de Oro: Actas selectas del XII Congreso de la Asociación Internacional de Teatro Español y Novohispano de los Siglos de Oro (julio 2005, Almagro)*, ed. G. Vega García-Luengos and R. González Cañal (Almagro: Ediciones de la Universidad de Castilla La Mancha, 2007), 333–44.
88. Francisco Manrique Cabrera, *El negro en la literatura española*, 81–84.
89. See Baltasar Fra-Molinero, *La imagen de los negros en el teatro del Siglo de Oro*, 77–101; Benedetta Belloni, "'Soy turco firme roca incontrastable': Sobre la conversión del protagonista musulmán en la comedia *El santo negro Rosambuco* de Lope de Vega," *Artifara* 17 (2017): 181–99.; Moses E. Panford, "La figura del negro en cuatro comedias barrocas: *Juan Latino* (Jiménez de Enciso), *El valiente negro en Flandes* (Claramonte), *El santo negro Rosambuco* (Lope de Vega) y *El negro del mejor amo* (Mira de Amescua)" (PhD diss., Temple University, 1993), 151.
90. Panford, "La figura del negro en cuatro comedias barrocas," 145.
91. Fra-Molinero, *La imagen de los negros en el teatro del Siglo de Oro*, 54–76; Lope de Vega y Carpio, *El prodigio de Etiopia*, ed. John Beusterien (Pontevedra: Mirabel, 2005).
92. Lope de Vega de Carpio, *El prodigio de Etiopia*, 73.
93. Ibid., 47.
94. Antonio Sánchez Jiménez, "Raza, identidad y rebelión en los confines del Imperio hispánico: Los cimarrones de Santiago del Príncipe y *La Dragontea* (1598) de Lope de Vega," *Hispanic Review* 75, no. 2 (2007): 113, 121–23, 127–128. See Manrique Cabrera, *El negro en la literatura española*, 66.
95. Sánchez Jiménez, "Raza, identidad y rebelión en los confines del Imperio hispánico," 125–30.
96. See Lope de Vega y Carpio, *La Dragontea*, ed. A. Sánchez Jiménez (Madrid: Cátedra, 2007), vv. 3293–3296; Also see Manrique Cabrera, *El negro en la literatura española*, 39; Sánchez Jiménez, "Raza, identidad y rebelión en los confines del Imperio hispánico," 120.
97. Luis Pacheco de Narváez, *Libro de las grandezas de la espada en que se declaran muchos secretos del que compuso el comendador Jerónimo de Carranza*, 259r.
98. Manrique Cabrera, *El negro en la literatura española*, 38. Sánchez Jiménez, "Raza, identidad y rebelión en los confines del Imperio hispánico," 126–27.
99. On Lope de Vega's Marrons as an "exception," see Baltasar Fra-Molinero, "Los negros como figura de negación y diferencia en el teatro barroco," 9.

100. For examples of these two points of view, see Marta Hidalgo Pérez, "Alianzas atlánticas en Armas Antárticas: Corsarios y cimarrones en la obra de Juan de Miramontes y Zuázola," *Nuevo Mundo Mundos Nuevos* (2018): 21; Rodrigo Miró, *Itinerario de la poesía en Panamá* (Biblioteca de la Nacionalidad y Autoridad del Canal de Panamá, 1999), 13, respectively. See also Juan de Miramontes, *Armas Antárticas* (Caracas: Biblioteca Ayacucho, [c. 1609] 1978), 80, 191; Hidalgo Pérez, "Alianzas atlánticas en Armas Antárticas," 22.

101. Jean-Pierre Tardieu, *Cimarrones de Panamá. La forja de una identidad afroamericana en el siglo xvi* (Madrid: Iberoamericana, 2009), 16–17.

102. Olmedo Gobante, "'El mucho número que hay dellos,'" 74; Sánchez Carranza, *Libro de Jerónimo de Carranza*, 233r-v.

103. Joseph A. Karbowski, "Aristotle's Scientific Inquiry into Natural Slavery," *Journal of the History of Philosophy* 51, no. 3 (2013): 331.

104. Tardieu, *Cimarrones de Panamá*, 12–20; Fra-Molinero, "Los negros como figura de negación y diferencia en el teatro barroco," 9.

105. Elvezio Canonica, "La figura del negro santo y su contrapunto burlesco en *El santo negro Rosambuco* de Lope de Vega," in *Pratiques hagiographiques dans l'Espagne du Moyen Age et du Siècle d'Or*, ed. F. Cazal, A. Arizaleta, and C. Chauchadis (Toulouse: Université de Toulouse-Le Mirail, 2005), 301.

106. See, respectively, Manrique Cabrera, *El negro en la literatura española*, 96; Margarita García Barranco, "Correlaciones y divergencias en la representación de dos minorías: Negroafricanos y moriscos en la literatura del Siglo de Oro," in *La esclavitud negroafricana en la historia de España: Siglos xvi y xvii*, ed. A. Martín Casares and M. García Barranco (Granada: Editorial Comares, 2010), 167.

107. Fra-Molinero, *La imagen de los negros en el teatro del Siglo de Oro*, 81.

108. See García Barranco, "Correlaciones y divergencias en la representación de dos minorías," 167; Canonica, "La figura del negro santo y su contrapunto burlesco en *El santo negro Rosambuco* de Lope de Vega," 321.

109. In Olmedo Gobante, "'El mucho número que hay dellos,'" for example, I argue that Juan de Mérida, the Black hero of *El valiente negro en Flandes*, cannot be considered exceptional for a number of reasons.

110. Manrique Cabrera, *El negro en la literatura española*, 97, 60.

111. See Olmedo Gobante, "'El mucho número que hay dellos,'" 73; Nicholas R. Jones, *Staging Habla de Negros: Radical Performances of the African Diaspora in Early Modern Spain* (University Park: Pennsylvania State University Press, 2019); Larissa Brewer-García, *Beyond Babel: Translations of Blackness in Colonial Peru and New Granada* (Cambridge: Cambridge University Press, 2020).

112. Curiously, the Alba-Medranos filed their lawsuit in Úbeda, only six miles away from the Narváez's birthplace, Baeza. See Laguna Fernández, "Luis Pacheco de Narváez," 211–344.

113. Pedro Andrés Porras Arboledas, "Los moriscos en el archivo municipal de Úbeda," *Etudes d'Histoire Morisque* 23 (2003): 326–27.

114. For the concept of citizen (*vecino*) and the rights conferred by it in early modern Spain, see Herzog, "Beyond Race," 153–56.

CHAPTER 4

On Enslaving and Impalement

The "Life" and Death of Chicaba, Black Woman Saint in Empire

JEROME BRANCHE

> Ahorran y dan libertad a sus negros cuando ya son viejos y no pueden servir, y echándoles de casa con título de libres, los hacen esclavos del hambre, de que no piensan ahorrarse sino es con la muerte.
>
> Miguel de Cervantes

In the recent documentary *Gurumbé: Afro-Andalusian Memories* (2016), the director Miguel Angel Rosales declares his intention of recuperating the centuries-old African musical presence in Spain and of highlighting the importance of its cultural and historical contribution to the larger national heritage.[1] Rosales's project is driven particularly by his awareness of the wide popularity enjoyed historically by a variety of Afro-originated genres and the emergence of flamenco, a cultural form institutionalized by practitioners and intellectuals alike since the nineteenth century, as an "official" and "national" folkloric genre. In his vindication of the now forgotten Black element to the cultural mix that produced flamenco, associated today with the marginalized Romani people, he hints at a larger racist national sense of self in Spain that cannot, in his words, conceive of Blackness as representative of the Spanish "esencia," or essence, taking into consideration the official "Whiteness" of European identity as a whole.[2] His methodological challenge is, of course, a formidable one, especially bearing in mind the scant demographic presence of the descendants of slavery-era Blacks in Spain today, the lack of easily available historical documentation on their musical practices or such hypothetical "items of proof" as musical instruments, along with the long-standing assumption that Africans had left no cultural trace in the country.[3]

Given his stated objectives, the question arises as to how to capture a reality for which there is not only minimal material evidence, but whose manifestations, besides, are to be found mainly in the expressive register and embedded into a contemporary cultural form like flamenco, the performances of which purportedly represent a vernacular ethos in which the bodies on stage are primarily non-Black. To be sure, as one of Rosales's interviewees puts it, as recently as the 1990s, common knowledge in Spain had it that slavery involving Black Africans was something that had happened elsewhere. And this was in spite of the fact that Africans were imported into the country over hundreds of years and that the neighboring Portuguese, along with the Spanish, were the initiators of the maritime outthrust that devolved into the transatlantic slave trade, colonialism, and the global maritime commercial networks that subsequently developed. In taking on the nickname "el negro Curro" in his documentary, Rosales assumes the identity of a sixteenth-century subset of free Blacks (*curros*) who once constituted a visible faction of Sevillian vernacular life, were associated with musical performativity, and existed alongside such other Black social groups as the "Black Brotherhoods," or *cofradías negras*, Black swordsmen, and so on (see Olmedo and Valerio in this volume), all of whom were part of the larger process that forcibly brought some ninety-five thousand Africans between the fifteenth and the nineteenth centuries to Seville and to other Spanish cities. In exhuming a value that, to all appearances, had been lost in time and covered over by a multiplicity of material and non-material elements, Rosales the researcher undertook a quest that required in the end a multidisciplinary approach employing anthropologists, archeologists, historians, and musicians, as well as a long-distance visit to the Serer people of Senegal.[4]

Considering the Afro-diasporan content and significance of the documentary, and the scarcity of workable leads, Rosales's project may well have put into operation what Sabine Broeck refers to, in a similar context, as a "hermeneutics of absence," occasioned by the cumulative effect of the interment of Black subjectivity across the Atlantic world, the social death suffered by its victims, and the ensuing *lacunae* created by slavery's inherently violent and destructive machinery.[5] Working on the premise that transatlantic slavery has been undertheorized in its global outreach and impact, in spite of a transgenerational afterlife with all-too-visible effects on Black existence, Afropessimists like Broeck see slavery's corollary, anti-Black racism, as integral to the very fabric of modernity and articulated transhistorically in a multiplicity of discourses and practices aimed at the perpetuation of Black abjection, a process which she dubs "enslavism" in an attempt to capture its trajectory through time and space. The construction of the racial dichotomy of Whiteness/Blackness, of personhood and subpersonhood, of being and thingness, is not only at the heart of the modern social contract, Afropessimists contend, but its continuance is also a requirement of the networks that constitute civil society and its dynamics of anti-Blackness today. From this standpoint, while standard social subalterns, marginals, women, and even insurgents are acknowledged, theorized, and interpellated within the Symbolic Order, the Black, on both sides of the Atlantic, and notwithstanding the promise and premise of Enlightenment, Emancipation, anticolonial Independence, Civil Rights, and other purportedly universal liberatory gestures, remains object and abject to the unremitting and prelogical violence that sustains the libidinal infrastructure of modernity.

Broeck's proposal of a study of "enslavism" would move toward connecting the dots between the Black as slavery-era abject and the Black as contemporary abject, constituted transhistorically outside of the Human and kept there by way of anti-Black racism as praxis. Frank B. Wilderson III, for example, reflecting on a 1970 political communiqué penned by former Black Liberation Army (BLA) member Assata Shakur, observes that such revolutionary declarations as Shakur's can only be successful as legitimate political statements to the degree that their proponents are recognized by their ostensible interlocutors (the State, civil society) as having "the right of authorization," and ongoing racist epistemic and ontological banishment disables this. In an analogous declaration on behalf of, say, an anticolonial insurgent or a labor protestor, who have land or improved relations of production as their objects of political desire, the existence of dialogue and negotiation itself implies a mutual recognition, while the Black is excluded from this "gated community." Indeed, appropriate recognition of Shakur as a BLA member, Wilderson argues, would prove calamitous to the Symbolic Order. For such an individual, given the contours of her enunciation, her very subjectivity is at stake.[6]

For the present discussion, whose subject is situated at the extreme end of the spectrum between Black rebellion and Black integration, one asks: What might author/ization mean if instead of a declaration of self-assertion or insurgency, à la BLA, we have one of apparently extreme assimilation, as in the ostensible life story of a nine-year old African girl, Chicaba? Captured in Ewe country and brought to seventeenth-century Spain, Chicaba grew up to become such a paragon of religiosity through her vows and their enactment that her biography was written to stand as a model of Christian piety and propriety and proof of the transcendence of the Church and its universal evangelical mission.[7] Under what terms might such an extended narrative declaration of selfhood (in Christ) be made? What are the contours surrounding the creation of the narrative? What is the agenda of the ubiquitous amanuensis, her confessor, Father Carlos Miguel de Paniagua, in the story? What is to be made both of his omissions and his accretions in fashioning her *Vida Ejemplar* or *Exemplary Life* (1752), even considering the conventions of the genre of hagiography?[8] What are the ostensible implications of recuperating her persona as a Black saint for Spain as a nation, or as the erstwhile seat of Empire, in a manner that might be analogous, even if loosely so, to Rosales's project described earlier? And in the final analysis, what significance might be culled from Chicaba's lone diasporan voice, albeit by way of ventriloquism, in the context of other auto/biographies of the enslaved across the Black Atlantic, whether Afro-Hispanic or not?

Chicaba, or the Venerable Madre Sor Teresa Juliana de Santo Domingo (c. 1676–1748), as per her *Vida*, was brought to Spain as a child and lived in slavery in the household of Spanish nobles Juliana Teresa Portocarrero y Meneses, Duchess of Arcos (Chicaba's original purchaser), and her future husband, Antonio Sebastián de Toledo, the Marquis of Mancera. The marchioness provided for her instruction in literacy and in the principles of the Catholic faith, and upon her death, after seventeen years of domestic service, she left Chicaba a life annuity of fifty ducats on condition that she take religious vows and enter a convent. When Chicaba herself died, forty-four years after professing at the Santa María Magdalena de la Penitencia, a Dominican convent for nuns at Salamanca, the Theatine priest Carlos Miguel de Paniagua wrote an obituary in her honor based on conversations the two had sustained in the latter months of her life and on the scattered fragments of her own writings, which spoke of her spiritual strivings.[9] Indeed, Chicaba's ostensible claim to being both the first Afro-Hispanic woman writer and a candidate for beatification lies as much on De Paniagua's eulogy as it does on the subsequent *Compendio de la vida ejemplar* that he edited a few years later.[10] It turns out that the second account is not only a garrulous extension of the first, framed in hyperbolic trajectory in the fashion of the traditional Christian hagiography, with its typical tropes of Christlike suffering and sacrifice and of pain and persecution for the spiritual purification of the protagonist, together with the requisite examples of miracle-making that would establish their eventual qualifications for sainthood. The book also aims to exemplify evangelical outreach, through Chicaba's persona as "cultural import," and the power of the Church in its capacity for extramural and ultimately transatlantic outreach and conversion in a way that would befit Spain's imperial project in the latter seventeenth and early eighteenth centuries. This operation, in which religion is instrumentalized through the evangelical idea for what I would call "colonial capture," that is, coloniality in its material and epistemic aspects, is what primarily animates this discussion and analysis.

Two important rhetorical strands become immediately evident in De Paniagua's enlarged version of the Chicaba story as outlined in his obituary for her. They concern the fraught protocols of publication in a time of ongoing heightened vigilance, surveillance, and censorship over questions of religious orthodoxy in Spain and, secondly, the writer's evident concern over the cultural capital that might accrue to *his* persona as writer within the emerging Hispanic and the larger Western canon.[11] In the process of narrative and rhetorical overlay(er)ing in which the two pages of the obituary are expanded one hundred-fold to satisfy the formula for the protagonist's canonization (Maseo's edition is 203 pages long), any notion of Chicaba as captive, as forced migrant, or as enslaved arrivant in the process of transition into (Afro-)Spanishness, as might be told from her own unfiltered perspective, is lost. Instead we see De Paniagua's evangelist triumphalism unfolding throughout the narrative, with the resulting epistemological obscuring of the slave exile, all of which underscores, from our standpoint, the importance of the associated hermeneutics of absence, following Broeck's observation above.

Carlos Miguel de Paniagua, the priest, in his role as amanuensis and editor, is meticulous in his courtship of the local and national academic and ecclesiastic authorities and in establishing his conformity to principles governing potentially problematic publications such as this one, whose subject is a foreign, Black African female. There are multiple authorities who endorse him in the biography. They include Cayetano Vergara y Azcárate and Gabriel Rodríguez, lecturers in the Salamanca College of the Theatine Regular Clerks; Melchor de Arbuistante y Ondeano, the Visitor General of the Regular Clerks; and José Garcés, their secretary, along with Manuel Bernardo de Ribera, professor of philosophy and chair of theology in the college and the author of the book's very favorable preface, or "Opinión."[12] Bernabé de la Torre, ecclesiastical judge writing on behalf of the bishopric; Sebastián Flores Pavón, among other things governor of the bishopric of Salamanca and prosecutor-elect of the tribunal of the Inquisition of Valladolid; and Ignacio de Igareda, senior chamber secretary to the king and of the council government, also approvingly underwrote the *Vida* in its introductory section.[13] Of these, Ribera's recommendation of the manuscript is perhaps the most illustrative, in that it both establishes De Paniagua's erudition and writerly skill by comparing him with famous historians of ancient Rome and with the contemporary writerly luminaries of France and Spain and underscores the orthodoxy of the book's form and content:

> En suma, la vida que quiere dar a luz el Rmo. P.M.D. Carlos Miguel de Pan y Agua y en la que (habiédola leido sin omitir sílaba) no he encontrado un ápice contra el candor de la sta. fe, buenas costumbres, ni Reales Prágmaticas, está como la vivió la *Negrita* de la Penitencia, esto es; ajustada, perfecta, admirable; sin más distinción, que haver vivido la M. Teresa con mucha pobreza y escribir el Rmo. Pan y Agua con mucha propiedad.

> *In conclusion, I have read without missing a syllable, The Life to which the Most Reverend Father Carlos Miguel de Paniagua wants to give birth. In it, I have not found a single iota against our Holy Faith, good customs, or royal authorities. The Life is just as the Little Black Woman of La Penitencia lived it. Like hers, it is fitting, perfect and admirable, the only difference being that Mother Teresa lived with total poverty, and the Most Reverend De Paniagua wrote with all the riches of proper style.*[14]

But as in so many other areas of the narrative, it is Chicaba's specificity in race, as a feature of coloniality and colonial capture, that differentiates hers from the typical (White) hagiographies and the mental and bodily sacrifices inherent to the saintly qualifications that inspire their "vidas." De Paniagua, entranced by the prospect of additional fame as he reflected upon the successful circulation of his initial publication not only in Spain but also in its New World colonies, was inscribing himself into a larger evangelical project even as he underscored the potential for publicity and evangelical propaganda in his planned *Vida* of Chicaba and in his negotiations for its sponsorship and publication. We recall that evangelical outreach, whose objective was to "conquistar almas para su reino, que no es de este mundo" (conquer souls for His kingdom, which is not of this world), had been formalized between 1622 and 1627 by Pope Gregory XV and Urban VIII as the Sagrada Congregación de Propaganda Fide, subsequently the Sagrada Congregación para la Evangelización de los Pueblos, or the Holy Congregation for the Evangelization of Peoples.[15] The project, which had installed a training college for missionaries in acute awareness of the burgeoning interimperial challenges from the Dutch and the English in regards to Asia, Africa, and even the Americas and with an appropriately distributed curriculum in linguistic, cultural, and doctrinal training designed for Muslims, Jews, and other assorted heretics and unbelievers from the Near East and Europe, had itself grown out of thirteenth-century, pre-imperial papal projections aimed at infidels and heretics.[16]

The long fifteenth century, from 1415 to 1513, in effect, would see the emergence and maturation of a politics of empire that combined militarism, evangelicalism, and massive material expropriation and forced labor in a genocidal and epochal parting of the historical waters that not only left the indigenous "New World" civilizations decimated but also depopulated untold African societies and laid the objective and subjective bases for their future underdevelopment.[17] Inspired in and underwritten by a series of papal bulls that authorized, blessed, and legitimized colonial expansion, Iberian monarchs and their armies of discoverers and colonizers took advantage of plenary indulgences, hospitable natives, expansive cartographic premises, and martial and biological weaponry to "reduce" populations to domination, exploitation, and servitude. *Dum Diversas*, the 1452 bull of Pope Nicolas V, spoke of "perpetual slavery" for "all Saracens and pagans whatsoever," and the 1493 bull of Pope Alexander VI would self-consciously repeat the mandate even as it literally divided the world, known and unknown, between Spain and Portugal.[18] Twenty-one years after Columbus stumbled upon the natives at Guanahani, the 1513 royal Requirement, or *Requirimiento*, in directly addressing the ostensible *Other* for the first time for evangelical purposes, would make clear their destiny in death and enslavement unless they acknowledged the god of the Christians as their new (true) God and the Pope and the Castilian monarch as his representatives on this earth.[19] The entire process would confirm the larger soteriological premise that bringing all peoples into "salvation" as the "proper order" was what was intended by Christ's crucifixion.[20]

The Protestant challenge to orthodoxy in the form of the Reformation, finally, would produce a response in the Council of Trent (1545–1563), which would also create a strategic opening for current and future colonial figures in the role of saintly exemplars for their presumed non-White constituencies. Indeed, one of the most highly promoted of the handful of (new) Black saints would have been the beatification of Benedict of Palermo, future patron saint of enslaved Blacks in Spain, Portugal, and the New World, in 1743, the decade of Chicaba's death.[21] As an ostensible *alma*, or "soul," for conquest, two hundred-plus years into the process of imperial evangelization, Chicaba's life story has implications that have to do both with that which is discursive and that which is real, that which is religious and that which is political, and consequently with the levels of violence that characterize all of these registers of empire as a transhistorical event. Being an African girl/woman in the archive of the diaspora, she is therefore relevant both as *persona*, or figment of narrative, and in terms of her living personhood. The implications for these aspects of her lived and literary identity, therefore, are as much epistemic as they are ontological.

As is to be expected, the aspiration to saintliness that defines the hagiography must render extraordinary the otherwise ordinary life of its subject. Chicaba's trajectory from childhood through adulthood is thus appropriately marked by this distinction and the praiseworthiness it presupposes. Long before she took her vows as a tertiary at the monastery at Salamanca and gained a reputation for her exceptional devoutness and piety along with the occasional miracle, she had shown signs of the promises she was going to fulfill. Accordingly, De Paniagua presents her as coming from legitimate and noble parentage (a "princess" on account of the jewelry she wore at her abduction) and as a precocious child, given to philosophizing and theological speculation as she explores the natural world in and around her native village. For her, the streams, stars, and meadows are all an opportunity for inquiry into nature and the origin of things, as well as the perception that the local cosmogony was somehow deficient, wanting a loftier explanation than that provided by her culture or, more specifically, her father. Chicaba even has a vision of the Holy Mother and Child before her departure from her African homeland, and though yet a child, she decides to be a devotee, or a "Bride of Christ."[22] During her sea passage to Spain, via São Tomé, where she is officially inducted into Christianity by the sacrament of baptism, she is again shown divine favor as the miraculous Lady appears in the middle of a storm to allay her fears of shipwreck and the temptation to make a suicidal attempt to swim back to the African shore. Her life with the Manceras is likewise regularly marked by heavenly intervention, as she is miraculously saved from drowning at the Buen Retiro recreational park, and she grows in faith and spirituality to the degree that she is instrumental in converting a fellow captive, a young Turkish (Muslim) woman. Chicaba even serves as an example to the Marchioness, turning down, in the end, an offer of marriage from a reputed prince from her homeland and the freedom it promised. She would eventually take her vows at Salamanca upon Mancera's death, celebrating her "royal" (holy) marriage to Christ in the presence of both visible, earthly and invisible, celestial guests, and go on to a life of exemplary obedience, generosity, abstinence, and self-mortification, gaining notoriety as a seer and source of succor for all until her last days, thereby fulfilling the *telos* of suffering and salvation as per christological thought. As proof of the legitimacy of her transition into the heavenly realm, we are told that her face, "por su naturaleza negro" (black by nature), turned white just before death. It remained so, according to De Paniagua, "después de muerta perseveró así no poco tiempo" (for quite a while after her death).[23]

Notwithstanding the miracles and the tests and spiritual trials of the hagiography as genre, designed to be told as both entertainment and instruction among the faithful, it is inescapable that De Paniagua's *Vida* here turns textually and subtextually on a racial and cultural binary of Blackness and Whiteness, of a superior Spanish (or European) Christendom and an inferior Black (pagan) Africanness. This binary, as we know, is central to the discourse that sustains conquest and is key to its meaning-making function. It therefore operationalizes enslavism in that here it recycles the prejudiced dichotomous racial tropes of Spain's literary Golden Age and the contiguous establishment of Catholic patriarchalism as the foundation of Spanish nationness and simultaneously projects these negatives forward in time. The dichotomous framing is there from the beginning of the narrative, as we see Chicaba plucked from the masses of Black Africans among whom she is made to seem superior, ostensibly on the grounds of divine will for her to be the instrument of the "true" God, in order to effect the correction or rehabilitation of a universe contaminated by Lucifer or the fallen angel with whom her people's god is identified.[24] They all, according to the text, worship the mythical "Morning Star," as the narrator collapses their spiritual darkness into their bodily darkness.[25] The larger cultural contrast is reiterated at the more immediate level of her personal accession to the Christian world and is seen in the racialized specialness of the Christ figure and his Holy Mother at their first miraculous appearance to her, a contrast that is sustained throughout the narrative. At this meeting, beauty, grace, sweetness, and an emphatic Whiteness are all conflated to create a meaningful contrast with the "rostros . . . tan atezados" (oh so dark . . . faces) that had surrounded Chicaba all her life. Her submission to their seductive power is immediate and ongoing—punctuated by her declaration to her brother Juachípiter, who is anxious about royal succession, that he need not worry, because in the future she would marry a "Niño muy blanco" (very white child) in a land far away—and reaffirmed in her subsequent rejection of the royal African suitor once she is in Spain and has taken her vows.[26] The disavowals of Black culture and society evident in these and other instances not only serve to show her appreciation for and transition into Euro-Christian culture; their overt and covert judgements on racial value also underscore the narrative's imperialist and supremacist premises.

Beyond the hagiographer's more-or-less evident lyrical license in reporting on her life, Chicaba remains both putative princess and *pieza* of the transatlantic trade. Her doubled and paradoxical selfhood is one that is, in a sense, shared by all the captive Africans fallen into slavery and so speaks to their universal trauma.[27] But it is in her differing and overlapping names where her particular case is highlighted in dramatic fashion. Between "Chicaba," "La Negra de la Penitencia," or the "Venerable Mother Sister Teresa Juliana de Santo Domingo," one finds an evolving process of brutality and violent un-becoming that is only surpassed in gendered terms, perhaps, by the violence of field labor and rape that characterized slavery in the Americas.[28] De Paniagua reports the first of this chain of life events as taking place on the island of São Tomé, when Chicaba's original name is replaced at baptism with the Christian name of Teresa, on her way to Seville, Spain.[29] By then his readers have been appropriately prepared for this presumably joyful event by the subject's a priori enthusiastic acceptance of Christianity's enchantments through her pre-betrothal, through her abandonment of her parents and family, and through his own writerly dismissal of the rigors of the Middle Passage by his placement of the White Lady to comfort her and allay her fears when in a moment of panic she entertained the suicidal thought of swimming back to shore. Upon her arrival in Spain, we are told that she was "recibida... con notable agasajo" (greeted with a splendid meal of welcome) and displays of affection. There is even a miraculous communion with the Holy Mother and the Christ Child at the event that marks the arrival of the purportedly "honorable" outsider. The Christ Child descends from his mother's arms in the painting and briefly shares her afternoon snack with her.[30]

It is the correspondence between her persona as commercial *pieza*, however, and her identity as La Negra de la Penitencia, as she became known in Salamanca, where we find the essence of what Chicaba the captive came to be, over and above the fabrication/s of her amanuensis. Her commodification as captive and as article of exchange is a constant from the moment of her abduction and throughout her life in Spain and extends, paradoxically, into the afterlife of her *Vida*. After being delivered to Carlos II as a gift by the original slave traders who acquired her, she is subsequently re-gifted to the Manceras in what appears to be a not-uncommon exchange of favors among the nobility. The Manceras' extraction of her labor for the greater part of two decades would culminate in a bequeathal of freedom that, again paradoxically, denied her the ability to do with her life as she herself wished. As in so many slaveowners' last wills and testaments, the Marchioness's liberation of the twenty-seven-year-old Chicaba was a severely limited one. Instead of being "libre enteramente," or "entirely free," as the document states, her liberation was conditioned upon her transferal to a convent and assuming (or resuming) the life of enclosure there.[31] Negotiations in this process highlight the terms of barter and the benefits accruing to the parties involved in the transaction. If for Mancera it meant a sense of spiritual or moral release after years of holding a fellow human being in bondage, or better yet the guarantee that masses might be said in her honor in acknowledgment of the monies being paid the convent for accepting Chicaba, for the convent it meant, and turned out to be, a lifetime of dedicated (slave) labor from the newcomer, who was entering as a tertiary, a position assigned to lay sisters whose role traditionally was that of doing the menial work, as Fra-Molinero reminds us. What is more, the dowry that would pay for her anticipated expenses at La Penitencia was twice the amount that might be normally charged for a future Black veiled nun, her originally intended position.[32] Agency for the novice, it is clear, could only be found in the fissures of a racialized monastic order that was unbending in its (supremacist) orthodoxy.

In spite of the rhetorical and editorial cosmetics evident in Chicaba's life story, racial ordering in eighteenth-century Spain had little room for anything approaching Black autonomy. The church's role as guardian of "blood purity," or *limpieza de sangre*, within the broader, rigid hierarchy of the *sociedad de estamentos*, or social "estates," guaranteed that.[33] It is hardly surprising, then, that the stigmatizing that came with her racial otherness overcame even the aristocratic status of her agents the Manceras, as we learn that she is rejected by all of the convents in Madrid and by the Franciscan convent in Alba de Tormes before finally being accepted in Salamanca by the Dominicans of La Penitencia, a convent of low esteem on account of its origins as a home for women of morally questionable antecedents.[34] And it is at La Penitencia that we see the conflation of *pieza* and *negra* in its most telling aspect. If De Paniagua's verbiage is slippery in characterizing her Blackness as a "natural defecto" (natural defect), in explaining why she was refused entry at the Madrid convents, or an "accidente" (accident), in reporting on the Alba de Tormes episode, there could be no rhetorical avoidance of the day-to-day reality of her treatment in Salamanca.[35] At La Penitencia, Chicaba could not dine in the dining room, nor sing in the choir with the other nuns. She was neither provided a spiritual guide initially, as would have been the norm for newcomers, nor allowed to sleep in the dormitory with the others. Her placement instead in the infirmary, with a mattress made of stones and pebbles ("jergón de guijarros"), and her regular use of such instruments of self-mortification as a cross studded with sharp nails, which she would embrace daily, and a hairshirt with little chains and bits of tin, both evocative of asceticism's excesses, would seem to carry an additional, sinister psychological dimension when taken in the context of her other sufferings and privations.[36] At the home of the marchioness, in addition to being subject to verbal and physical abuse, she had been the "criada de todas, la primera a asistirlos en todas sus enfermedades" (everyone's servant, the first one to help out whenever they got sick).[37] At the convent, for decades after receiving her "freedom," the same expectations continued. Beyond the scourges and other self-inflicted tortures, she would be the one sweeping, cleaning everyone else's dishes, and fetching wood for the fire.[38] Being a *negra*, writes De Paniagua, naturalizing her purported servility and ignoring the superstructure of her ongoing martyrdom, "she *made herself* everyone's slave" (como negra, se hizo por todos esclava).[39]

There is little, indeed, to separate Chicaba's performance of saintly virtue and humility from supremacist humiliation and degradation, and we see her taken to the limit in her duties of tending to the sick.[40] For instance, she is made on one occasion to extract the pus from an odorous, infected wound on the leg of one of her White patients with her mouth. Bishop Francisco Calderón de la Barca had looked with "alguna repugnancia" (some repugnance) at the idea that Chicaba, qua *negra*, might be allowed entry at "La Penitencia," reports the amanuensis.[41] But as we see De Paniagua's fellow churchmen and academics refer to her both with the honorific of "Venerable Madre" (Venerable Mother) and with the dismissive racial diminutive of "La Negrita" (the Little Negress) in endorsing the book of her ostensible (posthumous) celebration, the permanency of the racial marker and its ossifying effect in Spanish culture of the time become clear.[42]

To the extent that the protagonist's multiple names point to a splitting of her persona (or her personality), her particular condition at La Penitencia underscores the psychic instability brought on by captivity, enslavement, and exile. The symbol of an S cut through from top to bottom by an elongated nail served customarily as a hieroglyph to identify slaves in Spain. To indicate ownership and the individual's social condition, it might be burned into the recently arrived captive's cheek, as might the fleur de lis, the owner's initials, or even the owner's entire name. *Esclavo*, which literally means "slave," articulates a double entendre in this hieroglyph, in the sense that the latter two syllables (*clavo*) also mean "nail," so aside from pointing to the literal meaning alluded to in the sign (*es/clavo*), "he is / a slave," the additional embedded word also alludes to the impalement of the subject within his or her condition, that is, to the permanence of his or her condition in slavery. The *esclavo* hieroglyph was also used to signify Christ's crucifixion and suffering and the dedication and devotion of one of the many seventeenth-century Spanish religious confraternities, who referred to themselves as "The Slaves of the Holy Christ" (Los Esclavos del Santo Cristo). From its origin among the nobility, the icon became ubiquitous under the Habsburgs, appearing on banners, clothing, and even the jewelry of the rich.[43]

While there is no indication in the *Vida* that Chicaba bore this particular physical brand of slavery, her double impalement, as slave to the other nuns, all potentially "Christ's slaves," as well, is undeniable. Ensuing traumatic effects, likewise, are inescapable. Fracchia also alerts us to an alternative reading of the hieroglyph as recorded in Sebastián de Covarrubias's 1611 *Tesoro de la lengua castellana o española*, which sees an S and an I in the icon, representing the Latin phrase *sine iure* (without legal rights) and the associated assumption that the enslaved was also *sine patrie* (without country).[44] Chicaba, as an individual *sine iure*, is made to sign over her inheritance to La Penitencia in the paperwork that documents her acceptance into the convent.[45] Her abduction into slavery would have left her *sine patrie*, as well, and therefore bereft of home and family, but also liminal, by definition, in Spanish society. This distancing from the potential effect of her African parents and siblings is compounded by the fact that, as a woman, her religious vows also foreclose the possibility of future offspring. Exile in Spain and the enclosed world of the convent thus contribute to an existential and geographical culmination of her genealogical isolation and her social death, following Orlando Patterson's famous characterization of the institution and its effects.[46]

It is more than a little ironic that Bernardo de Ribera, in his "Opinión," would congratulate De Paniagua, another churchman, for "birthing" the quasi-fictional Chicaba in his narrative. Their masculinist collaboration goes to the core of the question of power in representation and to the ability to re/make a (Black) persona in their Whitened image.[47] A consideration of the racialized power on display in Chicaba's *Vida*, and the way this enslaved person is molded in her editor's third-person narration, seems emblematic of Fanon's famous insight that the Black "has no ontological resistance" in the eyes of the White man.[48] It may be impossible to (re)construct a real (auto)biography of Chicaba based on the fragments of her story that she would have shared with De Paniagua, particularly taking into consideration the elements of selection, omission, self-censorship, exaggeration, or even deception on her part and the obligation of nuns to provide detailed accounts of their spiritual lives to their confessors. In the final analysis, though, it is as the "Black bride of Christ," the metaphor which provides the title for the most recent iteration of her life story, that we see the protagonist revealing, in her own unfiltered words and within the framework of a single poem, the drama of her search for the elusive Christ figure, at once aspirational object of desire in the traditional lyric of the Spanish mystics and the marker of her own transition from "paganism" to the Christian community. Unsurprisingly, this poem, the only one of hers that we know of, speaks of abandonment and longsuffering, of envy and alienation:

> Aih Jesús, donde te has ido
> Que un instante no puedo
> Verme sin tigo;

> Aih Jesús de mi alma,
> Donde te has ido,
> Que parece que no vienes
> Y te has perdido.
>
> *Oh Jesus, where have you gone?*
> *I cannot for one instant*
> *Suffer your absence;*
> *Oh Jesus, of my soul,*
> *Where have you gone,*
> *It seems that you will not come*
> *And are lost.*[49]

Apart from the poem's sublimated eroticism, characteristic of the genre and exhibited most notably in the work of St. John of the Cross, there is precious little of the cultural insider's spiritual confidence and fortitude.[50] Rather than proclaiming in faith, as does Chicaba's namesake, St. Teresa of Ávila, that "I die for not dying" (Muero poque no muero), or making an affirmation of life outside the self, "Vivo ya fuera de mí," or speaking of life as a "Divine prison" (divina prisión) on account of her adoration of the Holy Beloved,[51] Chicaba's poem proclaims in tears and unfulfillment and speaks of the Beloved's absence. While references to Christ's life and his followers are conventional within the genre, Chicaba's suspicion of Christ's dismissal and preferential treatment to others, namely the biblical Martha and María, may just as plausibly identify the lyrical subject as a lonely voice crying in the wilderness of exile and confusion:

> A Marta y María
> Las has querido.
> Aih Jesús, donde te
> Hallaré yo?
> Pues tan tonta me tiene
> Quando te tengo . . .
>
> *You have loved*
> *Martha and Maria.*
> *Oh Jesus, where*
> *Will I find you?*

Oh such a fool I am
When I'm with you . . .[52]

The poem, indeed, sputters to its conclusion in a tone of despair and defeat as the lyrical voice repeats "no más, no más, no más" (no more, no more, no more).[53]

If one were to speculate on a hypothetical life for Chicaba as forced immigrant or as first-generation Afro-Spanish outside the convent, the possibilities would not be particularly promising. Enslaved Black women in eighteenth-century Spain executed such domestic chores as cooking, cleaning, doing the laundry, feeding children, and taking care of the sick in the homes of their owners. Outside the home, they brought in firewood and fruits and vegetables for the household, served travelers in inns and taverns, and could even be put out to prostitution by their owners.[54] The culture of sexual exploitation was such that as many as 90 percent of biracial children in the sixteenth century were fathered by White slave owners.[55] Outside of slavery, however, in what one might imagine as an Afro-Hispanic "nation" extending across Sevilla, Valencia, Málaga, Palmas, and Gran Canaria, there existed a vernacular tradition of word and thought, expressed in work songs and carols (*villancicos*), that affirmed Black humanity by insisting, against the dominant discourse, that "we have souls, notwithstanding our skin color" (aunque negros, gente somos / alma tenemos) and that the Black presence within the Christian myth around the Nativity sullies neither the Nativity nor the Christ child.[56] As early as 1700, coterminous with Chicaba's arrival, this Black vernacular tradition confronted the epistemic elimination fostered by the local narrative tradition by dismissing the racial determinant in declaring their essential humanity.

The recent research into Black voicing of the period, most particularly the culminating declarations around "aunque negros, gente somos" as part of a lyrical declaration by an Afro-Hispanic subject himself, in which African origin and Black selfhood are celebrated and the greed and tyranny of slaveownership and its ideological moorings are harshly critiqued ("Song of a freedman," 1700),[57] is not only of value as a counterdiscourse to the spectrum of mockery and dehumanization associated with *guineo* characterization in the representation of Blacks in the dominant narratives of Renaissance and baroque Spanish literature.[58] From the standpoint of the diasporan archive, it goes to the heart of the struggle against an anti-Black racist and patriarchal ethic born in and continued by colonialism and empire and their afterlives. De Paniagua's 1762 *Vida* of Chicaba, on the contrary, sticks religiously to the christological architecture that animates it. In it, Black African culture is proposed as a tabula rasa of no epistemic or ontological value, slavery in Europe is presented as better for the Black subject than freedom in Africa, the Black is subjected to a religious politics wherein slavery's cruelties are to be accepted in exchange for posthumous heavenly rewards, and the indifference and moral complacency of White antagonists are written off as mysteries of God's will. As narrative, it presents important elements of an evolving narrative enslavism, which would over time normalize Black victimization and inferiority and contribute to the long-lasting, anti-human legacy of racism. In the twenty-first century, when the Church is beginning to be confronted with some of the moral contradictions of its officials high and low, the call for beatification of the nine-year-old "bride" of Christ has remained unanswered. For this putative Black Spanish saint, it is probably as it should be. A contemporary initiative such as that of Miguel Angel Rosales, in its inclusionary, identitarian trajectory, which would in effect re-imagine Spain as a national community, not only has to contend with the cultural production of enslaved African immigrants as a historical abstraction but also faces the unavoidable challenge of dealing with those individuals sacrificed on the altar of White racial supremacy and colonial capture in its material, ideological, and libidinal aspects, with all its implications for the present and the future.

NOTES

Epigraph: "They free their slaves when they are already old and can no longer work, and tossing them out of the house with titles of freedom, they make them slaves of hunger, from which only death will free them." Miguel de Cervantes Saavedra, *El ingenioso hidalgo Don Quijote de la Mancha* (México: Espasa Calpe, 1998), 448. All translations by the author except as noted.

1. *Gurumbé: Afro-Andalusian Memories*, directed by Miguel Ángel Rosales (Mexico, Spain, and Portugal: ArtMattan Productions, 2016).
2. For a long time the Spanish have had to contend with the racially discomfiting idea, associated with Napoleon, Alexandre Dumas, and others, that Africa starts at their border with France, that is, "at the Pyrenees."
3. Antonio Domínguez-Ortiz, "La esclavitud en Castilla durante la edad moderna," in *Estudios de historia social de España*, ed. Carmelo Viñas y Mey (Madrid: CSIC, 1952), 369–427. Today's Black population in Spain is estimated to be around one million, consisting mostly of twentieth and twenty-first century immigrants from sub-Saharan Africa and their offspring.

4. Rosales's research brought him to Havana, Cuba, where the original Sevillan "negros curros" relocated and became a colorful presence in the nineteenth century. Cirilo Villaverde, contemporary *costumbrista* writer, declared the *curro* to be "desde su nacimiento . . . destinado a la penca, al grillete o a una muerte violenta" (destined from birth . . . to the whip, shackles, or a violent death) on account of his criminal tendencies. Cirilo Villaverde, *Cecilia Valdés o La Loma del Angel* (Madrid: Ediciones Cátedra, 1992), 535 (my translation). In quoting Villaverde in *Los negros curros*, Fernando Ortiz was hardly more charitable in his assessment in spite of his ostensibly good intentions, saying that "En la carne de los curros . . . está siempre la sombra de Africa, pero en su alma está la luz de España" (The darkness of Africa . . . is always in the flesh of the curros, but the light of Spain is in his soul). Fernando Ortiz, *Los negros curros* (Havana: Editorial de Ciencias Sociales, 1995), 4 (my translation).
5. Sabine Broeck, "Lessons for A-Disciplinarity: Some Notes on What Happens to an Americanist When She Takes Slavery Seriously," in *Postcolonial Studies across the Disciplines*, ed. J. Gohrisch and E. Grünkemeier (Amsterdam: Brill, 2013), 349–57; Broeck, "Legacies of Enslavism and White Abjectorship," in *Postcoloniality-Decoloniality-Black Critique: Joints and Fissures*, ed. S. Broeck and C. Junker (Frankfurt: Campus, 2014), 110–28.
6. Frank B. Wilderson III, "The Black Liberation Army and the Paradox of Political Engagement," in *Postcoloniality-Decoloniality-Black Critique: Joints and Fissures*, ed. S. Broeck and C. Junker (Frankfurt: Campus, 2014), 175–207. Shakur's communiqué was a critique of American imperialism and racism and the multiple forms of state-supported violence marking Black existence in the United States. Assata Shakur was added to the FBI's Most Wanted Terrorist List in 2013, almost half a century after the events that led to her escape and exile.
7. Elvira M. Melián, "Chikaba, La primera monja negra en el sistema esclavista finisecular español del siglo XVII," *Hispania Sacra* 64, no. 130 (2012): 568. Melián places Chicaba's place of origin as Ifsini, on the border between present-day Ghana and the Ivory Coast, in a general area referred to as the Mina Baja del Oro during the long period of slave trafficking.
8. For this study I will be using Juan Carlos Miguel de Paniagua, *Compendio de la vida ejemplar de la Venerable Madre Sor Teresa Juliana de Sto. Domingo*, 2nd ed. [1764], transcribed and edited by María Eugenia Maeso (Salamanca: Imprenta Calatrava, 1999); and the edited and translated version by Baltasar Fra-Molinero and Sue E. Houchins, *Black Bride of Christ: Chicaba, an African Nun in Eighteenth-Century Spain* (Nashville, TN: Vanderbilt University Press, 2018).
9. The eulogy was first read at her funeral and incorporated into the minutes of the Dominican national assembly at Toro in 1749.
10. Melián, "Chikaba," 565–81.
11. For a discussion on power and privilege and status of writers as "authors," see Michel Foucault, "What is an Author?" in *Critical Theory since 1965*, ed. H. Adams and L. Searle (Tallahassee: Florida State University Press, 1986), 138–48.
12. De Paniagua, *Black Bride of Christ*.
13. Ibid., 127–36. See also, De Paniagua, *Compendio de la vida ejemplar*.

14. De Paniagua, *Compendio de la vida ejemplar*, 17. Translation from De Paniagua, *Black Bride of Christ*, 132 (emphasis added).
15. Ángel Santos Hernández, "Orígenes históricos de la Sagrada congregación 'De Propaganda Fide,'" *Revista española de derecho canónico* 28, no. 81 (1972): 520.
16. Santos Hernández, "Orígenes históricos de la Sagrada congregación 'De Propaganda Fide,'" 512.
17. See Walter Rodney, *How Europe Underdeveloped Africa* (Washington DC: Howard University Press, 1982); Eduardo Galeano, *Las venas abiertas de América Latina* (Montevideo: Ediciones del Chanchito, 2004).
18. Frances Gardiner Davenport, trans., *European Treaties bearing on the History of the United States and its Dependencies to 1648* (Washington, DC: Carnegie Institution of Washington, 1917), 23. See Jerome C. Branche, *Colonialism and Race in Luso-Hispanic Literature* (Columbia: University of Missouri Press, 2006), 46. See also Luis N. Rivera Pagán, *Evangelización y violencia: La conquista de América* (San Juan de Puerto Rico: Editorial CEMI, 1991), 53.
19. According to the conquistadors' ultimatum to the American natives, "If you don't do it, with the help of God I will enter powerfully against you and I will make war everywhere and everyway I know how, and I will subject you to the yoke and obedience to the Church and Their Highnesses, and I will take you and your women and children, and I will make slaves of them, and as such will I sell them . . . and I will take your goods, and I will do all the harm and evil that I can" (Rivera Pagán, *Evangelización y violencia*, 53).
20. See Willie James Jennings, *The Christian Imagination: Theology and the Origins of Race*, (New Haven, CT: Yale University Press, 2010), 29.
21. Saint Benedict of Palermo was not African; his enslaved parents were. Fracchia (2019) and Rowe (2016) stress the role of iconography in relation to the much-circulated image of this Italian saint. Chicaba, in turn, would join the archive of Black saints through the medium of discourse. See Carmen Fracchia, *'Black but Human': Slavery and Visual Art in Hapsburg Spain, 1480–1700* (Oxford: Oxford University Press, 2019), 71; Erin Kathleen Rowe, "After Death, Her Face Turned White: Blackness, Whiteness, and Sanctity in the Early Modern Hispanic World," *American Historical Review* 121, no. 3 (2016), 728–30.
22. De Paniagua, *Compendio de la vida ejemplar*, 46. That the material instrument in Chicaba's holy "seduction" at nine is a shiny pretty ribbon ("una cinta tan resplandeciente como vistosa"; Ibid., 43), bears an ironic parallel to the implements of exchange in the larger trade for humans between Europeans and Africans.
23. De Paniagua, *Compendio de la vida ejemplar*, 195. The trope of a metaphysical inner whiteness that matches the outer whiteness of Whites is a constant in Spanish Golden Age literature in its references to a purported lack in Black Africans, which they must overcome.
24. Ibid., 33–35.
25. "Mas aunque tan oscuros sus aspectos, eran mucho más negros sus ánimos. Adoraban ciegos el lucero de la manana" (But as dark as their faces were, their hearts were even darker. They blindly worshipped the Morning Star; Ibid., 32).

26. Ibid., 43, 46.
27. The *pieza*, or "piece," was the unit of measurement applied to captives in an effort to mathematically quantify them for sale. In practical terms it could vary from one person to more than one person or a fraction thereof, depending on size, gender, or presumed usefulness.
28. Lamonte Aidoo's study on same-sex rape very usefully complicates the women-only assumptions surrounding sexual violation in the colonial Americas. See *Slavery Unseen: Sex, Power, and Violence in Brazilian History* (Durban: Duke University Press, 2018).
29. De Paniagua, *Compendio de la vida ejemplar*, 42. Actually, this would have been her second baptism. She is quoted as having been baptized first by an angel at the foot of a fountain in her African homeland. However, the baptism by men is the one that matters, since it can be recorded.
30. Ibid., 51, 54
31. De Paniagua, *Black Bride of Christ*, 278.
32. Ibid., 196.
33. The idea of blood purity sought to separate the old Christians from new Christians, or Jewish and Muslim converts and their descendants in Spain. It became an early instantiation of racializing genealogies to justify politico-religious rule. See Branche, *Colonialism and Race*, 49–61.
34. The most categorical statement of rejection came not from the authorities at Alba de Tormes but from a resident nun, scion of the aristocracy. "Ni en mis días" (Not while I'm alive), she is reported to have declared. "[N]o está fundada esta casa para negras" (This house was not founded for Black women). De Paniagua, *Compendio de la vida ejemplar*, 100.
35. Ibid., 96, 99.
36. Ibid., 128.
37. Ibid., 123.
38. De Paniagua is careful to place Chicaba's handlers, her confessors, in a morally and ethically "safe" position in describing their role in relation to her apparent zeal in her practices of self-mortification. In pointing out that they could restrain her only with difficulty ("no hacían poco los directores en contenerla"; Ibid., 128), he absolves them of guilt in her possibly self-destructive behavior, making her responsible for it, and simultaneously underscores her devotion.
39. Ibid., 171 (emphasis added).
40. Fracchia's discussion of the "Miracle of the Black Leg," preserved in Castilian sixteenth-century iconography, which depicts the grafting of the leg of a healthy Black male subject onto that of a White patient under the watchful gaze of Damian and Cosmas, patron saints of surgeons, doctors, and pharmacists, highlights the essential killability of the Black body, here in the service of Western medical practices. See Fracchia, *'Black but Human,'* 121–53. Here in the United States more recently, the Tuskegee Syphilis Experiment (1932–1972), in which treatment was withheld from unsuspecting Black male subjects in order to observe the natural history of the untreated disease, is another reminder of the longevity of this gruesome racist practice.

41. De Paniagua, *Compendio de la vida ejemplar*, 111, 172.
42. Ibid., 13–23.
43. Fracchia, *'Black but Human,'* 107–8.
44. Ibid., 105.
45. De Paniagua, *Black Bride of Christ*, 270.
46. Orlando Patterson, *Slavery and Social Death* (Boston: Harvard University Press, 1982).
47. Linda M. Alcoff, "The Problem of Speaking for Others," in *Who Can Speak: Authority and Critical Authority*, ed. J. Roof and R. Wiegman (Urbana: University of Illinois Press, 1997), 97–119.
48. Frantz Fanon, *Peau noire masques blancs* (Paris: Imprimerie Firmin-Didot, 1971), 89. In the original: "Le Noir n'a pas de résistance ontologique aux yeux du blanc."
49. Quoted in Melián, "Chikaba," 577.
50. Miguel Herrero García, *San Juan de la Cruz: Ensayo literario y El cantico espiritual* (Madison: University of Wisconsin, 1942).
51. Universidad Externado de Colombia, *Santa Teresa de Jesús, Que muero porque no muero: Antología* (Bogotá: Universidad Externado de Colombia, 2015), 9.
52. Melián, "Chikaba," 577.
53. Ibid., 577.
54. Fracchia, *'Black but Human,'* 113. See also Aurelia Martín Casares, "Evolution of the Origin of Slaves Sold in Spain from the Late Middle Ages till the 18th Century," in *Serfdom and Slavery in the European Economy, 11th -18th Centuries*, ed. S. Cavaciocchi (Firenze: Firenze University Press, 2014), 409–30; Arturo Morgado García, "The Presence of Black African Women in the Slave System of Cadiz (1650–1750)," *Slavery and Abolition* 34, no. 1 (2013): 61–76.
55. Fracchia, *'Black but Human,'* 113.
56. Ibid., 11.
57. Ibid, 192–94.
58. Branche, *Colonialism and Race*, 61–80.

PART II

CONTINUING EXPANSIONISM AND THE CIRCUM-ATLANTIC

CHAPTER 5

Facing the Enslaved

Explorations for a Transatlantic Archive

AGNES LUGO-ORTIZ

Preliminaries: Bodies, Faces, Portraits, and Archives

Alongside a rich and complex cultural legacy, the four-century-long history of the enslavement of Africans in the Americas—with the brutalities of the transatlantic trade in humans and the violent regimes of plantations—also left in its wake a troublesome image: the anonymous, besieging, and ghostly legacy of millions of faceless beings. Our visual memory of slavery has been, in no small measure, structured by an unequal distribution of the visible. It is an imaginary asymmetrically inhabited by the intense (hypervisual, if you will) inscription of the unfathomable suffering of an infinite number of nameless bodies, on the one hand, and, on the other, by blurry faces whose profiles are cast, like shadows, onto an amorphous yet agonic mass. This dissolution of the face into the body—integral to the desubjectifying logic of the modern slaveholding plantation system and to its technologies for the production of historical amnesia—was equally at work in the voyeuristic, and often paternalistic, visual rhetoric of the abolitionist movement that inflects our current imaginaries of slavery.

In its zeal to make slaveholding violence one of the most abject chapters in the universal history of infamy, the visual culture of liberal abolitionism (from its early antitrafficking struggles in the late eighteenth century to its fight against slavery itself throughout the nineteenth) would insist precisely on the ostentatious display of the vulnerable body as evidence of the criminal nature of the regime, making it its emblem. This is apparent in some of the most iconic images produced, or resignified, within these campaigns, and in which the face of the enslaved appears already diluted in undifferentiated masses of subjected bodies, such as in "Stowage of the British Slave Ship 'Brookes'"; or weighed down under the burden of a wounded body, as in *Harper's Magazine*'s "Marks of Punishment Inflicted Upon a Colored Servant in Richmond, Virginia"; or erased altogether by the spectacle of masks used for punishment and torture, denounced in 1807 by Thomas Branagan in *The Penitential Tyrant* and a few years later recorded within the picturesque aesthetics of Jean-Baptiste Debret during his travels in Brazil.[1] This visual archive of torturous subjugation has dominated our imaginaries of the slaveholding past, making it difficult to conjure up other forms of visuality that might register unsuspected modalities within the cultures of slavery. For instance, what other narratives of enslavement might emerge if, instead of focusing our attention on the body, we were to turn for a moment to the face, toward the sparse and rather intractable record that, at specific junctures in the history of transatlantic slavery, has provided an account of the singular appearance of an enslaved's face within the realm of visual portraiture? What sort of archive, even in its disarray, would become visible? And what different practices of slaveholding domination might be delineated in tandem with or alongside those that are more frequently spectacularized in the deployment of chains, masks, stocks, and whips? (See Figures 5.1, 5.2, 5.3, and 5.4.)

There is no doubt that within the concrete and symbolic logics of plantation slavery—as well as in a significant portion of the abolitionists' re-semanticizations—the body of the enslaved was materialized in extremely restrictive ways, all congruent with a rigidly instrumental rationality: a body destined to inhabit the eternal present of production; a body for labor, reproduction, and punishment; a body for disciplinary exemplarity. Within this logic, the body of the enslaved was assumed to house a non-subject, an entity devoid of memory and history. The enslaved here was conceived as mere corporeality and immanence, one whose history, if at all, was only that of a working, suffering body, more body than face. Contrary to this logic, portraiture (in its varied and problematic permutations) has long been conceived in Western art historical traditions as one of the privileged pictorial technologies for the production of the subject in its metaphysical fantasies of singularity, stability, autonomy, sovereignty, and transcendence. These are exactly the features that may be said to constitute "the other" of enslavement. Thus, the presence of enslaved subjects in portraiture lends it, as David Bindman has suggested, an oxymoronic character.[2]

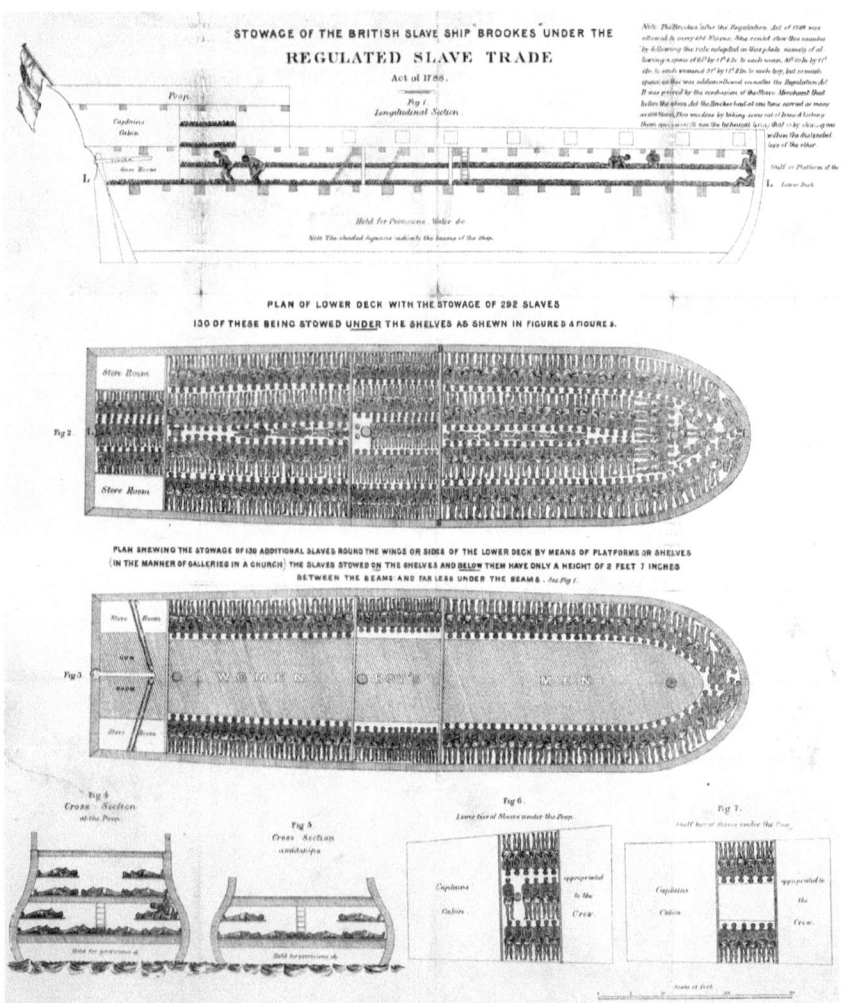

FIGURE 5.1. "Stowage of the British Slave Ship 'Brookes' under the Regulated Slave Trade, Act of 1788." First published in 1789.

Given this apparent philosophical contradiction between the early presuppositions of portraiture as a genre and the modern racialized condition of enslavement, one may ask what accounts for the infrequent yet consistent insertion of the enslaved's face within the sphere of modern visual representations, of which oil portraiture was, from the first, its epitome, though it was later reconceptualized under new epistemological regimes by

FIGURE 5.2. "Marks of Punishment Inflicted upon a Colored Servant in Richmond, Virginia." *Harper's Weekly*, July 28, 1866, 477.

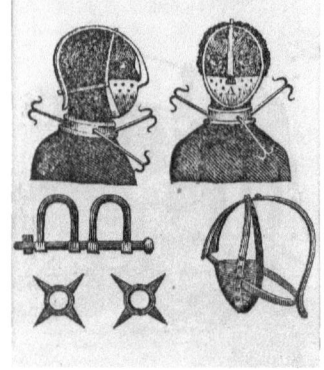

FIGURE 5.3. "Iron Mask, Neck Collar, Leg Shackles, and Spurs." From Thomas Branagan, *The Penitential Tyrant, or, Slave Trader Reformed* (New York, 1807), 271.

FIGURE 5.4. Jean-Baptiste Debret, *Masque de fer-blanc que l'on fait porter aux nègres qui one la passion de manger de la terre*. Circa 1820–1830. Pencil and watercolor on paper.

photography? What conditions enabled that appearance and to what effects? What archival practices have ruled, in various instances, the visualization and preservation of those faces in the field of symbolic production? To clarify, "archive" here is understood not just in its conventional usage but also, and primarily, in Foucault's more complex theoretical sense. Conventionally, we understand the archive to be the "sum of all the texts [or the images, for our purposes] that a culture has preserved as documents of its own past, or as testimony of its identity," as well as the institutions that house them. Yet, the archive for Foucault also carries with it the force of law. This is the law of what can be said (the sayable), the system that rules the appearance of utterances as singular events and the artifacts that prevent them from becoming an undifferentiated conglomeration—a device for discursive regulation and organization. For our purposes (that is, for an inquiry into the constitution of the archive of the enslaved as a face), what most concerns us here pertains to the discursive regimes and laws that made it possible, at particular historical moments, for the enslaved's face to become visible (the law of its visualization, of its becoming seeable) and to the systems and rules that would allow us to organize this archive. It should be stressed, as Foucault makes plain, that this system carries within it the potential for its own disarticulation and dissemination—the potential to deviate from the rules that, in the first instance, made that visibility possible.[3]

Without any pretense of completeness, four discursive scenarios may preliminarily help account for the apparition of the enslaved's face in the realm of portraiture in circum-Atlantic history, allowing us to identify some of the principles and modalities of its heterotopic archiving:

1) discourses on legitimacy and genealogical prestige that were associated with courtly cultures since the sixteenth century and that later, by the eighteenth century, were appropriated by the triumphant commercial bourgeoisies, in which the insertion in portraits of the figures of enslaved pages were deployed as signs of distinction;

2) discourses concerning artistic mastery that, at different junctures in the history of the entanglements between art and slavery, made the ability to paint the face of an enslaved person (endowing it with nobility or materializing its pigmentation) a demonstration of the painter's superior artistic skills;

3) the discourse of the law, with its evidentiary imperatives, for which the precise description of the enslaved's features (capturing his or her

"likeness"), including above all the face, became a necessary element for visualizing his or her identity, first as a "criminal" and later, within abolitionist rhetoric, as a subject of truth and innocence; and

4) the early development of ethnography and of discourses that today we recognize as "scientific racism" and within which the detailed description of the enslaved body also registered, against its own classificatory goals, the singularity of a face, one which, in its specificity, at times, defied the conventions of the "type" to touch upon those of the "portrait."

Each of these discursivities inadvertently generated "files" about the face of the enslaved or the enslaved as a face. Obliquely, they offer us the traces of a rather disorganized (and hypertextual?) corpus with which to elaborate the archive of its visualizations—of its seeability—and to complicate our understanding of the heterogeneous logics that shaped the visual cultures of transatlantic slavery, with its modern variation on the theme of the human as property. These different scenarios (as I denote them here because of their powerful performativity) allow us to draw a historical arc that stretches from the early intersection of courtly culture and the African slave trade in the sixteenth century to the enduring carcelary logic of the plantation, through the intersections of politics, aesthetics, visual technologies, and science that served both to legitimate and to critique the dying order of the slaveholding plantation in the nineteenth century. It also allows us to sketch a map of the places where these works were produced and housed (the archive in its most conventional sense): palaces and manors, studios and private collections, government buildings, libraries and laboratories, and, of course, museums. The goal here is simply to schematize each of these four paradigmatic scenarios, examining a series of exemplary materials that may help bring to the fore (however insufficiently) some of the problematics at stake in their constitution. This essay is only that, an attempt to rehearse and imagine the contours of the archives that give us the possibility of seeing the enslaved in the singularity of a face by means of portraiture.[4]

Scenario 1: Genealogical Discourses and Courtly Symbols

The first scenario that enabled the appearance of the enslaved's face in the "high" genre of oil portraiture relates to discourses of genealogical prestige that emerged within courtly cultures in the sixteenth century, associated with ideas of legitimate political succession and inheritance of property. The triumphant bourgeoisie later reappropriated these visual languages during the eighteenth century to signify their recently acquired power through the prestigious symbols and accoutrements of the waning aristocracy. The presence of slaves in these canvases was key to the visualization of hierarchy, lineage, and social distinction but—given the bodily intimacy many of them register—also an index of their perversions. Before hanging in museum galleries (or manors converted into museums), these portraits primarily decorated domestic and semi-private interiors of the aristocratic elite and, later, of the mimetic bourgeoisie. On occasion, they also served as objects of exchange (as gifts) among the powerful to consolidate alliances and effective political bonds. A significant number were family portraits, but many were also individualized images of gentlemen and ladies, who systematically appear as the object of admiration, and often adoration, of the enslaved figure in the composition. Placed either in the background or in a lower register, usually dressed as elegant pages, the enslaved characters (mostly children or young adults) always look up toward their masters, literalizing in that gesture their owners' superior position.[5]

Historically, the first of these courtly portraits is, ironically and significantly, the image of a woman of plebeian origin: the concubine of the Venetian Duke of Ferrara, Laura de Dianti, painted by Titian in the 1520s (see Figure 5.5). It has mistakenly been understood to portray Dianti after she had become the third wife of the powerful Duke Alfonso I d'Este (widowed in 1519 upon the death of the legendary Lucrezia Borgia) and that the portrait was a testament to her social ascendance. However, there is no evidence that their union was ever officialized. What is well established is that Dianti ("Signora Laura," as Vasari called her in his life of Titian) became the respected mistress of the Ferrara household, giving birth to two male heirs, whose descendants carried the weight of the duke's legacies.[6] More than a testament to her rise, the portrait was in fact a technology for its production: for the visualization of her upward mobility, the sedimentation of her newly acquired social identity, and a projection of continuities. Her sumptuous clothing, in vaporous blues and yellows, her exotic hairpiece (evocative of the emergent Orientalist fashions of the time), the very fact of being the portrait's central subject, but, especially, the presence of the Black page, so lovingly and intimately leaning against her (maternal?) body—all of these elements produce the image of a dignified person

FIGURE 5.5. Titian, *Laura de Dianti*, 1520s. Oil on canvas. Kisters Collection, Switzerland.

of elevated social stature. "None but a princess in those days indulge in the luxury of an Ethiopian page," said Crowe and Cavalcaselle.[7] And, no other portrait before Titian's *Laura Dianti* had indulged in the portrayal of such a tender Black face.

Despite references to "Ethiopia," this painting registers a foundational moment in the entanglements among the early modern economies of courtly visuality, portraiture, and the West African slave trade. Although spearheaded by the Portuguese, from the mid-1400s Italian capital was thoroughly invested in subsidizing many West African voyages, one of which produced the first full European account of the Guinea Coast (Alvise de Cadamosto's trip in 1455).[8] By the end of the fifteenth century, Venice had become a dynamic commercial entrepôt for the arrival and distribution of West African enslaved people to the rest of the Italian peninsula. There is plentiful evidence that the Ferrara clan enthusiastically participated in the acquisition of slaves, especially of enslaved women and children, and in mobilizing their semiotic functions.[9] Slavery, courtly social prestige, and portraiture were here beginning an association that endured for more than two centuries. Furthermore, in the compositional principles and innovations devised for his portrait of Laura Dianti, Titian inadvertently laid out a set of visual languages that progressively became constitutive of the modern imperial and colonial imaginaries, with their racial hierarchies.

In this early image, the semiotic/transformative functions of the enslaved's face (which are particularly dramatized by Dianti's plebeian origins) are clearly demarcated. In a sense, the portrait visualizes a new metaphysics of the subject by which the enslaved (the colonies, Africa) becomes "the other" in front of which the singularity, the essentiality of the European "one," is to be established. This visual paradigm is constituted (even with its fissures) by a series of inescapable dichotomies: White/Black, light/shadow, high/low, voluminous/small, maturity/infancy, essential/unessential. Here the face and gaze of the page only accrue meaning and consistency, so to speak, "outside" of himself: through his longing absorption in his mistress—a mistress who appears oblivious to the childish presence that requires her attention and who conveys, with her distant and distracted demeanor, a fiction of total self-possession. Moreover, due to the intense bodily proximity between the mistress and the outward-looking slave, and despite (or perhaps due to?) the performance of oblivion, the portrait cannot escape a subtle tension in which the maternal verges upon the erotic.[10] For centuries, this visual economy undergirded the iconographic insertion of enslaved pages in oil portraits—for example, in the notable portraits of Princess Henrietta of Lorraine by Van Dyck of 1634 or in that of the Duchess of Portsmouth by Pierre Mignard of 1682.[11] Self-control and simulated indifference (that is, a performance of self-possession and mastery) in front of "the other" are key elements in the gestures of domination figured in these kinds of portraits, and this gesticulation was emphatically displayed for one who was seldom identified by name in the documentary record of the portrait (which is another convention of this paradigm; see Figures 5.6 and 5.7).[12]

Toward the end of the eighteenth century—with the political and cultural crisis of the Ancien Régime and the emerging campaigns against trafficking and slavery—portraits of enslaved pages would begin to disappear as prestigious signifiers within both aristocratic and bourgeois visualities all across the transatlantic world. It is remarkable, though, that in the midst of this revolutionary juncture (one that was ideologically structured by ideas of liberty, equality, and fraternity), the patrician hero of North American independence, George Washington, reactivated this waning iconography in order to fix in portraiture his image as the heroic founder of the new nation. Two images record, with different inflections and resonances, the re-functionalization of the face of the enslaved in that moment of political liminality. It is also tempting to see those pseudo-courtly inscriptions as a kind of symbolic figuration of the stubborn continuity of slavery in the United States well into the second half of the nineteenth century. The first of these portraits relates to the homosocial scenario of war and the second to the hetero-domestic space of the familial interior. With these Washington portraits, the presence of the enslaved's face in the visualizations of courtly chivalry comes to a close; but, in a perverse way, they also mark a turn in the visualization of the type of corporeal intimacy between mistress and slave that had been inaugurated with the portrait of Laura de Dianti.

In 1780, artist-patriot John Trumbull made a Romantic military portrait in which Washington appears with his personal slave (his "valet") William "Billy" Lee. This full-length portrait was designed to commemorate the decisive military actions led by Washington in 1775, when patriot forces managed to control the Hudson River Valley, dealing a serious blow to the royalist forces and to their navy's strategic power. In the image, Washington appears relaxed and self-assured, at cliff's edge atop a rocky promontory, confronting the viewer with a dreamy yet confident gaze while pointing out the site of the battle. Behind him, like a shadow, is the enslaved

FIGURE 5.6. Anthony van Dyck, *Princess Henrietta of Lorraine*, 1634. Oil on canvas. The Iveagh Bequest, Kenwood House, London, UK / English Heritage Photo Library / The Bridgeman Art Library.

FIGURE 5.7. Pierre Mignard, Louise Renée Penancoet de Kéroüalle, *Duchess of Portsmouth*, 1652. Oil on canvas. National Portrait Gallery, London. Photo © National Portrait Gallery, London.

boy, dressed elegantly in the courtly garb of a page. He wears a dress coat and fashions a red Orientalist headdress, so popular among the European aristocracy. The shades of his skin are similar to the horse's coat, and holding the bridle, he seems to be one with the animal (note that the horse also wears a small red ornament on his head, near the left ear, echoing the headdress of the enslaved. Both slave and animal are properly adorned within the hero's portrait). We know that Lee actively participated in the War of Independence at the side of his master (and that he was the only slave that Washington freed in his will "for his services in the revolutionary war,"

FIGURE 5.8. John Trumbull, *George Washington*, 1780. Oleo sobre tela. Metropolitan Museum of Art, New York. Bequest of Charles Allen Munn. 1924. © Metropolitan Museum of Art / Art Resource, NY.

and not for services rendered to him personally).[13] Yet, here we do not see him as the warrior and horseman of repute but rather wearing an apprehensive, even anguished, expression, with his body partially hidden by the horse. Following the conventions of courtly portraiture, he gazes up toward the master/hero, who remains undaunted amid the frenzy of the war—perched there at the precipice—and indifferent to the timid presence of his subordinate (see Figure 5.8).

Ironically (given their different ideological perspectives), this image is not so different, with regard to visual languages and composition, from the extraordinary portrait of the first Lord Byron by William Dobson, painted around 1643 to commemorate his triumph over pro-parliamentarian forces in the Battle of Newberry. For Byron's services in the defense of the absolute prerogatives of the monarch, Charles I rewarded him with the title of baron. Akin to Trumbull's work, in this portrait of an English aristocrat, the enslaved figure is compositionally aligned with the axis of distinction that visually separates the human from the animal, though in this case the association slave/horse is marked by a contrast in color (i.e., Black page and white animal). Like Washington, Byron turns his back to his slave/animal and looks confidently, even arrogantly, at the viewer while indicating the field of his victories. Similar to Billy Lee, the enslaved here is dressed sumptuously in silk garb and looks upward, with a hint of apprehension in his gaze, at a master who ignores him. In addition, like the Titian painting and most known courtly portraits featuring enslaved pages, the servant in Dobson's picture also lacks a name. By contrast, in Washington's portraits nearly all of the enslaved pages who appear are named, and for most of them there is some extant documentation, even if incidental, that allows us to grasp pieces of their identities. What accounts for this particularity in Washington's portraits versus the archival vacuums in previous courtly formations? When was the enslaved's name able to follow the visual fictions of his or her face, a name that until today remains lost, displaced by the archival rubrics of "Black servant" or "page" (and sometimes under the most violent: "slave") in courtly portraiture? What archival practices enabled the reunification of the name and the face? (See Figure 5.9.)

Starting with Washington's portraits around the end of the eighteenth century, the paradigm of courtly portraiture met a disarticulating limit associated with the rise of republican nationalisms and the democratizing discourses that sustained them, as well as with the progressive institutionalization of local and national archives that organized and preserved the new nation's documents. Accounting for national origins through the meticulous documentation of its founding heroes and, selectively, its collective deeds was a fundamental task of this endeavor. However, in their eagerness to narrate the preeminence of the patricians—either by the systematic or the erratic gathering of documentation (of which portraiture was a part)—such efforts inadvertently produced a margin for the mostly

FIGURE 5.9. William Dobson, Portrait of John, 1st Lord Byron, ca. 1643. Oil on canvas. © Tabley House Collection, University of Manchester, UK / The Bridgeman Art Library.

random recompilation of materials that would eventually enable the telling and the identification of otherwise subjugated or invisibilized histories and knowledge. This is how we know about not only Washington's military prowess and political deals but also his prosthetic dentures (and the pain they caused him), along with debates regarding whether they were made of wood or ivory; his inclination or disinclination toward truth, when as a child (according to the legend) he cut down a cherry tree on his father's land; as well as the names of his enslaved cook Henry (who ran away during the war) and others under his authority (half of whom also escaped from his plantation), including his loyal valet Billy Lee. Following Marcia Pointon's observations, within the legacy of courtly portraiture, the *habitus* of the anonymous enslaved was the well-documented identity of the master or mistress, and here, by extension, at the ambiguous frontiers of republican nationalism, the metonymic gesture that construed the *national body* in the body of the patrician hero also bequeathed us his shadows, his hidden prostheses, and his protuberances.[14] This is where we find, without any original intent, the name of the enslaved.

Regarding this republican liminality, it is key to consider a second Washington portrait, which superficially appears to reverse Trumbull's painting, allowing us to pose another important question related to the archives of the enslaved's face, one that will survive its courtly modalities: the question of slaveholding intimacy and its visualization. It is a family portrait, an oil painting by Edward Savage made between 1789 and 1796 that depicts an idealized domestic interior overlooking the Potomac River. The portrait is also a political scene, in the sense that it represents the establishment of the nation's new capital, the District of Columbia, on the map that the women in the image casually examine. From the late eighteenth century onward, this image circulated widely through several engravings based on the oil painting, including one by Savage himself in 1798, as well as many more lithographs made later in the nineteenth century. In Savage's engraving, he not only reproduces the painted image but also includes an inscription in English and French indicating the title of the work (*The Washington Family / La Famille de Washington*), as well as names identifying the family members that appear in the image (*George Washington, his Lady, and her two Grandchildren by the name of Curtis*). The only figure that is not acknowledged in the inscription is the domestic slave, who appears standing at right (almost at the image's edge, behind Martha Washington), although we now know his name was Christopher Sheels. He was Billy

Lee's nephew and ended up replacing him as Washington's valet once the old page became physically handicapped.

Like Trumbull's portrait, Savage's work adopted some conventions of courtly portraiture but muted them. Sheels is shown elegantly dressed, but without Orientalist exoticism, and with a hand inside his vest, following masculine poses in fashion at the time. In this domestic interior, the enslaved is placed not behind his male master but in front of him, as if ready to respond to his gaze and orders. If anything, he is Martha's shadow (he was originally among her domestic slaves). It is difficult to miss the iconographic inversion in the compositional arrangement of the mistress and the enslaved that traditionally structured courtly portraiture. Older than the pages that served as lap dogs to aristocratic ladies (or as gentlemen's valets on the battlefield), Sheels's presence is rather sober and dignified in its servility. He inhabits the familial interior, but his contact with the bodies of the masters has been modified, neutralizing the intimacy of contact that characterized the dyad page/child with the body of the mistress and establishing a new distance with the male master. Thus, this image alters two of the main axes that had organized the bodily economies between masters and the enslaved in courtly portraiture: 1) the ostensibly visualized homosocial couple in which the enslaved appears as the shadow of his male master, as a projection of his body, and therefore indissociable from him; and 2) the intensely visible physical intimacy between the mistress and the enslaved child found in portraits of ladies, which were not exempt from libidinal suggestions under the rhetorical veil of maternity.

Sheels's hieraticism intensifies that difference, serving as a metaphor for a symbolic cesurae that suggests the passage from (but also continuities with) courtly cultures to national republicanism, a move that demands further inquiry. What new reorganizations in the visualization of the proximity between masters and slaves are being demarcated here? Does it actually represent a break? What would account for it, and what might its meanings be? Such an exploration could perhaps provide some historical density to the trajectory of the visualization of the enslaved's face, which goes from the libidinal maternity of Laura de Dianti in the sixteenth century to those spectacular economics of bodily contact staged later in the nineteenth century in the portraits of wet nurses and *amas de leite* found all across slaveholding societies in the Americas and in which, at first sight, one notes an inversion of the iconographic legacy of courtly portraiture, as in the portrait of *Fernando Simões Barbosa com ama de leite*. In these images,

FIGURE 5.10. Edward Savage and David Edwin, after Edward Savage. *The Washington Family 1798*. Stipple engraving. National Portrait Gallery, Smithsonian Institution, Washington DC. Photo: National Portrait Gallery, Smithsonian Institution / Art Rescource, NY.

the enslaved woman appears as a maternal figure and shadow of the White infant. What histories, not only of prestige and distinction but also of the relations between intimacy, eroticism, and power, are visualized and sublimated in the emergence of the enslaved as a face within this persistent genealogical rhetoric that does not entirely disappear with the waning of courtly cultures?[15] (See Figures 5.10 and 5.11.)

Scenario 2: Dominion over the Face of the Enslaved as a Sign of Artistic Mastery

The second scenario that accounts for the "apparition" of the face of the enslaved in portraiture concerns discourses that—at brief but meaningful junctures in the historical entanglements between art and slavery in

FIGURE 5.11. Eugnio & Mauricio, *Fernando Simões Barbosa com ama de leite* [Fernando Simões Barbosa with wet nurse], undated. Carte de visite. Coleção Francisco Rodrigues, Fundação Joaquim Nabuco, Recife, Pernambuco, Brazil.

the circum-Atlantic—made the ability to paint a dark face a demonstration of the painter's superior artistic skills. These instances often occurred in contexts where the artist's authority, worth, or commercial potential were either contested or in need of special display. While courtly portraiture has a long and complex history that allows us to trace an arc through inception, permutations, and exhaustion, as well as to identify certain ideological and aesthetic principles that persisted within various modalities, this second scenario is narrower and fragmentary yet no less distinctive. Within it are two of the most extraordinary portraits made in the history of art: 1) Diego Velázquez's *Juan de Pareja* of 1650 and 2) a work exhibited under the title *Portrait d'une négresse* (portrait of a negress) in the Paris Salon of 1800, painted by the Comtesse de Benoist, Marie-Guillemine de DeLaville-Leroulx. Later, to avoid the pejorative term "négresse," Benoist's portrait was renamed *Portrait d'une femme noire* (portrait of a Black woman) by the Musée du Louvre, where it is permanently housed. However, most recently, in 2019, the name of the sitter appeared to have been recovered, and a special exhibit at the Musée d'Orsay legitimized a new retitling of the painting as *Portrait de Madeleine* (portrait of Madeleine).[16] The two-century-long history of the naming and renaming of this work (from the typological "négresse" to the proper name "Madeleine") is emblematic of Black subjects' fate—not only in art but, more broadly, within modern discursivities on the singularity of the human—and of the place of artistic representations within struggles for cultural recognition and political power and in contests for the reconstruction of collective memory (see Figures 5.12 and 5.13).

By crafting the faces of Pareja and Madeleine, Velázquez and Benoist, respectively, sought to display their artistic skills and prowess by defying what was then considered to be a subject deserving of portraiture, that is, what was "proper," dignified, and beautiful. Thus, the apparition of the enslaved as a face in these works is related both to transgressing properties of the portrait as a pictorial genre and to the self-constitution of modern artists themselves. Under this discursivity, the enslaved's face marked a border to be crossed. Unlike the faces inscribed within the regime of genealogical/courtly visuality, the enslaved persons in these portraits are highly individualized presences; they are the sole subjects of the paintings, occupying the entire canvas rather than appearing as part of a group or placed in a visibly dependent position in relation to their master or mistress. On the surface of these canvases, that face, and only that face, is the protagonist of its own visualization.

FIGURE 5.12. Diego Velázquez, *Juan de Pareja*, 1650. Oil on canvas. Metropolitan Museum of Art, New York. Purchase, Fletcher and Rogers Funds, and Bequest of Miss Adelaide Milton de Groot (1876–1967), by exchange, supplemented by gifts from friends of the Museum, 1971. Photo: Malcolm Varon. © Metropolitan Museum of Art / Art Resource, NY.

According to Antonio Palomino (one of Velázquez's first biographers) in a 1724 text, Velázquez painted Pareja's portrait as a sort of rehearsal and advertisement for his skills during his second trip to Rome. While he traveled there by order of King Philip IV of Spain to acquire new works of art for his collection, Velázquez also used the trip to boost his own prestige and patronage, including recognition from the Catholic court. Palomino recounts how Velázquez made Pareja's likeness in preparation for painting

FIGURE 5.13. Marie-Guillermine de DeLaville-Leroulx, Condesa de Benoist, *Portrait d'une Négresse*, 1800. Oil on canvas. Musée du Louvre, Paris. Photo: Thierry Le Mage / Réunon des Musées Nationaux / Art Rescource, NY.

Pope Innocent X's portrait, a commission he had just secured. He wanted to "prepare himself beforehand by painting a head from life as an exercise." That head was Pareja's. When Velázquez sent Pareja's portrait to some of his friends "by means of Pareja himself," they stood looking "in awe and wonder, not knowing to whom they should speak and who would answer them." Palomino concludes by relating that Velázquez exhibited Pareja's portrait in the Pantheon, where the likeness between image and model "received such universal acclaim" that it earned him membership in the prestigious and exclusive Roman Academy.[17] Carmen Fracchia and other scholars have clarified that Velázquez was in fact already a member of the Academy when he painted Pareja's portrait (otherwise he would not have been allowed to exhibit in the Pantheon). The whole performance was a strategic device by the artist to enhance his reputation and secure additional commissions in the capital of the art world at the time, as well as to ensure that, with the support of the pope, the king of Spain would grant him the title of nobility he so eagerly sought (and eventually received).[18] All of this occurred at a time when mimetic likeness in portraiture had begun to be highly valued as an aesthetic in European artistic circles. Pareja's likeness was a chip in Velázquez's play to bolster his own authority and prestige.

In this composition, Velázquez painted Pareja—who was a painter in his own right, learning the trade from the master while working as his enslaved studio assistant—in a proper half-length portrait, with a dignified bearing in three-quarter view.[19] His intelligent gaze is serene, meeting the eyes of the viewer; his unblemished forehead is illuminated. According to the laws of the period, his status as a slave prevented his being represented on canvas as a painter. However, his right hand, robust and prominent, is clearly shown holding an undefined object under his left arm (part of his cape, a folded hat, or a bag with his painting tools?). That working hand—a hand for manual labor—cannot help but index Pareja's own artistic talents as well, which Velázquez could not make fully visible. The only conventional element in the portrait that reminds the viewer of Pareja's "lowly" status is the frayed fabric at his right elbow, the same arm that features his strong hand. In that subtle detail—and through Velázquez's forceful visual fiction of presence, one enhanced by the sumptuous white collar that illuminates the dark clothing—the painting suggests the humble condition of someone who otherwise appears as a noble being. It is precisely that ability to produce ennobling metamorphoses that Velázquez presented as evidence of his exceptional mastery and, perhaps, also as an allegory of his own being, one ready to be transformed from court painter into a newly consecrated knight of the exclusive Order of Calatrava. Not without some irony (given the highly stratified society in which Velázquez lived), his extraordinary artistic capacities for ennobling the ignoble were here deployed to further demonstrate his worthiness to be granted a noble title. Although the details of how it came about are not fully clear, shortly after the completion of his dignified portrait, Velázquez also gave Pareja his freedom. Almost as counterpoints, Velázquez would become a knight, Pareja a freedman. It is as if the portrait had served as a preliminary stage for undoing the condition of bondage, literally envisioning and materializing the possibility of a new social status.

A century and a half later, within the tumultuous struggles for the abolition of slavery in France and its colonies, Marie-Guillemine de DeLaville-Leroulx, Comtesse Benoist, would perform a similar appropriation of the enslaved's face, different in its political resonances and meanings but still akin to Velázquez's will to demonstrate artistic mastery through aesthetic dominion over the enslaved's image and being. The Comtesse Benoist was a student of Jacques-Louis David and Elisabeth Vigée-Lebrun. With *Portrait d'une négresse*, Benoist achieved unprecedented success in the 1800 Paris Salon, during that liminal period just six years after the abolition of slavery in France and its colonies (in 1794) but in the ominous prelude to Napoleon's reactionary restitution of the regime in the overseas territories (in 1802). Slavery would not be entirely abolished in all French holdings until 1848. The conscripted sitter, an enslaved woman from the island of Guadeloupe, was the property of Benoist's brother-in-law, a former colonial official from the Caribbean who had recently returned to the metropolis. Thus, for Viktoria Schmidt-Linsenhoff, the portrait conveys an allegory of the incorporation of Black womanhood and colonial subjects into the recently (and precariously) amplified sphere of citizenship. Note, for example, the subtle deployment of the colors of the French Republic's flag (blue, white, and red) that frame the figure and the Caribbean or African styled headdress that in its arrangement evokes a Phrygian cap, as James Smalls has convincingly argued.[20] Nonetheless, and in opposition to this allegorical reading, for critics such as Darcy Grimaldo Grigsby, Helen Weston, and Smalls himself, the image constitutes, in a profound and, to a certain degree, perverse manner, an instance in which Benoist negotiated her place as a woman artist in the competitive art world of early nineteenth-century Paris by defying certain aesthetic principles associated with established theories on color and regarding the suitability of Black faces as sites of beauty.[21]

Resistance to such aesthetic and political defiance was well articulated by one of the most acerbic critics of the portrait, as soon as the Salon of 1800 opened: "These African faces are, by nature, so uniformly ugly that it is impossible for art to give them any species of beauty; they lend themselves only weakly to the art of harmony with a light ground; it is impossible to make that air circulate around it, because it does not lend itself to the gradation of color and light necessary to produce this effect."[22] With such colorful subtleties of tautological intellect did critics in the early nineteenth century repeatedly assert the inadequacy of the Black face for rendering in oil painting, and especially for the high genre of portraiture. Nevertheless, as Grigsby has accurately pointed out in *Extremities*, her brilliant study of the relationships between painting and empire in nineteenth-century France, under this conception, to paint a Black face became—not without a certain degree of paradox—the proof of artistic mastery, of domination of coloristic techniques.

Smalls, on the other hand, has argued that with this work Benoist also aimed to alter established conventions for the imagining of bourgeois femininity—typically delicate and languid—by mobilizing, through that defiance, political connotations such as slavery that were considered, if at all, only suitable for the realm of history painting, which was the masculine pictorial genre par excellence. Though the woman in the portrait appears to recline on a divan (the privileged locus for the display of fragile femininity), several elements in the composition pull the figure in an opposite direction: her muscular, strong body, the uncovered breast, the outstretched arm (a signifier of a body for labor) that ends in an atrophied hand (reminiscent of an animal hoof), which so disturbed the public at the Salon. All of these coexist on canvas with the beautiful visage, the melancholic yet direct gaze, the inescapable presence of a force of being. These dissonant elements drive the image to disrupt the horizons against which "femininity" and "Blackness" were made legible. Aesthetically, then, Benoist's provocation was to produce a "monstrosity," a "beautiful monster," in front of which viewers were not to remain indifferent, and they were not. Similar to Velázquez's own gesture in his portrait of Juan de Pareja, Benoist engaged in a kind of visual promiscuity with regard to what was acceptable and forbidden, not only in terms of what was seeable in art but also of her own potentialities as a woman artist. The face of the enslaved woman, Madeleine, until recently nameless, was the scenario for that successful rehearsal.

Thus, if for Velázquez his visual prestidigitation dwelled in the ennoblement of the "lowly," for Benoist it resided in making the obscene (in its etymological sense: what was deemed to remain invisible, the off-scene) a spectacular aesthetic challenge. These faces of the enslaved, so masterfully painted, returned to both Velázquez and Benoist, like a mirror, the image of their artistic possibilities and daring, the potential for their own metamorphosis and monstrosity. Perhaps this is the reason that Benoist (despite having fewer resources than the court painter Velázquez) never sold "her" *négresse*, keeping the painting in her studio until her death (*'til death do us part?*). Perhaps like Velázquez, she was *the face* of her own desire. This desire is another possible condition for the enslaved as a face to join the transatlantic visual cultural archive.

Scenario 3: The Face of the Enslaved in the Archive of the Law

The incorporation of the enslaved into the discourse of the Law, especially, though not only, in the Anglo-Saxon world, has taken place to a large degree as a subject of guilt. Among many others, Angela Davis, Saidiya Hartman, and Colin Dayan have theorized this from various angles.[23] In the Ibero-American case, however, enslaved persons have historically and nominally enjoyed certain juridical considerations (distinct from the territories colonized by the British) in which masters, or White people in general, did not hold absolute or semi-absolute authority over the life and death of the enslaved. This also applied to the provisions for negotiating their liberty on a contractual basis with their masters, known as *derecho de coartación*.[24] Despite this, from the very first, slaveholding laws and codes elaborated across the Americas established an intimate relationship between enslaved existence and criminality. Rather than a subject of rights and justice, the law tended to understand the enslaved's condition mostly as an object of regulatory power (both soft and hard) and punishment. It is worth recalling that, in the case of Ibero-American jurisprudence, precedents in Roman and Hispano-medieval law (i.e., Alfonso X's *Siete Partidas*) only viewed testimony given by the enslaved as credible when it was extracted through torture. Suffering guaranteed the veracity of the enslaved's word since it was presumed that the condition of enslavement itself undermined truth, unless procured through terror. Akin to those philosophical and political precedents—which developed in varied and divergent ways within juridical systems across the colonial- and republican-era Americas—crime and untruth came to be seen as constitutive of the condition of enslavement in the context of the carceral order that defined the slaveholding plantation. To a great extent, these notions laid the foundation for the enslaved as a face to emerge, not only within the visual practices of slaveholding legality, but within the counter-discursivities of abolitionism, as well.[25]

The clearest instances of these legal idioms in visual terms were the runaway slave ads published in gazettes and newspapers beginning in the eighteenth century. These can be seen as a type of ekphrastic portraiture in which the detailed description of runaways was designed to register their features with exactitude in order to facilitate capture and re-enslavement. To some degree, they are the equivalent of our contemporary "wanted" ads, their verbal strategies endowed with a descriptive/visual zeal that was later transferred to and condensed in the photograph of the pursued.

The format of these ads varied, and not all of them focused exclusively on the face. However, among their common features are the runaway's name, age, height, skin color (mulatto, light or dark, etc.), a description of the clothing, and the reward offered for capture. Often, in order to provide the most exact description possible, the ads shamelessly registered the traces of brutality, of abuse and torture. This, for instance, is the case with Peter and his sadistic master Samuel Sherwin:

> a mulatto fellow named PETER: he is about 5 feet 6 inches, well set, and about 25 years old. The said slave run [sic] away once before, and was out [about one year], he was brought home the 14th, on which day I branded him S on the cheek, and R on the other, though very probably he will endeavor to take them out, or deface them. I likewise had his hair cut off, which is long, when grown out, and very black [. . .] Samuel Sherwin. (*Virginia Gazette*, May 9, 1771)[26]

As punishment for a previous escape, Peter's master mutilated his face, branding him, like cattle, with initials that signified ownership ("S" and "R"). Thus, when looking at Peter's face what was first seen was not his "face" but the signs of his condition as punished property. Within this visual regime, Peter was to have no other identity beyond this. His face was not supposed to reveal any identity other than the power of his master. This form of punishment could be seen as a perverse inversion of African cultural practices in which belonging to a cultural collectivity was made visible through the marking of the face (i.e., with scars or tattoos). In this sense, it is important that Peter, as we learn from the ad, may have been able to remove Sherwin's marks in order to reclaim his face, from which he had been partially dispossessed through branding. Significantly, the unmaking of the master's violent expropriation of Peter's face is described here as an act of "defacement" ("he will endeavor to take them out, or deface them").

In the visualization of the face of the enslaved enabled by slaveholding law and ekphrastic publicity, what was at stake was a regime that would facilitate the restitution of the enslaved's condition as property through a perverse *facialization*. Thus, at the core of the runaway's resistance was indeed a profound act of defacement.[27]

This particular appearance of the face of the enslaved within the law, associated with his or her criminalization, has a counterpart in some of the visual practices of the anti-slavery movement, especially in the frontispieces that served as paratextual elements to both slave narratives and the collections of poetry composed by enslaved writers. Perhaps the best known is the portrait of Frederick Douglass that appeared in the first edition of his famous *Narrative* of 1845. If runaway ads summoned the face of the enslaved as a manifestation of a criminal condition, these frontispieces summoned it as a source of evidence. At stake in that visualization—and against the grain of pro-slavery arguments—was the constitution of the enslaved as a subject of truth.

One of the main goals of slave narratives was to offer testimony of and to bear witness to the criminal nature of slavery, as well as to demonstrate the enslaved's capacity for literacy and "civilization," and, in consequence, for citizenship. In this sense, these frontispieces had a legal, evidentiary character. They showed the face of the author, and through that visualization they attempted to certify the truth of the narration—i.e., that the text was indeed written by an identifiable slave and not by a White person trying to pass for one. Let's recall that published slave narratives usually included prologues by recognized leaders of the abolitionist movement (the majority of them White men) who further pledged to the actual existence of the enslaved author, the authenticity of the portrait, and the truth of the story. The narrative, therefore, was not the product of the feverish imagination of a fanatical abolitionist, but the experience of an enslaved being who truly existed—and there was the portrait to prove it. In this operation a curious circular logic seems to legitimize the truth: White authority certifies that the enslaved author exists and that a White person is not the author of the text. The text is certified as true because it conveys the real experience of an enslaved being who exists (whose image we have and that they personally know). However, the existence of the enslaved, in turn, becomes the source that purportedly erases any suspicion of imposture (i.e., that a White abolitionist may have authored the text, that a liar concocted the story), so that, again, this White authority can be upheld as the legitimate force that certifies the enslaved as a subject of truth and as a being that truly exists. This circular logic, partly mediated by portraiture, paved the way to imagining the enslaved as a legitimate subject of language, witness to and victim of a regime of terror, and to affirming his or her rational capacities against arguments formulated by pro-slavery ideologues about the impossibility of eradicating "African barbarism."

The frontispiece portrait is, to some extent, an inversion of the ekphrasis found in runaway ads. These announcements had a de-subjectifying function (to return the enslaved to a condition of thingness and property), while the frontispieces aimed to certify the existence of a subject of language and suffering (or of language because of suffering). Nonetheless, despite their different valences, both participate in a legal discursivity deeply structured by notions of crime and truth, punishment and juridical indictment. This legal framework is a condition of possibility (for the seeable and the sayable) regarding the apparition of the face of the enslaved, with all its complex contradictions, in the archives of transatlantic visuality (see Figure 5.14).

Scenario 4: Between Type and Portrait:
The Enslaved's Face in Light of Scientific Racism

In the context of global anticolonial struggles in the twentieth century—of which the US Civil Rights movement was one manifestation—the emergence of alternative intellectual sensibilities demanded the construction of new archives to critically engage the legacies of racialized colonial thought and structures, excavating subjugated memories and fostering divergent epistemologies. Among these was the critical revision of nineteenth-century anthropology, a discipline that was central to the development of theories on racial differences and hierarchies and in which the new medium of photography played a crucial role, given the belief at the time in its capacities to truthfully capture the "reality" of a presence. The intimate collaboration established between photography, anthropology, and portraiture in the production of racial taxonomies set a problematic scenario for the appearance of the face of the enslaved.[28]

One example of these dynamics is found in the collection of images "discovered" in the 1970s, buried in the archives of the Peabody Museum at Harvard University: a group of fifteen daguerreotypes taken by the photographer Joseph T. Zealy in the 1850s. Commissioned by the Swiss zoologist Louis Agassiz, they were made to document his medico-anthropological

FIGURE 5.14. Frederick Douglass, frontispiece and title page of *Narrative of the Life of Frederick Dougass, an American Slave Written by Himself*. Boston: Published at the Anti-Slavery Office, 1845. Schomburg Center for Research in Black Culture / Manuscripts, Archives and Rare Books Division, New York, Public Library Digital Gallery.

investigations on comparative anatomy. A renowned scientist in Europe, Latin America, and the United States, Agassiz joined the Harvard faculty in 1846 with a well-established international reputation in the field of zoological classification. Significantly, his arrival in the United States coincided with a moment of heightened tension in the debates on American slavery, a prelude to the Civil War, which would begin fourteen years later. At that time, two "scientific" theories made competing claims for the truth regarding the origins of the human species and its varieties, each with serious political implications. The first, the theory of *monogenesis*, was partly based on the biblical myth of creation and, ironically, also on theories of Darwinian evolution. It argued that humanity had but one single origin and that the variations found in nature were related to environmental and historical factors. The second theory, known as *polygenesis*, argued that, on the contrary, such differences were due to divergent biological origins; the different races did

FIGURE 5.15. J. T. Zealy, *Renty, Congo, Plantation of B. F. Taylor, Esqu.* Columbia, SC, March 1850 (fontal). Daguerreotype. Peabody Museum of Archeology and Ethnology, Harvard University 35-5-10/53037, Cambridge, MA.

not share common ancestry, for each belonged to a different species.[29] The American School of Ethnology supported this second theory, and Agassiz played a fundamental role in its intellectual justification. It was in the midst of these debates that Zealy produced his now-famous daguerreotypes, featuring the powerful faces of enslaved human beings (see Figure 5.15).

Brian Wallis has offered a detailed account of the history and logic of these images' production.[30] With the goal of collecting evidence for his scientific hypotheses, Agassiz secured access to a plantation in South Carolina and recruited Zealy to take images that would allow him to keep a visual record of his meticulous anatomical analyses. These images were divided into two series: one in which the slaves appeared naked at full length, posing from the front, back, and both sides, and a second series that focused on the head and face, with front and profile shots. Wallis highlights how these images, far from being portraits, were rather intended to be "generic types," designed to exemplify anatomical categories based on the principles of physiognomic and phrenological analysis. Nevertheless, the face is there. It is there with its reality effects, revealing, in that slippery and rhetorical but still present *there*, the image of a contingent singularity: the sad, frightened, or anguished—or perhaps already resigned and absent—gaze, together with the inescapable gestures of defeat and suffering. And the name is also there. These images are not titled with exotic Latin nomenclatures, those used, according to Linnaeus's complex classificatory system, to name a species (e.g., *Felis catus, Felis silvestris catus*, which are the terms to classify different kinds of domestic, or European, wild cats), but rather with proper names: Jack, Renty, Delia, Alfred. Besides stating their ethnic affiliation and the plantation to which they belonged (along with the owner's name), their identification included, in some cases, their trades and even indications of kinship among some of them.

Undoubtedly, the epistemological and political project that gave rise to these daguerreotypes, as Wallis insists, had nothing to do with the subjectivizing rhetorics of the portrait genre but with the dispossessions of colonial ethnography and the delusions of scientific racism. What was at stake was building types, not capturing the uniqueness of a face. However, in the eagerness to record the peculiarity of the specimen and to register its details and physical specificity, the appearance of the contingent places typology under pressure, which is precisely the rhetorical place of the portrait. In the intended production of a taxonomical generality, the anthropological photograph (with its pact of referentiality) invariably had to contend with the potential disarray of forms and meanings presented by the singularity of the face. If the African American artist Carrie Mae Weems was able to re-appropriate Zealy's daguerreotypes in her work and turn them into the indicting face of the ancestors (as Wallis himself notes), this was due to the untamed potentiality contained in the images themselves. By recognizing the inescapable force of their gaze, Weems articulates a linguistic and intersubjective interpellation, speaking to them as "you" through the subtitles she etches across their surface: "You became a scientific profile / A negroid type / An anthropological debate / & a photographic subject." The subtitles both tell and dismantle the history produced by the theoretical abstractions of the knowledge/power dyad (scientific profile and anthropological debate) with its classificatory generalizations (the negroid type) and the modes of visualization that have left us a trace and only that, a material trace: a trace of existences that were instrumentalized to produce "scientific truths" through the means of photography. With no illusion of recovering a referent—from which Weems's images already appear forever removed by virtue of the hyperreal, spectral red superimposed onto the daguerreotypes—the works nevertheless evoke the idea of a lost subject,

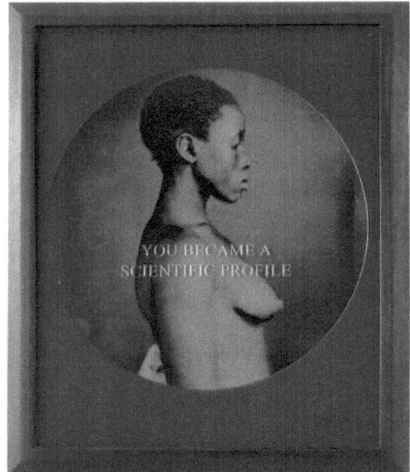
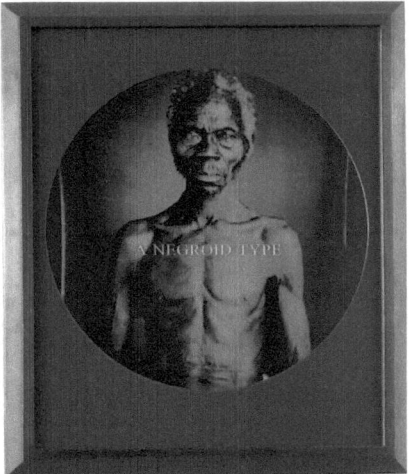
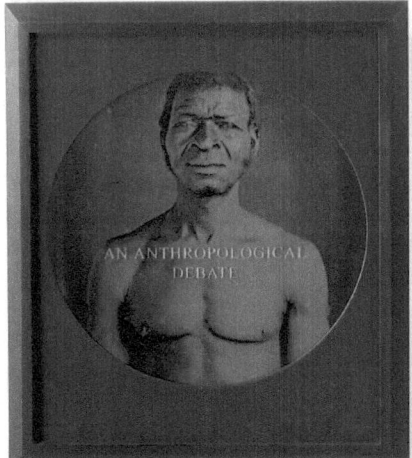
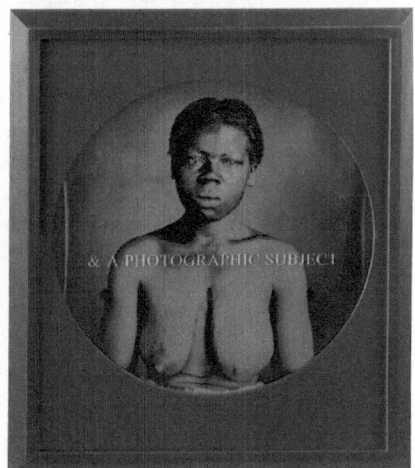

FIGURE 5.16. Carrie Mae Weems, *From Here I Saw What Happened and I Cried*, panels 2–5 (You became a scientific profile / a negroid type / an anthropological debate / a photographic subject), 1995–96. Toned prints. Courtesy of the artist and Jack Shainman Gallery, NY.

instantiating its shadow through the recovery of the "portrait" that has been buried, but still remains throbbing, under the "type." This is why one could say that the discourses of scientific racism, in their intersections with photography, and even against themselves, are a fourth scenario for the appearance of the face of the enslaved and for a possible investigation of the enslaved as a face in the transatlantic world (see Figure 5.16).[31]

Coda: Toward the Archives of the Enslaved's Face

Scattered in palaces, private collections, churches and museums, newspapers, gazettes, and *cartes-de-visite*; forgotten in dusty drawers and yellowed family albums; inhabiting the body of their masters like shadows, confused in allegorical figurations; lost between the production of prestige and the assaultive notions of crime and animality, between ignominy and justice. These are some of the places where the cultural logics of transatlantic slavery have located the enslaved's face and in which a consideration of their archives, inevitably, will need to further dwell.

NOTES

An earlier version of this essay appeared in *e-misférica* 9.1–9.2 (2012). I am grateful to the Hemispheric Institute of Performance and Politics for authorizing my use here of that material.

1. On visual culture and abolitionism, see Sara Thomas, *Witnessing Slavery: Art and Travel in the Age of Abolition* (New Haven, CT: Yale University Press, 2019); on the British Slave Ship "Brookes," see Marcus Wood, *Blind Memory: Visual Representations of Slavery in England and America, 1780–1865* (New York: Routledge, 2000), 14–77 and Cheryl Finley, *Committed to Memory: The Art of the Slave Ship Icon* (Princeton, NJ: Princeton University Press, 2018), 19–107; on slavery and visuality in Brazil and the Unites States, see Marcus Wood, *Black Milk: Imagining Slavery in the Visual Cultures of Brazil and America* (Oxford: Oxford University Press, 2013), and the bibliography on Debret is rich; among recent relevant works are Valéria Lima, *J. B. Debret, historiador e pintor: A Viagem pitoresca e histórica ao Brasil (1816–1839)* (Campinas, Brazil: Editora Unicamp, 2007) and Thiago Costa, *O Brasil pitoresco de Jean Baptiste Debret: Ou Debret, artista-viajante* (São Paulo: Editora Multifoco, 2015).
2. David Bindman, "Subjectivity and Slavery in Portraiture from Courtly to Commercial Societies," in *Slave Portraiture in the Atlantic World*, ed. A. Lugo-Ortiz and A. Rosenthal (Cambridge, UK: Cambridge University Press, 2013), 70–87. I want to clarify here that I am not interested in the vindication of the philosophical notion of "the subject" (especially in its liberal connotation as a coherent, highly individualized, self-possessed, and self-conscious entity) but rather in the historical dynamics by which enslaved people have been conceived or not within that category.
3. Michel Foucault, *The Archaeology of Knowledge*, trans. A. M. Sheridan Smith (New York: Pantheon Books, [1969] 1972), 128–31.
4. In this account I do not examine the possible appearance of the face of the enslaved within religious portraiture. Much research remains to be done on this front. Among others, recent scholarship by Cécile Fromont, *The Art of Conversion: Christian Visual Culture in the Kingdom of Kongo* (Chapel Hill: University of North Carolina Press, 2014) and Larissa Brewer-García, "Imagined Transformations: Color, Beauty, and

Black Christian Conversion in Seventeenth-century Spanish America," in *Envisioning Others: Race, Color, and the Visual in Iberia and Latin America* (Leiden: Brill, 2016), 111–41 may help shed light in this direction.

5. See Bindman, "Subjectivity and Slavery in Portraiture from Courtly to Commercial Societies" and Bindman, "Am I Not a Man and a Brother? British Art and Slavery in the Eighteenth Century," *Anthropology and Aesthetics* 26 (1994): 68–82.

Other relevant works include the chapter titled "Male Portraits, Property, and Colonial Might" in Kim Hall, *Things of Darkness: Economies of Race and Gender in Early Modern England* (Ithaca: Cornell UP, 1995), 226–53; Peter Erickson, "Representations of Black and Blackness in the Renaissance," *Criticism* 35, no. 4 (1993): 499–527; Erickson, "Invisibility Speaks: Servants and Portraits in Early Modern Visual Culture," *Journal of Early Modern Cultural Studies* 9, no. 1 (2009): 23–61; Paul Kaplan, "Italy, 1490–1700," in *The Image of the Black in Western Art*, vol. 3, *From the "Age of Discovery" to the Age of Abolition*, part 1, *Artists of the Renaissance and Baroque*, ed. D. Bindman and H. L. Gates Jr. (Cambridge: Belknap Press, 2010), 93–190; Simon Gikandi, *Slavery and the Culture of Taste* (Princeton, NJ: Princeton University Press, 2011); David Bindman and Helen Weston, "Court and City: Fantasies of Domination," in Bindman and Gates Jr., *The Image of the Black in Western Art*, vol. 3, part 3, *The Eighteenth Century*, 125–70; Kate Lowe, "Visible Lives: Black Gondoliers and Other Black Africans in Renaissance Venice," *Renaissance Quarterly* 66 (2013): 412–52; Lowe, "The Lives of African Slaves and the People of African Descent in Renaissance Europe," in *Revealing the African Presence in Renaissance Europe*, ed. J. Spicer (Baltimore: The Walters Art Museum, 2012), 13–33.

6. Giorgio Vasari, *Lives of Artists*, trans. George Bull (NY: Penguin, [1550] 1985), 448. Vasari introduced the idea that Ferrara had indeed married Dianti. However, current scholarly consensus contends that there is no credible evidence to support this assumption. See Paul Kaplan, "Titian's 'Laura Dianti' and the Origins of the Motif of the Black Page in Portraiture," *Antichità viva* 21, no.1 (1982): 11–18; Diane Yvonne Ghirardo, "The Topography of Prostitution in Renaissance Ferrara," *Journal of the Society of Architectural Historians* 60, no. 4 (2001): 402–31, 425 and notes 145, 431; Jane Fair Bestor, "Titian's Portrait of Laura Eustochia: The Decorum of Female Beauty and the Motif of the Black Page," *Renaissance Studies* 17, no. 4 (2003): 628–73.

7. Joseph Archer Crowe and Giovanni Battista Cavalcaselle, quoted in Herbert Cook, "The True Portrait of Laura de' [sic] Dianti by Titian," *Burlington Magazine for Connoisseurs* 7, no. 3 (1905): 449–51, 454–55.

8. G. R. Crone, Alvise Cà da Mosto, Antonio Malfante, Diogo Gomes, and João de Barros, *The Voyages of Cadamosto* (London: G. Crone Editor, 1937), quoted in Kaplan, "Titian's 'Laura Dianti,'" 18n57.

9. Paul Kaplan, "Isabella d'Este and Black African Women," in *Black Africans in Renaissance Europe*, ed. T. F. Earle and K. J. P. Lowe (Cambridge: Cambridge UP, 2005), 125–54.

10. As will be examined shortly, these visual dynamics found in portraits of ladies with pages will also be found, with different gender inflections, in portraits of gentlemen.

11. On the question of Whiteness in the images by Van Dyck and Mignard, see Angela Rosenthal, "Visceral Culture: Blushing and the Legibility of Whiteness in Eighteenth-Century British Portraiture," *Art History* 27, no. 4 (2004): 563–92.
12. For a critical take on the apparent rigidity of this courtly model of portraiture, see my essay "Between Violence and Redemption: Slave Portraiture in Early Plantation Cuba," in *Slave Portraiture in the Atlantic World*, ed. A. Lugo-Ortiz and A. Rosenthal (Cambridge: Cambridge University Press, 2013), 201–26. The subtle reading of Titian's image by Jane Fair Bestor in "Titian's Portrait of Laura Eustochia" (628–73) is also worth noting here. In this reading she underscores how the many visual languages and textual referents that structure the portrait walk a fine line between the desire to portray Dianti as a person of dignity and the attempt to avoid (due to her plebeian origins) portrait conventions that were reserved for aristocratic authority. For example, Bestor points out that earrings had not yet become fashionable among the nobility. On the contrary, they were associated with "the other": Jews, Moors, Africans, slaves. Thus, she claims that it is significant that the portrait shows Dianti with a single pearl earring in her right ear, while the page wears his, ostentatiously, in the left—establishing a system of identity and correspondences between the two figures. Bestor claims that this portrait creates "a complex dynamic of similarity in difference." This is not incompatible, however, with the idea that the portrait laid out a series of compositional dichotomies that will later be signified through, as Bestor herself acknowledges, "an aestheticized connection between darkness and vice in mind" (673). In this sense, a judgment made in 1565 by Giovan Battista Giraldi (tutor of Dianti's younger son), probably with Titan's portrait in mind, is revealing: "It is common opinion of the wisest people in the world, very illustrious lady, that a contrast placed near another is recognized more clearly than if it is considered by itself. And in truth, experience shows that this is indeed the case, because white beside black is revealed much lighter, and dark, which carries with it vice, makes the very bright rays of virtue appear much more than they would appear without comparison constructed in this way." *De gli hectommithi*, 2 vols. (Monte Regale, 1565), quoted and translated in Bestor (673).
13. Fritz Hirschfeld, *George Washington and Slavery: A Documentary Portrayal* (Columbia: University of Missouri Press, 1997).
14. Marcia Pointon, "Slavery and the Possibilities of Portraiture," in *Slave Portraiture in the Atlantic World*, ed. A. Lugo-Ortiz and A. Rosenthal (Cambridge: Cambridge University Press, 2013), 41–69
15. On the familial gaze, see the collection *The Familial Gaze*, ed. Marianne Hirsch (Hanover: University Press of New England, 1999). Especially pertinent are the essays by Deborah Willis, 107–23; Elizabeth Abel, 124–52; Laura Wexler, 248–75; and Andrea Liss, 276–92. Also relevant here is Laura Wexler, *Tender Violence: Domestic Visions in the Age of US Imperialism* (Chapel Hill: University of North Carolina Press, 2000). On the question of "the amas de leite in Brazil," see Rita Laura Segato, *O Édipo Brasileiro: A Dupla Negação de Gênero e Raça* (Brasília: Série Antropologia 400, 2006), which diverges from the idealizing views of Gilberto Freyre in his classic *Casa-grande e senzala* (Rio de Janeiro: Maia and Schmidt, Ltda., 1934).

16. "Musée d'Orsay Retitles Marie-Guillemine Benoist Painting for 'Black Models' Show," *ARTnews*, March 26, 2019, www.artnews.com/art-news/news/musee-dorsay-black-models-marieguillemine-benoist-12230. The exhibition in question was curated by Denise Murrell and opened at the Wallach Art Gallery of Columbia University in October 2018 under the title "Posing Modernity: The Black Model from Manet and Matisse to Today." Exhibition catalogue of the same title (New Haven, CT: Yale University Press, 2018). For the painting's entry at the Louvre, see Musée du Louvre (website), accessed June 15, 2020, cartelen.louvre.fr/cartelen/visite?srv=car_not_frame&idNotice=18871&langue=en.
17. Antonio Palomino, *El museo pictórico y escala óptica*. (Madrid: M. Aguilar, [1715–1724] 1947). English translation: *Lives of Velázquez: Francisco Pacheco and Antonio Palomino*, trans. Nina Ayala Mallory (Los Angeles: The Paul J. Getty Museum, 2006), 123–24. This somewhat apocryphal text is nonetheless relevant given the light it sheds on what might have made a dignified oil portrait of Pareja plausible at the time.
18. Carmen Fracchia, "Metamorphoses of the Self in Early Modern Spain: Slave Portraiture and the Case of Juan de Pareja," in *Slave Portraiture in the Atlantic World*, ed. A. Lugo-Ortiz and A. Rosenthal, 147–69 (Cambridge: Cambridge University Press, 2013). See also Fracchia, *'Black but Human': Slavery and Visual Art in Hapsburg Spain* (Oxford: Oxford UP, 2019); Victor Stoichita, "El retrato de Juan de Pareja: Semejanza y conceptismo," in *Velázquez*, ed. S. Alpers (Madrid: Galaxia Gutenberg, 1999), 367–81; Stoichita, "The Image of the Black in Spanish Art: Sixteenth and Seventeenth Centuries," in Bindman and Gates Jr., *The Image of the Black in Western Art*, vol. 3, part 1, 191–234.
19. Carmen Fracchia, "The Fall into Oblivion of the Works of the Slave Painter Juan de Pareja," trans. Hilary Macartney, *Art in Translation* 4, no. 2 (June 2012): 63–84.
20. Viktoria Schmidt-Linsenhoff, "Who Is the Subject? Marie-Guilhelmine Benoist's *Portrait d'une Négresse*," in *Slave Portraiture in the Atlantic World*, ed. A. Lugo-Ortiz and A. Rosenthal (Cambridge: Cambridge University Press, 2013) 315–43; James Smalls, "'Race,' Gender, and Visuality in Marie Benoist's *Portrait d'une négresse*," *Nineteenth-Century Art Worldwide* 3, no.1 (2004): 1–22.
21. See Darcy Grimaldo Grigsby, *Extremities: Painting Empire in Post-Revolutionary France* (New Haven, CT: Yale UP, 2002), 42–46; Helen Weston, "The Cook, the Thief, His Wife, and Her Lover: LaVille-Leroulx's *Portrait de Négresse* and the Signs of Misrecognition," in *Work and the Image*, ed. V. Mainz and G. Pollock (Aldershot: Ashgate, 2000), 53–74; James Smalls, "'Race,' Gender, and Visuality."
22. Quoted in Grigsby, *Extremities*, 42.
23. Saidiya Hartman, *Scenes of Subjection: Terror, Slavery, and Self-Making in Nineteenth-Century America* (Oxford: Oxford UP, 1997); Angela Y. Davis, *Abolition and Democracy: Beyond Empire, Prisons, and Torture* (New York: Seven Stories Press, 2005); Davis, "From the Prison of Slavery to the Slavery of Prison: Frederick Douglass and the Convict Lease System" and "Racialized Punishment and Prison Abolition," in *The Angela Y. Davis Reader*, ed. J. James (London: Blackwell, 1998), 74–95, 96–107; Colin Dayan, "Legal Terrors," *Representations* 92, no.1 (2005): 42–80.
24. Since the publication of Frank Tannenbaum's *Slave and Citizen* (New York: Alfred A. Knopf, 1946), there have been important debates about the differences between

Anglo-American and Ibero-American slave laws, comparing the different margins for juridical action on the part of the enslaved within these diverse systems. The question of slave law, however, cannot be separated from the socio-economic structures that are called to legalize it. Thus, despite differences in legal traditions, the regime of the large slaveholding plantation, with its grand-scale production of commodities for the international marketplace and with its brutal demands for intensive labor, brought into closer proximity notions of policing and punishment across different sub-areas of the Americas, especially in the period that Dale Tomich describes as "the second slavery." By "second slavery" he refers to the reorganization of the regime in the context of the ideological triumph of bourgeois liberalism (with ideas of freedom and rights), industrialization, and the emergence of new disciplines of knowledge in the nineteenth century; see Dale W. Tomich, *Through the Prism of Slavery: Labor, Capital, and World Economy* (Oxford: Rowman and Littlefield Publishers, 2004). There is an extensive bibliography on this subject. Relevant here are Gwendolyn Midlo Hall, *Social Control in Slave Plantation Societies: A Comparison of St. Domingue and Cuba* (Baton Rouge: Louisiana State University Press, 1976); Alejandro de la Fuente, "Slaves and the Creation of Legal Rights in Cuba: *Coartación* and *Papel*," *Hispanic American Historical Review* 87, no. 4 (2007): 659–92; de la Fuente, "From Slaves to Citizens? Tannenbaum and the debates on Slavery, Emancipation, and Race Relations in Latin America," *International Labor and Working Class History* 77 (2010): 154–73; Brodwyn Fisher, Keila Grinberg, and Hebe Mattos, "Law, Silence, and Racialized Inequalities in the History of Afro-Brazil," in, *Afro-Latin America: An Introduction*, eds. Alejandro de la Fuente and George Reid Andrews (Cambridge: Cambridge University Press, 2018), 130–76.

25. Titles of property were one of the first legal documents in which the existence of the enslaved, as a private possession, was inscribed and imagined. They also legalized the dispossession of African names and advanced the crushing machinery of enslavement with its volition to erode cultural bonds and memory. In the British colonies of North America toward the end of the eighteenth century, silhouettes of slaves' heads were made as attachments to bills of sale. In these documents, the silhouettes could not mimetically capture the defined factions of the face, only its contours. They mostly had indexical value for a general type, one that nonetheless inaugurated in the shadowy portraits the existence of the enslaved not as a subject but as an object of property. For a detailed discussion of these silhouettes, see Angela Rosenthal and Agnes Lugo-Ortiz, "Envisioning Slave Portraiture," in Lugo-Ortiz and Rosenthal, *Slave Portraiture in the Atlantic World*, 19–22; Gwendolyn Dubois Shaw, *Portraits of a People: Picturing African Americans in the Nineteenth Century* (Andover: Addison Gallery of American Art and University of Washington Press, 2006), 45–55.

26. "Runaway from the Subscriber, Runaway Advertisements, 1745–1775: A Selection," *National Humanities Center Resource Toolbox, The Making of African American Identity,* Vol. I, 1500–1865, nationalhumanitiescenter.org/pds/maai/index.htm. (Grammar has been modernized.)

27. In the Iberian colonies, where slave literacy was not legally forbidden, we find runaway ads that mention another recourse enslaved people used to disguise their iden-

tities: faking the master's written permission required by law for a slave to leave the plantation or the owner's house. Thus, in 1829, we have the following ad:

> Three months ago a black man named Mateo escaped from Don Manuel Pegudo, who acquired him from Don Manuel Sanchez, saddler, average height, thin, he is missing one or two teeth, of serious demeanor, has scars on his hands as the result of strong dyes, moves in a hurry, always dirty with a vest of coquillo [a light fabric] or a jacket of handkerchiefs, and it is likely that he carries a fake license, because he knows how to write although he hides it: the person who turns him in to the Royal Consulate, or gives correct notice of his whereabouts, will be rewarded in the house on Oficios Street, no. 29, and he who protects him will face charges. (qtd. in Linda Rodríguez, "Free Cuba: Runaway Slave Advertisements from Colonial Havana," *The Appendix* (2013), accessed June 16, 2020, theappendix.net/posts/2013/07/free-cuba-runaway-slave-advertisements-from-colonial-havana)

On the concept of *facialization* see Gilles Deleuze and Félix Guattari, "Year Zero: Faciality," in *A Thousand Plateaus: Capitalism and Schizophrenia*, trans. B. Massumi (Minneapolis: University of Minnesota Press, 1987), 167–91.

28. For a good compilation of texts on the relationship between anthropology and photography see Juan Naranjo, *Fotografía, antropología y colonialismo (1845–2006)* (Barcelona: Editorial Gustavo Gil, 2006); Christopher Pinney, *Photography and Anthropology* (London: Reaktion Books, 2012).

29. Thomas McCarthy, *Race, Empire, and the Idea of Human Development* (Cambridge, UK: Cambridge University Press, 2009). For a discussion of monogenesis and polygenesis and their presence in Brazilian debates about race, see Lilia Moritz Schwarcz, *The Spectacle of Races: Scientists, Institutions, and the Race Question in Brazil, 1870–1930*, trans. L. Guyer (New York: Hill and Wang, 1993), especially 44–70. Also pertinent for this discussion is Pedro Pruna and Armando García González, *Darwinismo y sociedad en Cuba. Siglo XIX* (Madrid: Consejo Superior de Investigaciones Científicas, 1989); Enrique Beldarraín Chaple, *Los médicos y los inicios de la antropología en Cuba* (La Habana: Fundación Fernando Ortiz, 2006), 139–49.

30. Brian Wallis, "Black Bodies, White Science: Louis Agassiz's Slave Daguerreotypes," *American Art* 9, no. 2 (1995): 38–61. Wallis points out that the desire to craft a photographic archive of the human races was not Agassiz's invention. Years before, his colleague, the French scientist Étienne-Reynaud-Augustin Serres of the Academy of Sciences in Paris, had proposed a similar project, and in 1845 a French daguerreotypographer named E. Thiesson had already taken photographs of Brazilian slaves and of Portuguese people in Lisbon with the aim of constructing an archive of races.

31. Angela Rosenthal and I have devoted more attention to this problem of "the type and the portrait" that haunts images of the enslaved (and of Blackness, more generally) in our "Envisioning Slave Portraiture," in *Slave Portraiture in the Atlantic World*, 8–11. Also important for this discussion is the chapter titled "Illustrious Americans" in Alan Trachtenberg, *Reading American Photographs: Images as History, Mathew Brady to Walker Evans* (New York: Hill and Wong, 1989), 21–70.

CHAPTER 6

A Postcard from Wakanda to the King of Spain

The Portrait of the Mulatos de Esmeraldas *(1599)*

BALTASAR FRA-MOLINERO

The famous 1599 portrait of Don Francisco de Arobe and his two sons, Don Pedro and Don Domingo, by Andrés Sánchez Gallque is the first work of art produced in the American continent depicting historical Blacks. Its location in the Museo de América in Madrid is part of the history of this painting and its Afro-diasporic content. Located on the second floor of the museum amid a disparate collection of objects and paintings, it has not lost its treatment as a curiosity and a spectacular attraction. Its reproduction graces the admission ticket for the museum (see Figure 6.1).

The purpose of this essay is, in the words of William B. Taylor, to find more meaning in the painting.[1] It will address three issues that arise from the contemplation of the painting as a physical and ideological object. The first one is the present-day housing of the painting in the Museo de América, an institution created in the early years of the Franco regime. The second issue is the history of the painting's composition, that is, what the painting depicts and what it hides in plain view. It is a documented history of violence with many and changing sides: Blacks, Indigenous nations, newly formed mulatto groups, and the Spanish empire. The third issue is the representation in the painting of an imagined political future with Black people in it that can be read through an Afrofuturist lens. The

MUSEO DE /// AMÉRICA

Museo de América

Gracias por su visita

FIGURE 6.1.
Admission ticket to
the Museo de América

origin of this reading is an anecdote during a visit I made to the Museo de América that reflects the perception and the reaction of early twenty-first century viewers to the image of Black men in the possession of weapons within the context of the African diaspora and the transnational.

The painting, known variously as *Los mulatos de Esmeraldas* or *Los zambos de Esmeraldas* represents a moment in the early history of the Maroon societies of Spanish America. Maroon political formations represented times and spaces that negated the universal claim of the Spanish and Portuguese imperial project in which Blackness equaled slavery. The representation of free Blacks in a painting, and carrying weapons, soon became a riddle.[2] In the sixteenth century, the province of Esmeraldas was a territory in dispute. The Spanish administration had assigned it to the jurisdiction of the Audiencia de Quito (corresponding to what is now Ecuador and parts of northern Peru and southern Colombia all the way to Cali), but the reality on the ground confirmed the existence of a province whose inhabitants had not submitted to the imperial rule of the Spanish monarchy. The officers of the Audiencia had tried military raids, settlements with the unwilling would-be subjects, even contracts with private elements to enslave anyone who stood in their way, all to little or no effect. Yet in 1596 the oidor (judge) Juan del Barrio de Sepúlveda arrived in Quito with a new plan. He would pacify Esmeraldas by reaching agreements with the Black and mulatto groups, who in turn would help secure the province through a form of indirect rule.[3] The mulattos would preserve their freedom from slavery as individuals and as a collective, as well as keep their political autonomy. The heads (*caciques* in the Spanish terminology toward non-Spaniards who exercised power and authority) of their clans, or *repartimientos*, would be

FIGURE 6.2. Andrés Sánchez Gallque, *Los mulatos de Esmeraldas*.
Museo de América, Madrid

designated governors. Oidor Juan del Barrio de Sepúlveda secured one such agreement with Don Francisco de Arobe, a prominent mulatto cacique. It was signed in 1599 in the city of Quito, where Don Francisco and his two sons, Don Pedro and Don Domingo, travelled. Previously, Don Francisco and his wife, Doña Juana, had accepted baptism.[4] The oidor commissioned the painting to commemorate and communicate across the sea a political achievement that culminated in his efforts to promote his new policy of indirect rule, called "pacification" in official terms. No other artistic production had been created to represent a similar political event before. The painting was to be sent to the king in Spain together with a series of documents explaining it. The oidor followed what was becoming a tradition: trying to explain America to Europe (see Figure 6.2).

The Museum

The painting was "discovered" in 1928 by Ecuadorian art historian José Gabriel Navarro. It was then housed in the Museo Arqueológico, also in Madrid, which displayed at that time a large collection of artifacts from Spain's former imperial territories. The language of mystery, of hidden treasure, used by Navarro in his essay announcing the discovery is reminiscent of the narratives of the Spanish conquest of America, which borrowed from the books of chivalry the concept of the "hidden" waiting to be uncovered. Twentieth-century Latin American intellectuals were involved in the recreation of national discourses that valued the Indigenous as the foundation of the modern nation. José Gabriel Navarro aptly connects the work to the early stages of the painting school of Quito, whose members were men of Indigenous descent, Andrés Sánchez Gallque among them.[5] But the painting would be moved more than a decade later to the new Museo de América, an institution created in 1941 in the early years of the Franco regime's neo-imperial aspirations.

After a failed attempt in July 2018 to visit the Museo de América in the Ciudad Universitaria of Madrid with Professor Jerome Branche one hot La Mancha afternoon, I returned by myself the next day. As I stood in front of the painting taking pictures, a child behind me was also looking at it. He made a comment that I was fortunate to capture in the videoclips that became two of the pictures I took: "Son los de Wakanda. Son wakandienses" (They are the ones from Wakanda. They are Wakandans). The depiction of three Black men richly dressed in clothes from a past time, wearing iron spears, prompted the child to establish a comparison of these men with images he had retained from the recently released Hollywood film *Black Panther*.[6] Meanwhile, the woman who was with him was trying to lead the child's attention to a less anachronistic interpretation of the painting by reading to him the explanatory note beside the canvas: "Francisco de Arove and his sons Pedro and Domingo symbolize the Maroon Blacks who led the Indigenous people of the region of Esmeraldas (Ecuador) in their resistance against the Spaniards. Once they were defeated, their portraits were made and sent to King Philip III."

The Museo de América misrepresents the content of the painting. It practices in real life what the fictional Museum of Great Britain in *Black Panther* does with the piece of vibranium, the extraordinary metal that allows the kingdom of Wakanda to have technological supremacy unbeknown to the rest of the world. The Museo de América is a modern museum that cannot fathom the idea of three Black men with weapons in their hands.[7]

This case of misrepresentation is ideological. First, the sign strips the three men of the honorific title of "Don" that appears before each of their names. This honorific title was inserted for reasons of political coherence at the time of the painting, as previous Black leaders of Esmeraldas reputedly had carried it.[8] Second, and following Oidor Barrio de Sepúlveda's report, these men were never *vencidos* (defeated). Rather, the opposite had happened. The peace treaty they came to sign, and which the painting celebrates, received the official name of *asiento*, a legal contract that presupposes the parties are legally capable and therefore free.[9] It was not, as the museum sign says, a capitulation. If anything, the presence of the raised spears is a demonstration of triumph. One has to remember the visual prominence of similar weapons in Diego Velázquez's painting *The Surrender of Brede* (1635), popularly known as *Las lanzas* (The Spears). In Velázquez's painting, the victorious soldiers of the Spanish army raise a forest of spears that contrasts with the way the Dutch, having lost the battle, carry theirs.

The exchange between the boy and the woman that I witnessed during my museum visit bears an ironic resemblance to a scene early in the movie *Black Panther*. The fictional Museum of Great Britain, located in London, has misclassified an artifact from Africa and cannot identify it as coming from the fictional country of Wakanda. The explanation of *Los mulatos de Esmeraldas* in the Museo de América is equally wrong because it contradicts—reinterprets—the words written by Juan del Barrio de Sepúlveda in the documents that accompanied the painting to Spain in 1599:

> Una de las quales es la de las esmeraldas tan nombrada y poseida de los mulatos de mas de setenta años a esta parte sin se aver podido allanar ni conquistar por gran numero de capitanes y gente de guerra que aello an entrado y todos an salido perdidos—y aora el dicho doctor [Juan del Barrio de Sepúlveda] los a sacado por bien a dar la paz y obediençia a V. Md. [Vuestra Majestad] como lo an hecho y a que sean xpnos [cristianos] con todos los yndios dellas.... Por parecerle V. Md. gustaría Ver Aquellos barbaros retratados (que asta agora an sido invençibles,) y ser cossa muy extraordinaria los embia con su carta y este memorial a V. Md.... Son hombres bien dispuestos ágiles y mui sueltos. Acostumbran traer de ordinario argollas de oro llanas al cuello y las narigueras, oregeras, beçotes y sortijas en la barba y botones en las narizes y aun otros en los carrillos todo de Oro.

> *One of those [provinces] is Esmeraldas, so famous, and under the possession of the mulattos for more than seventy years to this day. And a great number of captains and people of war have not been able to invade or conquer it when they entered it because they all came back in defeat. But now the aforesaid doctor [Juan del Barrio de Sepúlveda] has brought them out here in good faith for them to offer peace and obedience to Your Majesty, as they have done, and to be Christians together with all the*

Indians living there. . . . And because he thought Your Majesty would take pleasure in seeing a portrait of these barbarians (who until now have been invincible), and it is a truly extraordinary thing, sends them with his letter and this memorandum to Your Majesty. . . . They are men of good disposition, nimble and of easy movement. They wear, as a custom, flat rings made of gold around their necks and golden pieces in their noses, their ears, and their mouths, and also small rings in their beards, and buttons in their noses and even in their cheeks, all made of gold.[10]

Hidden History in Plain Sight

The painting is full of names: Andrés Sánchez Gallque, the creator of the painting, signs his work. He is an artist of Indigenous ancestry.[11] Oidor Juan del Barrio de Sepúlveda's name is inscribed above the artist's signature. He has paid for this unusual painting.[12] Finally, the names of the three depicted protagonists are inscribed over their heads, together with their ages.

What the painter represents is one scene and two viewpoints. Did the three Black men actually pose for the painter? The background in the painting is not well defined. It seems to be some sort of open space. The indefinite setting suggests that these men are not inside a house in Quito, a space dominated by the colonial authorities. Their clothes seem to indicate that they are about to start their way back home to Esmeraldas, because they did not come to Quito wearing such finery, or not all of it. The regalia these three men wear corresponds to the many places and people they represent in their implicit dialogue and negotiation with the imperial power.

Andrés Sánchez Gallque paints an epiphany more than a trophy. As someone who was not a Spaniard within the caste system, he had much in common with the three men he portrays. He occupied an intermediate position. As an Indigenous painter, he was knowledgeable of the cultural practices of the Spanish authorities.[13] He also interprets the three mulattos' racial and ethnic status. Neither he nor they could exercise or share the political authority coming from Spain and biologically situated in those who were defined as Spaniards. To be a Spaniard gave authority to those captains who had attempted to launch incursions into Esmeraldas to enslave its mulatto population. From the perspective of both the painter and the three men portrayed, the painting is less a trophy to King Philip III than a show of affirmation of a new political status as subjects. They are subjects by their own will and as a result of political calculation.

As a member of the painting school of Quito, Sánchez Gallque portrays the men following the Flemish style brought in the form of etches and copies from northern Europe.[14] He also Americanizes the Renaissance canon by using the iconic model of the private portrait of the human figure in three quarters with distinctively American subjects. The private portrait was reserved for official depictions of important subjects who were not the king himself.[15] Choosing this iconic model sends the message that these are three powerful men and serves as their introduction to another powerful man, the King. It is a "postcard from Wakanda" addressed to Philip III, so to speak. Of course, we do not know if this portrait was painted with any knowledge of the men portrayed in it, since the dates of their visit to Quito (1598) and the completion of the portrait (1599, before April) are separated by some months. However, the honorific title of Don preceding each of their names sends a message to the distant and invisible king. The elegant combination of Indigenous and Spanish clothes; the gold pieces that adorn their faces, necks, and breasts; and their phenotypic traits speak of their diasporic and transatlantic Africanity. And in their silent message, the iron spears they hold in their right hands imply that if the king does not want them to turn against his authority, he has to make his imperial officers in Quito comply and enforce what has been agreed upon, that is, that they are free and autonomous. A sign of this autonomy is the agreement these mulatto caciques make to help facilitate the evangelization of the Indigenous people by requesting the presence of priests in their towns.[16] This meant that they could register their children and their marriages in the parish books and be part of the lettered city, the colonial structure that would certify their freedom, a move that did not please some leading sectors of the Audiencia de Quito.[17] The exchange of iron was also an important marker of their autonomy.[18]

The gold they wear is not a gift or an enticement of riches to would-be conquistadors. It is now a visible sign of Afro-Indigenous autonomy. It is the work of goldsmiths, a cultural object and an adornment. It signifies that they own the land and the waters from where the gold has been extracted since a time prior to the Spanish conquest.[19] It is neither for sale nor to be taken, and neither are their bodies. They came to Quito with these object pieces that Barrio de Sepúlveda described in such detail, and they are going back to Esmeraldas with them.

Absent from the picture are the women who are intrinsic to these men's identities as mulattos. The gold decorations indicate their belonging in the

Indigenous society of Esmeraldas as much as they represent its transformation. They are a second, if not a third, generation. That the painter is an Indigenous man, even if at the service of the Spanish authorities in Quito, is no small matter, as the three men Andrés Sánchez Gallque was commissioned to portray are also Indigenous: the painter and his subjects share a common racial category, as they all have Indian mothers. The three men speak an Indian language and very little Spanish, as Oidor Juan del Barrio attests. The name *mulato* used by Juan del Barrio in his memorial was the appropriate name in the racial classification of the late sixteenth century. The chronicler Miguel Cabello Balboa had given them this classificatory name earlier.[20] *Mulatos* was the term used by a variety of authors, including the Inca Garcilaso de la Vega, to refer to the children of Blacks and Indigenous couples.[21] In *Los mulatos de Esmeraldas*, the three men's Black bodies and their golden decorations indicate that they have Black fathers and Indigenous mothers; these men are the children of those original marriages. Their cultural world was that of their mothers: they spoke their mothers' and grandmothers' language, and they wore the gold ornaments of their mothers' people.

The contact between Blacks and Indigenous, however, was not peaceful. *Los mulatos de Esmeraldas* is painted in the context of protracted decades of murder, inter-ethnic war, inter-familial conflict, and enslavement of Indigenous people by their mulatto conquerors. A few years after the completion of the painting and the signing of the peace treaty, everything collapsed. Don Pedro and Don Domingo de Arobe were involved in betrayals and massacres in the competition existing between Spaniards and the mulatto elites to gain control over Indigenous populations as a labor force.[22] Therefore, this is a painting that speaks of violence, stated by Barrio de Sepúlveda in his memorandum: "An sido grandes guerreros contra yndios de otras provinçias infieles. Témenlos mucho porque matan muchos y de los que cautiuan se sirven como de esclauos con gran señorio y son Terribles, determinados y crueles en el castigo. . . . Jamas an podido ser subjetados de españoles" (They have been great warriors against Indians from other infidel provinces. They fear them because they kill many and those they capture they make them serve as their slaves, ruling as their lords. And they are terrifying, determined, and cruel when they punish them. . . . They have never been subdued by the Spanish).[23]

As pointed out by Peruvian thinker Aníbal Quijano, race is the first social category modernity ever produced, and modernity produced race first in the American continent.²⁴ The category of race is born of a violent confrontation in which the losers, the dominated, were devalued to a perpetual condition of ontological inferiority. In this logic of domination and oppression, Blacks and Indians were dominated not because they lost the violent confrontation. The logic was reversed: they lost the confrontation because they were naturally inferior. The painting *Los mulatos de Esmeraldas* confounds this logic.

The three men with their spears upright do not send a message of subservience to the idea of their inferiority, no matter how their other hand makes a sign of reverence to a king they cannot see and who is thousands of leagues away from their land. The painting is meant to be a gift, as stated in the accompanying document that Juan del Barrio de Sepúlveda sent along. The concept of the gift is represented by these three Black men who appear deferent to a distant king, King Philip III, in front of whom their portraits will be displayed with their hats in their hands as a sign of respect, as part of a ceremony of homage. They proclaim themselves vassals of this king whom they have never seen but who sees them in portrait. Following a European tradition in representing Blacks in painting, these three Black men are a gift to the king. Andrés Sánchez Gallque must have been familiar with representations of the Adoration of the Magi of previous decades, in which the Black king appears younger, extravagantly dressed, and bearing an ornate gift. In the early period of the transatlantic slave trade, the reading is that of Blacks as gifts. Following the orders of Juan del Barrio de Sepúlveda, the artist decks the three subjects with gold. In this painting, however, the tables are turned: as confirmed by Juan del Barrio's document, it is the three Black men who are the recipients of the gift. Using Marcel Mauss's classical concept, a gift is something different from an offering.²⁵ A gift is to be kept by the recipient; it is not supposed to be an object of further transaction. The king of Spain's representative has made a donation to these men in the form of rich clothes. The mixture of Indigenous clothing and Spanish attire indicates their elevation to the upper Indigenous nobility, following the strict social hierarchy of the Viceroyalty of Perú.²⁶

But the gold is not for the king. The gold goes back to Esmeraldas with the three gentlemen after posing—if they ever did—for the painter. The king receives only a painted image of that gold, also made of gold, possibly by a hand different from that of Andrés Sánchez Gallque, the hand of a professional gilder.²⁷ As to the other finery, the clothes and the iron spears, these have been given to them by Barrio de Sepúlveda as tokens of goodwill. They are the king's gift to them. The painting, to a certain extent, is the representation of that donation. It is almost a receipt.

The three iron spears, or *chontas*, are an important component of the gift, a donation on the part of the Spanish authorities to these three men that speaks of their political ascendancy. They leave for Esmeraldas with weapons that they now own and know how to use. Iron spears represent the technological supremacy that has created this Spanish imperial order, the same one that created the category of Black as synonymous with slave. But the iron spears in the hands of these three mulattos signal toward the future, a future that starts with their travel back to their home in Esmeraldas. Their future will be a Black future in Esmeraldas, far from the surveillance of the Audiencia and its authorities.

The painting reorganizes the political geography of the Audiencia de Quito inasmuch as it depicts a journey. The *cimarrones* of Esmeraldas, as they were sometimes called, travelled from their homes to the capital, from the place where they were resisting conquest—read enslavement—to the place where the enslaving expeditions were coming from. The word *cimarrón* (runaway slave) adopts the point of view of the Spanish slavers. The other meaning of *cimarrón*, as Rocío Rueda Novoa points out, is that of individuals who flee slavery in order to construct freedom, a process she calls *des-esclavización*, or de-enslavement. The distinction is fundamental because de-enslavement is a radical rejection of the institution of slavery and the authority that practices and legitimizes it. It is the opposite of manumission, the granting of limited freedom by the enslaver to the enslaved, because it is an act of freedom that takes place before, and in spite of, an act of manumission.[28] The iron spears are the instruments of this process of de-enslavement. Their presence in the painting is a reminder that the king of Spain had to donate the instruments by which these Black men will ensure their freedom from now on.

The journey depicted in the painting, from Esmeraldas to Quito and back to Esmeraldas, is part of a continuum of diasporic experiences that gave Don Francisco, Don Pedro, and Don Domingo their degree of Black consciousness. This Black consciousness has been negated by Gutiérrez Usillos in his otherwise magnificent essay on the painting.[29] The story of the Black presence in Esmeraldas starts with two sea voyages that are as historical as they are legendary. The Spanish chronicler Miguel Cabello Balboa writes what should be considered the foundational narrative of these voyages. The first one involves a shipwreck in 1553 from which a group of twenty-four Blacks flee to the mountains of Esmeraldas "sin propósito ninguno de volver a servidumbre" (without any intention to go back to slavery).[30] We are most interested in the second sea voyage: Cabello Balboa tells the story of Don Francisco de Arobe's father, Andrés Mangache. His last name indicates that he was either an African or of African origin.[31] Andrés Mangache had emerged as one of the caciques who conformed to the new ethnic structure of Esmeraldas. Mangache's wife was an Indigenous woman, but not from Esmeraldas. The story Cabello Balboa tells is one of rebellion and forbidden love. He describes how Andrés Mangache had fled with other slaves in Esmeraldas after a shipwreck, accompanied by the one who would become his wife, an Indigenous woman from Nicaragua. Both had been enslaved and were travelling together. The decision to flee was provoked by the mistreatment Andrés Mangache had received as punishment for their relationship:

> llegó a aquella costa un navío que venía de Nicaragua, tierra de la Nueva España, y aportó a la bahía de San Mateo y saltaron en tierra los pasajeros con los negros e indias de servicio que traían, y entre los demás era uno que venía amancebado con una india de aquellas, por la cual había sido maltratado y como estos se vieron en tierra, quisieron hurtar su libertad y quitarse de servidumbre. . . . Parió allí aquella india de Nicaragua dos hijos, el uno llamado Jhoan y el otro Francisco.

> *A ship arrived at that coast that came from Nicaragua, a land in New Spain. It sought harbor in the bay of San Mateo. The passengers jumped from the ship to the land with the Blacks and Indian women who served them. Among them there was one who lived in sin with one of those Indian women. For this reason, he had been mistreated. When they saw themselves on shore, they wanted to steal their freedom and quit their servitude. . . . There the Indian woman from Nicaragua gave birth to two sons, one called Jhoan and the other Francisco.*[32]

The story Cabello Balboa tells comes from an origin narrative that the descendants of the Mangache and the anonymous Nicaraguan Indigenous woman had to tell him. The narrative establishes that the child Francisco, the future Don Francisco de Arobe in the painting, was born free in a free territory. He is the son of a Black man and an Indigenous woman, and these two were free by their own decision, "stealing" (*hurtando*) their freedom from those considered their owners, including the unnamed Spaniard who also subjected Andrés Mangache to violence as punishment for exercising sexual freedom. Their two sons and their descendants remember the narrative and repeat it. They also practice their parents' resistance by defeating all the expeditions sent to reduce them to slavery. They know from experience that black was the color of slavery in these lands. The details of the story Cabello Balboa tells establish Andrés Mangache and his wife as the foundational couple representing an idea of future, freedom, and being Black and Indigenous.

Afrofuturism

Los mulatos de Esmeraldas can be read through the esthetic and philosophical lens of Afrofuturism. The painting imagines a utopian Afro-diasporic world in which Blacks have access to power, and this power is political, economic, and based on technological superiority. Afrofuturist speculations create imagined futures that look back into the historical past, and in the past slavery is central as both a site of trauma and the origin of the audience's present conflict, an audience that is imagined to be Black. This present is also dangerous, a continuation of the slavery-era past, when the destiny of Blacks was annihilation and destruction. *Los mulatos de Esmeraldas* represents a stand against Black annihilation by Quito's powerful proslavery and anti-Black elites. Afrofuturism imagines a future with Blacks in it, and in power. Being the most Afro-diasporic painting of the Renaissance, *Los mulatos de Esmeraldas* invokes a powerful reaction in Black viewers who have seen it in recent exhibitions around the world.[33]

Los mulatos de Esmeraldas and *Black Panther* are in an aesthetic continuum from the point of view of modernity. Both are works of art that represent Black resistance, each in a different setting. As an early exponent of Afrofuturism, *Los mulatos de Esmeraldas* shares the aesthetic proposal that dominates the film *Black Panther*, which made the Spanish boy in the museum call the three Black men "wakandienses." The painting is portraying the future, and with it the Indigenous painter Andrés Sánchez Gallque is making a statement that can be interpreted through the proposals of Afrofuturism, which recovers the past that the perpetrators of a historical horror/error have erased. The implicit recipient of Afrofuturism is identified as a child, a teenaged Black person. Their gender is not exclusively masculine, as proven by women practitioners of Afrofuturism, from writers like Octavia Butler to Hip Hop artists like Janelle Monáe, Eryka Badu, and Missie Elliott to other creators like Beyoncé and Ava DuVernay.[34]

In Afrofuturism, power is represented as an intersection of race and technology, as Alondra Nelson has theorized.[35] The three Black protagonists being portrayed in the painting, all of them figures of authority, allow themselves to represent a moment in the history of Blacks in the Americas that looks toward a future of freedom and hope through the exhibition of high technology and the aspiration to political power through self-rule. Technological superiority is materialized by the presence of the iron spears. These three Black men have won their new social status through continuous acts of resistance that include violence and the future threat of more violence. Their violence is a challenge to the monopoly of violence claimed by the colonial state. But their violence cannot be shown, as in a battle scene, as this would be unseemly. Instead, we have a scene of stately restraint, the certification of peace and peace making. The three spears they hold stand for a degree of pessimism, Afropessimism being an inescapable aspect of Afrofuturism.[36]

The three spears stand in a metonymic relation with the notion of sovereignty. They are the result of the acquired sovereignty of these three Black men and the people they belong to and represent. Sovereignty is the power to decide over life and death by an individual (a king, a sovereign) or by a nation. Social and cultural critic Imani Perry has focused on the relation between masculinity and violence in one of the chapters of her latest book, *Vexy Thing*. Sovereignty is all about the legitimate use of violence, and the three men portrayed in the painting are all about what Perry calls "the uses of weapons." Perry states the obvious: weapons are tools used to dominate and escape domination.[37] The Black Panther Party understood it in this way. The prerogative to use weapons has traditionally belonged to men. Masculinity seems to be a prerequisite to use violence, and therefore sovereignty, the legitimate power to use violence, is a masculine power in a patriarchal order. The racialized colonial slave regime distributed power among men. The masculinity of these three Black men is the necessary currency they can use to have power bestowed on them.

Their spears signify that they are the authority figures in their homeland. It is necessary for the Spanish authorities in Quito to present the gift of spears and expensive, luxury garments to these Black men. Their allegiance to King Philip III will not be given for free. The political autonomy they expect to gain needs a physical token, which they wear on their bodies. The clothes and spears dress three Black bodies that otherwise would be naked, and nakedness is the sign of the slave. They are not slaves, and they will not be slaves. The painting, thus, contains this message to the king: your far-flung empire cannot be conceived without us, without free Black people. Their stance is an invitation to the king to imagine the world he reigns as one in which Black people think of themselves as political beings, that is, as people with a future, not people slated for enslavement and annihilation. The painting is the spectacular, and ceremonial, aspect of the *asiento*, or agreement, between the Black-Indigenous clans represented by the three Arobe men and the representatives of King Philip III in Quito. The promise to keep peace is made from a position of strength. Breaching this agreement will mean war. While the authorities in Quito know that many Spaniards wished to enter Esmeraldas on a war path and conquer and enslave the people living there, they decide to share sovereignty with these cimarrones as the only way to stop those other Spaniards in whose vision peace can only be achieved after the destruction of this Black society.

Los mulatos de Esmeraldas portrays three Black men who are in the process of building a free society for themselves as part of a community that is being created. They have to create a new people, a new ethnos, by joining Africanity and Indigeneity, and this formation is not peaceful. In their conquest of freedom, they have to resort to war. War is the immediate consequence of freedom in a slave society. Freedom has to be defended in a slave society, because a slave society does not recognize freedom; in fact, a slave society operates against freedom. A slave society needs more slaves and fewer free people, as it divides the population between the free and the slave. The painting *Los mulatos de Esmeraldas* portrays a contradiction in the racialized society in which it was produced—Blacks, that is, people destined to be slaves, who are free and armed. Three Black men displaying sovereignty. A sovereign people owning and displaying weapons. Wakanda, the mythical kingdom in the middle of Africa, possesses a magical weapon. But vibranium is only magical because its owners use it to maintain freedom. The mulattos from Esmeraldas, and the people of Wakanda, choose isolation. The historical isolation of the Black communities of Esmeraldas in the late sixteenth century and the mythical isolation of Wakanda belong to the same logic, one of defense against a world dominated by colonialism and white supremacy.

The three men in Sánchez Gallque's canvas tell an impossible story of an American world in which Blacks imagine themselves—and are imagined—

not as slaves. An Afrofuturistic reading of *Los mulatos de Esmeraldas* investigates the gaze of the subject directed at the king himself. This interpretation asks us to put ourselves in the eyes of the three mulatto gentlemen. It also asks us to think of the position of the artist, an Indigenous man who creates an official painting in which the people representing authority are not the usual ones. This authority on canvas is the formulation of a future that is possible. The descendants of Blacks and Indians see themselves sharing power, or at least a portion of that power. These three figures of authority that travel from the Indies to Spain represent a moment of crisis in the Spanish structure of power that opens a future in which the racial hegemonic system may be challenged.

Los mulatos de Esmeraldas becomes a pictorial fiction in which a multitude of voices tells different stories that share traits with the speculative fictions of Afrofuturism by contemporary writers like Octavia Butler and Samuel Delaney. All are epistemological projects imbued with an Afrodiasporic historical perspective. They state that Blacks will exist in the future and not as heralds of chaos. Afrofuturism imagines Blacks inhabiting the future; Blacks are the future.[38] *Los mulatos de Esmeraldas'* portrait of three Black men in luxurious attire, each holding an iron spear, proposes a narrative in which Blacks will exist as free people in the future. It stands in opposition to the imperial slave order. The painting is an artifact for present-day Black communities in the rural areas of Esmeraldas to recognize themselves and their struggle to acquire recognition for their home as Black ancestral territory.[39] *Los mulatos de Esmeraldas* is a tool of history that allows imagining a future of plenitude for Black people in the Americas.

NOTES

1. William B. Taylor, "Pensar en imágenes," *Letras libres* (30 June 1999). www.letraslibres.com/mexico/pensar-en-imagenes. This essay owes a debt of gratitude to Tom Cummins for his influential essays analyzing the painting and the documents that accompanied it on its journey to Madrid soon after it was completed. The pioneer in analyzing this painting in detail after its "discovery" by José Gabriel Navarro in 1928 was A. Szászdi, who provided the first account of the historical events surrounding this painting based on archival information. He is the first one to mention and study the Oidor Juan del Barrio de Sepúlveda and the three sets of documents he sent to Madrid regarding this painting. See Adan Szászdi, "El trasfondo de un cuadro: *Los mulatos de Esmeraldas* de Andrés Sánchez Gallque," *Cuadernos Prehispánicos* 12 (1986–1987): 98.
2. The different catalogs in the archives of the Spanish Royal Collection in the eighteenth century reflect the changing perceptions of the three men represented in the

painting, which was referred to as "negros con lanzillas" (Blacks with small spears), "Tres negros indios" (Three Indian Blacks), or even "negros indios," "indios," or "indios bozales" (non-Spanish speaking Indians). See Andrés Gutiérrez Usillo, "Nuevas aportaciones en torno al lienzo titulado *Los mulatos de Esmeraldas*. Estudio técnico, radiográfico e histórico," *Anales del Museo de América* 20 (2012): 10, 53. The label "indios bozales" is perhaps the most confusing. The term *bozal*, or in its old spelling *boçal*, referred to Black enslaved people born in Africa who could not speak standard Spanish. It was not normally used for Indigenous people. The double racialization of the label speaks of a new ethnicity, one that is composed of Blacks and Indigenous people who do not speak Spanish. It "blackens" their Indigenousness by accentuating their perceived non-participation in the Spanish-speaking *koine*.
3. Raúl Hernández Asensio, "Los límites de la política imperial: El oidor Juan de Barrio de Sepúlveda y la frontera esmeraldeña a inicios del siglo XVII," *Bulletin de l'Institut français d'études andines* 37, no. 2 (2008): 331.
4. Manuel Gracia Rivas, "El oidor D. Juan del Barrio de Sepúlveda y la exploración de la Costa de las Esmeraldas (Cuatro mapas curiosos del Siglo XVI en un archivo borjano)," *Cuadernos de Estudios Borjanos* 50–51 (2008): 417. Also, Don Francisco de Arobe was the son of Juan Mangache, one of the original groups of Black settlers who arrived in a ship to the coast of Esmeraldas in 1553. A Mercedarian friar, Juan de Salas, had contacted him with the purpose of establishing a relationship that would include the evangelization of his people. After being baptized, Don Francisco de Arobe allowed the construction of a church near his house and the establishment of a *padrón*, or baptismal register. Ibid., 416–17. This *padrón* was a significant instrument in the hands of the Audiencia authorities for marking the difference between people of peace (*de padrón*) and those at war or unwilling to sign agreements with the Audiencia. See Charles Beatty Medina, "Caught between Rivals: The Spanish-African Maroon Competition for Captive Indian Labor in the Region of Esmeraldas during the Late Sixteenth and Early Seventeenth Centuries," *The Americas* 63, no. 1 (2006): 130.
5. José Gabriel Navarro, "Arte hispanoamericano: Un pintor quiteño y un cuadro admirable del siglo XVI en el Museo Arqueológico Nacional," *Boletín de la Real Academia de la Historia* 94 (1929): 468–69, www.cervantesvirtual.com/obra/arte-hispano americano-un-pintor-quiteno-y-un-cuadro-admirable-del-siglo-xvi-en-el-museo-arqueológico-nacional/
6. *Black Panther*, directed by Ryan Coogler (Burbank, CA: Walt Disney Pictures, 2018).
7. Editor's note: This observation is of particular importance, given the control of access to arms (swords) by the enslaved and free Blacks during the colonial period (see Chapter 3). One notes the museum's contemporary effort to preserve this episteme by controlling the image of the past.
8. Tom Cummins renamed the painting *The Three Gentlemen from Esmeraldas* to reflect the position of honor they had inherited from their ancestor Alonso de Illescas, who had received it from Miguel Cabello Balboa, the first chronicler of the Esmeraldas province. See Cummins, "Three Gentlemen from Esmeraldas: A Portrait Fit for a King," in *Slave Portraiture in the Atlantic World*, ed. A. Lugo Ortiz and A. Rosenthal (Cambridge: Cambridge University Press, 2013), 124.

9. Andrés Gutiérrez Usillos, "Nuevas aportaciones en torno al lienzo titulado *Los mulatos de Esmeraldas*," 20. *Asiento*: "tratado o ajuste de paces" (peace treaty or arrangement) in definition ten for the term in *Diccionario de la lengua española* (Real Academia de la Lengua). dle.rae.es/asiento. The term *asiento* would come to mean the contract signed between the king of Spain and different private individuals to provide enslaved Africans to the Americas.
10. Archivo General de Indias, "Fondo Quito 9 R3 N21," *El oidor Juan del Barrio Sepúlveda sobre varios asuntos*, bloque 2, f. 1v, pares.mcu.es/ParesBusquedas20/catalogo/show/412625 (my translation). In another document, dated a few days before, Juan del Barrio mentions the painting he is about to send to the king. Archivo General de Indias, "Fondo Quito,9, R.2,N.15," *Juan del Barrio de Sepúlveda sobre varios asuntos*, April 12, 1599, pares.mcu.es/ParesBusquedas20/catalogo/show/412619. Barrio de Sepúlveda was himself the owner of enslaved Blacks, as shown in a document signed ten years before the painting's commission. Archivo General de Indias, "Fondo Panamá, 237, L.12, F.121V–122R," *Licencia de esclavos a Juan del Barrio de Sepúlveda*, pares.mcu.es/ParesBusquedas20/catalogo/description/1860836.
11. Andrés Sánchez Gallque belonged to a school of Indigenous and mestizo painters formed at the convent of Santo Domingo in Quito and to a confraternity of Indigenous painters as early as 1588. Susan V. Webster, "Of Signatures and Status: Andrés Sánchez Gallque and Contemporary Painters in Early Colonial Quito," *The Americas* 70, no. 4 (2014): 608. His known works are of religious subjects, like most paintings by School of Quito artists. See José de Mesa and Teresa Gisbert, "The Painter, Mateo Mexía, and His Works in the Convent of San Francisco de Quito," *The Americas* 16, no. 4 (1960): 393. His name appears as "Galque" in numerous academic citations, although he signed it "Gallque" in different archival documents. See again, Webster, "Of Signatures and Status," 604n3.
12. The full Latin inscription reads, "Philippo Catholico / Regi Hispania[rum] / India[rum] Q[ue] D[omi]NO svo / Doctor Ioannis Del Barrio / a Sepvlveda Avditor Svae / Cancellariae Del Qvito / Svis Expensis Fieri / Cvravit / Anno 1599" (Doctor Juan del Barrio de Sepúlveda, Oidor of His Chancery (Audiencia) of Quito, had it made at his own expense and directed his execution for Philip, Catholic King of the Spains and the Indies, and his Lord. Year 1599).
13. Sánchez Gallque was the most prominent participant in an ideological program in which some Indigenous leaders became patrons and promoters of art. The cacique Don Diego Pilamunga commissioned Sánchez Gallque for the painting of the main altar in the church of Santiago de Chimbo. Webster, "Of Signatures and Status," 614.
14. José de Mesa, "La influencia de Flandes en la pintura del área Andina," *Revista de Historia de América* 117 (1994): 70.
15. Andrés Gutiérrez Usillos, "Nuevas aportaciones en torno al lienzo titulado *Los mulatos de Esmeraldas*," 22–23.
16. Rocío Rueda Novoa, *Zambaje y autonomía. Historia de la gente negra de la provincia de Esmeraldas, siglos XVI–XVIII* (Quito: Abya-Yala, 2001), 71.
17. The pacification policy promoted by Oidor Barrio de Sepúlveda hurt the interests of those who preferred a policy of conquest and enslavement. Some of the authorities

in Quito used the case of the Trinitarian friar Alonso de Espinosa. He had lived in Esmeraldas for a considerable time and had promoted some of the earliest agreements with the mulatto leaders. He was formally accused of conniving with the English corsairs at the time Francis Drake and others had set their eyes on Panama. Father Espinosa was expelled to Panama, and upon his unauthorized return to Esmeraldas, he was also accused of homosexual practices among the Indigenous people ("pecado nefando con los yndios"). Archivo General de Indias, "Quito 8 R22 N65," *La Audiencia de Quito sobre diversos asuntos*, f. 5.

18. Raúl Hernández Asensio, "Los límites de la política imperial," 337.
19. The types of gold pieces the three men wear have been only partially identified. They are similar to pieces found in the archeological site of La Tolita, between Esmeraldas and Tumaco, in today's Colombia. See David Scott, "The La Tolita–Tumaco Culture: Master Metalsmiths in Gold and Platinum," *Latin American Antiquity* 22, no.1 (2011): 65–95.
20. Miguel Cabello Balboa, *Descripción de la provincia de Esmeraldas*, ed. J. Alcina Franch (Madrid: CSIC, 2001), 71.
21. Cummins, "Three Gentlemen from Esmeraldas," 23.
22. Charles Beatty Medina, "Caught between Rivals: The Spanish-African Maroon Competition for Captive Indian Labor in the Region of Esmeraldas during the Late Sixteenth and Early Seventeenth Centuries," *The Americas* 63, no. 1, *The African Diaspora in the Colonial Andes* (2006): 125.
23. Archivo General de Indias, "Fondo Quito 9R3 N21a," El oidor Juan del Barrio Sepúlveda sobre varios asuntos, 2r. pares.mcu.es/ParesBusquedas20/catalogo/show/412625.
24. Anibal Quijano, "Colonialidad del poder, eurocentrismo y América Latina," in *La colonialidad del saber: Eurocentrismo y ciencias sociales. Perspectivas Latinoamericanas*, comp. E. Lander (Buenos Aires: CLACSO, Consejo Latinoamericano de Ciencias Sociales, 2000), 202.
25. Marcel Mauss, *The Gift: Forms and Functions of Exchange in Archaic Societies*, translated by Ian Cunnison (London: Cohen and West, 1966). 44
26. Andrés Gutiérrez Usillos, "Nuevas aportaciones en torno al lienzo titulado *Los mulatos de Esmeraldas*," 31.
27. José Gabriel Navarro, "Arte hispanoamericano," 461.
28. Rocío Rueda Novoa, "Des-esclavización, manumisión jurídica y defensa del territorio en el norte de Esmeraldas (siglos XVIII–XIX)," *Procesos: Revista ecuatoriana de historia* 43 (2016): 11.
29. Andrés Gutiérrez Usillos, "Nuevas aportaciones en torno al lienzo titulado *Los mulatos de Esmeraldas*," 21.
30. Miguel Cabello Balboa, *Descripción de la provincia de Esmeraldas*, 49.
31. The last name "Mangache," also spelled "Manganche," gestures to the term "malgache," an inhabitant of Madagascar. However, another hypothesis is that of an Indigenous name, after a place name, the Estero Mangachi, located between Guayaquil and Portoviejo. See Adam Szádszdi, "El trasfondo de un cuadro: *Los Mulatos de Esmeraldas* de Andrés Sánchez Gallque," *Cuadernos Prehispánicos* 12 (1986–1987): 99.

32. Miguel Cabello Balboa, *Descripción de la provincia de Esmeraldas*, 52 (my translation).
33. The painting was exhibited in Quito in 2019. See "*Los mulatos de Esmeraldas* vuelve a España tras exhibirse en Quito," *Agencia EFE*, August 3, 2019, www.efe.com/efe/america/cultura/la-obra-los-mulatos-de-esmeraldas-vuelve-a-espana-tras-exhibirse-en-quito/20000009-4036761. The Ecuadorian press celebrated the exhibition as a major cultural event, as in the article by Evelin Caiza, "Los tres mulatos de Esmeraldas en el MuNa," *El Comercio*, May 6, 2019, www.elcomercio.com/tendencias/intercultural-pintor-mulatos-esmeraldas-muna.html. Another newspaper, *Ecuador 24*, however, brought up the issue of Ecuadorian national ownership of the painting. See "Obra 'Los mulatos de Esmeraldas' finaliza su exposición en Ecuador," *24 Ecuador*, August 5, 2019, www.24ecuador.com/cultura/obra-los-mulatos-de-esmeraldas-finaliza-su-exposicion-en-ecuador/108486-noticias.
34. See, for example, Janelle Monáe's short film and album *Dirty Computer* (2018); Ava DuVernay's futuristic fantasy film *A Wrinkle in Time* (2018), and Jay-Z's music video for the song "Family Feud," featuring Beyoncé (2017).
35. Alondra Nelson, "Afrofuturism: Past-Future Visions," *ColorLines* 2 (June 2002): 35. culturetechnologypolitics.files.wordpress.com/2015/11/afrofuturism_past_future_visions_colorli.pdf.
36. For Jared Saxton, Afropessimism is rooted in the historical context of the transatlantic African Diaspora. For him, to be a slave is to be paradigmatically Black, as the practice was to equate the condition of slave with the outer sign of black skin, thus collapsing the two concepts of being African with being Black. The historical subjects of the painting are fighting their social death in a colonial society ruled by white supremacy. They are trying to dissociate Frank Wilderson's concept of "slaveness," the condition predicated by the equation of Blackness and Africanness. Quoted in Annie Olaloku-Teriba, "Afro-Pessimism and the (Un)Logic of Anti Blackness," in "Identity Politics," special issue, *Historical Materialism* 26, no. 2 (2018), www.historicalmaterialism.org/articles/afro-pessimism-and-unlogic-anti-blackness#_ftn18.
37. Imani Perry, *Vexy Thing: On Gender and Liberation* (Durham, NC: Duke University Press, 2018), 156.
38. Susana M. Morris, "Black Girls Are from the Future: Afrofuturist Feminism in Octavia E. Butler's 'Fledgling,'" *Women's Studies Quarterly* 40, no. 3/4 (2012): 155.
39. Juliet Hooker, "Indigenous Inclusion/Black Exclusion: Race, Ethnicity and Multicultural Citizenship in Latin America," *Journal of Latin American Studies* 37, no. 2 (2005): 295.

CHAPTER 7

A Transhistorical and Translocal View of the Luso-Brazilian Imperial/Colonial World through the Poetry of Gregório de Matos (1636–1695) and Domingos Caldas Barbosa (1740–1800)

LÚCIA HELENA COSTIGAN

"For formerly colonized peoples," according to Jerome Branche, "particularly . . . those whose Spanish or Portuguese vernaculars are inflected by ancestral languages of non-European provenance, what is taken as 'natural' about the way they speak is often brought into tension when confronted by the metropolitan model/s, whose claim to superior linguistic 'correctness' and 'purity' has all too often proved to be an existential challenge for them as writers, politicians, or just ordinary citizens, marginalized by space and race within the larger polities created by empire."[1]

Despite the fact that Gregório de Matos (1636–1695) and Domingos Caldas Barbosa (1740–1800) lived in different centuries and belonged to two distinct ethnic groups of different socioeconomic backgrounds, both poets experienced discrimination in Portugal for being born in Brazil, a place regarded as a marginal space of the empire, ethnically and linguistically associated with Africa. Other aspects that connect these two colonial writers are the facts that, disillusioned with the Portuguese social and political establishment that discriminated against those born in the empire's overseas dependents, both De Matos and Caldas Barbosa rebelled against the strict linguistic and literary norms imposed by the Portuguese academy and embraced the language spoken by the inhabitants of the Lusophone empire's marginalized areas.

Because they existed at a time when the Portuguese crown prohibited the establishment of universities and printing presses in Brazil, many of their writings were displaced and lost, and some were published only long after their deaths. Additionally, between the sixteenth and the eighteenth century, writings by colonial subjects who lived outside Portugal were regarded as inferior to the metropolitan models, so their works were generally considered unfit for publication. Even the texts produced by writers born in Brazil but who had studied at the famous Universidade de Coimbra and spent most of their lives in the metropole were subject to strict censorship by the Portuguese Inquisition and by the crown.

Fortunately, in the case of Brazil, perhaps due to the absence of printing presses and universities, a rich oral tradition that blossomed there during the sixteenth, seventeenth, and eighteenth centuries allowed for the verses and songs that were popular during these authors' lifetimes to be repeated orally, and thereby retained. Scribes transcribed some of these texts and collected them in special volumes that eventually were published after the writers and assumed authors were no longer living. The satirical poems believed to have been written by the Bahian poet Gregório de Matos are examples of apocryphal texts that were published posthumously. Because of their popularity, the verses attributed to the Bahian *letrado* were kept alive orally throughout the centuries and published for the first time only in the second half of the nineteenth century, after Brazil had gained independence from Portugal and finally had access to a printing press. Paradoxically, even in 1850, when for the first time some of the satires attributed to the Bahian poet were published by the historiographer Francisco Adolfo de Varnhagen in his famous collection of poetry, *Florilégio da poesia brasileira*, the strict moral and grammatical rules inherited from the Portuguese academy which, as Branche emphasizes, have "too often proved to be an existential challenge for formerly colonized peoples," led Varnhagen to delete words, verses, and entire stanzas from De Matos's satiric poetry. The editor considered the poet's language improper for the Portuguese academy's high standards and offensive to educated readers' moral values. Since *Florilégio da poesia brasileira* was published for the first time in Portugal, it is quite possible that it was the Portuguese editor who censored some of the poems attributed to De Matos, because Varnhagen calls attention to the importance of the Bahian poet's work to Brazilian literature. He finds

De Matos's satiric verses very humorous and admits that they are examples of the innovative literary expressions that blossomed in Brazil and in the Americas during colonial times.

Between the years 1923 and 1933 the Academia Brasileira de Letras attempted to publish a collection of the complete work attributed to Gregório de Matos, but even this time Afrânio Peixoto, the editor responsible for selecting the poems, did not allow the inclusion of the verses and stanzas that had been deleted from Varhnagen's *Florilégio*. In fact, Peixoto was even more incisive in his censorship. He explained that to prevent offending the readers' moral values, he had eliminated all the satires considered to be licentious and unfit for publication. Finally, it was only in 1969, during the first decade of the military dictatorship in Brazil, that, in a gesture of protest against the military regime, a group of intellectuals from Bahia led by James Amado managed to collect a series of sixteen different codices of the apocryphal works attributed to the seventeenth-century baroque poet. The poems found in these different codices were published without censorship in a collection of seven volumes titled *Obras completas de Gregório de Matos: Sacra-Lírica-Satírica-Burlesca*. Because James Amado neither censored the poems nor deleted any part of the apocryphal verses included in the sixteen codices attributed to De Matos, I have used James Amado's special edition as the major source of the poems cited in my work.[2]

Caldas Barbosa's experience in Portugal and the way he has generally been treated by the literary academy has been even more negative than that of Gregório de Matos. The discrimination and condescending behavior of the Portuguese writers and critics who were his contemporaries can be explained through the fact that Caldas was a mulatto, and his compositions follow the vernacular and rhythms that were popular in eighteenth-century Brazil, especially among the mixed-race individuals who formed the majority of the Brazilian population. The Portuguese language as spoken in Brazil in colonial times was regarded as inferior to the model that followed the baroque and neoclassical Peninsular norms. Because Brazilian critics, who included some of Caldas Barbosa's works in the anthologies published in Brazil after the founding of the Brazilian Literary Academy in 1896, continued following the hierarchized, racialized, and conservative perspective inherited from the Portuguese literary academy, they insisted on portraying his work in a negative light. The majority of the critics who have written about this mulatto poet and musician from Rio de Janeiro base their comments on the book *Viola de Lereno: Collecção das suas cantigas offerecidas a seus amigos*. This special collection of verses and songs that were popular in Brazil and Portugal during the eighteenth century was published in Lisbon in 1798, two years before the death of the Afro-Brazilian poet.

A Translocal View of the Seventeenth Century Luso-Brazilian Context through the Case of Gregório de Matos

Known from the seventeenth century onward as Boca do Inferno (Hell's Mouth) and described by critics as *maldito*, or damned and evil poet, and by others as *herói*, or hero, Gregório de Matos is without doubt the most polemical poet of colonial Brazil. The controversy that originated from the satiric poetry attributed to him has divided Brazilian critics throughout the centuries. The Bahian poet has also become a major character in some fictional novels, but apart from Fernando da Rocha Peres, we do not know of any scholars who have produced a biography of him based on archival research.

According to Fernando da Rocha Peres, Gregório de Matos was born on December 20, 1636, in the city of Salvador da Bahia de Todos os Santos, known in the seventeenth century simply as the city of Bahia (a cidade da Bahia). During the poet's lifetime the city of Bahia was the capital of the Estado do Brasil, later known as Brazil. Similar to other distinguished seventeenth-century literary figures who lived in the New World, including Sor Juana Inés de la Cruz and Juan del Valle y Caviedes, who followed the Iberian poetic tradition, De Matos used the Spanish baroque writers Francisco de Quevedo and Luis de Góngora as models for his writings. As a member of an influential Portuguese family that moved to Bahia during the first decades of the seventeenth century, when Brazil became a wealthy overseas possession due to the sugar-cane boom, De Matos received the best education available to a son of a plantation-owning Portuguese. After completing his primary studies with the Jesuits, in 1650 he was sent to Portugal to study law at the University of Coimbra.

Due in part to the fact that Portugal and its overseas colonies were part of the Spanish Empire from 1580 until 1640, the Spanish baroque poets Quevedo and Góngora exerted a strong influence on poets of the Iberian world. For this reason, De Matos and other Portuguese writers of the seventeenth century could not escape the *culteranismo* of Góngora, with its erudite imagery, or the similarly elitist *conceptismo*, or wit. Culteranismo is present in De Matos' religious poetry, and especially in his amorous verses that explore the baroque theme of carpe diem. Quevedo's conceptismo is the primary source behind the Bahian poet's satirical verses. As I have observed elsewhere, De Matos adapted Quevedo's rhymes but not the content.³ Sometimes he even surpassed the Spanish satirist in wit and in the musicality of his rhymes. Because he was able to interweave Tupi and African vernacular and sounds with the Iberian poetic tradition, contemporary critics, including Haroldo de Campos, consider De Matos the first *antropófago*, or an avant-gardist of Brazilian poetry.⁴

Although the works attributed to the Bahian poet were published posthumously, and the apocryphal ones do not indicate the publication date, a close reading of the satirical poems found in the volumes edited by James Amado allows us to establish a chronological profile of the poet and to trace his experiences as a student in Coimbra during the early 1650s and as a lawyer in Lisbon during the turbulent years of 1661–1682, when the Lusitanian empire was under the monarchy of Alfonso VI of Portugal. However, the bulk of De Matos's apocryphal satires seemed to have been written between 1683 and 1694, years after the poet's return to Bahia. In the pages that follow I will focus on a few satirical verses that shed light on his biography, including the discrimination that De Matos endured in Portugal and the disappointing experiences he faced upon returning to Bahia in 1683.

Starting with some of the verses from one of the sonnets that describe De Matos's experience as a student in Coimbra, one can see the discrimination that Portuguese students directed against Brazilians and other students who were born outside of the metropole:

> Adeus Coimbra inimiga
> Dos mais honrados madrasta,
> Que eu vou para outras terras,
> Onde viva mais 'a larga!⁵

> *Goodbye enemy Coimbra*
> *Stepmother to the upright,*
> *I am going to other lands,*
> *Where I can live as I please!*

After receiving a degree in canon law, De Matos moved to Lisbon and worked in the Portuguese imperial court serving as a lawyer to the Portuguese king. Unfortunately, even in Lisbon, De Matos could not live as he expected. In Lisbon he was discriminated against for being born in Brazil, lost the favor of the king, and was classified as a *mazombo*, a word of very negative connotation, synonymous with "sullied," "lazy," and "melancholic."[6] As a result of the discrimination that he encountered in the metropole, De Matos decided to return to Bahia. But because in the seventeenth century Brazil did not offer many opportunities for lawyers, prior to leaving Portugal he prepared for a religious career. Upon receiving the tonsure, he was designated to serve in Bahia as treasurer of the See. When De Matos arrived in Bahia, he was filled with optimism:

>   Mudei-me de ponto a ponto
>   De Portugal ao Brasil
>   Lá deixo infortúnios mil,
>   Acho cá ditas sem conto[7]

>   *I moved from point to point*
>   *From Portugal to Brazil*
>   *There I leave a thousand sorrows,*
>   *To find here infinite bliss*

Contrary to his expectations, De Matos was no more successful in Brazil. Shortly after arriving in Bahia, he was removed from his ecclesiastical position because of his refusal to wear a cassock. Another major factor that made the poet's life very difficult was the economic hardship that Brazil suffered in the last decades of the seventeenth century because of the loss of the sugarcane monopoly that occurred when the Dutch were expelled from Pernambuco in 1654 and took their knowledge of sugar production to the Caribbean. They also took with them many Africans they had enslaved after taking control of the maritime trade routes that had previously been dominated by Portugal. The loss of the sugar monopoly, combined with the loss of some African territories and the control of the maritime routes to the Dutch, led the Portuguese crown to impose heavy taxes on Brazil's landowning rural elite, especially those in Bahia, including the family of Gregório de Matos. The wars with Spain, known in Portugal as the Restauração (Restoration), which lasted from 1641 to 1668, also caused economic disruption in the metropole and led many Portuguese men to move to Brazil. Some of the Portuguese migrants who arrived in Bahia, then the Brazilian capital, were single men who tried to make a living through trade and commerce. According to historian Caio

Prado Jr.,[8] many of them became rich because the new commercial regulations favored Portuguese subjects and penalized the landowners who were born or had previously settled in Brazil. The argument made by Prado Jr. can be expanded through the research by Flory and Grant Smith on "Bahian Merchants and Planters in the Seventeenth and Eighteenth Centuries," a study that shows that the majority of migrants that arrived in Bahia in the second half of the seventeenth century came from the lower sectors of Portuguese society.[9] Upon their arrival in Brazil, they made a living in small business and commerce. Eventually many of them were able to ascend the social ladder by marrying the daughters of local landowners. The sonnet "À cidade da Bahia" (To the city of Bahia), illustrates these historic arguments. It can also be seen as a typical example of seventeenth-century poetry that conveys the idea of the *desengaño barroco* (baroque disillusion), through Gregório de Matos's disillusionment or sadness about the transformation that he found in Bahia upon his return to Brazil. Here the poet compares the negative changes that occurred in his hometown of Bahia to those of his own life.

> Triste Bahia! Oh quão dessemelhante
> Estás e estou do nosso antigo estado!
> Pobre te vejo a ti, tu a mim empenhado,
> Rico te vi eu já, tu a mi abundante.[10]

> *Sad Bahia! Oh how different*
> *You and I are from what we once were!*
> *I see you poor, you see me in hock,*
> *I saw you rich then, you saw me wealthy.*

In the same poem, De Matos expresses his resentment against tradesmen and their mercantile deals that transformed Bahia into a deteriorated place and that negatively affected his own life:

> A ti trocou-te a máquina mercante,
> Que em tua larga barra tem entrado.
> A mim foi-me trocando e tem trocado,
> Tanto negócio and tanto negociante.[11]

> *The mercantile machine,*
> *That anchored in your bay changed you.*

All that business and all those businessmen,
Changed me and change me still.

As a White man born from Portuguese parents at a time when Brazil was not regarded as a colony of Portugal but as an extension of the Lusophone empire, Gregório de Matos believed that as a Coimbra-educated lawyer he should have the right to occupy a position in the Bahia government. Since that was not the case, and the Portuguese crown discriminated against those born outside of the metropole, calling them *mazombo*, or inferior, melancholic, good-for-nothing people, De Matos rebelled against the government and mocked the incompetence of the representatives of the Portuguese crown in Bahia.

A cada canto um grande conselheiro,
Que nos quer governor cabana, e vinha,
Não sabem governar sua cozinha,
E podem governar o mundo inteiro.[12]

At every corner a great counselor,
That wants to govern our home and our land,
Uncapable to manage their own kitchen,
They hope to govern the entire world.

Apparently, De Matos's disillusion and frustration with the abuses of the members of the court, and with the ignorance and various vices he observed in Brazil upon his return in 1683, led him to use satirical verses to expose everything and everybody he perceived as being wrong, including the Portuguese immigrants' opportunism, the mulattos' and women's impudence, the clergy members' lack of charity, and, above all, the Portuguese government's corruption.

Se souberas falar, também falaras,
Também satirizaras, se souberas,
E se foras Poeta, poetizaras.[13]

If you knew how to speak, you would speak,
You also would write satires, if you knew how to do it,
And if you were a Poet, you would write poetry.

He compares the city of Bahia to a crib of beasts, a stable, or an animalistic party house:

> A nossa Sé da Bahia,
> Com ser um mapa de festas
> É um presépio de bestas,
> se não for estrebaria.[14]

> *Our See of Bahia,*
> *For being a map of festivities*
> *Is also a cradle of beasts,*
> *Or stall of horses.*

After losing or abandoning his positions as a lawyer and a treasurer in the city of Bahia, De Matos moved to the state interior, where he mingled with people of different races and social levels. Apparently, it was during the decade of 1683 to 1693 that Gregório de Matos became an itinerant poet, embraced popular culture, and produced the larger portion of his poetry.

> Ausentei-me da cidade
> Porque este povo maldito
> Me pôs em Guerra com todos
> E aqui vivo em paz comigo
> Visita-me o lavrador
> Sincero, simples e liso.[15]

> *I escaped the city*
> *Because these evil people*
> *Put me at war with everybody*
> *And here I live at peace with myself*
> *The peasant, sincere, modest, and loyal*
> *Visits me.*

His satires and *liras maldizentes* earned him the sobriquet Boca do Inferno. In fact, De Matos's invectives against the representatives of the Portuguese crown almost cost him his life. As punishment for his scathing criticism of Governor Câmara Coutinho in 1694, De Matos was deported to Angola. In the last year of his life, he was granted permission to return to Brazil, but his return was only possible on the conditions that he would never return to the city of Bahia and that he would no longer write poetry, especially satirical verses. In 1695, De Matos died in Recife shortly after returning from his exile in Africa.

As a result of De Matos's sharp tongue and his verses' fierce satire directed at the different sectors of the Luso Brazilian society, especially his attacks on the members of the Portuguese government, the critics who have written about him and his work from the nineteenth century onward present very different points of view. Some portray him as a villain, others as a hero. Examples of the contradictory points of view about the Bahian poet and his work can be seen through the works of Sílvio Romero and José Veríssimo, two major nineteenth-century Brazilian critics and historiographers. In his *História da literatura brasileira*, published for the first time in 1888, Romero sees Gregório de Matos as one of the first poets who used his verses to express his dissatisfaction (and that of the inhabitants of Brazil) with the metropole. Romero identifies in the satiric poetry of the Bahian poet an embrace of the popular language spoken in Brazil and evidence of an incipient Brazilian difference or consciousness.[16] Contrary to Romero's opinion, in his *História da literatura brasileira* published in 1915, José Veríssimo does not see any positive aspect in Gregório de Matos's poetry. In fact, he thinks that De Matos was a mere imitator of Quevedo and that his poetry is inferior to that produced by other seventeenth-century poets.[17] Critics like Haroldo de Campos use an anachronistic approach to the Bahian baroque poet and see him as a precursor of Brazil's concrete poetry movement, or the *movimento de poesia concreta in Brazil*. Others see De Matos as a protonationalist poet who was alerting his countrymen to Portugal's abuses and exploitation two centuries before Brazil's independence.[18]

Although some of the satiric verses attributed to De Matos describe Bahian mixed-race people in a negative light, what is admirable in his case is his satire's opening a space for popular language and traditions and the voices of the marginalized sectors of the Brazilian population. As one can observe through some of his satiric poems, apparently after his first years in Brazil, De Matos decided to abandon the literary norms imposed by the Portuguese academy and embraced the popular culture that he encountered in his wanderings through the interior of Bahia: "Cansado de vos pregar cultíssimas profecias hoje das culteranias quero o hábito enforcar" (Tired of expressing myself in elaborate discourse, today I want to give up the habit of using cultured and sophisticated language).[19]

As Gonzalo Aguillar observes in the "Prólogo" of his anthology *Sátiras y otras maledicencias*, as a "musa praguejadora" (muse of the uncouth),[20] Gregório de Matos relies on popular and vulgar language to be understood by everybody, even the less educated, including mulattos, ladinos, Indigenous captives, and slaves who were already becoming familiar with the Portuguese language spoken in Brazil.[21] The racial diversity in the colony, which was much larger than that of Portugal, fragmented and changed the spoken language. Contact with the popular sectors led him to embrace the Afro-Brazilian culture and to act as a chronicler who used the pen to describe and document all aspects of Bahian life, including the processions and dances of Afro-Brazilians. In many of his verses we can detect a certain admiration for the charm and grace of the *mulatas*. This can be seen in the following poem that describes the *paturi*, a local indigenous dance performed by women of African heritage:

> Ao som de uma guitarrilha,
> que tocava um colomin
> Vi bailar na Água Brusca
> as Mulatas do Brasil:
> ¡Que bem bailam o Paturi!
>
> Não usam de castanhetas,
> porque com os dedos gentis,
> Fazem tal estropeada,
> Que de ouvi-las me estrugi:
> ¡Que bem bailam as Mulatas!
> Que bem bailam o Paturi.[22]

> *At the sound of a small guitar,*
> *Played by a Young Indian boy*
> *I saw dancing in Água Brusca*
> *The Mulatas from Brazil:*
> *How well they dance the Paturi!*
>
> *They do not use castanets,*
> *For with their delicate fingers,*
> *They produce such loud sounds,*
> *That I was fascinated listening to them:*

> *How well the Mulatas dance!*
> *How well they dance the Paturi.*

It seems that in these verses the mulatas are appropriating the Indigenous paturi dance and transforming it into a kind of music and dance that reminds us of the *umbigada* and *lundu*, a music and dance that became popular among descendants of enslaved Africans in the eighteenth century and that later transformed into samba music and dance. As José Wisnik suggests in his preface to *Poemas escolhidos de Gregório de Matos*, after becoming disillusioned with the political system, De Matos wandered through the Bahia interior with a rustic guitar singing satiric verses about the society as a whole, including the negative and positive aspects of daily life in colonial Brazil, to claim, subsequently: "E pois, cronista sou" (Therefore, I am a chronicler).[23] We can see, then, through some of the satires attributed to Gregório de Matos, that the Indigenous and African songs such as the *paturi* and the *lundu* that were becoming popular in Brazil during the second half of the seventeenth century crossed the Atlantic and reached Lusitanian lands in the eighteenth century.

A Translocal View of Eighteenth-Century Portugal and Brazil through Domingos Caldas Barbosa's Poetry and Songs

Apparently, it was Domingos Caldas Barbosa, an Afro-Brazilian poet from Rio de Janeiro, who introduced the *lundu* in Portugal when he was sent by his father to study in Coimbra. Similar to Gregório de Matos's case, despite having received a classical education from the Jesuits, Caldas Barbosa embraced the spoken language and the cultural expressions that he had learned as a child and young adult from other Afro descendants and mixed-race people who lived in Rio de Janeiro. Born in Rio de Janeiro in 1740, Caldas Barbosa was the son of the Portuguese merchant Antonio de Caldas Barbosa and Antónia de Jesus, a previously enslaved woman brought from Angola. After completing his studies with the Jesuits during the years of 1750 to 1760, Caldas joined the incipient Brazilian army and fought against the Spaniards in the battle of Colonia do Sacramento. With Spain's victory in 1762, Caldas's father decided to send him to study in Portugal. In 1763, when the poet was twenty-three years old, he began studying canonical law at the University of Coimbra. Unfortunately, because of the unexpected death of his father in 1764, Caldas Barbosa was unable to continue his studies and faced many misfortunes in the metropole, including poverty, illness, and homelessness. Out of necessity Caldas Barbosa became a minstrel, or *griot*, who used praise singing as a way to survive. As an itinerant singer, he succeeded in receiving the patronage of José de Vasconcelos e Sousa, count of Pombeiro and brother of Dom Luís de Vasconcelos, a member of the Portuguese aristocracy who became viceroy in Brazil during the second half of the eighteenth century.[24]

During the time that Caldas Barbosa was under the protection of the Vasconcelos e Sousa family, he was introduced to the royal circles of the Lusitanian Empire and joined the Portuguese literary academy known as Arcádia de Roma. It was then that the poet from Rio de Janeiro wrote many compositions praising his patrons and other members of the court for the favors received. In addition to these neoclassical verses aimed at gaining or receiving favors, the poet of African origin improvised popular verses known and *lundus* and *modinhas* that were performed in the Portuguese court with the accompaniment of his rustic viola. With these popular compositions, whose rhythm and content were associated with Africa, Caldas Barbosa gained celebrity in Portugal and opened a space in the metropolitan society for Afro-Brazilian culture and literature.

Until recently, most of the information about Domingos Caldas Barbosa and his work that has been anthologized was based on negative comments by some of his contemporary Portuguese poets and writers. Generally, these comments have a negative tone, possibly because many of these authors were jealous of Caldas's talents and certainly because they were prejudiced against him for being a dark-skinned Brazilian of African descent. Due to Portugal's strong influence on the Brazilian academy, even after the printing press was established in Brazil following the Portuguese court's arrival in Rio de Janeiro in 1808, some Brazilian critics who wrote about the work of the mulatto poet from Rio de Janeiro continued to repeat the negative views of Manuel Maria Barbosa du Bocage and Filinto Elysio, two Portuguese writers who, envious of Caldas Barbosa's talents and full of hatred and prejudice against Brazilians and African descendants, directed racist attacks against him.[25]

In Brazil José Veríssimo was one of those critics who viewed Caldas Barbosa's literary production as inferior to the work written by other poets of his time. In his *História da literatura brasileira*, he describes the poet from Rio de Janeiro as a social parasite and a mediocre poet without any creativity.

Because Veríssimo considered only the intrinsic aesthetic value of works that followed the European literary norms, he did not regard Caldas Barbosa's verses, inspired by popular tradition, as a significant contribution to Brazilian literature or an important step in the development of Afro-Brazilian literature. In fact, Veríssimo regarded Caldas Barbosa's popular verses as an affront to the linguistic and vernacular purity and the moral values established by Portugal. Because the mulatto minstrel used a rustic guitar to play and sing his verses, Veríssimo regarded Caldas Barbosa's popular poetry as extremely inferior and very negative to the image of Brazil in Portugal, describing it as follows: "Cantados à viola, com os requebres e denguices da musa mulata, e o sotaque meloso do brasileiro, versos tais teriam em Portugal o sainete do exótico, ... Não enriquecem a poesia brasileira" (Sung with the accompaniment of the viola, such verses that had the swing and charm of the mulatto muse and the Brazilian sugary accent had in Portugal the stamp of the exotic, and they do not enrich Brazilian poetry).[26] Differing from Veríssimo, Sílvio Romero recognizes the importance of Caldas Barbosa's works and regards the *modinhas* and *lundus* found in *Viola de Lereno*, a collection of poems and songs published by Caldas Barbosa in 1798, as evidence of the impact of mixed-race people's popular language and culture on Brazilian literature.

Because many of the literary critics who wrote about Caldas Barbosa do take into consideration the fact that the lundus and modinhas that he performed in the Portuguese court were written out of necessity and that his originality as a poet derives not from his neoclassical production found in *Almanak das Musas* (1793) but from the verses that originated from an oral repertoire, the evaluation of his work usually ends on a negative note. Another possible reason for the harsh evaluation of Caldas Barbosa is that many of his critics had never read his poem *A Doença* (The Malady), a lyric composition dedicated to those who saved him from starvation and dying from a large tumor that afflicted his body. This hybrid poem, which violates the rules of the epic through the insertion of scatological topics such as disease and the autobiographical element, is a fundamental piece in the construction of the poetic discourse of the Afro-Brazilian poet in Portugal. The most surprising fact related to this poem is that it has been completely ignored by those who have written about Caldas Barbosa. Perhaps because they did not read *A Doença* the misunderstandings and negative perception surrounding Caldas Barbosa have persisted throughout the centuries.

Fortunately, through some of the few recent studies about the Afro-Brazilian poet and musician, we have learned that besides the collection of songs and lundus that made him known across the Lusophone world, Caldas published many other texts that prove he was not only a minor poet but also an intelligent and erudite scholar. The false perception of the eighteenth-century Brazilian poet is gradually changing with works by José Ramos Tinhorão, Adriana Rennó, Luiza Sawaya, and also with the recent edition of the poem *A Doença* published as a special volume in 2018 by Editora 34.[27] This last edition, based on extensive historic research and including critical commentaries and notes, constitutes a major contribution toward the reevaluation of Caldas Barbosa and his work. Besides being the second time since 1777 that the poem has been published as a special volume, the accompanying critical and historical explanation and updated bibliography will allow scholars to learn from Caldas's own words about his experiences in Portugal, including the way he used his erudition, his kind manners, and his artistic talents to overcome discrimination and succeed as an artist in the Portuguese imperial society. Additionally, Caldas produced many plays that were performed in Lisbon during the last decades of the eighteenth century.[28] Some of the plays attributed to him, and that were performed in Lisbon in the last decade of the eighteenth century, include *Os viajantes ditosos*, *A Saloia namorada ou o remédio a casar*, *A vingança da cigana*, and *A escola dos ciosos*.

A Doença, a major poem that Caldas published twenty-two years prior to his *Viola de Lereno*, is a piece of art that paints a clear and vivid picture of the conflictive sociopolitical and economic context of the Portuguese empire and of the transhispanic context of the second half of the eighteenth century. The poem teaches us about the life of this Afro-Brazilian poet, his experiences in Brazil during his early years, and above all, the discrimination he endured during his first years in the metropole and the success he achieved there after being rescued from homelessness by a noble aristocratic family that offered him shelter and patronage. To this day, however, *A Doença* continues to be neglected by academia and unknown by readers and literary critics.

Published in 1777, *A Doença* is an important document that describes the Portuguese court society during the conflictive last decades of the eighteenth century, characterized by the death of King José I, followed by the ascension to the throne of the conservative Queen Maria I, and the firing of the famous prime minister José Sebastião Carvalho de Melo, a member of the new enlightened Portuguese society who became internationally known by his title, the Marquis of Pombal. During those politically convoluted times known as Viradeira, and following the death of his father in Brazil, Caldas Barbosa became a homeless beggar. To avoid succumbing to starvation, Caldas began to sing and play his rustic guitar in the streets of Lisbon and other major Portuguese cities. Between the lines of the poem one can perceive the discrimination and the mistreatment that Portuguese students at the University of Coimbra, and other inhabitants of the metropole, launched against the mulatto poet from Brazil. Through this autobiographical poem one can also detect that it was while Caldas wandered through Portugal singing lundus and modinhas in exchange for food that he was rescued by the brothers of Luiz de Vasconcelos e Sousa, who had learned to appreciate Brazilian popular music while serving as viceroy in Rio de Janeiro.

As indicated by the title and subtitle of the poem, *A Doença: Poema oferecido 'a Gratidão por Lereno Selinuntino da Arcádia de Roma / aliás D. C. B.*, the Brazilian poet reveals how he became forever grateful to the Vasconcelos e Sousa family for rescuing him from starvation and for protecting and promoting his talents among the circles of the Portuguese aristocracy and the members of the court society. Besides offering shelter to Caldas in his palace, Antonio de Vasconcelos, recognizing Caldas's erudition and literary talents, appointed him as chair of the Arcádia de Roma, the most prestigious Portuguese imperial literary academy of the eighteenth century.

In the poem, Caldas follows the classical tradition and rules of epic poems. He includes in his epic poem an array of mythological figures, as one sees in poems such as the *Aeneid* by Virgil and *Os Lusíadas* by Camões. Following the epic model, the poet opts for poetic verses of twelve syllables and divides the poem into "cantos." Caldas also follows the canonic model of the epic poem that includes a "Proposition," an "Invocation," a "Dedication," and a "Narrative" that begins in canto 3 in medias res.[29]

In canto 1, the poetic voice tells how Fate sought to punish the Vasconceloses through Caldas. It describes the good and protected life he enjoyed in the palace of the Vasconcelos family and among the powerful Portuguese noble families (around 1775–1776) and the vengeance that an infuriated Fortune launched against the Vasconcelos family for breaking the established social rules and hierarchies of the Portuguese imperial society by protecting a mulatto from Brazil. Fortune's punishment is a disease that materializes as a gross and horrible tumor that appears on the poet's back shoulder. Using the third person singular, he introduces himself as the protagonist who became victim of the envious and revengeful Fortune. He appeals to the reader's compassion:

> Se houver algum mortal que possa tanto
> Que ouvindo a minha voz reprima o pranto,
> Aplique o duro coração e ouvidos
> E ouvirá nos meus versos meus gemidos,
> Os tristíssimos ais e altos clamores,
> As duras aflições e agudas dores
> Que o miserável Caldas suportara
> Até que destra mão destrói, separa
> Com apressado e horroroso corte
> Grosso tumor que lhe ameaça a morte.[30]

> *If there be any mortal so stone-hearted*
> *That hearing my voice, represses his tears,*
> *Let him apply his heart and his ears*
> *And in my verses my cries he'll hear,*
> *The saddest sighs and the loud weeping,*
> *The terrible hardship and acute pain*
> *That miserable Caldas endured,*
> *Until a skilled hand, with a swift*
> *And hideous cut, destroyed, separated*
> *The gross tumor that threatened his life.*

In canto 2 we find information about Caldas's illness and the remedies sought by the Vasconcelos family to cure him. Canto 3 consists of the beginning of the narrative that describes the reasons that led Caldas to move from Brazil to Portugal. This in medias res part of the poem is a fascinating narrative that shows his love for Brazil, which the poetic voice describes as a happy and bright place "where Phoebe burns brighter." In this section one also learns about his transatlantic voyage, his first impression of Lisbon, and what happened to him upon his arrival in the Coimbra, including his father's death and the discrimination he suffered in Coimbra and everywhere in the metropole:

> Apenas se publica e se divulga
> A triste morte de meu Pai, se julga

(E acaso se acertou) que esta orfandade
Me poria em cruel necessidade
De depender dos mais, e dependente
Pouco me estima a orgulhosa gente.
Mendigo sempre, aflito e desgraçado,
De uns iludido, de outros procurado
E dos mesmos deixado frouxamente,
Vi a inconstância da mundana gente.[31]

As soon as my father's death
Became publicly known, all thought
(Perhaps rightly) that orphanhood
Would land me in cruel need
Of depending on others and as a dependent
By all the proud people I was judged.
Always a beggar, afflicted and unfortunate,
By some avoided, by others sought
And by the same very easily abandoned,
I saw the inconstancy of frivolous mortals.

Pelos campos que lava o bom Mondego,[32]
Sem certo asilo ter, sem ter sossego,
Errava vagabundo: quando um dia
Figura enorme a encontro me saía
De eriçado cabelo e acesos olhos
E de escarnadas faces que os abrolhos
Co'a famulenta boca devorava
Nem se sustinha, pelo chão rojava.[33]
Sobressaltei-me ao ver a dura fome
Que eu conhecia por figura e nome:
Três vezes quis soltar bramido fero
E fraca apenas disse: 'espero, espero . . .'
Quando quis escapar-lhe já me via
Seguro pela mão mirrada e fria.[34]

Through the fields washed by the Mondego,
Without certain roof, without rest,
I wandered as a beggar: when one day

> And enormous figure came my way,
> It had raised hair and burning eyes
> And a fleshless face and with its famished
> Mouth it devoured boulders,
> Though they did not sustain it,
> And so it crawled on the ground.
> I was stunned to see hard Hunger,
> Whom I knew in form and name:
> Thrice I tried to cry a loud scream
> And weakly only said: 'I still hope . . .'
> When I wanted to escape, I was already
> Secured by its bony and cold hand.

In canto 4 Caldas tells how an enlightened and skilled Brazilian surgeon cured him, a true medical breakthrough in eighteenth-century Portugal. The poet explains how the surgery helped him to regain his health, his voice, and his artistic talents as a poet and singer:

> A sábia experiência e arte ajudam,
> Não tarda tempo algum que não lhe acudam:
> Ela ilumina a mente e arma o braço.
> Nada então demora, em breve espaço
> Cortante bisturi na pele entranha
> Que separa do corpo a massa estranha.[35]

> His experience and his art,
> Are always there to help:
> She lights his mind and guides his hand.[36]
> No time is lost, in a brief moment
> The sharp scalpel enters the flesh
> Extracting the strange mass.

> A amizade, a saúde e arte
> Rodeiam duma parte e doutra parte
> Ao assustado Caldas: vai dispondo,
> Uma o ânimo, as outras vão compondo
> Os turbados humores: a doença
> Nas fuscas asas pelo ar suspensa

Se alonga mais e mais de junto ao leito.
Entra a alegria a habitar no peito
Donde os sustos e dores o expulsaram
Que também c'oa doença aos ar voaram.
Voz sonora outra vez sai da garganta
E ao som da doce Lira o Caldas canta
Nome dos Protetores e do amigo
Que o socorreram no maior perigo.
Piedade dos Ilustres Protetores,
Tu és digna de altíssimos louvores:
Sábio e destro Martins o Céu te ajude,
Tu seguras ao Caldas a saúde.[37]

Friendship, Health, and Art
On one side and the other, frightened
Caldas surround: one consoles
His spirit, the other restores
The disturbed humors: Malady
On dark wings, in space suspended,
Retreats farther and farther from the bed.
Joy enters to dwell in the bosom
Whence fright and pain expelled it,
Who, with Malady, took to the air.
A sonorous voice once more issues from his throat
And to the music of the sweet lyre Caldas sings
The name of his Protectors and his friend,
Who saved him from greatest danger.
Generosity of the Illustrious Protectors,
Thou art worthy of highest praise:
Wise and skilled Martins, may Heaven help thee,
For thou restored Caldas to health.

Through my studies of Caldas Barbosa's works, including *Viola de Lereno* and the poem *A Doença*, I make a case for resituating this Afro-Brazilian figure within the literary and artistic history of Brazil. My concern for Caldas Barbosa's case stems from the lamentable fact that despite the relevance of his writings for understanding Portuguese imperial society and the struggles colonial subjects of mixed race and dark skin color confronted in the metropole, Portuguese academics ignore him, and some Brazilian historiographers persist in portraying the poet from Rio de Janeiro in a distorted light.[38] Though unknown or misunderstood by many literary critics who have written about him, Caldas Barbosa's verses influenced Portuguese court society and opened a lasting space in Portugal as well as in Brazil for Afro-Brazilian music, literature, and culture. To strengthen my argument, I have carried out a close reading of *A Doença*, which underscores how he not only embraced Afro-Brazilian cultural traditions but also sought strategies for psychological survival in the hierarchized and racialized Lusitanian court society. I claim that Caldas Barbosa's poetic talents and personal qualities mark a watershed in the emergence and affirmation of Black culture and literature in both Portugal and Brazil.

Fortunately, the recent works by José Ramos Tinhorão, Luiza Sawaya, and other Brazilian and Portuguese scholars mentioned above, and the recent analysis of *A Doença* by Fernando Morato and Miguel Valerio under my guidance, are helping to bring more attention to the literary and artistic production of this creative poet and talented musician from Rio de Janeiro. Outside Brazil, only a few critics have written about Caldas Barbosa and his poetry. In the United States, Jane Malinoff seems to have been one of the first scholars to recognize the importance of his work.[39] Perhaps inspired by critics such as Roger Bastide, who sees Caldas Barbosa as "o primeiro poeta afro-brasileiro" (the first Afro-Brazilian poet), Malinoff embarked on a serious scholarly study of Caldas Barbosa and makes a convincing case that the modinhas and lundus (the latter being songs of African origin) brought together in *Viola de Lereno* constitute "the earliest articulations of a genuine Brazilian sensibility in a colonial literature largely characterized by uninspired imitations of models from the mother country" (195). She believes that Caldas Barbosa was the first to translate "Afro-Brazilian speech pattern and rhythms into the lyrics of his lundus" and that he was the creator of "an essentially separate black poetry which held great appeal for the audience of his day."

In her analysis Malinoff concludes that "the black worldview which takes shape in the earthy realism of his lundus makes these delightful songs of courtship and love-play the first examples of an authentic Afro-Brazilian literature." Apart from the poems that have *lundu* or *lundum*, from Angola's Kimbundu language, in their titles, such as "Lundum das cantigas vagas" (Lundum of undetermined melodic stories) and "Lundu em louvor de uma brasileira adotiva" (Lundu in praise of an adoptive Brazilian woman), which she considers to be a literary milestone in Afro-Brazlian poetry, Malinoff also elaborates on the negative perception that some envious Portuguese contemporaries of Caldas Barbosa, such as writers Manuel Maria du Bocage and Filinto Elysio, directed at the Afro-Brazilian poet.

Upon reflecting on the insults and such pejorative nicknames as *Bode* (Goat), *Neto da Rainha Ginga* (Grandson of Queen Nzgingha), *Orpheu de Carapinha* (Kinky-hair Orpheus), *Crespo Arion* (Nappy-hair Arion), and *Negro Peru* (Black Turkey), which Bocage and Elysio used to refer to Caldas Barbosa, Malinoff states: "If the Afro-Brazilian poet had ever been deluded by his fame as a minstrel into thinking that he was truly accepted in society, his illusions were shattered by the racist barbs of Bocage" (196).

If Malinoff had read some of the recent critical and biographical studies about Caldas Barbosa, she would have realized that he, in fact, never felt "truly accepted" in Portuguese society. It is quite possible that "the racist barbs of Bocage" hurt his feelings, but it is unlikely that "his illusions were shattered." Because he was a very intelligent Brazilian mulatto who had experienced discrimination and marginalization in the metropole since his first days as a student in Coimbra, he must have been fully aware of the fact that as a man of color he would be constantly confronted with the empire's racialized politics. The racist attacks that the metropolitan writers Elysio and Bocage directed at Caldas Barbosa illustrate Jerome Branche's argument about the existential challenges that colonial subjects faced in Spain and Portugal. As a Brazilian mulatto, "marginalized by space and race" in Portuguese imperial society, Caldas likely understood that the offensive insults by Bocage, Filinto Elysio, and other racist individuals of the time were part of these challenges.[40] Perhaps if Malinoff had had the opportunity to read Caldas Barbosa's autobiographical poem, *A Doença*, she would have seen that the mulatto poet did not feel deluded by his fame. In this poem Caldas clearly shows that he never thought that he was "truly accepted" in Lisbon society.

In *A Doença*'s canto 3, for example, the poet describes the discrimination and sufferings he endured during the first years of his arrival in Portugal. After his father's death in 1764, Caldas Barbosa was forced to abandon his studies at the University of Coimbra and become an indigent in the capital of the Portuguese empire. In the following lines he expresses his anguish: "Apenas se publica, e se divulga / A triste morte de meu Pai, [. . .] esta orfandade / Me poria em cruel necessidade" (As soon as my father's death / Became publicly known, [. . .] all thought / (Perhaps rightly) that orphanhood / Would land me in cruel need). In many parts of his autobiographical poem he uses the adjective *soberba* (haughty) and *vaidosa* (vainglorious) to describe Lisbon. Referring to Lisbon's inhabitants, he writes: "Pouco me estima a orgulhosa gente" (I am held in little esteem by such vainglorious people). In Coimbra and Porto, two other major cities of Portugal, he also experienced discrimination, hunger, and homelessness: "Pelos campos que lava o bom Mondego, / Sem certo asilo ter, sem ter sossego, / Errava vagabundo" (Through the fields washed by the Mondego, / Without certain roof, without rest, / I wandered as a beggar).[41]

These verses show that, following the strategy for psychological survival that marks the emergence of Black culture and literature, to escape hunger and homelessness the mulatto Caldas embraced Afro-Brazilian traditions. In his wanderings through Portugal, he decided to play his rustic guitar and improvise songs with African words and rhythms that he had learned in Brazil: "Valeu-me o Dom de Phebo, fui ouvido / Fez-me ser estimado, e aplaudido / E nas margens do Cavado, e do Lima / Eu vivi do louvor da minha Rima" (The gift of Phebo inspired me, and I was heard / He allowed me to be appreciated and applauded / And on the banks of the Cavado and Lima rivers / I lived from the praises of my rhyme).[42] The popular verses that he improvised and sang with the accompaniment of his rustic guitar helped Caldas Barbosa to survive and to receive the protection from the Counts of Pombeiro: "Mudei o humilde tom de desgraçado / E como não pedia, era escutado" (I altered the humble tone of a disgraced person, / And since I was not begging, I was heard).[43] It was only when he embraced the happy tunes of popular African tradition that Caldas Barbosa escaped his miseries and attracted the attention of a Portuguese count. It was under the patronage of José and Luis de Vasconcelos that the Afro-Brazilian poet was introduced to the court of Queen Maria I.

The fact that Caldas Barbosa relied on his Afro-Brazilian experience to escape hunger corroborates Heloisa Toller's point of view that oral and written expressions of Afro-Brazilian literature and culture were born under circumstances of repression and social tension.[44] Nevertheless, despite suffering discrimination the poet and singer from Rio de Janeiro was able to take advantage of his talents to transform the environment that surrounded him. While his autobiographical poem *A Doença* allows us to see that his embracing of the Afro-Brazilian culture occurred at a time when he was facing misfortune and illness, verses written after he found health and protection also reveal that his affirmation of Afro-Brazilian culture never faded. This can be illustrated with the poem "Lundú em louvor de uma brasileira adotiva," published in his *Viola de Lereno*, which describes the seductive effect that his lundus and modinhas had on the people of Lisbon. The composition depicts a Portuguese woman who, charmed by the poet's song, becomes an "adoptive Brazilian" capable of moving her body and dancing like a Brazilian woman, probably a mulatto one:

> Uns olhos assim voltados,
> Cabeça inclinada assim,
> Os passinhos assim dados
> Que vem entender com mim.
> Ai! Companheiro,
> Não será ou sim será,
> O jeitinho é Brasileiro.
> Quem me havia de dizer,
> Mas a coisa é verdadeira;
> Que Lisboa produziu
> Uma Linda Brasileira.[45]

> *Eyes thus turned gazing,*
> *Head thus inclined,*
> *Steps thus taken*
> *He comes to communicate with me.*
> *Oh! Companion,*
> *It cannot be or yes it will be,*
> *The moves are those of a Brazilian.*
> *Who could have told me?*
> *But it is true;*
> *That Lisbon produced*
> *A Pretty Brazilian Woman.*

In the poem, even the Tagus, Lisbon's major river, could not resist the seductive rhythm of the lundu: "Eu vi correndo hoje o Tejo, / Vinha soberbo, e vaidoso; / Só por ter nas suas margens / O meigo Lundum gostoso" (Today I saw the Tagus flowing, / It did so proudly, and flauntingly; / Only because on its banks it had / The pleasingly gentle Lundum).[46] In addition to his verse, another illustrative example of Caldas Barbosa's cleverness is the fact that he appropriated and rendered innocuous the negative epithets such as *orangotango* (orangutang), *Orfeu de carapinha* (Kinky-haired Orpheus), *bode* (goat), *chusma Americana* (American riffraff), with which envious Portuguese writers characterized him and other Brazilian mulattos. These and many other examples found throughout Caldas Barbosa's compositions show that he embraced his African color and heritage in the realm of an emerging Afro-Brazilian literature.

Literary and historical documents written in Lisbon at that time reveal that Caldas Barbosa's modinhas and lundus had a profound impact in all sectors of Portuguese society. The comments written in 1796 by Antonio Ribeiro dos Santos, a member of the Portuguese elite who became the first director of the Biblioteca Nacional de Lisboa, may clarify my argument: "[S]ó se ouvem cantigas amorosas [. . .] Isto é com que embalam as crianças; o que ensinam aos meninos; o que cantam os moços, e o que trazem na boca donas e donzelas" (Nowadays you only hear amorous songs. . . . It is with them that babies are being rocked to sleep; that the children are being taught; that the youth is singing, and that married and single women bring in their mouths).[47] In a gesture of reprimand and in a tone of sarcasm Ribeiro dos Santos continues:

> Que grandes máximas de modéstia, de temperança e de virtudes se aprendem nestas Canções! Esta praga é hoje geral depois que o Caldas começou de pôr em uso os seus romances, e de versejar para as mulheres. Eu não conheço um poeta mais prejudicial à educação particular e pública do que este trovador de Venus e de Cupido: a tafularia do amor, a meiguice do Brasil, e em geral a moleza Americana [. . .] encantam com venenosos philtros a phantasia dos moços e o coração das Damas.[48]
>
> *What great maxims of modesty, of temperance and virtues they are learning in these songs! This plague is today general after Caldas began to make use of his rhymes and to compose verse directed at women. I know of no poet more harmful to the private and public education than this troubadour of Venus and Cupid: the nonsense of love, the sweetness of Brazil, and in general the American softness . . . enchant with their poisonous filters the fantasy and the heart of the ladies.*

These derogatory comments made by Ribeiro Santos demonstrate that despite the prejudice that Caldas Barbosa suffered in Portugal, which a few times caused him to lament the fact that he was born with dark skin, he overcame anguish and frustration and eventually succeeded in transforming the metropolitan society into a space where the elite class began to incorporate elements of the African and Afro-Brazilian culture into their daily routine, as well as into their artistic and literary expressions. By operating within the aristocratic circle, a social sector that in principle was hostile to popular culture, the mulatto poet from Brazil succeeded as a cultural negotiator.

At a time when philosophers such as Hegel and scientists such as Linnaeus were portraying Africa and Blacks in a negative light, Caldas Barbosa was able to use his talent as a minstrel or *griot* to introduce in the European court society influential aspects of the African and Afro-Brazilian culture.

Conclusion

As a brief way to conclude this comparative study about Gregório de Matos and Domingos Caldas Barbosa, two formerly colonized Brazilian writers who faced discrimination and marginalization within the larger context of the Portuguese empire, I would like to refer again to Branche's exhortation that we: "reveal how empire works in the creation of social relations and racialized identities, especially those relating to diasporan Blackness."[49] As one can see in this study, the two writers analyzed in this chapter are examples of "racialized identities" created by the Portuguese empire. Both Gregório de Matos and Domingos Caldas Barbosa were born in Brazil, but because the Portuguese monarchs did not allow universities in the colonies, they had to migrate to the metropole in order to pursue university studies and find better opportunities in the center of the empire. As diasporic colonial subjects, they both experienced discrimination and marginalization in the metropole due to their linguistic skills and physical appearances.

Despite the fact that Gregório de Matos was the son of White Portuguese parents, because he was born in Brazil, a place that was associated with Africa in the social imaginary of the metropolitan people, the Bahian satirist was racially classified as a mazombo, or a person of dark complexion and bad character. In addition to being born in Brazil, Caldas Barbosa was a dark-skinned mulatto, so the discrimination that he confronted in eighteenth-century Portuguese imperial society proved to be an even more intense "existential challenge" than the prejudices experienced by Gregório de Matos in the seventeenth century.

Caldas Barbosa's autobiographical poem *A Doença*, still unknown by scholars in the fields of Iberian, Lusophone, and Afro-Brazilian studies, is one of the best examples of literary texts produced by an eighteenth-century Afro-Brazilian writer. Besides documenting the poet's "existential challenges" and his strategies for survival in the Portuguese imperial society, this epic poem, the title of which translates in English as "disease" or "malady," offers insights toward the understanding of the "'longue durée' of modern raciology and its effects on Black diasporan subjectivity during and after the Iberian empires."⁵⁰

NOTES

1. Jerome C. Branche. Excerpted from the invitation to the symposium "Empire and its Aftermath: Transhispanic Dialogues on Diaspora," which took place on April 4–6, 2019, at the University of Pittsburgh. With the forgoing excerpt in mind, I intend to discuss in this chapter the extent to which Gregorio de Matos and Domingo Caldas Barbosa confronted as writers the existential challenges Branche highlights.
2. See Gregório de Matos, *Obras Completas de Gregório de Matos*, ed. J. Amado (Salvador: Janaína, 1969). Although some critics do not regard this collection as a very reliable source because of the lack of evidence that the poems found in the codices were written by De Matos, most of the poems cited in this chapter are found in the special edition published by James Amado. In fact, he considers his edition as an extra codex of Gregorio de Matos's works.

   Besides James Amado's edition, I also cite a few poems found in anthologies published by José Miguel Wisnik and other contemporary critics. See Gregório de Matos, *Poemas escolhidos. Introdução de José Miguel Wisnik* (São Paulo: Cultrix, 1971).
3. Lúcia Helen Costigan, *A sátira e o intellectual criollo na colônia: Gregório de Matos e Juan del Valle y Caviedes* (Lima-Pittsburgh: Latinoamericana editores, 1991).
4. This is based on the theory put forward by the Brazilian Modernist Oswald de Andrade in his *Manifesto Antropofágico*, which argues that Brazilian literature and culture are both similar to and different from that of Europe, because the one has ingested and assimilated the other, thus becoming stronger, in a process that is similar to that of the country's first inhabitants, who ate the Europeans, not necessarily as an act of cannibalism, but in order to become stronger by assimilating them. Haroldo de Campos thus defends the thesis that Gregorio de Matos can be considered the first "anthrophogous" Brazilian, because he was able to combine the different elements of the European baroque to create a new and miscegenated poetic language that expressed the cultural melting pot of seventeenth-century tropical Brazil. For additional information about his thesis, see De Campos, *A arte no horizonte do provável* (São Paulo: Perspectiva, 2010).
5. Gregório de Matos, *Obras Completas de Gregório de Matos*, 173. This, and the translations of the poems that follow, are mine.
6. *Mazombo*, a word from the African Kimbundo language, was used by the inhabitants of Portugal to refer to a White person of Lusitanian origin born in Brazil and other marginal spaces of the Portuguese empire. Similar to the case of White Spaniards

who were born in the Spanish American colonies, the term *criollo*, derived from the Portuguese word *crioulo*, was adopted by Peninsular Spaniards to refer to descendants of Castilians born in the Americas. During the colonial period, the terms *mazombo* and *criollo* carried a negative associated White descendants of settlers from the Iberian Peninsula with Africa and with Blacks.

7. Gregório de Matos, *Obras Completas de Gregório de Matos*, 185.
8. See Caio Prado Jr., *História econômica do Brasil* (n.p.: Editora Brasiliense, 1945).
9. Rae Flory and David Grant Smith, "Bahian Merchants and Planters in the Seventeenth and Eighteenth Centuries," *Hispanic American Historical Review* 58, no. 4, (1978): 571–94.
10. Gregório de Matos, *Obras Completas de Gregório de Matos*, 428.
11. Ibid.
12. Ibid., 3.
13. Ibid., 460–70.
14. Ibid., 234.
15. Ibid., 170–71.
16. In Romero's words, "Gregório de Matos é a mais perfeita encarnação do espírito brasileiro" (Gregório de Matos is the most perfect example of the Brazilian spirit). Sílvio Romero, *Historia da literatura brasileira*, vol. 2, 3rd ed. (Rio de Janeiro: José Olympio [1888], 1943), 31.
17. José Veríssimo, *História da literatura brasileira* (Rio de Janeiro: Editora Record, [1915] 1998).
18. Initiated by the brothers Haroldo and Augusto de Campos and by Décio Pignatary around the middle of the twentieth century in Brazil, a time of the innovative, abstract architecture of Oscar Niemeyer as expressed in Brasilia, the new capital city of the country, the Movimento de Poesia Concreta blossomed. Besides putting emphasis on the ability to translate abstract ideas into visual images and encouraging creativity in all artistic forms, including architecture, graphic design, sounds and visual elements of the word, the Campos brothers and Décio Pignatari also took advantage of the ideas and manifestos that appeared in São Paulo during the Semana de Arte Moderna (Week of Modern Art) of April 22, 1922, the centenary of Brazil's independence from Portugal in 1822. Due perhaps to the fact that some of the participants of Brazil's Modernist movement recognized the dissident and creative aspects of Gregório de Matos's satirical poetry, including the playful aspect of his words in his verses, the brothers Augusto and Haroldo de Campos regard Gregório de Matos as a "concretista" avant-la-lettre. For additional information on this topic, see Gonzalo Moisés Aguilar, *Poesia concreta brasileira: As vanguardas na encruzilhada modernista* (São Paulo: EDUSP, 2005).
19. Gregório de Matos, *Obras Completas de Gregório de Matos*, 1 (my translation).
20. See José Wisnik's preface to *Poemas escolhidos de Gregório de Matos* (São Paulo: Companhia das Letras, 2010). Also the prologue to *Gregório de Matos. Obras Completas*, ed. J. Amado.
21. Gonzalo Aguilar, *Gregório de Matos: Sátiras y otras maledicencias: Antologia del poeta conocido como "Boca del Infierno,"* ed. G. Aguilar and J. N. Terranova (Buenos Aires: Editora Corregidor, 2001).

22. Gregório de Matos, *Obras Completas de Gregório de Matos*, 581.
23. Gregório de Matos, *Obra poética*, ed. James Amado (Rio de Janeiro: Editora Record, 1990). See the introduction by Emanuel Araújo.
24. The capital of Brazil was moved in 1776 from Salvador da Bahia to the city of Rio de Janeiro, and Luiz de Vasconcelos was sent as viceroy to Rio, where he lived from 1778 to 1790.
25. For detailed information about the prejudices Caldas Barbosa endured in Portugal, and the racist attacks that Bocage and F. Elysio directed at him, see the introductory critical study found in *Domingos Caldas Barbosa, A Doença*, organized and introduced by Lúcia Costigan and Fernando Morato (São Paulo: Editora 34, 2018).
26. José Veríssimo, *História da literatura brasileira*, 133.
27. José Ramos Tinhorão, *Domingos Caldas Barbosa: O poeta da viola, da modinha e do lundo (1700–1800)* (São Paulo: Editrora 34, 2004) underscores Caldas Barbosa's intelligence and creativity and recognizes Caldas as the artist who transformed the lundo and the modinha, two musical genres practiced by Afro-Brazilians, into widely popular styles of dance and song accepted by Brazilians of different races and social backgrounds. Prior to the publication of Tinhorão's book, Adrianna de Campos Rennó had already called attention to the innovative and creative qualities of Barbosa's work in her book *Violando as Regras: Uma releitura de Caldas Barbosa* (São Paulo: Editora Arte e Ciência, 1999). Luiza Sawaya, *Domingos Caldas Barbosa: Herdeiro de Horácio* (Lisboa: Esfera do Caos, 2015) notes that besides writing about popular Brazilian verses and songs, Caldas Barbosa also produced classical Renaissance poetry. See also the Costigan and Morato edition mentioned above.
28. As a result of a graduate seminar on imperial/colonial literature and culture of the Lusophone and Luso-Hispanic world that I taught at the Ohio State University, and which included Caldas Barbosa's poem in the syllabus, Fernando Lima e Morato and Miguel Valerio, two former graduate students who enrolled in the seminar, have embarked with me on a scholarly project that involves an English translation of the poem. We expect to publish this project as a book sometime soon.
29. Caldas Barbosa begins the narrative with a "Proposição" (vv. 1–10), where he explains to the reader the poem's theme, followed by the "Invocação" (vv.11–18), where the poet invokes the deities' help in accomplishing his proposed task; the "Dedicatória" (vv. 19–32) is another major aspect of the poem, because here he dedicates his work to an important figure. Only then does the poet begin the Narration.
30. Domingos Caldas Barbosa, *A Doença*, 45.
31. Ibid., 76–77.
32. Reference to the lands around the city of Coimbra washed by the Mondego River.
33. Allegorical representation of Hunger.
34. Domingos Caldas Barbosa, *A Doença*, 84.
35. Ibid., 87–88.
36. "She" in the line refers to medicine, Martins' art.
37. Ibid., 102–3.
38. I would like to thank my colleague Isis Barra-Costa for reading a preliminary version of this chapter and for sharing her forthcoming article "Other Forests: The

Afro-Brazilian Literary Archive." Dawson's concept of "Deficit Model," she challenges the opinion expressed by some racialized critics "that #BlackWritingMatters: Literary Interventions in the Afro-Américas (1959-Present).

39. See Jane McDivitt Malinoff, "Domingos Caldas Barbosa: Afro-Brazilian Poet at the Court of Dona Maria I," in *From Linguistics to Literature: Romance Studies Offered to Francis M. Rogers*, ed. B. H. Bichakgan (Amsterdam: John Benjamins, 1981), 195–204.
40. In José Ramos Tinhorão, *Domingos Caldas Barbosa*, the author states that Caldas Barbosa had always been a kind person with a generous heart. He also suggests that Caldas Barbosa did not protest against Bocage's and Elysio's offensive and aggressive insults because he was a gentleman with a noble character. I agree that Caldas seems to have been a very intelligent, amicable, and generous person. However, I believe that the poet knew that, since he was a Brazilian-born mulatto, nobody in Portugal would defend him against a White person's insults.
41. Domingos Caldas Barbosa, *A Doença*, 37.
42. Ibid., 38
43. Ibid., 39.
44. Heloisa Toller Gomes, "Afro-Brazilian Literature: Spaces Conquered, Spaces In-between," in "Lusophone African and Afro-Brazilian Literatures," special issue, ed. Lúcia Helena Costigan and Russel Hamilton, *Research in African Literatures* 38, no. 1 (2007): 152–62.
45. Caldas Barbosa, *Viola de Lereno*, ed. A. Barbosa and S. Valença (Rio de Janeiro: Civilização Brasileira / Instituto Nacional do Livro, [1798] 1980), 278.
46. Ibid.
47. Quoted in José Ramos Tinhorão, *Domingos Caldas Barbosa*, 171.
48. Ibid.
49. Jerome C. Branche, "Empire and Its Aftermath," accessed May 12, 2021, www.hispanic.pitt.edu/events/empire-and-its-aftermath.
50. Ibid.

CHAPTER 8

Silences and the Corporeal

The Enslaved Body in (Historical) Pain

CASSIA ROTH

In 1845, an enslaved woman named Ignacia went into labor in the city of Rio de Janeiro, Brazil. Her owner called a physician who later published the clinical report of Ignacia's delivery in the country's leading medical journal, the *Annaes de Medicina Brasiliense* (Annals of Brazilian Medicine).[1] According to the physician, Ignacia had carried her pregnancy to term, and at around four o'clock in the afternoon of August 16, she began to experience contractions. Ignacia gave birth to a daughter one hour later. The short span between contractions and birth demonstrates that Ignacia probably went into labor earlier in the day or during the night before, but her owner only called a physician late in the delivery (a common practice for women of all races and classes in nineteenth-century Brazil).

After Ignacia gave birth, the newborn girl was "picked up by another Black woman [*preta*] who followed the parturient [Ignacia] to the bedroom, where a bed was prepared."[2] Nevertheless, Ignacia did not expel the placenta, and "the uterus remained very voluminous." The physician realized that Ignacia was delivering twins, but as the second infant was not crowning, he felt it "prudent to leave things as they were." Several hours later, around 9:00 p.m., the physician returned, just in time for Ignacia to deliver her second and, to everyone's surprise, third infant, both boys. In his clinical report, the obstetrician noted only in passing that all three newborns died during the night. Although Ignacia initially recovered from the delivery, four days later, "without appreciable cause," she began suffering from a uterine infection. The obstetrician most likely had caused the puerperal infection. Between the delivery of her first and second infants, he had performed an internal manual exam, and it was likely he had not washed his hands. He was practicing medicine in the 1840s—before the medical profession understood the nature of infections and adopted antisepsis and asepsis practices.[3]

This chapter explores enslaved women's reproductive experiences like that of Ignacia's in nineteenth-century Rio de Janeiro city and province—an important coffee-producing region and economic center and then Brazil's capital and largest city. The city was also home to the country's first national medical association, the Imperial Academy of Medicine (Academia Imperial de Medicina), founded in 1829 as the Society of Medicine of Rio de Janeiro (Sociedade de Medicina do Rio de Janeiro; it changed names in 1835), and one of the country's only two medical schools (the other was located in the northeastern city of Salvador da Bahia). Thus, many of the country's leading physicians trained and practiced in the city and surrounding province. Their published reports provide a valuable source for understanding the medical treatment available to and practiced on enslaved people in both urban and rural areas in nineteenth-century Brazil. This included gynecologic, obstetric, and maternal-infant health care.

But these experiences are difficult, if not impossible, to access. Ignacia's labor and delivery are a case in point. Did it come as a surprise to Ignacia that she was delivering triplets? How did she experience the death of her three newborns, which the attending physician only mentioned in passing? How did it feel to survive a puerperal infection? Who was the father of her children? These are questions that the medical documentation does not answer. Through careful reading, however, we know that a physician only attended Ignacia late in the pregnancy, that another enslaved woman assisted during the delivery and thus perhaps accompanied her throughout her previous labor pains, and that Ignacia had her own bed at least for the postpartum recovery period. In the case of Ignacia, her owner cared enough about her health, the health of her children, or both to call a physician. Ignacia's life (and reproductive potential) was important enough to merit the cost of medical care.

Nonetheless, medical attention did not save the lives of Ignacia's newborns (and, in fact, the physician's intervention almost caused her death). Rather than being an anomaly, however, the death of Ignacia's triplets was the norm in nineteenth-century Brazil, a period when miscarriage, stillbirth, and infant mortality rates were elevated for all women but particularly among the enslaved population.[4] In Brazil, as in most Atlantic slave societies, the slave population was reproduced through imports and not natural growth, with some regional and temporal exceptions.[5] For Rio de Janeiro city and province, historians have argued that harsh labor regimes, disease, and sex imbalances were the main reasons for negative growth. In other words, mortality, not natality rates, were the most important factor.[6] Ignacia's tragic delivery highlights this point.

In Brazil, as in slave societies across the Americas, enslaved women's experiences with miscarriage, stillbirth, and infant death shaped how they viewed themselves as mothers, their partners, their living children, and their enslaved status. Their reproductive experiences are thus crucial in understanding the history of the institution across the hemisphere. Recently, historians have turned toward the history of emotions to analyze this complex topic.[7] Approaching the enslaved experience through the lens of emotions creates a space in which we can understand enslaved women as mothers, partners, and sisters.[8] This approach rejects an either/or approach that emphasizes resistance *or* submission; celebration *or* grief; courage *or* fear—it starts from a place of ambiguity and contradiction.

As Sasha Turner has demonstrated for Jamaica, for example, infant death shaped how enslaved women experienced and practiced motherhood, and this emotional toll "manifested [itself] in invisible scars." That is, the probability that most enslaved infants would not survive their infancy, rather than the joy of raising children, was the primary definer of enslaved motherhood. Turner found that in Jamaica, some enslaved women ignored or abandoned their offspring, which shielded them "from the vulnerability of the almost inevitable death of their children."[9] But this did not mean that enslaved women did not grieve the loss of their infants, even those they neglected for lack of ability to care for them. Mothering under slavery was a complex endeavor with contradictory emotions and actions coexisting within enslaved women's lives.[10] Did Ignacia feel relief that her infants did not survive childbirth, that they would not be enslaved? Did she feel grief? Perhaps she felt both.

The historiographical turn toward understanding the emotional history of slavery thus complicates past histories that have overemphasized either victimhood or resistance.[11] For example, the emotional reframes the debate over enslaved women and reproductive resistance—or the hypothesis that enslaved women purposefully practiced abortion and infanticide as acts of resistance.[12] By underscoring the traumatic context in which enslaved women labored productively and reproductively, we can imagine that an enslaved mother could both let her infant starve and grieve its death; could both search for familial ties through raising children and feel relief when she miscarried.[13]

In nineteenth-century Rio de Janeiro, for example, sources do not tell us if enslaved women's practices of fertility control had an impact on the negative biological growth of the enslaved population. Thus, it is important to not read resistance into a document simply because we want it to be there.[14] In Brazil, physicians and slave-owners considered the increase or decrease of the enslaved population's numbers within the framework of bondwomen's overall poor reproductive health. Elites referenced both enslaved women's calculated efforts to end pregnancy and their poor health, and the subject was present in public debate over the future of slavery.[15] As I have argued elsewhere, Brazilian enslaved women's alleged practices of abortion and infanticide played an important *symbolic role* in how elites and the enslaved understood and approached slavery and abolition itself. Disparate actors with varying goals used the specter of reproductive resistance to justify their position.[16] In this sense, this stereotype worked to empower both slave-owners and abolitionist elites as it furthered their respective projects of power.[17] The possibility of enslaved women's fertility control played a central role in debates about Brazilian slavery, which demonstrates the power enslaved women had in shaping their own future, the future of their children, and the end of the institution of slavery.

This chapter builds upon the emotional history of slavery to look at a more material reality: physical pain. Medical sources emphasize the physical, often manifested in the experience of pain, and thus reading them brings a different question to the fore. How does the historian approach, analyze, and write about the experience of physical pain in history?[18] This chapter thus focuses on how we read historical sources in relation to this question, specifically, the reproductive pain of enslaved women. In medical documents detailing enslaved women's pregnancies, labors, and deliveries, bodily pain is a constant and prominent feature.

Enslaved women's physical reality, after all, was one of harsh labor regimes, torture, sickness, and exhaustion. I argue that in addition to the emotional, we must also bring their physical experience into the history of enslaved reproduction. I want to suggest two ways we can read dominant sources like medical reports for bondwomen's embodied experiences of the intensely physical (and emotional) events of pregnancy, miscarriage, and labor and delivery. The first involves reading the silences through comparison. Only by looking at how physicians treated White women, and then comparing that to their treatment of enslaved women, can we find the silences and absences that reveal the specific nature of the enslaved experience. The second method relates particularly to the history of pain. I suggest we employ what I call a practice of "corporeal reading" in that we operationalize our own physical reactions to the violence of the sources to study enslaved women's historical experience of pain. As a way of reading historical texts for the embodied subjects that those same documents often (or always) elide, this methodology expands upon the evidence provided by those in power, here physicians and slave-owners (often one and the same), thus decentralizing their telling of the past. It goes beyond the history of slavery and as a methodology applies to the study of the body more generally.

The Silence in the Documents

Marisa Fuentes, in her analysis of slavery, gender, and the archive, contends that enslaved women often only "emerge from the archives" through their interactions with violent power, which has left fragmentary mentions of their lives.[19] These fragments continue to constrain enslaved women's lives by dictating what we can know—and not know—about them. Scholars of the British Caribbean in particular have faced these problematic archives.[20] In Latin America, enslaved peoples had some level of personhood under the law and within the church, and thus they left a richer documentary history through court cases, wills and testaments, and baptismal and marriage records.[21] In relation to reproduction and slavery, scholars of the United States have found oral histories such as the WPA narratives helpful in understanding enslaved women's physical experiences while still noting that traditional medical sources are as fragmented and violent as they come.[22] In Brazil, where almost no oral histories of formerly enslaved peoples exist, medical reports, books, and dissertations—along with newspaper advertisements, plantation manuals, and hospital records—are some of the only sources available for historians of medicine.[23]

In response to this fragmentary reality, both literary scholars and historians have turned toward silence as an historical source in the field of slavery studies. Saidiya Hartman, for example, asks us to "listen to the unsaid," a practice for which Lamonte Aidoo argues requires that we be "willing to listen."[24] Ula Taylor broadens this out from one single document to the entire archive, asking us to pay attention to what she calls "archival voids."[25] Other scholars, however, have celebrated archival voids, arguing that the silences are an example of the success of those enslaved "fugitives" who escaped the violence of the archive of slavery.[26] Here, however, I contend that silences and voids perhaps tell us more than actual documentation does.

Thus, I propose that we read the silences in elite medical writings in the realm of pregnancy and childbirth. In relation to enslaved women's reproductive health, these erasures come into sharp focus when we compare clinical notes of White and Black patients. In the early to mid-nineteenth century, medical practitioners in Rio de Janeiro advised slave-owners to treat pregnant and postpartum enslaved women with less severity than they would otherwise.[27] For example, in 1857 one physician attended an unnamed enslaved woman who was miscarrying, and, as a result, hemorrhaging profusely. He managed to stop the bleeding with ergot (*ergotina*), a plant used in controlled doses both to induce abortions and to stop postpartum or post-miscarriage hemorrhaging. The physician then advised the enslaved woman to rest "for six or eight days," after which she could return to work.[28] In the case of another bondwoman who was hemorrhaging during a miscarriage, the same physician only required three days of rest, even though she was "already compromised by other sufferings."[29]

The physician detailed that these enslaved women should be allowed to rest after their miscarriages. But was it a general prescription, given to Black and White women, enslaved and free alike? Or was this specific to these women's enslaved condition? Here, we can compare this physician's approach toward the two enslaved patients to his care for a White married woman (*senhora*) who was also miscarrying. On the surface, it appears that the physician treated his patients the same. When Senhora D., married and already with two children, began miscarrying, the physician once again used ergot to stop the bleeding. However, after successfully treating the senhora, the physician did not explicitly prescribe rest as he did for his enslaved patients. It went without saying that this woman would have as much rest as she required.

The physician's description of his patients' pain also underscores his differential attitude. When discussing his treatment of the White senhora, the physician noted "the displeasure that such an uncomfortable state caused the sick woman." When he performed a manual exam on the senhora, she exhibited a "great sensitivity."[30] In his notes, the physician highlighted her embodied experience of the medical treatment; she felt sensitivity and pain, experiences that he supposedly took into account when treating her.

The physician also performed physical exams on his enslaved patients. And while he described the enslaved women's pain, he did so in a disembodied manner. For example, when he pressed on the abdomen of one enslaved woman, he noticed that "the hypogastric region was as if tense and with some sensitivity."[31] The physician *treated* his three patients similarly; he gave them similar doses of medicine and attended to their progress regularly. But the physician described the senhora as a *person* experiencing pain, while the enslaved women were merely sums of their (reproductive) body parts. As historian Dierdre Cooper Owens has found for gynecological practice in the antebellum United States, "gynecological operations were the same for black and white patients, even if the bedside manner and medical treatment differed because of racism."[32]

Although these voids in the medical documentation can provide clues to the enslaved experience of reproduction, they are still methodologically challenging.[33] Here, we do not know the enslaved women's names (although we also do not know the name of the senhora). We do not know their full life histories or if they went on to bear more children (and perhaps watch them die young or be forcibly removed from their care). But a careful comparison between enslaved and free White women actually shows us the power of the silences in historical methodology. We begin to see exactly how enslaved women of reproductive age had experiences very distinct from those of White women.

Corporeal Readings

Often, the callous manner in which the physician described his enslaved patient's pain could become total disregard. For example, in February of 1848, another prominent obstetrician wrote about the labor and delivery of thirty-five-year-old Felicidade, the domestic slave of his medical colleague. Felicidade had been pregnant various times, once with twins, and all but one of her pregnancies had resulted in miscarriages or stillbirths. Her only living infant had been born prematurely at seven months.

During this delivery, Felicidade was in painful labor for two days before she "committed the imprudent act of throwing herself onto her belly in desperation."[34] Only then did her owner feel it necessary to call his obstetric colleague. When the obstetrician arrived, he found Felicidade "unconscious" and with a weak pulse. He tried to extract the infant with forceps twice, with no luck. By that time, "as the Black woman [preta] had already expired," he delivered the stillborn infant. The obstetrician detailed the various causes of death, which included a ruptured uterus (from a prolonged labor), a small pelvis, and a fused lower lumbar vertebra. Perhaps unsurprisingly, he also cited one cause of both Felicidade's and her infant's death as "the wretched attitude and the violent force employed by the parturient during the birth, in particular the blow upon her belly."

While the report erases Felicidade's subjective, embodied experience, we still know that her owner (a physician) did not believe it necessary to call a doctor to attend to his slave's suffering until she had been in labor for nearly forty-eight hours. We also know that Felicidade suffered terrible pain during this delivery—pain that caused her to throw herself onto the ground in desperation. It appears that her owner disregarded her distress and that the attending physician refused to acknowledge, at least in his clinical notes, her embodied experience of pain. This is in part due to the sterile nature of medical reports, but as we saw, physicians did describe and acknowledge White women's pain.

Felicidade's pain pervades the archive—the source is at once only about her pain and a complete erasure of that physical experience. So how do we read this archival source that violently disregards Felicidade's pain? Archival studies scholars have questioned the underlying power structures that create the archive.[35] Now, we understand the archive as a "contact zone," one that requires scholars to examine our own place in recreating the violence of the past in our current research and writing.[36] The body takes center stage in this approach. Zeb Tortorici, for example, in his study of queer sexuality in colonial New Spain (current-day Mexico), argues that "textual imperial power . . . was enacted both on and through the body."[37] As Tortorici writes, the power inscribed upon the bodies of colonial subjects through the bureaucratic processes of colonial authorities, and the paperwork that resulted from the enactment of that power, maintained colonialism.

But part of centering the body in history requires an analysis of our own embodiment. Tortorici, for instance, asks us to think about both the "archiving and the writing of history as embodied practices."[38] One way to do that is to foreground the concept of viscerality. Tortorici is interested in viscerality at two moments: both when the act was inscribed into document form in the past and when we as scholars read that document in the present. Asking how a scribe's or denouncer's visceral reaction to, say, an interrupted act of necrophilia or anal penetration makes us consider how the act was inscribed in the first place, which shapes what we know of it today. Tortorici asks us to center "our own emotional responses" through the use of speculation, to "analyze how certain affects, in relation to some specific event in the past, can and do reverberate across individuals who are separated by place, time, and experience."[39] In the archives of slavery, perhaps we simply need to rethink our understandings of historical time, rejecting an idea of linear progress in which we are separated from the violence and power of the dehumanizing institution.[40]

In the realm of the archive, the context of studying slavery brings up a complicated problematic. How does one begin to mediate the experience of enslaved women in relation to physical pain? How does one do so in a manner that centers their embodied experience without verging on the voyeuristic and sensational? How does one make the body whole in an archive defined by silence and fragments? As Hartman asks: "How does one revisit the scene of subjection without replicating the grammar of violence?"[41]

Fragments do not mean we turn away. Despite the numerous erasures and silences in the documents on sexual violence in Brazilian slavery, for instance, Aidoo still finds "a vivid picture of extreme violence" and asks us to "validly wonder what more was left out."[42] Here, I ask if part of this "wondering," this "visceral reaction," involves including our own *physical* responses—the way we react to reading these sources. For what we are reading—punishment, torture, pain—is inherently physical, an embodied experience of violence.

My suggestion here introduces a second approach toward dealing with physicians' disregard for enslaved women's pain, what I call a corporeal reading. One way to do this is to draw upon, but never center, our physical reactions to violent obstetric interventions. For example, in an 1856 medical lecture, a physician discussed the case of one unnamed "Black woman [*preta*]."[43] During childbirth, a colleague had applied forceps so forcefully that he ruptured the woman's vagina and crushed her cervix, causing her death. To pause here, to sit with our immediate embodied reactions to how painful that must have been for that woman, is one approach toward subjective experience from a historical lens. This historical attempt at "embodied listening," in the words of anthropologist Lyndon K. Gill, considers the "contextualized subjectivity" of the historical actor in question while attending to the connected commonness of material bodies.[44] If, as literary scholar Gladys M. Francis argues, "The text becomes a device that stores embodied memories," a corporeal reading of those texts for the embodied memories that lie beneath is necessary.[45]

But this is dangerous territory—assuming you understand the physical experience of an enslaved woman. Are we reproducing the violence of their lives? Are we inappropriately centering our own experience? This method, if done carelessly, will further disembody the woman and sensationalize her pain. But I suggest that one way we can fight against this dehumanizing tendency is to listen to our physical understandings of what we are reading. Of course, our physical reactions are not those of Felicidade—or the millions of women who experienced the pain of slavery. But perhaps if we place our reactions within the realm of the "subjunctive and the rhetorical" we can incorporate them as another tool to approaching archival sources.[46]

Hartman asks us "How does one listen to for the groans and cries" in the historical documents on slavery and then "assign words to all of it?"[47] Or, are words even appropriate? Elaine Scarry has argued that "physical pain does not simply resist language but actively destroys it, bringing about an immediate reversion to a state anterior to language, to the sounds and cries a human being makes before language is learned." Scarry contends that when the person undergoing pain begins to come out of their physical experience and express their feelings in speech, it is almost "the birth of language itself."[48] But here, we do not even have Felicidade's own words or the words of the unnamed enslaved woman whose body was exploited for an anatomy class. We only know how slave-owning physicians described their experiences. If Felicidade, for example, dictated how she felt to her owner or the physician, they never listened. Felicidade was from the Cabinda nation, modern-day Angola. Perhaps she did not speak Portuguese. They certainly did not write her expressions down. Thus, the language we as historians have to work with is further filtered through how this White, male, enslaving physician believed Felicidade experienced pain. The language is not attached to Felicidade's body or mind.

I suggest here, then, that we can draw on our own embodied reactions when reading these sources because we cannot become desensitized to the historical experience of pain. Of course, we must acknowledge and foreground that our own physical reactions are distinct from those of the women (or men) we are studying. But our readings cannot ignore these experiences. In fact, bringing in the physical can provide a new way to look at historical evidence—one that centers the embodied experience of the historical subject *and* the scholar. It implicates us in this history of violence—our reading of the archives of slavery inevitably reproduces its violent nature, but instead of ignoring this fact, our physicality can mean we reject the artificial divide between "now" and "then" and the fake neutrality and objective nature of scholarly inquiry. It lays bare how we, just like the physicians who ignored Felicidade's pain, profit from that pain.

Racialized Medicine

The violent interventions that physicians practiced on pregnant enslaved women like Felicidade also require a deeper analysis of racialized medicine. Nineteenth-century Western obstetric medicine was a crude affair, with cesarean sections that almost always led to maternal death, fetal dismemberments in utero, and infection.[49] Physicians practiced invasive techniques on women of all colors. But slavery affected medical practice. Scholars have demonstrated that in nineteenth-century Rio de Janeiro, as in the United States and Jamaica, the bodies of enslaved and indigent women served as the training grounds for obstetricians.[50] Historian Lorena Telles argues, for example, that although childbirth was not a medical event in the first half of the nineteenth century in the city of Rio de Janeiro, obstetricians still practiced limited medical interventions on enslaved women at the behest of their owners. The cases of Ignacia and Felicidade demonstrate this trend. While physicians attempted to save the lives of enslaved women and their children, they also practiced rudimentary and painful treatments that they would not have used on upper-class White women.[51]

But both race and legal status mattered. While a physician might have viewed a free woman of color and an enslaved woman in a similar light, he only had unfettered access to the latter. For example, one physician's published clinical notes mentioned that he practiced his intervention—applying ergot to stop obstetric hemorrhage after a miscarriage—"on a slave woman who was in my house."[52] The fact that he wrote up his report as a case study in the leading medical journal further highlights how his access to her body, although saving her life, violated her bodily autonomy while furthering his own career. My findings thus confirm those of scholars of the Southern United States and the British and French Caribbean. Enslaved women's (and men's) bodies served as the training grounds for physicians, but Western medical practitioners did not necessarily experiment on Black bodies simply to advance scientific and medical knowledge.[53] The issue at stake was access—which bodies were available—and who had a say over the medical treatment.

But legal status was not the only factor in determining the care enslaved women received. Racist science still underpinned these treatments—and had direct implications for medical understandings of pain. Throughout the nineteenth century, Brazilian physicians, like their counterparts in slaveholding societies across the Americas, expressed racist views of both Africans and enslaved Blacks.[54] Brazilian physicians described women of African descent as closer to an alleged animalistic sexuality and nature.[55] For instance, in 1833 one medical student in Rio de Janeiro likened African women to animals in his discussion of their care for newborn infants. He noted how "the Hottentots, similar to mammiferous animals, not only cut the umbilical cord of their children with their teeth but also lick them for a long time."[56] The physician used the generic term "Africans" to refer to women living on the African continent before applying this reasoning to enslaved practices of mothering in Rio de Janeiro. In a medical dissertation published a few years later, another doctor-in-training discusses how various African tribes, while differing in their level of debauchery and savagery, all lived premature lives due to their licentious habits of selling their neighbors, engaging in promiscuous sexual activity, and succumbing to laziness.[57]

In the latter half of the century, physicians began arguing that the institution of slavery and not enslaved women's "inherent nature" erased their familial or maternal instincts. The problem was not any intrinsic racial inferiority but rather the institution of slavery itself. In 1857, a medical student asked, "Can the slave have love? No, because he cannot have a family, because he does not have a country, he does not have friends. There is no moral tie that binds him to society. Slavery, under its black mantle of iron suffocates honor, modesty, valor, virtue."[58] It was not an innate lack of morals and love that caused the brutality of the slave but enslavers' denial of those rights.[59] After all, how could abolitionists argue that enslaved people deserved freedom (and perhaps even citizenship) if there was a biological difference that made them "incapable" of achieving White civilization?

But the gradual shift from biological to social explanations was tempered by the rise of scientific racism in the late nineteenth century, which reinvigorated a biological position within the obstetric profession. Thus, even in the latter part of the century, when enslaved women were using their legal maternal identities to fight for the rights of their children in the courts, physicians continued to believe they were inherently "stupid" when it came to raising children.[60] On the eve of abolition, Brazilian obstetricians reiterated the dominant mode of scientific thought that Afro-descended peoples were closer on the evolutionary scale to animals than Europeans.[61]

Enslaved women's actions, on the other hand, demonstrate a different reality. As Camillia Cowling has shown, enslaved and freed women of color employed gendered discussions of motherhood to fight for their children in the courts in the decades leading up to abolition in Brazil.[62] While these women relied on discourses of women's traditional nurturing and maternal roles because these arguments would gain the most traction within the judicial system, the fact that they were fighting for their children's autonomy demonstrates that both their maternal identity and their children's wellbeing were central to their lives and worldviews.[63]

Racist science also purported that race affected the experience of pain. For example, Cooper Owens has demonstrated how, in the nineteenth-century Southern United States, White male physicians viewed enslaved Black women as "impervious to pain."[64] We have seen that Brazilian physicians' clinical practice throughout the nineteenth century implicitly relied on a similar understanding. But in the late nineteenth century, these theories became more explicit. In 1887, one student published the only medical thesis in Rio de Janeiro to specifically address the alleged physical differences between White and Black women in relation to reproduction and childbirth. Justo Jansen Ferreira reinforced the idea of inherent biological differences between the races, the supposed animal-like bodies of Black women, and their "natural" propensity to tolerate pain. Here, he was not as interested in legal status but rather race, thus reifying a hierarchy that could endure long after slavery ended. For example, when arguing that Black and White women had different sized pelvises, he likened the pelvis of the "Venus Hottentot" to that of a monkey and discussed how the typical lower lumbar curve of the "black race" facilitated delivery.[65] Moreover, Ferreira believed that "civilized" women who lived in cities had longer deliveries than their counterparts in rural areas: "Among the savages it has been observed that . . . childbirth is not very painful, that right after the delivery of the placenta women take to their harsh labor."[66] In dividing city and rural areas, Ferreira racialized these women and contributed to the scientific racist belief that Black and Indigenous women were closer to nature than their White counterparts.

Ferreira's observations from his time as an intern at the maternity hospital associated with Rio de Janeiro's medical school underscore this racist view. Ferreira described the labor and delivery of one Black woman, who "without any painful phenomenon indicating the proximity of birth," was actually "surprised by the birth of her child, not having even any time to return to her bed!"[67] In equating the ability to tolerate pain to "savage races," Ferreira reinforced the medical idea that Black women were less than human, an idea that underpinned the long history of slavery across the hemisphere and which became more important in the face of full emancipation. Paradoxically, he overlooked the fact that this Black woman lived in a city.

These descriptions of Black women's almost painless experiences of labor and delivery stand in stark contrast to Felicidade, who was in so much pain she threw herself on her belly, or the unnamed Black woman whose maimed body was used to educate future physicians. Medical documents show how intense pain was for enslaved women. Physicians, in fact, often could not complete their surgical obstetric interventions because of enslaved women's physical reaction to the painful experience. In 1831, for example, one physician described the case of an "almost complete congenital obliteration of the vagina." According to the case notes, this "*preta* from the Calabar nation" worked in a rural household where she had been raped while working in the fields. The unnamed enslaved woman became pregnant, but due to her vaginal deformation, the physician was unable to examine her. He tried to dilate her vagina, introducing "the thinnest canula" before using a scalpel to help with dilation. He was forced to stop, however, by "the shock of the patient."[68]

The same physician also described the case of Venancia, a "dark brown" enslaved woman of around thirty years of age. Venancia complained of pain when trying to evacuate her bowels, and the physician, after performing a rectal exam, found fetal bones in the colon. He pulled one out with the help of tweezers, but then the patient "tortured by pain [*mortificada de dores*] did not allow him to perform any other action on that occasion."[69] Carneiro's inability to continue with painful surgical interventions on enslaved women's bodies demonstrates that physicians did witness in their clinical practice that enslaved women felt pain—intense, excruciating pain. Yet this clear evidence of enslaved women's pain did not sway physicians' racist depiction of Black women as having a higher pain tolerance. Physicians were able to ignore the pain of enslaved women—even when they experienced firsthand bondwomen's cries of agony. They could not imagine that pain. Can we? The feeling of a scalpel cutting into tissue in an era before anesthesia? Can this reaction influence our reading and writing about the past? Should it?

Conclusion

I want to end here with a note about the implications of these historical tendencies. The ideologies and clinical routines forged in the late nineteenth century paved the way for modern attitudes toward race, pain, and the at times violent role of the obstetrician in all Brazilian women's labors and deliveries, but particularly those of poor women of color. Today's racial health disparities in Brazil should alone give us pause.[70] For example, Black infant mortality rates are twice as high as White ones.[71] Numbers, however, can gloss over the *quality* of clinical treatment and the experiences of people of African descent. Studies from across the Americas, for example, show that racial disparities exist in the quality of (and not just the access to) treatment and that physicians' understandings of pain influence this treatment. Researchers in the United States demonstrate that some North American medical practitioners still hold "false beliefs about biological differences between blacks and whites" that then "inform [their] medical judgments" and approach toward pain treatment.[72] Some medical students simply believe Black Americans feel less pain.

This is also the case in Brazil. In the realm of labor and delivery, Black women in Brazil face lower-quality obstetric care, resulting in what historian Okezi Otovo calls an "abject devaluation of black reproduction."[73] Data from a nationwide study demonstrate that when compared to White women of their same social class, education level, region, and healthcare (public or private), Black women received less information during pre-natal care about childbirth, including any possible complications. The study found that Black women were less likely to undergo cesarean sections or painful interventions during vaginal delivery (including episiotomies, or the cutting of the perineum to facilitate vaginal delivery, and the use of oxytocin, a drug used to accelerate contractions) than their White counterparts. But when they did undergo an episiotomy, Black women received less local anesthesia.[74] As the authors write, although the study of race and quality of medical treatment in relation to pain is understudied in Brazil, they found in their own research that "there were occasions, such as was the case in obstetric clinics in Rio de Janeiro, in which health professionals mentioned the supposed better pelvic adequacy of black women for giving birth, a fact that justified the nonuse of painkillers [during childbirth]."[75] Justo Jansen Ferreira's racist musings on enslaved women's superior "lower lumbar curve" continue to structure the type of medical care Black women in Brazil receive during childbirth. The issue of racialized medicine is alive and well in Brazil today, and it has a long history that requires unpacking.

NOTES

1. The publication, associated with the country's main medical association, changed names several times throughout the century. See Casa de Oswaldo Cruz/Fiocruz, "Sociedade de Medicina do Rio de Janeiro," *Dicionário Histórico-Biográfico das Ciências da Saúde no Brasil (1832–1930)* (blog), accessed June 18, 2019, www.dichistoriasaude.coc.fiocruz.br/iah/pt/verbetes/socmedrj.htm.
2. José Pereira Rego Filho, "Obstetricia. Parto de 3 crianças, uma do sexo feminino e duas do masculino," *Annaes de Medicina Brasiliense* 2, no. 6 (1845): 137. All translations are my own unless otherwise noted.
3. These sterile practices resulted from Louis Pasteur's discovery of the pathological basis for infections, and Joseph Lister first recorded its surgical use in 1867 in England. Jaime L. Benchimol, *Dos micróbios aos mosquitos: Febre amarela e a revolução pasteuriana no Brasil* (Rio de Janeiro: Editora Fiocruz, 1999).
4. Mary C. Karasch, *Slave Life in Rio de Janeiro, 1808–1850* (Princeton, NJ: Princeton University Press, 1987); Cassia Roth, "From Free Womb to Criminalized Woman: Fertility Control in Brazilian Slavery and Freedom," *Slavery and Abolition* 38, no. 2 (2017): 269–86; Luiz Lima Vailati, *A morte menina: Infância e morte infantil no Brasil dos oitocentos (Rio de Janeiro e São Paulo)* (São Paulo: Alameda, 2010).
5. Laird W. Bergad, *Slavery and the Demographic and Economic History of Minas Gerais, Brazil, 1720–1888* (New York: Cambridge University Press, 1999); Manolo Florentino and José Roberto Góes, *A paz das senzalas: Famílias escravas e tráfico atlântico, Rio de Janeiro, c. 1790–1850* (Rio de Janeiro: Civilização Brasileira, 1997); Robert W. Slenes, "The Demography and Economics of Brazilian Slavery: 1850–1888" (PhD diss., Stanford University, 1975); Michael Tadman, "The Demographic Cost of Sugar: Debates on Slave Societies and Natural Increase in the Americas," *American Historical Review* 105, no. 5 (2000): 1534–75.
6. Herbert S. Klein and Francisco Vidal Luna, *Slavery in Brazil* (Cambridge: Cambridge University Press, 2010); Karasch, *Slave Life in Rio de Janeiro, 1808–1850*.

7. On emotions in history, see Barbara H. Rosenwein, "Worrying about Emotions in History," *American Historical Review* 107, no. 3 (2002): 821–45.
8. Sasha Turner, "The Nameless and the Forgotten: Maternal Grief, Sacred Protection, and the Archive of Slavery," *Slavery and Abolition* 38, no. 2 (2017): 234.
9. Ibid., 234–35.
10. Sasha Turner, *Contested Bodies: Pregnancy, Childrearing, and Slavery in Jamaica* (Philadelphia: University of Pennsylvania Press, 2017); Turner, "The Nameless and the Forgotten."
11. Stephanie M. H. Camp, *Closer to Freedom: Enslaved Women and Everyday Resistance in the Plantation South* (Chapel Hill: University of North Carolina Press, 2004); Marisa J. Fuentes, *Dispossessed Lives: Enslaved Women, Violence, and the Archive* (Philadelphia: University of Pennsylvania Press, 2016); Jennifer L. Morgan, *Laboring Women: Reproduction and Gender in New World Slavery* (Philadelphia: University of Pennsylvania Press, 2004); Turner, *Contested Bodies*.
12. Angela Davis, "Reflections on the Black Woman's Role in the Community of Slaves," *Massachusetts Review* 13, no. 1/2 (1972): 81–100; Maria Lúcia de Barros Mott, "Ser mãe: A escrava em face do aborto e do infanticídio," *Revista de História* 120 (July 1989): 85–96; Roth, "From Free Womb to Criminalized Woman."
13. Morgan, *Laboring Women*; Katherine Paugh, *The Politics of Reproduction: Race, Medicine, and Fertility in the Age of Abolition* (Oxford, UK: Oxford University Press, 2017).
14. Fuentes, *Dispossessed Lives*, 9.
15. Jane-Marie Collins, "Bearing the Burden of Bastardy: Infanticide, Race and Motherhood in Brazilian Slave Society," in *Killing Infants: Studies in the Worldwide Practice of Infanticide*, ed. Brigitte H. Bechtold and Donna Cooper Graves (Lewiston, NY: Edwin Mellen Press, 2006), 199–229; Mott, "Ser mãe"; Roth, "From Free Womb to Criminalized Woman."
16. Roth, "From Free Womb to Criminalized Woman."
17. Hazel V. Carby, *Reconstructing Womanhood: The Emergence of the Afro-American Woman Novelist* (New York: Oxford University Press, 1987), 22.
18. David B. Morris, *The Culture of Pain* (Berkeley: University of California Press, 1991); Roselyne Rey, *The History of Pain*, trans. Louise Elliott Wallace, J. A. Cadden, and S. W. Cadden (Cambridge: Harvard University Press, 1995).
19. Fuentes, *Dispossessed Lives*, 2.
20. Vincent Brown, *The Reaper's Garden: Death and Power in the World of Atlantic Slavery* (Cambridge: Harvard University Press, 2008); Fuentes, *Dispossessed Lives*; Morgan, *Laboring Women*; Diana Paton, *No Bond but the Law: Punishment, Race, and Gender in Jamaican State Formation, 1780–1870* (Durham, NC: Duke University Press, 2004); Orlando Patterson, *Slavery and Social Death: A Comparative Study* (Cambridge: Harvard University Press, 1982).
21. For example, Herman L. Bennett, *Africans in Colonial Mexico: Absolutism, Christianity, and Afro-Creole Consciousness, 1570–1640* (Bloomington: Indiana University Press, 2003); Camillia Cowling, *Conceiving Freedom: Women of Color, Gender, and the Abolition of Slavery in Havana and Rio de Janeiro* (Chapel Hill: University of North Carolina Press, 2013); Sandra Lauderdale Graham, *Caetana Says No: Women's Stories from*

a Brazilian Slave Society (New York: Cambridge University Press, 2002); Keila Grinberg, *Liberata: A lei da ambigüidade - as ações de liberdade da Corte de Apelação do Rio de Janeiro no século XIX* (Rio de Janeiro: Centro Edelstein de Pesquisa Social, 2010); Alejandro de la Fuente, "Slaves and the Creation of Legal Rights in Cuba: *Coartación* and *Papel*," *Hispanic American Historical Review* 87, no. 4 (2007): 659–92; Michelle A. McKinley, *Fractional Freedoms: Slavery, Intimacy, and Legal Mobilization in Colonial Lima, 1600–1700* (New York: Cambridge University Press, 2016).

22. Dierdre Cooper Owens, *Medical Bondage: Race, Gender, and the Origins of American Gynecology* (Athens: University of Georgia Press, 2017); Sharla M. Fett, *Working Cures: Healing, Health, and Power on Southern Slave Plantations* (Chapel Hill: University of North Carolina Press, 2002); Marie Jenkins Schwartz, *Birthing a Slave: Motherhood and Medicine in the Antebellum South* (Cambridge: Harvard University Press, 2006).

23. On oral histories, see Ana Lugão Rios and Hebe Mattos, *Memórias do cativeiro: Família, trabalho e cidadania no pós-abolição* (Rio de Janeiro: Civilização Brasileira, 2005). On medical sources, see Tânia Salgado Pimenta and Flávio Gomes, eds., *Escravidão, doenças e práticas de cura no Brasil* (Rio de Janeiro: Outras Letras, 2016).

24. Respectively, Saidiya Hartman, "Venus in Two Acts," *Small Axe* 26 (June 2008): 2–3; Lamonte Aidoo, *Slavery Unseen: Sex, Power, and Violence in Brazilian History* (Durham, NC: Duke University Press, 2018), 8.

25. Ula Taylor, "Women in the Documents: Thoughts on Uncovering the Personal, Political, and Professional," *Journal of Women's History* 20, no. 1 (2008): 189.

26. Greg Childs, "Insanity, the Historian, and the Slave Catcher: 'Capturing' Black Voices," *Black Perspectives* (blog), February 15, 2015, www.aaihs.org/insanity-the-historian-and-the-slave-catcher-capturing-black-voices/#fnref-1594-7.

27. João Gomes dos Reis, *Dissertação medico-legal sobre o aborto precedida de algumas considerações acerca dos motivos que em geral levão as mulheres a provocal-o e meios de o prevenir* (Nictheroy: Typ. Commercial de E. C. dos Santos, 1845), 3.

28. José Pereira Rego Filho, "Sobre os effeitos therapeuticos da ergotina, e do centeio esporado, nas hemorrhagias uterinas puerperaes; lida na Sessão Geral da Academia Imperial de Medicina do Rio de Janeiro, em 19 de outubro de 1857," *Annaes Brasilienses de Medicina* 11, no. 12 (1858): 343.

29. Ibid., 346.

30. Ibid., 345.

31. Ibid., 346.

32. Cooper Owens, *Medical Bondage*, 28.

33. Fuentes, *Dispossessed Lives*, 147.

34. Luis da Cunha Feijó, "Breves considerações acerca das rupturas do utero durante o trabalho do parto, seguido da importante observação d'um caso, em que existia, alem das causas communs de tal accidente, um vicio da bacia não descripto pelos autores. Memoria offerecida á Academia Imperial de Medicina do Rio de Janeiro," *Annaes de Medicina Brasiliense* 4, no. 5 (1848): 109.

35. Anjali Arondekar, *For the Record: On Sexuality and the Colonial Archive in India* (Durham, NC: Duke University Press, 2009); Carolyn Steedman, *Dust: The Archive and Cultural History* (New Brunswick, NJ: Rutgers University Press, 2002).

Silences and the Corporeal 209

36. On the archive as "contact zone," see Antoinette M. Burton, *Archive Stories: Facts, Fictions, and the Writing of History* (Durham, NC: Duke University Press, 2005); Mary Louise Pratt, *Imperial Eyes: Travel Writing and Transculturation*, 2nd ed. (London: Routledge, 2008). On examining our own place, see María Elena Martínez, "Archives, Bodies, and Imagination: The Case of Juana Aguilar and Queer Approaches to History, Sexuality, and Politics," *Radical History Review*, no. 120 (Fall 2014): 159–82; Zeb Tortorici, *Sins against Nature: Sexuality and the Archive in Colonial New Spain* (Durham, NC: Duke University Press, 2018).
37. Tortorici, *Sins against Nature*, 3.
38. Ibid., 24.
39. Ibid., 35–36.
40. Paton, *No Bond but the Law*, 18.
41. Hartman, "Venus in Two Acts," 4. See also Paton, *No Bond but the Law*, 17–18.
42. Aidoo, *Slavery Unseen*, 8.
43. Academia Imperial de Medicina, "Sessão Geral em 28 de Outubro de 1856," *Annaes Brasilienses de Medicina* 11, no. 4 (1857): 80.
44. Lyndon K. Gill, "Situating Black, Situating Queer: Black Queer Diaspora Studies and the Art of Embodied Listening," *Transforming Anthropology* 20, no. 1 (2012): 33.
45. Gladys M. Francis, *Odious Caribbean Women and the Palpable Aesthetics of Transgression* (Lanham, MD: Lexington Books, 2017), xvii.
46. Hartman, "Venus in Two Acts," 11.
47. Ibid., 3.
48. Elaine Scarry, *The Body in Pain: The Making and Unmaking of the World* (New York: Oxford University Press, 1985), 4, 6.
49. Cooper Owens, *Medical Bondage*; Irvine Loudon, *Death in Childbirth: An International Study of Maternal Care and Maternal Mortality, 1800–1950* (Oxford: Clarendon Press, 1992); Ana Paula Vosne Martins, *Visões do feminino: A medicina da mulher nos séculos XIX e XX* (Rio de Janeiro: Editora Fiocruz, 2004); Fabíola Rohden, *Uma ciência da diferença: Sexo e gênero na medicina da mulher*, 2nd ed. (Rio de Janeiro: Editora Fiocruz, 2009); Luiz Lima Vailati, *A morte menina*; Jacqueline H. Wolf, *Cesarean Section: An American History of Risk, Technology, and Consequence* (Baltimore: Johns Hopkins University Press, 2018).
50. Cooper Owens, *Medical Bondage*; Ana Paula Vosne Martins, *Visões do feminino*; Lorena Féres da Silva Telles, "Pregnant Slaves, Workers in Labour: Amid Doctors and Masters in a Slave-Owning City (Nineteenth-Century Rio de Janeiro)," *Women's History Review* 27, no. 6 (2018): 924–38; Turner, *Contested Bodies*.
51. Telles, "Pregnant Slaves, Workers in Labour."
52. José Maria de Noronha Feital, "Dous casos de pratica de partos," *Annaes de Medicina Brasiliense* 4, no. 7 (1848): 165.
53. Cooper Owens, *Medical Bondage*; Londa Schiebinger, *The Secret Cures of Slaves: Peoples, Plants, and Medicine in the Eighteenth-Century Atlantic World* (Stanford: Stanford University Press, 2017).
54. Rana A. Hogarth, *Medicalizing Blackness: Making Racial Difference in the Atlantic World, 1780–1840* (Chapel Hill: University of North Carolina Press, 2017); C. Riley Snorton,

Black on Both Sides: A Racial History of Trans Identity (Minneapolis: University of Minnesota Press, 2017), 17–53.
55. Agostinho Joze Ferreira Bretas, *A utilidade do alleitamento maternal e os inconvenientes que resultão do despreso deste dever* (Rio de Janeiro: Typographia e Livraria de J. Cremiere, 1838), 18–20; José Henrique de Medeiros, *A mamentação materna é quasi sempre possivel* (Rio de Janeiro: Typographia Imparcial de Francisco de Paula Brito, 1848), 10; Zeferino Justino da Silva Meirelles, *Breves considerações sobre as vantagens do aleitamento maternal* (Rio de Janeiro: Typographia do Diario de N. L. Vianna, 1847), 14; Pedro da Silva Rego, *Os cuidados que reclama a mulher depois do parto natural* (Rio de Janeiro: Typographia Imparcial de Francisco de Paulo Brito, 1838), 28; José Pereira Rego Filho, "Considerações sobre algumas molestias de crianças mais frequentes no Rio de Janeiro," *Annaes Brasilienses de Medicina* 6, no. 1 (1850): 4.
56. Francisco Julio Xavier, *Considerações sobre os cuidados e os soccorros que se devem prestar aos meninos na occasião de seu nascimento; e sobre as vantagens do aleitamento maternal* (Rio de Janeiro: Typographia Imperial e Constitucional de Seignot-Plancher e G., 1833), 7.
57. Bretas, *A utilidade do alleitamento maternal*, 19.
58. Luiz Delfino dos Santos, *Que regimen será mais conveniente á criação dos expostos da Santa Casa da Misericordia, attentas as nossas circumstancias especiaes, a criação em commum dentro do Hospicio, ou a privada em casas particulares?* (Rio de Janeiro: Typographia Universal de Laemmert, 1857), 56.
59. Luiz Augusto Corrêa d'Azevedo, *Do aleitamento natural, artificial e mixto e particularmente do mercenario em relação as condições em que elle se acha no Rio de Janeiro* (Rio de Janeiro: Typographia Academica, 1873), 67; José Rodrigues de Lima Duarte, *Ensaio sobre a hygiene da escravatura no Brasil* (Rio de Janeiro: Typographia Universal de Laemmert, 1849), 48–50.
60. Juvenal Martiniano das Neves, *Do aleitamento natural, artificial e mixto e particularmente do mercenario em relação as condições em que elle se acha no Rio de Janeiro* (Rio de Janeiro: Typographia da Reforma, 1873), 38.
61. Lilia Moritz Schwarcz, *O espetáculo das raças: Cientistas, instituiçõe e questão racial no Brasil, 1870–1930* (São Paulo: Companhia das Letras, 1993).
62. Cowling, *Conceiving Freedom*.
63. Camillia Cowling, "Debating Womanhood, Defining Freedom: The Abolition of Slavery in 1880s Rio de Janeiro," *Gender and History* 22, no. 2 (2010): 284–301.
64. Cooper Owens, *Medical Bondage*, 44. See also Miriam Rich, "The Curse of the Civilised Woman: Race, Gender and the Pain of Childbirth in Nineteenth-Century American Medicine," *Gender and History* 28, no. 1 (2016): 57–76; Snorton, *Black on Both Sides*, 17–52.
65. Justo Jansen Ferreira, *Do parto e suas consequencias na especie negra* (Rio de Janeiro: Laemmert, 1887), 17, 37–38.
66. Ferreira, *Do parto*, 33.
67. Ibid., 36.
68. João Alvares Carneiro, "Obliteração congenita e quase inteira da vagina, e concepção effeituada apezar d'ella," *Semanario de Saude Publica pela Sociedade de Medicina do Rio de Janeiro*, no. 10 (March 5, 1831): 56.

69. João Alvares Carneiro, "Caso de huma prenhez em que as partes osseas do feto forão extrahidas pelo intestino recto," *Semanario de Saude Publica pela Sociedade de Medicina do Rio de Janeiro*, no. 12 (March 21, 1831): 66.
70. Rosa Maria Soares Madeira Domingues et al., "Adequação da assistência pré-natal segundo as características maternas no Brasil," *Revista Panamericana de Salud Publica* 37, no. 3 (2015): 140–47; Fernanda Lopes, "Para além da barreira dos números: Desigualdades raciais e saúde," *Cadernos de Saúde Pública* 21, no. 5 (2005): 1595–1601.
71. Kwame A. Nyarko et al., "Explaining Racial Disparities in Infant Health in Brazil," *American Journal of Public Health* 103, no. 9 (2013): 1675–84.
72. Kelly M. Hoffman et al., "Racial Bias in Pain Assessment and Treatment Recommendations, and False Beliefs about Biological Differences Between Blacks and Whites," *Proceedings of the National Academy of Sciences* 113, no. 16 (2016): 4296.
73. Okezi T. Otovo, *Progressive Mothers, Better Babies: Race, Public Health, and the State in Brazil, 1850–1945* (Austin: University of Texas Press, 2016), 211.
74. Maria do Carmo Leal et al., "A cor da dor: Iniquidades raciais na atenção pré-natal e ao parto no Brasil," *Cadernos de Saúde Pública* 33, no. Sup. 1 (2017), sec.3, para.17.
75. Ibid., 10.

PART III
AFRO-LATIN AMERICA
Black Marginality in the New Century

CHAPTER 9

Racial Dynamics and Tensions in Twenty-First Century Post-Revolutionary Cuba

ALBERTO ABREU

Translated by Laura Colaneri

From the eighteenth century onward, panic at the Africanization of Cuba has constituted one of the primary impediments for elites attempting to move forward with the political, cultural, and social project that they have conceived as the *nation*. This phenomenon—which some Cuban historians have referred to as *el miedo al negro* (fear of Blacks)—is key for understanding not only the dilemmas that discourses of rationalism and the formative process of Cuban nationality contended with throughout the nineteenth century but also the marginal and understudied spaces that Black and mulatto men and women have been made to occupy even today in Cuba within those grand narratives that account for the formative processes of our national identity.

For the Afro-Cuban poet Gastón Baquero, el miedo al negro "es el eje, la constante sobre la cual gira la historia cubana. Hubo Pacto de Zanjón por miedo a los negros en armas" (is the axis, the constant around which Cuban history turns. The Pact of Zanjón was made due to fear of armed Blacks).[1] Baquero further explains how Cuba was left out of the Treaty of Paris "porque tanto los españoles como los norteamericanos y como los cubanos blancos, temían 'un nuevo Haití'" (because Spaniards, North Americans, and White Cubans all feared "a new Haiti"). In the aforementioned essay,

"El miedo al negro," he also notes the highly interesting fact that Simón Bolívar wrote to General Santander in 1826, with Spain defeated and the Congress of Panama approaching, that "La libertad de Cuba puede esperar; nos basta con un Haití en el Caribe" (The liberty of Cuba can wait; one Haiti in the Caribbean is enough for us).

Furthermore, little to nothing has been written about how enslaved and free Black and mulatto Cubans expressed those initial ideas of nationhood, which, for obvious reasons, were different from those of Whites but nevertheless contained a sense of belonging to the territory where they were born and lived. These ideas were manifested through the defense of their homeland against foreign aggressions; the will to acquire a respectable economic and social position based on their talents in their trades; the search for a citizenship status made evident by the large accumulation of legal claims presented before the authorities; and the decision to lead a model of community life relatively independent of the ordinances and prescriptions of White society.[2] In the marginal neighborhoods where they had been confined socially, they were able to share not only their aspirations of social realization and communal direction but also gain an awareness of the ethnic and social exclusion with which they were faced.[3]

The literature produced during the colonial period by both enslaved and free Black and mulatto authors is therefore the space that best informs us about this phenomenon. We must recall that the colonial literary text emerged as the ideal space for the staging of both a paradigm of modernity and an imagined nation that were continually refuted by precarious socioeconomic modernization, a model of production linked inextricably to slavery and our colonial status.

Such are the cases of Antonio Medina Céspedes (Havana, 1829), Néstor Cepeda, Juan Antonio Frías (Port-au-Prince, 1835), Mácsimo Hero de Neiba [Ambrosio Echemendía] (Trinidad, 1843), Manuel Roblejo, and Narciso Blanco [José del Carmen Díaz] (Güines, 1835). All of these authors were enslaved, save for Medina, who was born free. This new wave of Afro-Cuban poets emerged within the Cuban literary panorama in the 1850s and 1860s; almost all of them came from inland, urban, slave-holding communities. All, in one way or another, lend continuity to the complex process, begun by Plácido and Manzano in the first half of the nineteenth century, of imagining the nation from a marginalized and racially differentiated body and place of enunciation. Their textualities make manifest that tense relationship that the enslaved or Afro-descendant subject maintains with power and language.[4]

Bringing together this group of Black and/or enslaved poets is essential not only for studies on the formative processes of Cuban national identity but also for understanding the negotiations, intellectual practices, and gestures of resistance that, out of the absence of the individual voice, both enslaved and free Black and mulatto authors undertake in order to access the power of enunciation: efforts that have as their main setting our Republic of Letters.

Of course, these intellectual and symbolic practices are not exclusive to this group. In fact, many of them had already been outlined in the first half of the nineteenth century by Plácido and Manzano, in particular those involving a group of questions regarding the possibility or impossibility of these subjects to represent themselves without mediation, as well as those related to writing as a space of negotiation and rearticulation of the constructed identity designed by the colonial system for the Black and mulatto subject.

2

Manuel Moreno Fraginals, in a brief essay titled "Negrofobia" (Negrophobia), argues that el miedo al negro is a phenomenon with very deep roots in colonial Cuban society and associates its origins with the Haitian Revolution.[5] José Luciano Franco, for his part, shares the same point of view expressed by Fraginals concerning the Cuban origins of negrophobia in his book *La conspiración de Aponte 1812* (The Aponte conspiracy 1812).[6] However, in contrast to José Luciano Franco and Moreno Fraginals, other Afro-Cuban historians such as Enrique Patterson, Juan F. Benemelis, Gastón Baquero, Walterio Carbonell, and Tomás Fernández Robaina see el miedo al negro as a narrative rooted in the deep unity of the Cuban nation at that time.[7]

Based on these elements, I would like to form the first thesis that I'm interested in sharing with the readers of this essay. It is related to the order of the social production of discourse and its links with desire and power. I am referring to understanding el miedo al negro as the construction of a discursive field and imaginary of terror and catastrophe about the racialized Other.

In my judgment, what Luciano Franco, Fraginals, and other Cuban researchers define as *el miedo al negro* is only the tip of the iceberg,[8] in that we find ourselves faced with a phenomenon that transcends the elite *criollo*'s feeling of panic toward the Black subject; and it situates us within a discursive field about the racialized Other, in whose center are found the writings of Francisco de Arango y Parreño, José Antonio Saco, Domingo Del Monte, and the whole genealogy of illustrious aristocrats who were the founders of Cuban nationality.[9]

An appreciable group of essays devoted to the analysis of colonial subjects and discourses as related to events in Haiti is rather emphatic in situating el miedo al negro and the outbreak of the Revolution of Guarico as primordial instances for understanding the "exceptionality" of the Cuban nation-state's formation, or why the modality of the nation arrives late to Cuba.[10]

Rumor leaves its mark upon the stories that arrive from Haiti and spread throughout the island. It impregnates them with violent images, associated with terror and racial massacre. How much transformation of facts into truths and truths into rumors was there in the stories of exaggerated violence? Among the many documents amassed within the archives of Cuban historiography related to the Haitian Revolution, I will briefly pause at one where rumor is positioned as a privileged route for the transmission and circulation of news and a mobilizing agent of insurgency. Beyond its cruel humor, it allows us to hear the voice and aspirations of the slave within the historical text. The incident—recalled by Ada Ferrer in her study "Cuba en la sombra de Haiti: Noticias, sociedad, y esclavitud" (Cuba in the shadow of Haiti: News, society, and slavery)—reveals the imaginaries of disarticulation, fracture, and uncertainty that the Haitian Revolution introduced within colonial Cuban society, ultimately shaping a social landscape charged with contradictory, irrational tales, marked by symbolic and physical violence toward the racialized Other.[11]

The anecdote is fairly simple. It concerns a slave, of whose identity, significantly, no further indications are given; the report only tells us that he belongs to Don Fernando Rodríguez. He announces to his master that the French slaves had already won their freedom. The slave is sentenced to one hundred lashes and made to wear a sign around his neck that says: "Este es el fruto de la imaginada libertad de los Negros franceses. En la virtud se halla la verdadera libertad" (This is the fruit of the imagined freedom of the French Blacks. In virtue lies true freedom).[12] In this story are codified the emancipatory expectations from which the Black subject perceives the Haitian Revolution. The "childish" claim of the slave is contrasted with the sign's empty rhetoric and the excessive punishment of one hundred lashes, although Ada Ferrer's reading of this anecdote is intended only to attest to the knowledge that slaves in Cuba had about the events in Haiti. For me, on the other hand, the story suggests other interpretations, which derive from the potentialities of rumor: the transience of its action, the prohibition that compels it and makes it attractive. Let us remember that rumor is errant and inhabits the space excluded by regulations: it is that which is not authorized. In this anecdote, rumor confronts the apparent stability of institutions and social representations and does so to fill in and expose the spaces of silence left by the normative.[13]

Based on these ideas, it is possible to undertake a reverse reading of this tale. I am interested in the manner in which it operates as a counter-discourse that erodes the colonial elite's version of the Haitian Revolution as a bloody racial massacre, where Blacks and mulattos are described as savages whose actions are only explained by virtue of their primitivism and "lack of culture." The voice and claim of Don Fernando Rodríguez's slave undermine this hegemonic perception and bring to light the rhetorical mechanisms aimed at silencing and distorting the political and social content of this revolution.

The explicit setting of the discourse, as we see, is the confrontation of the master by his slave, but it is also that of the colonial authorities charged with punishing similar impudence in the subaltern. The severe punishment of one hundred lashes, in its irrational violence, illustrates the climate of terror that reigns over the island of Cuba stemming from the events in Haiti. Meanwhile, the sign underlines the abject condition of the slave, in need of both corporal and conceptual punishment. At the same time, the notion of liberty written on the poster hanging around his neck operates as an erasure of the perception that French slaves have thereof, and diverts the idea of freedom toward another, falsely spiritual and more manageable, meaning. On the other hand, the slave's assertion is verified by the Haitian referent. For him, the recent events on the neighboring island settle into the place of the emancipatory utopia, of a rumor that, although unlikely, is possible. However, for Don Fernando and the colonial Cuban authorities, his claim is an explicit call to subordination and insurgency.

Underlying the semantic micro-structure of this story are other no less revealing oppositions. For example, the space of the letter (the poster) corresponds to that of power (the master, the authorities), whereas the slave's claim navigates through a territory lacking authority like that of language (rumor). The latter, though, without a doubt is the space that best reflects the dynamic and feeling of the popular sectors, because, in all its deformity, it attempts to make up for the gap in the official version of the story about the events in Haiti; it is the reverse of institutional knowledge, the spirit of rebellion that produces new meanings.

Not by coincidence, the narrative and grammar of rumor respond to the phonocentric logic of speech as a general system of production of meaning. Spivak considers the power of rumor in the subaltern context to be derived from its participation in the structure of illegitimate writing rather than in the authoritative writing of the law: "Thus rumor is not error but primordially (originally) errant, always in circulation with no assignable source. This illegitimacy makes it accessible to insurgency."[14] This testimony allows us to read the slave as a political subject. Rumor (language) is the space where, on the one hand, the racial fear of the dominant classes and, on the other, the Black subject's desire for liberty and the utopias of social equality and emancipation converge and settle.

Slave uprisings on sugar and coffee plantations were not a novelty on the island. From 1810 onward, enslaved Blacks and mulattos, inspired by the Haitian Revolution, had demonstrated their insurgent spirit against Spanish domination and their will to build an emancipatory, anti-slavery project. Such was the case of the rebellion led by José Antonio Aponte in 1812. Nevertheless, it was only after 1843 that these uprisings acquired a significant dimension due to their extension and organization. This is corroborated by the uprisings that took place in the Alcancía, La Luisa, La Trinidad, Las Nieves, La Aurora, Triunvirato, and Ácana mills; the Moscú coffee plantation; and the Ranchuelo ranch. The forced laborers working on the construction of the Cárdenas-Bemba railway section also mutinied. The movement also spread throughout the entirety of the plains of Colón when slaves from the La Concepción, San Miguel, San Lorenzo, and San Rafael mills rose up. These events had their culmination in what is known as the Conspiracy of La Escalera. A total of 4,000 people, White, Black, and mulatto, free and enslaved, were involved in the trial of La Escalera. The repression exceeded 300 deaths by torture, 435 expulsions from the island, 182 prison sentences, and 78 death sentences. According to the judgments, 71.09 percent of those targeted were free Black and mulatto members of the petite bourgeois sector, 25.45 percent were slaves, and only 10.5 percent came from plantations.[15] I will take a moment to dwell on this shocking description for two fundamental reasons: First, because the rigor of these sentences illustrates the colonial authorities' terror at the prospect of a Black republic similar to Haiti, and second, because these data, in one way or another, are essential for understanding the climate of repression and social panic in the midst of which the interrogations of Plácido and others accused took place, as well as the drops of blood that quite literally dot the record of his statement.

According to Julio Le Riverend, the increasing economic activity of Black and mulatto freedmen during this period transformed them into a threat toward colonial power and the White criollo aristocracy. They "buscan insertarse en la jerarquía social, allí donde los blancos aún no quieren intervenir por considerarse ocupación degradante" (were looking to insert themselves into the social hierarchy in positions which Whites still do not want to take up due to considering them degrading occupations).[16] Furthermore, the existence of this petite bourgeoisie of Black and mulatto tailors, dentists, barbers, craftsmen, midwives, teachers, etc. has also been meticulously documented by Pedro Deschamps and Juan Pérez de la Riva via the analysis of the numerous freemen's wills present in our National Archives.[17] This group's small amount of capital figures among the major reasons motivating its inclusion in the case of *La Escalera*.

It was not by chance that the poet Gabriel de la Concepción Valdés (Plácido) was accused of being the head of the conspiracy and shot in 1844. Plácido remains at the center of numerous debates in the history of Cuban literature even today. He was born to a White mother and multiracial father; a poor craftsman, autodidact, and writer sought after by the elites, bridging two worlds marked, interchangeably, by orality and writing. On this question of writing and orality in the foundational period of the Cuban lettered city, I'll bring the aforementioned Juan Francisco Manzano, the formerly enslaved poet, back into the discussion, to briefly explore the writing of the Black literary subject through these two poets, highlighting the trajectory of their cultural maroonage and their impact on the hegemonic spaces. We recall that both of them work from the margins and use literature as a means of negotiating their abject citizenship and participating in the complex and arduous exercise of imagining the Cuban nation from a racially different point of enunciation.

Roberto Friol, in his book *Suite para Juan Francisco Manzano* (Suite for Juan Francisco Manzano), avoids making any sort of parallel between the enslaved poet Juan Francisco Manzano and Plácido.[18] What ethical, professional, or other impulses lead him to exhibit so much caution? Shouldn't this comparison be well known in Cuban literary historiography? Let us hear the answers to these questions in Friol's own voice: "La trampa racista abierta por Domingo del Monte con su paralelo entre Plácido y Manzano en el artículo 'Dos poetas negros' [. . .] aún no se ha cerrado, y voluntariamente, no he de caer en ella" (The racist snare set out by Domingo del Monte with his parallel between Plácido and Manzano in the article "Two Black Poets" [. . .] has still not been shut, and I will not fall into it willingly).[19] In the comparison by Del Monte—severely contested by Friol—judgments on the behavior of the Black subject are framed within a relationship of hegemony/domination, white-supremacist ideology/Black subaltern subject. It has permeated Cuban historiographical discourse to such an extent that still today our literary studies privilege the figure of Manzano, as a metonymic way of celebrating the bonds of subjection of the slave to the master or the loyalty of the Black Other to the enlightened aristocrat.

Let us approach Fina García Marruz's interpretation of the *Autobiografía de Juan Francisco Manzano* (Autobiography of Juan Francisco Manzano) in her essay, "Manzano y Del Monte" (Manzano and Del Monte). I would like to dwell especially on those moments where the behavior of the enslaved poet, in the face of the despicable treatment that he receives, is perceived as a kind of martyrdom:

> Qué ancestrales reservas de benignidad, de insondable paciencia, no debieron concentrarse en aquel que ve que le maltratan a la madre, a quien ama tanto que pide a Dios "que se quitase a mi primero la vida qª ella," o lo vejan delante de la joven esclava por la que siente "una angelical inclinación."
>
> *What ancient reserves of kindness, of unfathomable patience, must be concentrated in he who sees his mother being mistreated, who he loves so much that he asks God "that he might take away my life before hers," or who is abused in front of the young slave for whom he feels "an angelic inclination."*[20]

More than Manzano's docile behavior, what concerns me is García Marruz's celebration of his conduct, and the use of the terms "humility," "placid," "timid," "his ancient reserves of kindness," and "unfathomable patience" to describe his attitude before the disgraces of which he was a victim. In this way, Manzano is positioned as the reverse of Plácido's rebellious consciousness and of the Black men and women that at this time spearheaded numerous uprisings and escapes. The acceptance and entrance of Manzano into the Cuban lettered city is not only explained by virtue of the numerous cannibalisms of his work, but also the aforementioned descriptors.

By the time the enslaved Manzano arrives at the literary circle of Domingo del Monte and reads his moving poem "Mis treinta años" (My thirty years), he has already learned his lesson well: for the subaltern, access to the world of letters comes only with sacrifice. Hereafter, one must feign obedience and loyalty to the codes and norms of Whiteness. Del Monte and his friends had realized that, unlike Plácido, Manzano knew his place. And they weren't far from the truth. The Escalera events are illustrative. According to the official government report, the plot being hatched by a network of rebellious slaves and their allies was to exterminate the Whites in the island and establish a Black republic like Haiti, with the support of the British government. Thanks to their visibility as Black writers, and as members of the emerging Black middle class whose influence was seen by the authorities with increasing alarm, both Plácido and Manzano were caught up in the government's wave of repression. They were brutally tortured and eventually brought face to face to give testimony, in Del Monte's absence, as to his own participation in the alleged conspiracy. *Escalera*, or stair, which gives the name to the events, refers to the procedure of tying the bodies of the accused to the stair-like contraption and whipping them, often to death, under threats, false accusations, and empty promises.

Following the events of *La Escalera*, Plácido, aware that he had been used by the colonial authorities and the enlightened aristocrats to further their own agenda, reportedly denounced Del Monte's involvement in the conspiracy. Manzano, under questioning, denied it: "Manzano le repuso sosteniendo lo que había dicho, y no adelantándose otra cosa en esta confrontación, sosteniendo cada cual lo que había dicho se dio por concluido el acto, que por hallarlo conforme después de habérseles leído, lo ratificaron, firmado con dicho Sör y presente Escribano" (Manzano replied, standing behind what he had said, and nothing else moving forward in this confrontation, each standing by what they had said, the act was concluded, and, finding it accurate after having read it, they ratified it, in the presence of aforementioned Notary Public and Gentleman).[21]

Fina García Marruz's version of this episode is even more shocking than that of Martínez Carmenate and the one cited above:[22]

> El esclavo liberado por Del Monte y sus amigos resultó así a la postre su defensor y bastaría quizás estas palabras y estas lágrimas suyas, su "no señor, eso es falso," "el Sor Don Domingo no me ha hablado jamás de semejante cosa ni como tal le conozco," "el Señor Sor es demasiado savio para aventurar así su reputación (*sic*)."

> *The slave freed by Del Monte and his friends was thus, in the end, his defender, and perhaps his tears and words would suffice, his "No sir, this is false," "Mr. Don Domingo has never spoken to me of such a thing, nor do I know him as such," "the Gentleman is too wise to risk his reputation in this way."*[23]

Manzano represents the docile body of difference because, according to the analytical terms of traditional historiography and Cuban academic discourse, he meets all the demands to be a "good" object of knowledge, which certify the underlying relations of domination in the epistemological and institutional powers of these cases and which, historically, have deprived Black subjects of the power to signify their historical desire and establish their own oppositional discourse.

If Manzano is the docile body of difference, Plácido, on the contrary, embodies the rebellious consciousness: "the informer," "the pretender," "the indecisive one," and the subject unable to make a heroic gesture. According to these historiographic narratives, the former exists insofar as he highlights or alludes to the negativity of the Other. There is no doubt that such antimonies are constructed and enunciated from a colonial perspective in which the historical, cultural, historiographic, political, ethnic, and racial patterns of the aristocratizing imaginary of Whiteness converge and where the Afro-Cuban subject remains sequestered at the edges of this representational and discursive field, in those places where his performance is conceived only as a violation of the dominant symbolic order.

What I seek to bring to light is how *el miedo al negro* operates in the approach of the Cuban historiographical tradition during a period like this one, in which there is an attempt to diagram the definitive lines of Cuban nationality, where the formative processes of the Cuban literary field and our modernity intersect with pro-independence political positions. Similar perceptions about the Black and/or mulatto subject not only are generated from a hegemonic (literary and racial) space of enunciation but also possess, in addition, a prescriptive calling: to emphasize the subaltern condition of the racialized Other in these processes.

3

As you can see, the project of Cuban modernity needed, for its legitimation, a set of narratives that, from its hygienicist ideology, would operate as a metaphor for the good health of the body of the emerging nation at the same time as it confined Afro-Cubans and their culture on the side of the perverse and dirty. Blacks and mulattos, with their languages needful of correction, disturbed the order and were an expression of the island's chaos and barbarity—hence the urgency to silence them.

Consequently, our modernizing aristocrats—founders of the Cuban nation—articulated a discursive field about the Black Other, which was based on imaginaries of terror, catastrophe, and the disposable as its place within the project of the gestating nation. The construction of this discursive field was not only necessary to validate the aristocratizing imaginary of Whiteness but is also inseparable from the island's insertion into the process of establishing the capitalist world-economy and from its aspiration to insert itself into the international market in the vacuum left by France, as a major producer, after the revolutionary events in Haiti.

Let's not lose sight of the fact that the cementation of Whiteness as a racial and ethnic hierarchy is a global phenomenon that operates alongside the international division of labor, organized as relationships between center and periphery on a global scale. The merit of Francisco Arango y Parreño was, in his wisdom as a colonial statesman, unraveling the logic of these phenomena on an international level and articulating them along with the problematics and new national and international conjunctures the local economy found itself facing. Therefore, the creation of a discursive field for these racially exclusive practices has a strong foundation in the economic reality that it is seeking to transform, in the production of discourses centered on the social, economic, technical, and moral progress of a nation that, from its very genesis, is conceived as racially White. On a semiotic level, this desire for modernization is controlled and compensated by this end goal of racial exclusion. This is illustrated by the double transitive/intransitive movement from which Black raciality is inscribed in these grand narratives of progress and the new modes of production of the modern-colonial world system.

Not by chance, the rhetorical procedures to which, in the symbolic order of languages, Arango y Parreño appeals in order to validate his project of modernization have the function of warding off dangers, mastering fortuitous events, and avoiding the heavy and fearsome materiality that the Black subject represents for those who lust for power. The politics of terror, the account of catastrophe, and the culture of disposability that the presence of the racialized Black body in the emerging Cuban nation supposes, and the necessity of implementing social mechanisms that allow for the evacuation of the rubbish of the Other, constitute the ideological foundations upon which Arango y Parreño articulates this discursive field regarding the Black subject.[24] This discursive field forms part of the arsenal of political techniques that this aristocratic founding father of our nation leaves as his legacy to the burgeoning elites who will succeed him on the island.

The performative way with which panic toward the Black Other operates in his writings is relevant.[25] It is a fact that always must be alluded to or remembered so that the hegemonic group might preserve itself culturally and legitimate the processes of subalternization of the Other. In this way, el miedo al negro becomes a cultural phenomenon that is symbolically constructed through language. The entry of the racialized Black and mulatto body into the nation as imagined community has, therefore, a negative connotation. Within this process of the cementation of a discursive field on Blackness in terms of hegemony-domination, the writings of Francisco Arango y Parreño are fundamental. That is, the author is inscribed in the category of *founding subject* of these narratives of el miedo al negro, because of the range of procedures that his works, insistently, propose for the purposes of disciplinary control, repression, and the gradual elimination of the racialized Black body from the Cuban national imaginary.[26] Two aspects to which we should attend are: the configuration of the subject of enunciation in Arango y Parreño's essays (the place from which one speaks and thinks of the wellbeing of the nation and its interrelations with the Black subject) and the symbolic authority of the speaker in these texts to produce and impose new horizons of meaning over the *being* and *condition* of Black racial identity in the Cuban nation.

4

In his memorable essay, *¿Cómo surgió la cultura nacional?* (How did the national culture arise?), Walterio Carbonell demands a revision of the Cuban nineteenth century:

Es por todas estas razones que el siglo XIX necesita revisión. Dioses de barro superviven como una realidad en la conciencia de nuestro pueblo revolucionario. Figuras oscuras, esclavistas de la peor especie, como Arango y Parreño; esclavistas atormentados como José Antonio Saco y Luz Caballero, enemigos de las revoluciones y de la convivencia democrática, han sido elevados a la categoría de dioses nacionales por los historiadores, profesores y políticos burgueses.

It is for all of these reasons that the nineteenth century needs revision. Clay gods survive as a reality in the consciousness of our revolutionary nation. Dark figures, slave-holders of the worst type, like Arango y Parreño; tormented slave-holders like José Antonio Saco and Luz Caballero, enemies of revolutions and democratic coexistence, have been elevated to the category of national gods by bourgeois historians, professors, and politicians.[27]

And next he stresses: "La Revolución no puede tener por dioses nacionales a estos hombres, los mismos hombres que fueron elevados por la burguesía a la categoría de dioses nacionales" (The Revolution cannot have as national gods, the same men who were elevated by the bourgeoisie to the category of national gods.)[28] Walterio's book appeared in 1961, from which we can assert that it proposes a rewriting of Cuban national history at the same time that it attempts to sketch out a new revolutionary historiography in relation to those invisibilized events and subjects that bourgeois historiography excommunicated from the nation's memory.

But unfortunately, the re-readings of the texts of Francisco Arango y Parreño, José Antonio Saco, and Domingo Del Monte conducted by postrevolutionary historiography from the 1970s until the present reproduce, in the order of knowledge, a method of writing and a philosophy of history inherited from Eurocentric paradigms, which do not consider the scars, fractures, and exclusions produced by *colonial difference* in these subaltern subjects and identities. Said re-readings, on the contrary, attempt to silence the wounds and cursed memories in search of a falsely harmonious image of *us as a nation*. Furthermore, this is a dangerous endeavor, since it silences the diversity of racial, social, cultural, gender, and class projects that make up this expression, where different memories evaluate their past and propose diverse futures.

It is important to remember that, since its assumption of power in 1959, the Cuban Revolution has dedicated a large part of its efforts to constructing an *Other* nation and a new project of modernity, whose ideas about nationalism, identity, and national culture were summarized in the paradigm of a mestizo or mulatto nation, which subsumed all racial and cultural differences. At the same time, it allowed the White, Eurocentric cultural matrix to continue playing its hegemonic and exclusionary role through a cultural policy that operated as a device of ideological integration.

I propose that we examine a group of aporias and cultural extortions that transformed Black popular culture into an indicator of cultural degradation. For example: even as institutes, such as the Institute of Ethnology and Folklore, the National Seminary of Dramaturgy, and the National Folk Ensemble, were created with the charge of rescuing and preserving African cultural heritage, said culture remained constrained to the condition of archive, folklore, museum, patrimony. From this condition, the past could only be seen as something archaic. In other words, this same gesture of recognition of the national identity's African component implied a hijacking of its autonomy and cultural differences, of its secular gestures of challenge and resistance against the hegemonic culture that had allowed it to survive for centuries.

Not by chance, the heated debates that traversed the intellectual scene during these early years of the Revolution have among their pretensions the goal of outlining the place of the "people" within the cultural revolution. For example, Juan Blanco, in a text entitled "Los herederos del oscurantismo" (The heirs of obscurantism), published in *La Gaceta de Cuba* in April 1963, makes the following exhortation to Cuban intellectuals and artists:

> Luchar por lograr obras que contribuyan aún más a la integración de una verdadera cultura nacional que sea fiel a nuestro tiempo, fiel a nuestra Revolución y, por tanto, libre de prejuicios limitadores, de oscurantismos y coyundas, lograda a través de la aplicación de todos los conocimientos adquiridos, de todas las técnicas existentes y de las que podamos desarrollar para tan elevado fin.

> *To fight to achieve works that further contribute to the integration of a true national culture that is faithful to our time, faithful to our Revolution, and, therefore, free from limiting prejudices, from obscurantisms and limits, achieved through the application of all acquired knowledge, of all existing techniques, and those that we can develop for such high ends.*[29]

These words synthesize the archetype of cultural modernity and the new national subject that the Revolution sought to construct. However, this technical rationality of culture that Blanco proposes is contradicted by the cultural traditions of the African diaspora. Furthermore, the presuppositions of art and literature stemming from Marxist aesthetics, which seek to prevail in these struggles for interpretive power, not only attempt to validate the canons of realism and socialist realism, but also pose an antagonistic struggle between idealism and materialism, between bourgeois and proletarian culture.

This is how Mirta Aguirre formulates it, early on, in her essay "Apuntes sobre el arte y la literatura" (Notes on art and literature):

> Hoy, en manos del materialismo dialéctico, el arte puede y debe ser exorcismo, forma de conocimiento que contribuya a barrer de la mente de los hombres *las sombras caliginosas de la ignorancia*, instrumento precioso para la sustitución de la concepción religiosa del mundo por su concepción científica y apresurador recurso marxista de la derrota del idealismo.
>
> *Today, in the hands of dialectical materialism, art can and should be an exorcism, a form of knowledge that contributes to sweeping from the minds of men the caliginous shadows of ignorance, a precise instrument for the substitution of the religious conception of the world by its scientific conception and an urgent Marxist appeal for the defeat of idealism.*[30]

Aguirre's text, which appeared in October 1963 in the magazine *Cuba Socialista*, constitutes part of the debate held by a group of filmmakers regarding the models of representation that art and literature should follow within the nascent Revolution. The following text, "El Consejo Nacional de Cultura contesta a Alfredo Guevara" (The National Council of Culture answers Alfredo Guevara), also forms part of these struggles for the monopoly over representation. It consists of a document enunciated by an official body; therefore, their proposal should be read taking into account its normative, guiding nature within the cultural policy of those early years of the Revolution.[31]

I will dwell on the paragraph where we are informed that among the ten most urgent objectives proposed by the Revolutionary government in the cultural arena is found: "Despojar las expresiones folklóricas del campo y de la ciudad y las manifestaciones populares de nuestra cultura, de las mistificaciones de los elementos ajenos a su propia esencia, creando las condiciones necesarias para que puedan expresarse en toda su pureza" (To strip from the folkloric expressions of the countryside and city and the popular manifestations of our culture, the mystifications of those elements alien to their own essence, creating the conditions necessary for them to be expressed in all their purity).[32]

The renovating and democratizing projects that the Cuban Revolution promoted as part of its project of cultural modernity come into tension, in the first place, with the misfortunes, mixtures, and hybridizations of our colonial heritage.[33] Such dysfunction is understandable, if we consider that we are talking about a post-occidental context, where modernity never managed to work, and if it did so, only in a failed way, at the wrong time.[34] To this we must add the prejudices that, historically, White intellectuals have demonstrated toward *the masses* and their culture. For these elites, the cultural and religious practices of the Black subject are hoaxes that impede the project of modernization that the Revolution aspires to build. The following text, which appeared in the magazine *El militante comunista* in 1968, is revealing:

> La santería es una mezcla grosera de elementos mitológicos de ciertas religiones africanas [. . .] Se precian de sus supuestos conocimientos acerca de las virtudes de las plantas, el cual (sic) es más primitivo que por ejemplo, el que poseían los alquimistas medievales [. . .] Una religión es primitiva cuando no ha llegado ni siquiera a elaborar abstracciones. A nosotros nos revuelve el estómago, mas para una mentalidad primitiva tiene lógica.
>
> *Santería is a crude mix of mythological elements of certain African religions [. . .] They pride themselves on their supposed knowledge regarding the virtues of plants, which is more primitive than, for example, that possessed by medieval alchemists [. . .] A religion is primitive when it has not even managed to elaborate abstractions. Our stomach churns, but for a primitive mentality it is logical.*[35]

Decades later, evoking those years, Rogelio Martínez Furé points out the following:

> Si todavía hoy hay grandes tensiones, ¡imagínate en la década del 60! Y llega un momento donde comienza el movimiento de reivindicación de las minorías que controlaban el poder, entonces cada vez que tú hablabas de había que incluir historias de África o de afroamericanos te decían que

tú querías destruir la unidad del pueblo cubano, que tú querías destruir la cultura blanca, el discurso histórico que es el mismo en todo momento de crisis. Un discurso sovietizante donde las nacionalidades no tenían un papel fundamental, y la caída del capo socialista demostró que sí es importante tomar en cuenta los factores no solo étnicos sino también raciales

> *If there are still today huge tensions, imagine the '60s! There comes a time when the moment of vindication for the minority that controlled power begins, and then every time that you say that stories of Africa or African Americans should be included they tell you that you want to destroy the unity of the Cuban people, that you want to destroy White culture, the historical discourse that is the same in every moment of crisis. A sovietizing discourse where nationalities do not have a fundamental role, and the fall of the socialist leader showed that, yes, it is important to consider not only ethnic, but also racial factors.*[36]

For his part, the Cuban historian Juan Felipe Benemelis notes the following paradox: "Pese a que existía una política exterior de acercamiento al continente africano, sin embargo, la temática africana como tal era rechazada, o simplemente tenida como poco importante" (Despite the fact that there existed an approach to foreign policy for the African continent, however, the African subject as such was rejected, or simply considered unimportant).[37] And he recalls:

> En 1966 se denegó la celebración de los carnavales en toda la Isla, puesto que no se avenía a la nueva ética revolucionaria y no representaba al "hombre nuevo" que construía el socialismo. Este "hombre nuevo" no podía ser abakuá, no podía abrazar la fe de los orishas africanos, ni consultar el tablero de Ifá y, por supuesto, debía alejarse de la herencia africana enraizada en los carnavales.

> *In 1966, the celebration of carnivals throughout the island was denied, since it did not comply with the new revolutionary ethics and did not represent the "new man" that built socialism. This "new man" could not be Abakuá, could not embrace the faith of the African Orishas, nor consult the Ifá board, and, of course, should distance himself from the African heritage at the root of the carnivals.*[38]

We hear the following testimony from the Afro-Cuban playwright Tomás González, which he sent me several years ago via email, where he recounts the repression and exclusion from the country's cultural life that he and a group of Afro-Cuban intellectuals suffered after their attempts to place Cuban racial problems on the agenda for the First National Congress of Education and Culture in 1970. The email begins with these words: "Después de aquella vez, donde me ocurrieron cosas tan dolorosas como bestiales, quedé como en estado letal. Lo que era para mí la posibilidad de vivir feliz y realizado se me fue abolina, como un papalote de colores furiosos" (After that time, where things as painful as they were beastly occurred to me, I was left in a lethal state. The possibility of leading a fulfilled and happy life became abhorrent to me, like a furiously colored kite). The events that triggered such a witchhunt against him were the following:

> I presented a paper, written on two pages, in which I set out my criteria regarding the problems facing the development of national culture in our country. I said that Blacks and Whites were not on equal terms regarding the integration of their cultural contributions. Racial discrimination is not erased by decree. And in this paper we present various examples. From the blond doll in the arms of a Black girl, to the fact that on the cast for a show the actors and actresses couldn't be Black, the million ways that the Black person was considered a brute, savage being who "if he doesn't mess up at the beginning, will mess up at the end." The reaction against these arguments was extraordinary. A majority of White Cubans demanded, thumbs-down, that they throw me to the lions at the Roman circus. Of course, this had cutting consequences for me: I was without a job or salary for several years, during the time that Llanusa was minister. Because of that presentation I was considered the leader of a *Poder Negro* in Cuba, in the style of Black Power and with implications of the *negritude* movement of our friend Cesaire, the great poet of Martinique. From this moment on I was a pariah.[39]

The information that I have just offered reveals how the construction of the concept of *Black popular culture* has not only been at the mercy of tensions between intellectuals and the masses, but has also been subject to hygienicist perceptions and strategies of invisibility generated from the field of political power.

Institutional academic discourse, in complicity with the political arena, built a series of metaphor-concepts like *Cuban color*, *melting pot* [*ajiaco*], *transculturation*, *mulatez*, and *mestizaje*, which responded to the political goal of constructing a homogeneous national subject that allowed the state to reabsorb from its center of power the identity-based differences that presented an obstacle to its unified exercise of power. Consequently, these discourses and practices related to the staging of Black history and culture became unintelligible or "suspicious" in the face of the interpretive frameworks of the new hegemonic symbolic order stemming from Marxist-Leninist aesthetics and philosophy that, at best, viewed them as prejudice, ignorance, and superstition: "Black stuff."

As can be seen in the email from Tomás González quoted above, a truly inspiring and influential moment in the process of conscientization of the racial identity of a group of Afro-Cuban intellectuals, as well as others who formed part of the diplomatic and political circuits related directly with Africa and the Caribbean, was their contact with the leaders of the Black Power movement and the Black Panthers who visited Cuba beginning in the late 1960s, among whom were Robert F. Williams, Stokely Carmichael, and Eldridge Cleaver.[40] This is what many call the Cuban Black Power movement, whose existence has become something of a legend. Even researchers such as Linda S. Howe and Carlos Moore speak of the existence of a "Black Manifesto," or *Manifiesto Negro*.[41]

For his part, Juan F. Benemelis—in an interview that I conducted with him on Monday, October 11, 2011, in Miami—told me that the group: "tuvo dos tendencias o vertientes. Una, llamémosle cultural, cuyos actores provenían fundamentalmente del campo de la investigación etnográfica, y la creación artística y literaria como Sara Gómez, Tomás González, Pedro Pérez Sarduy" (had two tendencies or perspectives. One, we'll call them cultural, whose actors came fundamentally from the field of ethnographic research, and literary and artistic creation like Sara Gómez, Tomás González, Pedro Pérez Sarduy). The other tendency was closer to the political structures in those early years of revolution and was "el grupo del cual provengo, éramos dirigentes políticos y diplomáticos. Teníamos relación directa con África y el Caribe, sus líderes y pensadores. Por ejemplo: yo, trabajaba en el MINREX" (the group that I come from, we were political and diplomatic leaders. We had direct relationships with Africa and the Caribbean, their leaders and thinkers. For example: I was working in the Ministry of Foreign Relations [MINREX]).

Benemelis identifies as important "nuestra relación personal con líderes negros afronorteamericanos que estaban en Cuba como Williams, Bround de las Panteras Negras. Confluíamos muchos con ellos. Las discusiones y las conversaciones personales con otros intelectuales y líderes negros internacionales fueron determinantes" (our personal relationship with Black African American leaders that were in Cuba, like Williams, Bround from the Black Panthers. Many of us came together with them. Discussions and personal conversations with other, international Black leaders and intellectuals were decisive). And later he clarifies:

> No había en nosotros el ánimo de una rebelión violenta. Asumir el rótulo de Black Power era, por un lado, una forma de indicar una pertenencia racial, y por otra parte puede decirse que un modo simbólico de llamar la atención, visibilizarnos como grupo. Lo que, también te demuestra que se había llegado a un estado de asfixia en la búsqueda de un espacio para dialogar, debatir el tema. Ese momento fue más neurálgico si lo comparamos con el de hoy en día. Lamentablemente, nosotros no logramos ningún espacio. Según se entiende esto actualmente.

> *There was no spirit in us of violent rebellion. To assume the Black Power label was, on the one hand, a way of indicating racial belonging, and on the other we might say it was a symbolic way of attracting attention, making ourselves visible as a group. Which also shows you that a state of suffocation had been reached in the search for a space to dialogue, debate the issue. This moment was more nerve-wracking compared to today. Unfortunately, we didn't make any space. According to how this is currently understood.*[42]

From this complex scenario it's possible to understand the silence, fear, and frustration that permeated the approach to different topics related with Black racial identity in Cuba from the late sixties to the early years of the twenty-first century. This timid approach, with none but the slightest focus on the political-ideological discourse, remained confined to the symbolic field, thanks to the solitary labor and gestures of resistance of filmmakers such as Sara Gómez and Nicolasito Guillen Landrián; the poetry of Nancy Morejón, Pedro Pérez Sarduy, and Georgina Herrera; the theatrical works of Gerardo Fulleda, Eugenio Hernández, Tomás González, and Alberto Pedro; the poems and research of Rogelio Martínez Furé; and the narratives of Manolo Granados, all of whom had to deal with the silence and indifference of critics who refused to speak about them in the context of their condition as Afro-Cuban authors and artists. The strategy of these creators was concentrated on elaborating an aesthetic discourse that, although moving within the utopian and redemptive dimension of the Revolution, incorporated the most diverse topics related to the racial identity of Black and mulatto men and women. It was a meaningful project insofar as it allowed the thematization and consequent problematization of the racial not to die. These circumstances explain why, in the works produced by the groups of Afro-Cuban writers that emerged on the Cuban literary scene between the 1960s and 1980s, there are no Black heroes.

Another example that illustrates this problematic is the debate regarding the terms "Afro-descendant" and "Afro-Cuban." Above all, the latter has encountered some resistance within the Cuban intellectual community at the beginning of this new millennium. The detractors of the term "Afro-Cuban," in order to disqualify it and arouse childish political suspicions, resort to the argument that it is nothing more than a borrowed term from the African American movement. These objections are only explained by virtue of the absence of studies on the Afro-Cuban movement of the 1960s, a segment of time marked by the important ties and theoretical, ideological, and political influences that they exerted on Afro-Cuban intellectuals, not only via leaders of the Black Power and Black Panther social movements that resided in Cuba, but also due to encounters with important Black thinkers of the decolonization movement in Africa and the Caribbean.

In my view, this rejection of the term "Afro-Cuban" transcends the mere terminological question and presupposes not only a political but also an epistemological debate about the way in which the colonial legacy and its modes of thinking about the racialized Other continue reproducing themselves in the discursive paradigms of our humanities and social sciences. It is almost always associated with a "policy of interpretation" anchored to teleological perceptions of history, in a contradictory aspiration for homogeneity, where the categories of syncretism, *mulatez*, and *mestizaje* (which we will later question) respond to this desire to read the cultural processes of the Cuban nation in terms of succession, homogeneity, and racial harmony. In my case the term "Afro-Cuban" is perfectly coherent with my intellectual positioning and with my willingness to explore historical exclusions and differences whose public discussion has been largely silenced. For this reason, it is necessary to remember the role that this term has played in the different debates about the racial problematic in Cuba throughout the twentieth century. It is not a neologism but a theoretical space that the Cuban anti-racist and decolonizing tradition built up throughout the twentieth century, the place of enunciation from which the ties of Black and mulatto men and women with national identity, culture, and political power have been articulated and re-thought.

With everything that has been discussed up until this point, it is easy to understand why, since the beginning of the millennium, it is the space of activism and not that of the academy where the most stimulating contributions related to the recognition and revindication of Afro-Cuban identity are being carried out. The different groups and projects that make up Cuban anti-racist activism, out of the diversity of their agendas, have become important political actors oriented toward questioning the revolutionary social order and its concepts of liberty, citizenship, and democracy. Not by chance, their claims—within the ideologically walled precincts of the island—echo or are confused with heresy or political dissent. Hence, a fairly influential area of this activism—that which has been confined to and/or has preferred to be located in alternative, unofficial spaces—continually has to travel on the edge of a knife, under the scrutiny of political ideologies and actors that are suspicious of their actions, proposals, or demands as though they were a wolf in sheep's clothing.

This explains the delayed recognition—on the part of Cuban academic knowledge and discourse—of the work and existence of this activism. Let us recall that we are talking about an academy whose protocols are conditioned by or in continuous negotiation with a political arena that establishes a border between the focuses and themes considered politically correct and those that are not. It is not surprising, then, that from the beginning of the 1960s onward, Cuban anti-racist activism has been producing an Other knowledge than that of the academy, one which operates as a counter-discourse to it. This knowledge is born from a concrete reality: the direct contact of the activist with these subjects and their harsh reality. I am thinking of the texts and work of figures like Walterio Carbonell and Tomás González, to add only two other names to the list of authors mentioned above.[43]

5

Finally, I would like to refer to activism as a space that is producing new categories of knowledge enunciated *about* and *from* the racialized bodies of Black and mulatto men and women, and in a global context characterized by the effervescence of *post* accounts. Said discursive field stresses and poses new epistemological challenges for twenty-first century Cuban social sciences. I speak of an Other epistemology, of new intellectual and symbolic practices, and of behavioral models derived from post/trans/national subjects, immersed in an environment of mass media and traversed by a range of *post* discourses (post-theoretical, post-racial, post-colonial, post-occidental); where Black and mulatto racial identity are redefined in intersection and dialogue with other identities (gender, sexual, generational, group, class, etc.); whose practices and imaginaries, at present, exceed for the social scientist the limits of disciplinary knowledge.

The production of knowledge or new categories of knowledge out of activism is distinguished by the plurality of positions, subjects of enunciation, practices, and agendas. They have a cross-disciplinary and anti-disciplinary focus. Owing much to decolonial, subaltern, and cultural studies, they erode, deconstruct, and problematize the old analytical frameworks and paradigms of representation legitimized by historiography and academic knowledge in Cuba, as well as the devices and technologies that have historically determined the subalternization and exclusion of the Black subject, whether from the foundational stories of the Cuban nation or from other settings. Hence, their positions regard the monolithic notion of national identity, as a colonial remnant of that aspiration for an integral and universal subject postulated by Western modernity.

Contrary to this image of consensus that official spaces attempt to construct, the math of Afro-Cuban thought and its discursive struggles, in the last ten years, is a territory traversed by various decenterings and disseminations. In the first place, its enunciative support is not only limited to print but also includes others such as those from rap music, graffiti, spoken word, the visual arts, and those produced by new information technologies like the blogs *negracubanateniaqueser, afrocubanas, afromodernidades y afromodernidad*, and other digital sites like *afrocubaweb*. And, secondly, because of its discursive translocation, it is not only limited to the enunciative Afro-Cuban community within the island but is also affected by the phenomena of migration, political dissent, and alliances with other movements of the African diaspora in Latin America and the Caribbean, such as Articulación Regional de Afrodescendientes de América Latina y el Caribe, ARAAC (Regional Articulation of Afro-descendants of Latin America and the Caribbean).

Another significant aspect is related to the deconstruction of the doubly subaltern place that Black women and dissident sexualities have held in the tradition of Black thinkers and in movements of an eminently patriarchal and heteronormative character, such as *negritude*, *negrismo*, Marcus Garvey, the Harlem Renaissance, Black Power, Pan-Africanism, etc. Said deconstructive exercise—beyond all essentialization of identity—is related with the intersectionality of our struggles. Therefore, no natural basis (woman, Black, lesbian) exists to legitimize political action. For example, Norma Guillard Limonta, in her essay "Lesbian Afro-descendants Enrich their Identity: Cuba in the Process of this Development," refers to the multiple forms of discrimination experienced by Black, lesbian, and sometimes masculine women in the face of the norms of the heterosexual imaginary. This fact, according to her, operates out of an intersectionality that puts dominant identities in check.[44]

Of course, this type of viewpoint is not exempt from confrontations such as the one that this area of Cuban Afro-feminist discourse sustains with queer theory and its uncritical appropriation in the local context, crying out for the need to imagine conceptual tools that emanate from the particularities of our own post-occidental contexts of the periphery in a country where the alliance between the anti-racist and LGBTI movements is still a pending issue on the agenda of both movements. If accepting oneself as Black or Afro-Cuban today in Cuba is to establish a radical political difference that attempts to counteract the degrading stereotypes, invisibility, and dynamics of social stigmatization to which the racialized Black body has historically been subject in the Cuban nation, to live as a Black gay or lesbian person supposes a doubly defiant political posture, as it challenges heteronormativity and racialized designs.

Let us recall that the Western-colonial imaginary constructed a myth around the supposed virility of the African man and his offspring: the unusual proportions of his member and his almost primitive sexual ardor, capable of transgressing the limits of all morals and prohibitions and which historically has aroused the sexual anxiety of the White man and woman. The popular imaginary, for a long time, has taken charge of feeding into this sexual representation of the Black man with all kinds of gossip. Said perception makes up part of the foundational myths of the Cuban nation. Many gay men that I know have constructed their sexual tastes from these stereotypes. On the other hand, the excessively performative nature from which masculinity is constructed in the Black social, religious, and domestic spheres turns homosexual existence into a more problematic and violent fact. Furthermore, among all this cartography that I have attempted to outline throughout these pages, the public debate about racism and racial discrimination in Cuba continues to be one of those silenced chapters of the Cuban Revolution. So far, it has been limited to the academic sphere and to social media in a country that, as has been recognized, has one of the lowest rates of Internet connectivity in the world.

NOTES

1. Gastón Baquero, "El miedo al negro" [Fear of the Black], in *La memoria y el olvido. Syllabus Afrocubano* [Memory and forgetting. Afro-Cuban syllabus], ed. J. F. Benemelis (Kingston: Ediciones Ceiba, 2009), 10–11.
2. See the significant study by Jorge Ibarra, "Del sentimiento de Patria a la conciencia de nación (1600–1868)" [From patriotic feeling to national consciousness (1600–1868)], in *Patria, etnia y nación* [Homeland, ethnicity, and nation] (La Habana: Editorial de Ciencias Sociales, 2007).
3. Ibid., 25.
4. Gabriel de la Concepción Valdés, also known as Plácido (Havana, 1809), was accused of being the leader of the "Escalera" antislavery conspiracy and executed in Matanzas on July 28, 1844. Juan Francisco Manzano (Havana, 1797–1854) was famous for his sonnet "Mis treinta años" (My thirty years) and for his autobiography, which was written in 1835 and appeared first in London under the title *Poems by a Slave in the Island of Cuba*, ed. and trans. Richard Madden (London: Ward, 1840).
5. Manuel Moreno Fraginals, "Negrofobia," in *Orbita de Manuel Moreno Fraginals*, ed. Alfredo Prieto (Havana: Ediciones Unión, 2009), 44.
6. José Luciano Franco, *La Conspiración de Aponte 1812* (La Habana: Editorial Ciencias Sociales, 2006).
7. See Enrique Patterson, "Cuba: Discursos sobre la identidad," in *La memoria y el olvido. Syllabus afrocubano*, ed. Juan F. Benemelis (Kingston: Ediciones Ceiba, 2009); Walterio Carbonell, *Cómo surgió la cultura nacional* (Havana: Biblioteca Nacional José Martí, 2005); Tomás Fernández Robaina, *El negro en Cuba 1902–1958* (Havana: Editorial de Ciencas Sociales, 1990).
8. Enrique Patterson, "Cuba: Discurso sobre la identidad"; Gastón Baquero, "El negro en Cuba," in *Indios, blancos y negros en el caldeo de America* (Madrid: Cultura Hispánica, 1991), 91–116.
9. Francisco de Arango y Parreño, *Obras* (Havana: Editorial Ciencias Sociales y Casa de Altos Estudios Don Fernando Ortiz, 2005); José Antonio Saco, *Memorias sobre la vagancia en la Isla de Cuba* (Havana: Editorial de Ciencias Sociales, [1830] 2006); Domingo del Monte, *Escritos*, Introduction and notes by José Fernández de Castro (Havana: Cultural S.A., 1929). Enrique Patterson, in "Cuba: Discurso sobre la identidad," presents the thought-provoking thesis that Arango y Parreño "es el ideólogo

que introduce el 'miedo al negro' como una categoría política y sociológica que marcará la conducta de la élite cubana, y el primero que propone medidas para eliminar paulatinamente al negro como grupo futuro social de peso mediante el estímulo de la inmigración blanca" (is the idealogue that introduces "fear of the Black" as a political and sociological category that will mark the behavior of the Cuban elite, and the first to propose measures to gradually eliminate Blacks as a significant social group in the future through the stimulation of White immigration). Patterson distinguishes two moments in Arango y Parreño's position which "pueden ser rastreados como una conducta constante de la élite cubana" (can be tracked as a consistent behavior of the Cuban elite). In the first of these moments, "los negros deben ser *usados* cuando sean necesarios" (Black people should be *used* when they are necessary), while the second moment establishes that Black people should in some way be "*eliminados* al pasar esta necesidad" (*eliminated* once this necessity has passed; emphasis in original).

10. See, for example, Ada Ferrer, "Cuba en la sombra de Haití: Noticias, sociedad y esclavitud" and Consuelo Naranjo Orovio, "La amenaza haitiana, un miedo interesado: Poder y fomento de la población blanca en Cuba," in *El rumor de Haití en Cuba: Temor, raza y rebeldía. 1789–1844*, ed. D. González-Ripoll, C. Naranjo, A. Ferrer, G. García, and J. Opatrny (Madrid: Consejo Superior de Investigaciones Científicas, 2004), 179–231.
11. Ada Ferrer, "Cuba en la sombra de Haití: Noticias, sociedad, y esclavitud."
12. Ibid., 215.
13. Mario Rufer, "Huellas errantes: Rumor, verdad e historia desde una crítica poscolonial de la razón" [Errant traces: Rumor, truth, and history from a postcolonial critique to reason], *Version* 23 (2009): 41.
14. Gayatri Spivak, "Subaltern Studies: Deconstructing Historiography," in *The Spivak Reader: Selected Works of Gayatri Chakravorty Spivak*, eds. Donna Landry and Gerald Maclean. (New York: Routledge, 1996), 203–37.
15. See René Méndez Capote, "El proceso de la Escalera," in *4 Conspiraciones* (Havana: Instituto Cubano del Libro, 1972), 97–113.
16. Julio Le Riverend, *La Habana. Biografía de una provincia* [Havana: Biography of a province] (La Habana: El siglo XX, 1960), as cited by Pedro Deschamps Chapeaux, *El negro en la economía habanera del siglo XIX* [The Black man in the nineteenth-century Havanan economy] (La Habana: Ediciones Unión, 1971), 15.
17. Pedro Deschamps Chapeaux and Juan Pérez de la Riva, *Contribución a la Historia de la gente sin Historia* [Contribution to the history of the people without history] (La Habana: Editorial de Ciencias Sociales, 1974). See also Deschamps Chapeaux, *El negro en la economía habanera del siglo XIX*.
18. Roberto Friol, *Suite para Juan Francisco Manzano* [Suite for Juan Francisco Manzano] (La Habana: Biblioteca Básica de Literatura Cubana-Editorial Arte y Literatura, 1977).
19. Ibid., 66–67.
20. See the chapter "Manzano y Del Monte" [Manzano and Del Monte] in Fina García Marruz, *Hablar de la poesía* [To speak of poetry] (La Habana: Editorial Letras Cubanas, 1986), 336.

21. See the section "Acta del Careo entre los pardos libres Juan Francisco Manzano y Gabriel de la Concepción Valdés" [Proceedings of the confrontation between the free Blacks Juan Francisco Manzano and Gabriel de la Concepción Valdés] in Roberto Friol, *Suite para Juan Francisco Manzano*, 203.
22. Urbano Martínez Carmenate, *Domingo del Monte y su tiempo* (Havana: Ediciones Unión, 1997).
23. Fina García Marruz, *Hablar de la poesía*, 334–35.
24. On these categories and their role in the dynamics that interweave center-periphery relations in the current global Latin American context, see Daniel Castillo Durante's essay, "Culturas excrementicias y postcolonialismo" [Disposable cultures and postcolonialism], in *El debate de la postcolonialidad en Latinoamérica. Una postmodernidad periférica o cambio de paradigma en el pensamiento latinoamericano* [The debate on postcoloniality in Latin America. A post-modernity of the periphery or a change in the paradigm of Latin American thinking], ed. A. de Toro and F. de Toro (Madrid: Vervuert Iberoamericana, 1999), 235–57.
25. I use the term *performative* in the sense described by Judith Butler, "Performative Acts and Gender Constitution: An Essay in Phenomenology and Feminist Theory," *Theatre Journal* 40, no. 4 (1988): 519–31; Butler, "Precarity, Performativity, and Sexual Politics," *AIBR. Revista de Antropología Iberoamericana* 4, no. 3 (2009), i–xiii.
26. I borrow this "founding subject" category from Foucault. According to him, the founding subject is he who takes charge of encouraging, directly, with his objectives the empty forms of language, he who founds a horizon of meanings that future history will not have to make explicit later. See Michel Foucault, "An Aesthetics of Existence," in *Foucault Live. Collected Interviews, 1961–1984*, ed. S. Lotringer (New York: Semiotext(e), 2006).
27. Walterio Carbonell, *Cómo surgió la cultura nacional* [How did the national culture arise?] (La Habana: Ediciones Bachiller-Escribanía Collection-José Martí National Library, 2005), 22.
28. Ibid.
29. Juan Blanco, "Los herederos del oscurantismo" [The heirs of obscurantism], in *Polémicas culturales de los 60* [Cultural controversies of the '60s], ed. G. Pogolotti (La Habana: Editorial Letras Cubanas, 2006), 5.
30. Mirta Aguirre, "Apuntes sobre el arte y la literatura" [Notes on art and literature], in *Revolución, Letras, Arte* [Revolution, letters, art] (La Habana: Editorial Letras Cubanas, 1980), 201 (italics in original).
31. Vincentina Antuña, "El Consejo Nacional contesta a Alferedo Guevara," in *Polémicas culturales de los 60*, ed. Graziella Pogolotti (Havana: Editorial Letras Cubanas, 2006), 189–94.
32. Ibid., 191.
33. I follow here the model of analyzing Latin American modernity proposed by Néstor García Canclini, who establishes four processes or movements: emancipation, renovation, democratization, and expansion. García Canclini, *Hybrid Cultures: Strategies for Entering and Leaving Modernity* (Minneapolis: University of Minnesota Press, 1995).
34. In place of the term "post-colonial," I prefer to use the term "post-occidentalism," suggested by Roberto Fernández Retamar in his essays, "Para una teoría de la

literatura hispanoamericana" [Toward a theory of Spanish-American literature] and "Algunos problemas teóricos de la literatura hispanoamericana" [Some theoretical problems of Spanish-American literature], in *Para una teoría de la literatura hispanoamericana* (Santa Fé de Bogotá: Instituto Caro y Cuervo, 1995). Further reference in Fernández Retamar, "Nuestra América y el Occidente" [Our America and the West], in *Nuestra América y el Occidente* (México: UNAM, 1978). See the essay by Roberto Schwarz, "Las ideas fuera de lugar" [Misplaced ideas], originally published under the title "As idéias fora do lugar," in *Estudos, CEBRAP*, no.3 (1973), and as the first chapter of *Ao vencedor as batatas* (San Pablo: Duas cidades, 1977), 13–28, the version upon which this translation is based. www.ffyh.unc.edu.ar/modernidades/II/Mod2Contenidos/Main-Traducciones.

35. Jesús Barquet, *Ediciones El Puente en La Habana de los años 60: Lecturas críticas y libros de poesía* [Havana in the '60s: Critical readings and books of poetry] (Chihuahua: Ediciones del Azar, 2011).
36. Quoted in Barquet, *Ediciones El Puente en La Habana de los años 60*, 156.
37. Juan Felipe Benemelis, "El Black Power en la Cuba de los sesenta y setenta. Conversación con Juan Felipe Benemelis" [Black Power in Cuba in the sixties and seventies: Conversation with Juan Felipe Benemelis], Interview by Alberto Abreu, *Afromodernidades* (blog), October 20, 2012, www.afromodernidades.wordpress.com.
38. Benemelis, "El Black Power en la Cuba de los sesenta y setenta," para.14.
39. Tomás González in discussion with the author, January 08, 2007. Original Spanish: Presento una ponencia, redactada en dos cuartillas, en la que exponía mis criterios sobre los problemas para el desarrollo de la cultura nacional en nuestro país. Dije que negros y blancos no estaban en igualdad de condiciones para la integración de sus aportes culturales. La discriminación racial no se borra con un decreto. Y en esa ponencia presentamos diversos ejemplos. Desde la muñeca rubia en los brazos de una niña negra, como en un reparto para una novela o para un clásico los actores y actrices no podían ser negros, las mil formas de considerar al negro un ser salvaje y bruto que "si no la hace a la entrada, la hace a la salida." La reacción en contra de estos argumentos fue extraordinaria. Una mayoría de cubanos blancos pedían para mí, con el pulgar hacia abajo, que me echaran a los leones del circo romano. Por supuesto, esto me trajo una tajante consecuencia, me quedé sin empleo y sueldo durante algunos años, durante el tiempo los que Llanusa fue ministro. Por aquella ponencia me consideraron como el líder de un Poder Negro en Cuba, al estilo del Black Power y con ramificaciones en la "negritude" de nuestro amigo Cesaire, el gran poeta de Martinica. A partir de ese momento fui un apestado.
40. As is well known, Williams arrived in Cuba fleeing from the United States government and falsely accused of kidnapping. He remained on the island from 1961 to 1965, where he directed the program Radio Free Dixie, from which he propagated his radical ideas toward the United States. In September 1966 he sent a letter to Fidel Castro from China, where he went after experiencing certain tensions with officials of the Ministry of the Interior. As María Isabel Alfonso has been able to verify by tracing these sources:

En la misiva, se refiere a conflictos con Osmany Cienfuegos, el comandante René Vallejo y el viceministro del Interior Manuel Piñeiro, quienes desatendieron y boicotearon, según Williams, su lucha por la causa afroamericana. No llega a hablar de racismo en dicha carta, pero he encontrado en el archivo Robert Williams Papers otras cartas suyas refiriéndose a que fue discriminado por las autoridades cubanas.

In the letter, he refers to conflicts with Osmany Cienfuegos, Commander René Vallejo, and Deputy Minister of the Interior Manuel Piñeiro, who neglected and boycotted, according to Williams, their fight for the African American cause. He does not speak of racism in said letter, but I have found in the archive of the Robert Williams Papers other letters of his referring to the fact that he was discriminated against by Cuban authorities.

See María Isabel Alfonso, "Ediciones El Puente y las dinámicas raciales de los 60: Un capítulo olvidado de la historia literaria cubana" [El Puente Editions and racial dynamics of the 1960s: A forgotten chapter of Cuban literary history], *Temas* 70 (2012): 110–18.

Carmichael was a member of the Black Panthers. In 1967 he visited Cuba and was disappointed by the way racial issues were treated. For Carmichael, it was nonsense to think that the dissolution of social classes was the way to gradually eliminate racism.

As William Brent relates, the Cuban government enthusiastically invited Eldridge Cleaver to Cuba in 1968, until he decided to organize a Cuban Black Panthers. Then, under official pressure, he had to abandon the island and went to Algeria. See William Lee Brent, *Long Time Gone* (New York: Time Books, 1996), 174.

It is significant that one of the arguments put forth by Cuban literary historiography for a long time to justify its banishment of the El Puente literary group (1961–1965) from the nation's literary memory was that it wanted to foment a Black Power movement in Cuba, an accusation that is only sustained by virtue of the prominent presence of young Black writers and the revitalization of the African legacy within this group, since at the time these African American movements emerged, official policy had already decreed the death of El Puente. Said argument, in addition to lacking any historical basis, illustrates the racist bases on which the post-revolutionary literary canon is being built.

41. Linda S. Howe, *Transgression and Conformity: Cuban Writers and Artists After the Revolution* (Madison: University of Wisconsin Press, 2004); Carlos Moore, *Castro, the Blacks and Africa* (Los Angeles: University of California, 1989). For his part, Benemelis, in the interview quoted above, assured me of the existence of the Manifesto:

Sí, recuerdo que Manolito Casanova llegó una tarde a mi casa enarbolándolo. Eso fue antes del congreso del 68. Walterio estaba muy estimulado con este congreso y con la idea de crear una comisión para discutir el problema racial cubano. El manifiesto se centraba en cuestiones relativas a las trampas de la mulatez, la equidad. Estimábamos falsa la afirmación de que en Cuba habían entrado las ideas del movimiento de la negritud en la década del cuarenta.

> *Yes, I remember that Manolito Casanova arrived one afternoon to my house brandishing it. This was before the congress in '68. Walterio was very encouraged by this congress and with the idea of creating a commission to discuss the Cuban racial problem. The manifesto was centered around questions relative to the pitfalls of mulatez, equity. We considered the claim that the ideas of the negritude movement had entered Cuba in the forties to be false.*

Pedro Pérez Sarduy, for his part, affirms that it is a paper of which he keeps a typed copy and where everyone "participamos en la elaboración de ideas. Sobre todo Sarita [Sara Gómez] quien fue muy aguda. El llamado Manifiesto Negro nunca fue tal cosa. . . . Fue una ponencia al Congreso" (participated in the elaboration of ideas. Above all Sarita [Sara Gómez] who was very sharp. The so-called Black Manifesto was never such a thing. . . . It was a presentation to the Congress). (qtd. by Benemelis in discussion with the author, May 9, 2017).

42. Juan Felipe Benemelis, "El Black Power en la Cuba de los sesenta y setenta."
43. See Walterio Carbonell, *Cómo surgió la cultura nacional* (Havana: Biblioteca Nacional José Martí, 2005); Tomás González, *El bello arte de ser y otras obras* (Havana: Editorial Letras Cubanas, 2005).
44. See Norma R. Guillard Limonta, "Afro-Descendant Lesbians Strengthen Their Identity," *Souls* 21, no. 4 (2019): 312–22. Also, "Ser mujer negra, lesbiana," paper read at the colloquium on "La nación que estamos imaginando, nuevas geografías de la racialidad negra" (The Nation that we are Imagining, New Geographies on Black Raciality), held at the Centro Cristiano de Reflexión y Diálogo de Cárdenas, May, 28–29, 2015. afromodernidades.wordpress.com/2015/07/15afromodernidfades-100.

CHAPTER 10

Senzalas e Quilombos Modernos
Evoking the Legacy of Slavery in Brazilian Hip Hop

ELISEO JACOB

On November 20, 1995, in the Vale do Anhangabú, in the center of São Paulo, a rap festival was organized in commemoration of Dia da Consciência Negra (Black Consciousness Day), a date that recognizes the anniversary of the death of Zumbi, leader of the *quilombo* (Maroon community) of Palmares during the seventeenth century, which became a symbol of resistance and Black pride in the 1970s with the rise of the *movimento negro*.[1]

The date of the rap festival was notable in that it not only marked the holiday that celebrates Black culture, history, and pride, but it was also the three-hundredth anniversary of Zumbi's death. Posse Mente Zulu, a little-known rap group outside of São Paulo's *periferia* (working class outskirts) and with no albums yet recorded, performed a song that would go on to symbolize hip hop's role in instilling what Derek Pardue would call "consciência" in Brazil's urban Black youth. The song, "Sou Negrão" (I'm really Black), can be read as a call to the audience to recognize the contributions of Black culture through a Pan-Africanist mapping of Black figures, musicians, and leaders not only throughout Brazil's history but within the African diaspora, as well:

> Vinte de novembro temos que repensar
> A liberdade dum que tanto teve de lutar
> O negro não é marginal, não é perigo
> Negro ser humano, só quer ter amigo

> Na antiga era o funk, agora é o rap
> Vem puxando o movimento como negro de talento
> O negro é bonito quando está sorrindo
> Como versou Jorge Ben, o negro é lindo.
>
> *November 20, we have to rethink*
> *The freedom of a Black man who*
> *fought so much*
> *Blacks are not criminals, not dangerous*
> *Black human beings, they only want to be friends*
> *In the past it was funk, now it's rap*
> *Moving forward the cause with talented Blacks*
> *Blacks are beautiful when they are smiling*
> *Like Jorge Ben sang, Black is beautiful.*[2]

The verb "repensar" used in the first line is important in that in Portuguese it does not just mean to rethink in the literal translation of the verb but to think over something again, to reflect, to reconsider. Posse Mente Zulu is calling to the audience and to Afro-Brazilians in general to rethink their value in a society that has frequently seen them as marginal or dangerous.

Other rap groups recorded songs in 1995 to recognize the tricentennial of Zumbi's death as a way to evoke Black pride and consciousness. Thaíde and DJ Hum, the rap duo that emerged in the early days of 1980s Brazilian hip hop, produced the song "Afro-Brasileiro" (Afro-Brazilian) with a refrain that repeatedly asks listeners if they know who they are in terms of their racial/ethnic ancestry. Thaíde ends the refrain with a powerful statement: "Afro-brasileiro / Somos decendentes de Zumbi / Grande guerreiro" (Afro-Brazilian / We are descendants of Zumbi / Great warrior).[3] These two rap groups' homage to a key historical Afro-Brazilian figure on the anniversary of his death raises the question of what is the aesthetic value of popular, Afro-centric musical productions, and what do they show us about the politics of Black cultural productions in Brazil? I argue that they reflect the role of *quilombismo* in Brazilian rap in using references to slavery and revolt as a way not only to make sense of the extreme poverty and violence that impacts urban Afro-Brazilian populations but also to conceptualize other possibilities for social and political empowerment due to a deeper understanding of these systemic inequities, or what Derek Pardue observes among Brazilian hip hoppers as being "informados" (informed) about their material reality and then deciding to finds ways to engage with it differently.[4]

Abdias do Nascimento proposed and developed the concept of quilombismo during the rise of the MNU in the 1970s as a way to deal with the systemic racism that has impacted Black communities in Brazil. In his essay "Quilombismo: An Afro-Brazilian Political Alternative," Nascimento makes the assertion that contemporary Blacks' condition has not improved since abolition in 1888 because of being segregated from economic opportunities, being subjected to police brutality, and living in substandard conditions. It is because of this reality for the Afro-Brazilian population that Nascimento uses the metaphor of the *quilombo*, or Maroon community, for Afro-Brazilians to "ensure their survival and assure their existence as human beings."[5] He names Black cultural organizations, such as *terreiros*, brotherhoods, *confrarias*, *afoxés*, and samba schools as examples of modern-day quilombos, or what Niyi Afolabi categorizes as cultural *quilombolas*.[6] I include hip hop as another iteration of these cultural quilombolas, as it too circulates discourses that call attention to the historical oppression experienced by Afro-descendants while proposing a politics of social engagement. Ultimately, quilombismo is a constant process of revitalization and modernization rooted in anti-imperialist practices and Pan-Africanism.[7]

This study, therefore, examines how Brazilian rappers can be seen as part of this *quilombista* tradition by calling upon the legacy of slavery to 1) critique the effects of anti-Black racism and state violence in the urban periphery and 2) to advocate cultural resistance through an Afro-centric aesthetic that values Black traditions and histories. In particular, I look at how rappers use the dialectic of the *senzala* (slave quarters) and the *quilombo* (Maroon communities) as a way to reframe the experiences of their communities, the *periferias* (working class communities on the outskirts) and *favelas* (shantytowns), which have a predominately Afro-descendant population.[8] While Brazilian rappers critique how the periferia and favelas continue to experience discrimination and a lack of social mobility by drawing parallels with their ancestors enslaved in the senzalas, they also look to acts of resistance, calling upon the mythos of the quilombo to draw attention to the genocide of Black people in Brazil's major cities and to efforts to preserve and celebrate Afro-Brazilian history, culture, and identity. To better understand this dialectic, I will analyze four rap songs: "Antigamente Quilombos, Hoje Periferia" (2002) by Z'África Brasil, "Boa Esperança" (2015) by Emicida, "Crime Bárbaro" (2017) by Rincon Sapiência, and "Psicopretas Vol. 1" (2018). All the rap artists belong to what Derek Pardue categorizes as the fourth phase of *negritude* in Brazilian Hip Hop (1999–present), which combines a working-class Afro-centric discourse with narratives on the harsh life in the periferia.[9] I consider Brazilian Hip Hop not only as a cultural production that generates narratives and uses language reflective of periferia life but also as belonging to a larger Afro-Brazilian tradition rooted in quilombismo, which includes the Teatro Experimental do Negro, Movimento Negro Unificado, blocos Afros, and Quilombhoje.[10] My study on this newer generation of rap is framed by Imani Perry's important work *Prophets from the Hood: Politics and Poetics in Hip Hop*, which analyzes rap lyrics and images as "text to illuminate and examine an oral and auditory art form."[11] By focusing on the aesthetics of hip hop, the goal is to understand how it functions as a discourse that engages politically, not only critiquing state violence but also functioning as a liberatory practice from an Afro-centric positionality.

Periferia as Senzala: State Violence and Anti-Black Racism

Before examining how recent hip hoppers in Brazil call upon the image of the senzala and quilombo in their songs, it is essential to understand how the periferia, or urban periphery of São Paulo – the principal setting for many of these songs – is construed as a space that evokes the legacy of slavery and racial violence. Teresa Caldeira, in her book *City of Walls: Crime, Segregation and Citizenship in São Paulo*, historically contextualizes how the periferia developed through state and municipal policies that not only segregated different social classes, but also perpetuated discourses having to do with crime and danger associated with the working-class, urban population.[12] The history of how the periferia developed frames how hip hoppers use a rhetoric tied to the senzala and slavery to make sense of their current living conditions of being pushed to the outskirts of the city, segregated from educational and economic opportunities, and subjected to state violence via law enforcement.

Rappers frame the periferia as a contemporary senzala as a way to process what João Vargas observes as Black genocide and anti-Black racism in Brazil's urban communities. Vargas contends that genocide is not limited to the killing of the physical Black body but is also a social death through the systematic destroying of Black communities via economics, education, and citizenship.[13] While I examine more recent rap productions, the idea of calling upon the reality of genocide in the Black community is not new to Brazilian rap. One of the foundational rap albums, *Holocausto Urbano* (1990), released by the iconic Brazilian rap group Racionais MCs, addresses the poverty and state violence that impacts these marginalized communities. In one of the key songs from the album, "Pânico na Zona Sul" (Panic in the South Zone), the group describes with vivid imagery how residents who live in the southern periphery of São Paulo are constantly the target of physical violence at the hands of vigilante groups: "Justiceiros são chamados por eles mesmos / Matam humilham e dão tiros a esmo." (They call themselves vigilantes / They kill, humiliate, and shoot at random).[14] The *justiceiros* are death squads made up primarily of off-duty policemen who operate with impunity in the favelas and periferias of São Paulo, Rio de Janeiro, and other major Brazilian cities. These extra-judicial killings carried out by the police since the 1980s are a legacy of the paramilitary groups that were known as *Esquadrão da Morte* (death squads) that emerged in the late 1960s during the military dictatorship. The death and destruction that Racionais MCs narrate in their lyrics reflects the double negation of Black life in urban Brazil—being neither human nor citizen—leading to the periferia becoming what Jaime Alves labels as a Black necropolis.[15]

The legacy of the senzala, in particular how Afro-descendant populations in Brazil have been negatively affected throughout the twentieth century by state policies, has been mapped out by rap groups. Z'África Brasil's 2002 song "Antigamente Quilombos, Hoje Periferia" (Formerly Quilombos, Today Periphery) mentions Brazil's history of scientific racism to openly denounce the long history of racial oppression that has impacted Afro-Brazilians since abolition. The refrain to the song clearly illustrates this history:

> A que sentido flores prometeram um mundo novo?
> Favela viela morro tem de tudo um pouco,
> Tentam alterar o DNA da maioria.
> Rei Zumbi! Antigamente Quilombos Hoje Periferia!
> Levante as caravelas aqui nâo daremos tréguas nâo, nâo
> Entâo que venha a guerra
> Zulu Z'África Zumbi aqui nâo daremos trèguas nâo, nâo
> Entâo que venha a Guerra.

> *How have flowers promised a new world?*
> *Favela, alley, hill there is a little bit of everything,*
> *They tried to alter the DNA of the majority.*
> *King Zumbi! Formerly Quilombos Today Periphery!*
> *Raise your caravelles we won't give a truce, no, no*
> *So, bring on the war*
> *Zulu Z'África Zumbi we won't give a truce, no, no*
> *So, bring on the war.*[16]

The reference to altering the DNA of Brazil's majority Afro-descendant population evokes the history of the country's eugenics policy of *branqueamento*, or racial whitening, at the turn of the twentieth century. This racial ideology gained significant legitimacy during the height of racist thought among Brazil's intellectual elite from 1880 to 1920.[17] During this time, policies were enacted to encourage immigration from predominately White, European nations as a counter measure to the large, recently freed Afro-descendant population. Intellectuals and policy makers also endorsed the idea of *miscigenação*, or miscegenation, among different racial groups as a way to supposedly lighten the overall population, since White genes were thought to be stronger.[18] While eugenics may no longer be an accepted scientific method, the ideology of racial mixing as a way to negate Blackness has continued into the present with the metanarrative of racial democracy that attempts to downplay racism in Brazil as well as minimize an individual's African ancestry.[19]

The rap group's listing of locations with majority Afro-descendant populations—the *favela*, *viela*, and *morro*—brings attention to additional policies enacted by the state to attempt to neutralize and contain the Black population through the pathologization of criminality in relation to the inhabitants of these spaces. At the same time as the rise of racist ideologies, such as branqueamento, Brazilian physicians and researchers adopted similar ideas to do with criminal anthropology and phrenology as a means of proving their hypothesis about Blacks and *mestiços* being more susceptible to social degeneration and criminal behaviors. Raimundo Nina Rodrigues's studies on criminology and its relation to the Black subject at the turn of the twentieth century reflect the valuing of ideas rooted in eugenics. Rodrigues believed that it was a natural order for Afro-descendant populations to be in an inferior position due to their unequal development in relation to other human groups, and because of this they were more susceptible to degenerate behaviors, including crime.[20] Z'África Brazil's lyrics connect these racist ideologies of the past with the present, since residents of their communities continue to be categorized as populations affiliated with criminal activities due to their racial and social class background.

Brazilian rap artists make sense of the violent impact of the criminalization of periferia and favela residents, particularly of Black youth, through the metaphor of the ship used in the transatlantic trade. Z'África Brasil references the caravelles used by European colonizers as a symbol of the state's sending agents to subdue the predominately non-White communities in the urban periphery. One of the most popular rappers from São Paulo's periferia, Emicida, develops this metaphor further when critiquing the carceral state and its impact on his community. The song "Boa Esperança" (Good Hope) references the names given to *navios negreiros*, or slave ships, during Brazil's colonial period. Many navios negreiros had similar names, including *Feliz Dia a Pobrezinhos* (Happy Day to the Unfortunate), *Feliz Destino* (Happy Destiny), *Caridade* (Charity), and *Boa Intenção* (Good Intentions).[21] These names were not random but rather reflected the traffickers' belief that they were doing a service for the betterment of enslaved Africans by bringing them to a land where their souls could be saved. Naming was not limited to the ships, as the Portuguese prohibited enslaved Africans from embarking on their ships without being baptized first. Following group baptisms, the enslaved would be given Christian names by a Catholic priest.[22] The vile irony of these names reflects a logic that the Black subject will benefit from subjugation in a system rooted in White, Christian values and norms. This irony is not lost on Emicida, as the modern state uses the system of mass incarceration as a way to justify a logic rooted in social conditioning via punishment. The astute observations made by Emicida can be found in the song's refrain:

> Por mais que você corra, irmão
> Pra sua guerra vão nem se lixar
> Esse é o xis da questão
> Já viu eles chorar pela cor do orixá?
> E os camburão o que são?
> Negreiros a retraficar
> Favela ainda é senzala, Jão!
> Bomba relógio prestes a estourar

> *However much you run brother*
> *They won't care about your war*
> *That's the crux of the question*
> *Have you ever seen them cry over the orixá color?*
> *And the police vans what are they?*
> *Slave ships resuming trade*
> *The favela is still a senzala, bro!*
> *A time bomb ready to explode*[23]

Comparing the *camburão* (police van) to slave ships offers insight into the negative impacts of the criminal justice system by separating families and destroying whole communities. This continual threat of incarceration can be better understood when Jaime Alves, in his book *The Anti-Black City: Police Terror and Black Urban Life in Brazil*, observes a social condition unfolding among urban youth, which he labels as the favela-to-prison pipeline. This cycle of mass incarceration comes about because of unemployment/underemployment and residential segregation, creating a dynamic of Black captivity and disposability in the city.[24] Emicida is not the first Brazilian rapper to comment on the carceral state and its impact on Afro-Brazilians; however, the parallels between the transatlantic slave trade and the prison system create a powerful commentary on the social reality of Afro-descendant communities at the turn of the twenty-first century.[25]

The parallels of the favela and the senzala further illustrate the legacy of slavery as it manifests itself in the contemporary Brazilian carceral state. The metaphor of the time bomb ready to explode alludes to the extreme conditions of surveillance and confinement urban youth are subjected to in their home communities as well as in the prison system. Brazil has the fourth largest incarcerated population in the world with the prison population increasing by 410 percent, from 148,000 to 607,000 between the years of 1995 and 2015.[26] Scholars of Black studies would argue that the current Brazilian carceral state is "historically and ideologically linked to the 'peculiar institution' of slavery," similarly to how it has developed in the United States with the prison system becoming the new plantation as a way to control the Black population.[27] Emicida is fully aware of the historical connections between mass incarceration and Brazil's slavery past when he unequivocally describes prisons as "Tipo campos de concentração, prantos em vão" (Like concentration camps, weeping in vain).[28] The high rates of incarceration among favela youth reinforces Emicida's argument that his friends and family are being systematically targeted by the state as a way to criminalize Black life in Brazil, which has the ultimate goal of enacting racial domination over Brazil's majority Afro-descendant population.

Another form of state violence and control frequently overlooked in Brazilian rap is Black femicide. Historically, most rap songs have focused on experiences of violence related to the Black male body; however, in recent years a growing number of Brazilian female rappers have emerged, addressing issues of oppression experienced by Black women. One song that illustrates this shift in rap is the song "Psicopretas Vol. 1" (Black Psycho Women, Vol. 1). Recorded in 2018, the song is a collaborative effort among six female rappers who each have recorded their own solo albums and established themselves as "informadas" in the rap scene.[29] While issues connected to colorism are recurring themes in the song, what is salient is the focus on what the Afro-Brazilian intellectual Sueli Carneiro would label as *epistemicídio* (epistemicide), or the symbolic death of Black Brazilians through the denial or erasure of references to African and Afro-Brazilian culture.[30] The negation of Afro-descendants as subjects with knowledge comes about through the imposition of White or Euro-centric cultural norms and histories framed as the idealized standard for intelligence, beauty, and success. Bia Doxum, one of the collaborators on the song, raps about her own personal experiences of trying to erase physical traces of her African ancestry in order to fit in with the dominant White society:

> Quem me viu naquela estrada?
> Me diz, quem me viu naquela encruzilhada?
> Quando não era moda ser preta de quebrada
> Quer julgar minha história, não sabe minha
> Na mira da espingarda de algum escravocrata
> Sei que não fui aceita, fui tolerada
> Me camuflava nos teus espaços
> Alisando o cacho
> Fiz mó embaraço.
>
> *Who saw me on that road?*
> *Tell me, who saw me at the crossroads*
> *When it wasn't cool to be a Black woman from the hood*

> *You want to judge my history, you don't know my path*
> *In the sights of some slave owner's shotgun*
> *I know I was accepted I was tolerated*
> *I camouflaged myself in your spaces*
> *Straightening the curl*
> *I made a fool of myself.*[31]

Bia narrates about this notion of being tolerated and, because of the stigma she experienced, wanting to blend in with the White hegemonic society, "alisando o cacho" (straightening the curl). Kia Lilly Caldwell, in her monograph on Black women's attitude on hair in Brazil, notes how past studies on Brazil's racial dynamics focus on policies and ideologies of racial whitening but not how they contribute specifically to a sentiment of anti-Blackness not only among the general population but also among Black women themselves.[32] She makes the observation that, as opposed to Black men, Black women experience the mark of racial difference through their hair.[33] And we can see this in the song, since Bia herself has a lighter complexion but has *cabelo cacheado*, a marker of racial difference. The phrase stating that she is in the sights of a slave owner's shotgun is extremely powerful, as it not only comments on physical violence but also embodies Carneiro's idea of an epistemological violence against Black culture, beauty, and history.

The last phrase of Bia Doxum's stanza, "fiz mó embaraço" (I made a fool of myself) references the moment where she becomes "conscientizada," or her recognition in the present of how she was mentally colonized when she was younger. Her state of mind ties back to Frantz Fanon's idea of the violence of the colonizer that seeks to annihilate the body, culture, and psyche of the colonized. The sense of inadequacy and inferiority Bia internalizes reflects a larger pattern within Afro-descendant populations of their identity being framed by the colonizer, so much so that they will attempt to imitate the culture of the colonizer in the hope that social mobilization will ensue. The effort to master the colonizer's culture or, in the case of Bia, to take on beauty norms tied to White hegemonic culture results in her being able to metaphorically wear what Fanon labels as the "White Mask."[34] She is trying to fit into Western norms of beauty and fashion by transforming her hair to match the styles accepted and praised by society.

While Bia focuses on issues of erasure, Dory Oliveira, a member of a Black lesbian rap collective known as Les Queens, confronts the issue of state violence against Black women in peripheral communities. In the music video for the song, as Dory raps the lyrics "Preta de quebrada é Maria Eduarda / É Cláudia arrastada / Luana que teve sua vida arrancada por nada," (Black woman from the hood is Maria Eduarda / It's Cláudia being dragged / Luana who had her life taken away for nothing), the three women's names flash on the screens, juxtaposed with text from the news reports on how they were killed.[35] Maria Eduarda was a thirteen-year-old Black teenager killed by a stray bullet while at school in the Zona Norte of Rio de Janeiro. The bullet came from a police operation nearby that involved a gun battle with gang members. Cláudia Silva was a Black woman hit by a stray bullet while on her way to the store. The PM placed her in the back cab of an SUV to take her to the hospital. The video of her death went viral, as the back door to the vehicle flew open, and her body fell out to be dragged another three hundred meters. And Luana dos Reis was a Black lesbian mother who was beaten by a group of police officers. A witness to Luana's death states that "Foi uma coisa de terrorismo que eu nunca tinha visto na minha vida. Eles foram muito violentos. Deram bastante cacetada nela, nas pernas, mas muito. Batiam com o cassetete" (It was a thing of terrorism that I had never seen in my life. They were very violent. They beat her a lot, on the legs. A lot. They beat her with the nightstick).[36] What stands out is the phrase "Foi uma coisa de terrorismo" (It was a thing of terror) because of the ability of the witness, also a Black woman, to express the state apparatus of law enforcement not as an entity that serves and protects but one that takes on a necropolitical stance, using its sovereign power to decide who lives or dies. The three examples bring attention to how Black women are impacted by police brutality and, more significantly, how these female rappers' rhetoric echoes Abdias do Nascimento's argument that Black populations still experience the legacies of slavery.

Periferia as Quilombo: Afro-centricity's Role in Cultural Resistance

Rappers' denouncement of the reality experienced by their communities has a purpose that goes beyond a mere recognition or chronicling of Black pain and suffering. The hip hopper from the periferia recognizes the historical discrimination and racial inequality in Brazil, becoming what Derek Pardue labels as "informados," or the idea that because the hip hopper has knowledge of their social condition, they have something of worth in their lives to foment some kind of change, even on a micro level.[37] Hip hop notions of being "informado" or "consientizado" resonate with the concept of quilombismo—of being aware of the historical legacy of slavery and then deciding to engage in some kind of resistance to existing systems of oppression. Jaime Alves recognizes that a reaction emerges among urban Black communities in relation to the Black necropolis in the form of what he calls a "Blackpolis": "Yet, within the context of necropolitical governance, blackness appears as a spatially grounded praxis that enables victims of state terror to reclaim their placeless location as a political resource for redefining themselves and the polis."[38] The references used by Brazilian rappers to the quilombo and slave revolt can be framed as a kind of reclamation of the space of the periferia and subaltern identity to forge new ways to engage with "o sistema" not yet considered.

The image of enslaved Africans seeking freedom, whether through escape, violence, or open revolt, is a common trope used by Brazilian rappers as a way to reclaim a sense of political agency in their lives. This action can be seen in the title of Rincon Sapiência's first studio album, *Galanga Livre* (2017), which brings together references of the legendary African figure of Chico-Rei and the 2012 film *Django Unchained* (*Django Livre* in Portuguese).[39] In the album, Rincon Sapiência takes on the persona of Galanga in the opening sequence of the album before transitioning into the song "Crime Bárbaro." He not only references police brutality through the images in the music video but also incorporates a modern-day fugitive slave narrative to explain how he resists state oppression. I would argue that Rincon Sapiência's character, who engages in physical violence to gain his freedom, upends Django's narrative in Quentin Taratino's film, as he had to have his freedom purchased by a European:

> Boatos correm, eu também
> Me sinto como um herói, isso me faz bem
> Escravos me colocam como um rei
> Porque o senhor de engenho fui eu que matei!
>
> Meu crime a ele eu culpo
> Bateu em criança, cometeu estupro
> Proibiu a dança e a religião
> Gerou confusão interna entre o grupo
>
> *Rumors run wild, so do I*
> *I feel like a hero, it gives me strength*

Slaves see me as a king
Because it was the slave master that I killed!

I blame him for my crime
He beat children, committed rape
Prohibited dance and religion
Created confusion within my group.[40]

Rincon's lyrics offer a literal retelling of a slave revolt and an ensuing fugitive slave narrative; however, the killing of the *senhor do engenho*, or plantation owner, can be interpreted as a metaphor for what Derek Pardue observes among Brazilian hip hoppers as a critique of "o sistema."[41] Killing the slave master then can be understood as a form of resistance to the systemic oppression experienced by Rincon's community, what James Holston classifies as "insurgent citizenship," or periferia residents engaging in illegal and legal forms of civic engagement to meet their needs.[42] The decision to strike back at the system and create an alternate path for oneself resonates with Abdias do Nascimento's categorization of Afro-descendant organizations as contemporary quilombos, thereby transforming the space of the periferia into a site of political engagement.

The protagonist in Rincon's song openly states that his momentary freedom from these oppressions will probably end in death, but the act of resistance he performs gives him a brief sense of agency in a world with few, if any, opportunities. The refrain of "Crime Bárbaro"— "mesmo estando em desvantagem / a sensação é de poder" (despite being at a disadvantage, there is a sensation of power)—references the protagonist's momentary feeling of empowerment. He may not win the battle, but the decision to rebel, to engage in some form of resistance, points to the recognition of systemic inequality and to a politics of imagining new possibilities not considered before. The *senhor do engenho* committing rape, beating children, and prohibiting African-based cultural expressions again refers to the Brazilian state's efforts throughout the twentieth century to police Black, urban communities and to downplay, outside of state-sanctioned traditions like samba and Carnival, the value of Africa's influence in Brazilian culture. Therefore, the phrase "I blame him for my crime" reflects the narrator's acknowledgment that his marginalized condition is not of his own doing but rather the fault of a system that has continually oppressed him and his community. Dismantling the metanarrative of crime and danger associated with his community is a liberatory act in that the state, and not the populations on the margins of society, is now seen as the source of violence.[43]

One salient form of cultural resistance that Brazilian rappers call upon is the frequent reference to Zumbi dos Palmares as a model of leadership for their communities. Returning to Z'África Brasil, the rap group makes a direct appeal to Zumbi in their 2002 album and song, "Antigamente Quilombos, Hoje Periferia." The song's refrain functions as a call to arms to periferia youth to follow the example of Zumbi and resist the forces of poverty, state violence, and cultural erasure:

> A que sentido flores prometeram um mundo novo?
> Favela, viela, morro tem de tudo um pouco,
> Tentam de alterar o DNA da maioria.
> Rei Zumbi! Antigamente Quilombos Hoje Periferia!
> Levante as caravelas aqui não daremos tréguas não, não
> Então que venha a guerra.
>
> *In what way did flowers provide a new world?*
> *Favela, ally, hill, there's a little of everything,*
> *They try to alter the DNA of the majority.*
> *King Zumbi! Formerly Quilombos Today Periferia!*
> *Raise the caravelles, we won't give a truce, no, no*
> *So, bring on the war.*

By affirming Zumbi's status as a king, Z'África Brasil contests Brazil's legacy of erasing Blackness as it points to the rap group's epistemological work of instilling in periferia youth a sense of racial pride and to inform them that they come from a rich ancestry with great leaders and intellectuals. Z'África Brasil argues for open resistance now that the periferia is "informado," or informed, in order to follow Zumbi's example of transforming their community into a present-day quilombo, or using Niyi Afolabi's term, cultural *quilombola*.[44] Zumbi never ceded control of Palmares to the Portuguese.

Psicopretas also use Z'África Brasil's template, but they instead map out a genealogy of female warriors through references to women quilombola leaders during Brazil's colonial period. Sistah Chilli, in the opening stanza of "Psicopretas Vol. 1," highlights these key figures:

> Cê nem sabe que na minha veia tem sangue de
> Teresa Benguela.
> . . . .
> E parda é uma porra, respeita a minha história!
> Fiscal de melanina, nem vem que não faz glória
> Rainhas coroadas de corpo e mente blindada
> Exu guia minha estrada, por Dandara abençoada
> Da sua língua amaldiçoada, eu sigo forte e immune
> Respeita a minha trilha, herdeira de Aqualtune

> *You don't even know that in my veins I have the
> blood of Teresa Benguela.*
> . . . .
> *And mixed-race is fucked up, respect my history!*
> *Melanin inspector, don't even cuz it won't bring glory*
> *Queens crowned with armored bodies and minds*
> *Exu guide my path, through Dandara blessed*
> *From your cursed tongue, I continue strong and immune*
> *Respect my path, heiress of Aqualtune.*

The three women Sistah Chilli names in the song were important leaders of quilombos during the seventeenth and eighteenth centuries. Teresa Benguela became the queen of the Quilombo do Piolho following her husband's death. She led the quilombo for over two decades, until 1670, when it was eventually destroyed by the Portuguese military. Dandara was the wife of Zumbi dos Palmares but was a well-respected warrior in her own right. She committed suicide after being arrested in 1694 because she did not want to return to captivity as a slave. By including Teresa and Dandara in their song, Psicopretas is arguing that women must have leadership roles within community-based initiatives tied to social engagement. Afro-descendant populations in Brazil will never be fully free and empowered unless women play a central role in the labor of resistance and education. In addition to the two quilombola leaders, Aqualtune was born a princess in the Kongo kingdom and led an army of thousands of men in battle before being captured and transported to Brazil. She is best known as the mother of Ganga Zumba, one of the leaders of Palmares, and the grandmother of Zumbi. Aqualtune symbolizes the power of Black women in shaping their community's destiny through their ability to nurture and prepare future generations who will lead the struggle against oppression. Interestingly, Abdias do Nascimento argued for equal representation of women in quilombista organizations by pointing out the contributions of female leaders. And like Z'África Brasil, Psicopretas are offering a framework to periferia youth, especially young women, of how they are the descendants of great leaders who can serve as models in their development as future leaders.

An analysis of the aesthetics of Brazilian hip hop points to a project of social consciousness and political engagement through continual references to the legacy of the transatlantic slave trade in Afro-descendant communities in Brazil. Rap artists' references to slavery and quilombos is not necessarily new or innovative but rather illustrates how they belong to a larger tradition of politically conscious Afro-Brazilian cultural productions rooted in Abdias do Nascimento's concept of quilombismo. Afro-Brazilian writers, artists, and musicians throughout the twentieth century and into the twenty-first century have sought ways to make sense of their identity and the stigma experienced by their communities by exploring the relationship between the horrors of slavery endured by their ancestors and the contemporary material reality of racism, state violence, and poverty.

However, hip hop may have something new to offer in that its message about social inequity and social empowerment framed in the context of slavery reaches a larger number of Afro-descendant youth. Past organizations, such as Quilombhoje and the Movimento Negro Unificado, were primarily isolated to middle-class, educated Black populations in São Paulo. Hip hop has a working-class ethos and aesthetic, which speaks to the experiences of a significant portion of the Afro-descendant population in Brazil. Therefore, the potential to transform Black youth into "informado" subjects highlights Brazilian hip hop's political project among marginalized youth in Brazil's major urban centers, including São Paulo, Rio de Janeiro, and Salvador. In fact, rap songs can serve as a bridge to other Afro-Brazilian cultural traditions that engage in similar political work because of parallels in their aesthetics and ethics. Many rappers frequently reference Black writers, artists, and intellectuals in their songs as a way to recognize the formation of a genealogy of key figures rooted in a Black radical tradition.

The dialogue between hip hop and other Afro-Brazilian cultural productions in relation to the legacy of slavery and the work of social empowerment ultimately points to the need to consider hip hop as a legitimate art form that belongs to a rich tradition of socially engaged art and literature among Afro-descendant communities in Brazil. Additional studies need to be done on the aesthetics of Brazilian hip hop in order to further understand it as a discursive practice emanating from marginalized populations that use this musical genre to engage in serious discussions within the public sphere on pressing social issues tied to race, class, and violence impacting their communities.

NOTES

1. Black movements have emerged in Brazil throughout the twentieth century, including the Frente Negra Brasileira (Black Brazilian Front) in the 1930s, but it was not until the 1970s when new movements emerged on an unprecedented national level to address the political concerns of Afro-descendant communities through cultural and political initiatives. The most notable of these groups, the MNU, or the Movimento Negro Unificado (Unified Black Movement), became a national leader in São Paulo and Rio de Janeiro. For more information on the MNU, see Michael Hanchard, *Orpheus and Power: The "Movimento Negro" of Rio de Janeiro and São Paulo, Brazil, 1945–1988* (Princeton, NJ: Princeton University Press, 1994).
2. "Sou Negrão," Posse Mente Zulu, track 16 on *Revolusom: A Volta do Tape Perdido*, recorded December 2004, Unimar, compact disc (all translations of rap lyrics are mine).
3. "Afro-Brasileiro," Thaíde e DJ Hum, track 1 on *Afro-Brasileiro*, recorded 1995, Brava Gente, vinyl LP record.
4. Derek Pardue, *Brazilian Hip Hoppers Speak from the Margins: We's on Tape* (New York: Palgrave Macmillan, 2011), 98–99.
5. Abdias do Nascimento, "Quilombismo: An Afro-Brazilian Political Alternative," *Black Studies* 11, no. 2 (1980): 151.
6. *Terreiros* are sacred spaces where practitioners of *Candomblé* (Afro-Brazilian religion) congregate to perform rituals and ceremonies. *Confrarias* are Afro-Brazilian Catholic fraternities that started in the colonial period but continue in existence to the present. *Afoxés* are groups that come out during Carnival in Brazil. They are also known as *Candomblé de Rua* (Street Candomblé), since the members also belong to *terreiros de Candomblé*. See Niyi Afolabi, *Afro-Brazilians: Cultural Production in a Racial Democracy* (Rochester: University of Rochester Press, 2009), 302.
7. In defining Pan-Africanism, I am using Cedric Robinson's analysis of the rise of Black radical nationalists around the mid-twentieth century who were engaged in anticolonial and revolutionary struggles. In his book, *Black Marxism: The Making of the Black Radical Tradition* (Chapel Hill: North Carolina University Press, 1983), Robinson observes how these Black nationalist intellectuals, who included W. E. B. DuBois, C. L. R. James, and Richard Wright, engaged in a radical Pan-Africanism, or Black internationalism, that set about to recover the history of the revolutionary Black struggle rooted in the struggle of the Afro-descendant working-class masses (312–14).
8. Lourdes Carril argues in her monograph *Quilombo, Favela e Periferia: A longa busca da cidadania* (São Paulo: Annablume, 2006) that the *periferias* and *favelas* found in

contemporary Brazilian cities are a legacy of the *senzalas* and *quilombos* of the nineteenth century.

9. Pardue, *Brazilian Hip Hoppers*, 115–16. Pardue has divided Brazilian hip hop into what he calls the four phases of *negritude*: phase one (1988–1992) is marked by an *união* ideology, phase two (1992–1996) uses a working-class Afro-centric discourse, phase three (1996–1999) does not focus so much on race, instead giving preference to narratives of periferia life and marginality, and finally phase four (1999–present) is a negotiation of aspects of phases two and three. While I agree that the songs I will examine have characteristics of phases two and three, of looking at the challenges of living in the urban periphery juxtaposed with discourses that affirm racial pride, I argue that this more recent generation of Brazilian hip hop artists can also be seen as quilombista practitioners that employ Afro-centric discourses as a response to racism and state violence impacting their communities.

10. The Teatro Experimental do Negro (TEN) was a Black theater company founded and directed by Abdias do Nascimento from the 1940s to the early 1960s. The Movimento Negro Unificado (MNU) emerged in the late 1970s in response to racial discrimination against Black youth in São Paulo. The blocos Afros also started to form in the 1970s with well-known groups, such as Ilê Aiyê, Olodum, and Filhos de Gandhy. Quilombhoje was a literary group founded in 1980 in São Paulo to promote the importance of Afro-Brazilian literary productions. All of these different movements reflected the centrality of Afro-Brazilian cultural productions in affirming Black pride and critiquing the Brazilian state's inability to address racism in society. See Niyi Afolabi, *Afro-Brazilians: Cultural Production in a Racial Democracy*.

11. Imani Perry, *Prophets of the Hood: Politics and Poetics in Hip Hop* (Durham, NC: Duke University Press Books, 2004), 2.

12. Teresa Caldeira, *City of Walls: Crime, Segregation, and Citizenship in São Paulo* (Berkeley: University of California Press, 2000), 2–4.

13. João Vargas, "Genocide in the African Diaspora: United States, Brazil, and the Need for a Holistic Research and Political Method," *Cultural Dynamics* 17, no. 3 (2005): 269–70.

14. "Pânico na Zona Sul," Racionais MCs, track 1 on *Holocausto Urbano*, recorded August 1990, Zimbabwe Records, vinyl LP record.

15. Jaime Alves, *The Anti-Black City: Police Terror and Black Urban Life in Brazil* (Minneapolis: University of Minnesota Press, 2018), 41–42.

16. "Antigamente Quilombos, Hoje Periferia," Z'África Brasil, track 4 on *Antigamente Quilombos, Hoje Periferia*, recorded January 2002, Paradoxx Music, compact disc.

17. Thomas Skidmore, *Black into White: Race and Nationality in Brazilian Thought* (Durham, NC: Duke University Press, 1992), 46.

18. Ibid., 45–46.

19. "Racial democracy" is a term used to describe race relations in Brazil. The idea was advanced by sociologist Gilberto Freyre in his work *Casa Grande e Senzala* (The Master and the Slaves), which espoused the idea of a meta-race, or post-racial society, where Brazilians' identity is made up of the three main races: White, Black, and

Indigenous. See Gilberto Freyre, *The Masters and the Slaves*, trans. S. Putnam (New York: Alfred A. Knopf, 1946).
20. See Raimundo Nina Rodrigues, *Os africanos no Brasil* (Rio de Janeiro: Centro Edelstein, [1932] 2010), 300–302. This book was the result of studies he conducted from 1890 to 1905.
21. Caetano Manenti, "Lista com nomes de navios negreiros escancara cinismo dos comerciantes de seres humanos no Oceano Atlântico," *Geledés* (blog), April 24, 2015, www.geledes.org.br/lista-navios-negreiros-cinismo-comerciantes-seres-humanos-oceano-atlantico/
22. Kátia M. de Queirós Mattoso, *To Be a Slave in Brazil, 1550–1888* (New Brunswick: Rutgers University Press, 1986), 32.
23. "Boa Esperança," Emicida, track 10 on *Sobre Crianças, Quadris, Pesadelos e Lições de Casa*, recorded August 2015, Laboratório Fantasma, compact disc.
24. Jaime Alves, *The Anti-Black City*, 142–43.
25. Additional examples of Brazilian rap songs providing commentary on the carceral state include the classic "Diário de um detento," Racionais MC, *Sobrevivendo no Inferno*, recorded December 1997, Cosa Nostra Label, compact disc; and "Apologia ao crime," Detentos do Rap, *Apologia ao crime*, recorded 1998, Fieldzz, compact disc.
26. Jaime Alves, *The Anti-Black City*, 119–20.
27. Ibid., 120.
28. "Boa Esperança," Emicida, track 10 on *Sobre Crianças, Quadris, Pesadelos e Lições de Casa*, recorded August 2015, Laboratório Fantasma, compact disc.
29. Recent scholarship on Brazilian hip hop has focused more on the role of gender in this historically masculine-dominated music genre. Derek Pardue devotes a chapter, "*Mano/Mana*: The Engendering of the *Periferia*," in his 2011 monograph *Brazilian Hip Hoppers Speak from the Margins: We's on Tape*. Tanya Saunders also offers insights into the politics of gender, in particular for Black women, within the world of hip hop in her article "Towards a Transnational Hip-hop Feminist Liberatory Praxis: A View from the Americas," *Social Identities* 22, no. 2 (2016): 178–94.
30. Sueli Carneiro, *Escritos de uma vida* (São Paulo: Polén Livros, 2019).
31. "Psicopretas Vol. 1," Psicopretas, track 1 on *Psicopretas Vol. 1*, recorded March 2018, Narceja Produções, YouTube video, https://www.youtube.com/watch?v=bxqhlctLIZY.
32. Kia Lilly Caldwell, *Negras in Brazil: Re-Envisioning Black Women, Citizenship, and the Politics of Identity* (New Brunswick: Rutgers University Press, 2007), 85.
33. Ibid., 81.
34. Frantz Fanon, *Black Skin, White Masks* (New York: Grove Press, 2008).
35. "Psicopretas Vol. 1."
36. *Geledés* (blog), www.geledes.org.br/do-luto-luta-nao-esqueceremos-luana-barbosa-dos-reis-morta-por-pms-em-ribeirao-preto.
37. Pardue, *Brazilian Hip Hoppers*, 98.
38. Jaime Alves, "From Necropolis to Blackpolis: Necropolitical Governance and Black Spatial Praxis in São Paulo, Brazil," *Antipode* 46, no. 2 (2014): 323.

39. *Django Unchained*, directed by Quentin Tarantino (New York: The Weinstein Company, 2012).
40. "Crime Bárbaro," Rincon Sapiência, track 2 on *Galanga Livre,* recorded May 2017, Boia Fria Produções, compact disc.
41. Derek Pardue, *Brazilian Hip Hoppers*, 27.
42. James Holston, *Insurgent Citizenship: Disjunctions of Democracy and Modernity in Brazil* (Princeton, NJ: Princeton University Press, 2008), 34.
43. Marilene Chauí questions the belief that the populations living in poverty and substandard conditions are the root of violence in Brazil by positing the state as the perpetrator of violence in Brazilian society through its enactment of policies and laws that create conditions of social inequity. See Chauí, "A Não-Violência Do Brasileiro, Um Mito Interessantíssimo," *Almanaque: Caderno de Literatura e Ensaio*, no. 11 (1980).
44. Niyi Afolabi, *Afro-Brazilians: Cultural Production in a Racial Democracy* (Rochester: University of Rochester Press, 2009), 302.

CHAPTER 11

Honoring the Bones beneath Us

Conjuring Black Heritage in the Performances of "Intervenções Urbanas" in the Gamboa Neighborhood, Rio de Janeiro

MARIA ANDREA DOS SANTOS SOARES

Rio de Janeiro is at the epicenter of the narratives created and reproduced by writers, sociologists, filmmakers, and soap opera scriptwriters that have helped to sustain the "racial democracy" discourse through their descriptions of harmonious interactions between enslaved people and their owners. The city, which debuted as a tourist destination by the 1960s, gets a significant part of its touristic appeal from the exotification and hypersexualization of Black bodies and their cultural practices. Every advertisement for Rio shows nature, beaches, *capoeira*, and Carnival. More recently even the favelas appear as an attractive site to visit, meet the locals, and participate in their festivities. Black communities, however, have always been under siege by state policies. Spaces, places, and cultural practices associated with Black people are surveilled, controlled, forbidden, or eliminated. As different generations of scholars have shown from different angles, Black life holds little value, is the target of state necropolitics,[1] and the dynamics of tourism and cultural consumption work only to commodify Black cultural experience while simultaneously denying protagonism and economic autonomy to Afro-Brazilians.[2] From 2012 to 2013, while conducting ethnographic fieldwork in Rio de Janeiro, I had the opportunity to meet artists, cultural producers, and activists from the Brazilian Black

Movement. In March 2012, several Black artists from Rio de Janeiro mobilized to protest against what they believed to be their systematic exclusion from state-sponsored funding opportunities for arts projects. They named their mobilization "Akoben," a word for the *Adinkra* symbol meaning "war horn."[3] Hilton Cobra—"Cobrinha," as the head of the Akoben mobilization is known—has a long history of activism, artistic production, and political engagement.[4] He often works in collaboration with other cultural agents such as the Centro Afro Carioca de Cinema (Afro-Carioca Cinema Center), created by actor and director Zózimo Bulbul.[5]

In what follows, I will describe the event known as the "Herança Africana: Intervenções Urbanas no Caminho do Cais do Porto" (African Heritage: Urban Interventions along the Pathway to the Port), created by Zózimo Bulbul. We can connect this artistic event to the very history of the area where it happened: the Valongo Port and its surrounding neighborhood, a crucial place to understanding Brazil's imperial era, its relationship to slavery, and the spatialities of Black life, resistance, and cultural production in Brazil. The article also identifies those ways through which, in the process of nation building, the Brazilian state dealt with tensions arising from the presence of a large Black population, ideals of whitening, and the discourse of harmonious racial interaction and mixture. The aim here is to show how the Estado Novo era (1937 to 1946) created the conditions for appropriating symbols and practices from the Black community, using them as symbols of a unified and harmonious nation and denying African descendants any possibility for reparation and equality in the meantime. Subsequently, I intend to discuss the effects of tourism, more specifically heritage tourism, in sites of Black memory, pointing out the contradiction between discourses of conservation and/or preservation and the practices at sites like the Valongo Wharf and the nearby area. Finally, we address the subject of performance, more specifically, the subject of Black performances, examining what artistic performances have to offer in terms of potential for resistance against racialization, geographic displacement, and memory loss.

Locating Time, Space, and Agency

Zózimo Bullbul, actor and film director, was born in 1937 in the city of Rio de Janeiro. He worked in a few national cinema roles, such as *Cinco*

Vezes Favela (1962), *Quilombo* (1984), and *Sagarana* (1974). In 1988, already a member of the Black Movement, Bulbul directed his first movie, titled *Abolição*, marking the centenary of the abolition of slavery in Brazil. He continued developing short films such as *Aniceto em dia de Alforria* (Aniceto on Manumission Day, 1981) which narrates the daily life of Aniceto do Império, a man who was a wharf worker during the day but who was also the founder of a very traditional samba school (Império Serrano) located in the Madureira neighborhood, in the northern section of Rio. Together with his wife, Bisa Vianna, Zózimo founded the Centro Afro Carioca de Cinema in 2007, and since then this movie production center has created workshops, launched new generations of Afro-Brazilian filmmakers, and organized twelve editions of the cinema festival "Africa, Brasil, Caribe." Zózimo died in 2013, two months after the event described here, at the age of seventy-five.

In order to analyze the event organized by Zózimo Bulbul, it is necessary to contextualize the territorialities and temporalities of our existence as Afro-Brazilians, particularly in this case, as it relates to the Valongo Wharf. Located in the Gamboa neighborhood (downtown Rio) this old port area contains an underexplored archaeological treasure: there, under several layers of construction sediment from different eras, lay pieces of objects, clothes, pipes, and ornaments carried by new captives on their way to Brazil between 1811 and 1843. The entire Gamboa neighborhood, including the nearby Pedra do Sal (The Salt Stone), Largo da Prainha (Small Beach Square), and Cemitério dos Pretos Novos (Cemetery of the Newly Arrived Blacks), are places of Black memory and resistance. Some of them recently became historical preservation sites while simultaneously undergoing processes of urban remodeling.

The discovery of the Valongo Wharf occurred in 2011. This area underwent an intensive remodeling in 1920, during the great urban reforms carried out by Mayor Pereira Passos, a process that dislodged the communities of the so called "Pequena África" (Little Africa), which included the region around the neighborhoods of Gamboa, Santo Cristo, Mangue, Praça 11, Saara, and Saúde, and moved them toward the north region of the Madureira neighborhood. Pereira Passos's remodeling buried what was left of the Cais da Imperatriz (The Empress Wharf), built in 1843 over the Valongo Port to receive the empress Teresa de Bourbon, who was coming to Brazil to marry D. Pedro II. Based on the clues found in archives and old maps, the staff of the Museu Nacional, under the leadership of

Dr. Tânia Andrade Lima, found irregular stones seated in a rudimentary way twenty-four inches below the Empress Wharf's foundations. Those were the remains of the Valongo edifications, whose construction started, according to the documents, in approximately 1811, with the sole purpose of disembarking the newly arrived African captives to be sold at the slave market nearby. The estimated number of captives brought from 1817 to 1921 is 200,000 individuals.

In 2011, the former mayor, Eduardo Paes, authorized the construction of modern stairways in the area during the city's preparations for the mega events of the World Cup and the Olympic Games (2012 and 2014, respectively). The archeological exploration happened concomitantly to the process of remodeling. The findings—pipes, shells, fabric pieces, tableware, among other materials—were kept in an improvised hangar on a nearby street. By that time some entities, journalists, Black activists, and students had denounced the lack of care taken with these findings.[6] The stairways were finished in 2012. In the center of the construction, there is an open space where it is possible to see part of the Valongo's original construction.

The tourism economy and, more specifically, the economy of heritage tourism, provoke debates about the gentrification of urban areas under the pretext of preservation. Departing from an Urban Anthropology perspective, scholars such as Charleswell and Herzfeld discuss the ongoing social effects in spaces that were formerly undesired or considered unfit for tourism but then suddenly become highly desired tourist routes.[7] Authors such as Lees, Chin, and Lopes-Morales, approaching this question from the perspective of human geography and urban planning, consider gentrification as a global phenomenon bringing unequal social development.[8]

Thinking about this investment in culture and Black heritage while the area was simultaneously going through a revitalization process, we can only conclude that such investments were related to the city's preparation for the mega events of the World Cup and the Olympic Games, with the specific goal of attracting tourists to these sites. Such perception—of this being an investment in urban renovation in an impoverished area, as well as the political use of the heritage tourism trope as just a maneuver of the same capitalist order using memory to make profit—fits Paul Amar's description regarding state policies working in alliance with private capital. Amar describes how the projects valuing samba music and culture during the 1990s in the Morro da Serrinha neighborhood of North Rio de Janeiro were closely related to the discourses on the city's securitization that occurred in the early 2000s. According to him, these public policies constitute "a governance model based on projects that celebrate, moralize, and racialize the national history to sell it to the global touristic consumerism."[9] In this way, the celebration of Black memory and culture through the lens of historical conservation and preservation enters the spotlight of a city that has always been selling tourism, either in the form of its exuberant nature or in the form of Black tropical exoticism, sensuality, and rhythm and, now, through the remembrance of Black pain, death, and enslavement.

Herança Africana: Intervenções Urbanas / African Heritage: Urban Intervention

During the week of November 20, 2012, Zózimo Bulbul and his staff of Afro Carioca Center of Cinema made a series of interventions in the area of the Valongo Wharf. For the interventions, event staff attached to the light posts lining the street that goes from the Largo da Prainha to the Cais do Valongo large photographs of Black people who were/are a part of that area's history. The photographs were framed in *Capim Santa Fé*, a type of straw with ritual meaning in the *Candomblé* religion.[10] At the Largo da Prainha Square, I saw Zózimo, dressed all in white, seated in a straw chair. At his left were several large pottery vases with flowers and plants, *Espada de São Jorge* (Saint George sword) and white *Palmas* (Gladiolus). In front of the vases, there were ritual offerings of roots, seeds, and cereals such as yellow corn, popcorn, and yam. At Zózimo's right were chairs where several Candomblé priestesses and the actress Léa Garcia were seated.[11] In front of them, a semi-circle of candles was set. Hilton Cobra opened the "Urban Interventions" circuit by reading a text presenting the work goals while he reminded us of the meaning of the Valongo area to Black Brazilians and the importance of resisting cultural and spatial appropriation.[12]

When Hilton Cobra's speech was finished, the *jongo* group "Jongo da Serrinha" performed.[13] After the presentation, everyone started walking to the next event: the sit-in at the stairways of the Valongo. When we arrived at the port area, we sat on the new stairways looking at the wall where images of Bulbul's movies were being projected. The bartenders brought us *cachaça*, the strong liquor made from fermented sugarcane juice. A new jongo presentation began, and Jongo da Serrinha positioned themselves right next to the old stones of the Valongo Wharf, the stones recently excavated after having been forgotten for 166 years. This time the ensemble invited everybody to join the performance, creating a huge circle while three drums echoed in the night and the voices sang the chorus of some jongo lyrics. The Candomblé priestesses came in a van accompanied by their *ekedis*.[14] Some of the cinema producers and directors from different African and Caribbean countries presenting at the concurrent film festival arrived at the Valongo, too. Zózimo came with his family. I introduced myself, telling him how important it was to me to be there and to meet him and see so many Black activists together. He could only answer me with his kind smile and hand gestures. He was recovering from a delicate surgery and was not able to talk or walk. In fact, he died a month and a half after this event.

After the projections and jongo performance, we walked back two blocks and turned right, going to Pedra do Sal. It was close to 8:00 p.m. when around thirty of us arrived there. The bar serving drinks, beer, and appetizers was preparing the tables for that night's show, an atypical event: Pedra do Sal was hosting a night with *forró* rhythm—a northeastern Brazilian musical genre that became very popular in Rio with the immigration of people from the northeast states to Rio and São Paulo because of drought and the dream of making money in the country's biggest cities. In the last fifteen years, the genre has gained a new pace, accent, and lyrics and is now known as *Forró Universitário* (College Forro), as it is highly appreciated by middle- and upper-class college students. When all of these Black people, foreigners among them, in fancy and ritual clothing arrived there after leaving the Valongo event and sat at the tables to chat, but with a bunch of cameras and camcorders, it caused a surprise and a certain uneasiness among the few customers arriving to the forró show. The way they looked at us made me reflect on why Zózimo Bulbul's work was necessary. We were at one of the centers of Black history and resistance in the city of Rio de Janeiro, the place had been officially recognized as a *quilombo* just a few years before, and still our Black presence was looked upon as excessive, or as if it were disrupting the normalcy of this now touristic space.[15]

The attempt to resist gentrification and to preserve memory is evident in "Intervenções," but beyond that, beyond its socio-political connotations, there was an intangible dimension to this work—a dimension that speaks from its silence, from its intimate conversations, and from the ritualistic content of the work. In Alexander's book *Pedagogies of Crossing* we learn that: "African-based cosmological systems are complex manifestations of the geographies of crossings and dislocation. They are at the same time manifestations of locatedness, rootedness, and belonging that map individual and collective relationships to the Divine. The complexities derive in part from the fact that the Sacred energies that accompanied the millions who had been captured and sold for more than four centuries had indeed inhabited a vast geography."[16] The elements of Candomblé—the priestesses, the jongo dance and singing, and the large pictures of Black people—are somehow part of our history as Afro-Brazilians. All those elements, rhythms, colors, signs, ritual offerings, food, and drinks are operating diasporic memories, times and places that centuries have made part of who we are. As I see it today, the deepest meaning of this event was to create—or better, to recall—a bond between the living and the ones who are no longer in this world but whose spiritual energy, whose legacies, still remain. Sometimes I ask myself what it might have been like to everybody there, many of them longterm activists, friends, partners. I wonder what it was like to be there, knowing that the end of one of them was close. I wonder if Zózimo himself was feeling the imminence of his passing. As Hilton said, referring to the text he read during the "Intervenções" opening, during a gathering we had in late December of 2012: "I wrote that text thinking about the proximity of Zózimo's death." Would Zózimo Bulbul's last project be his way of making the crossing between the dimension of the living and the dimension of the ancestors?

Handling Blacks and Black Culture in Brazil

Cultural and religious traits related to the Black experience in Brazil are considered important sources of Afro-Brazilian identity, resistance, and resilience for the majority of Black activists and intellectuals. But we need to recognize that state institutions have often persecuted and criminalized these manifestations of Black existence. An easy example of persecution and criminalization of Black cultural expressions could be the psychiatric discourse of Raimundo Nina Rodrigues, the nineteenth-century physician, psychiatrist, and ethnologist in charge of the School of Medicine in Bahia. To Rodrigues, Candomblé religious practices were a manifestation of some kind of psychosis affecting the Black population, whose inferiority, he argued, placed these individuals as not capable of moral or ethical judgment.[17] Other good examples are laws prohibiting the practice of capoeira and samba meetings in the early 1900s.[18] Years later, however, it was exactly these manifestations that were held up as signs of an "African heritage," with capoeira and samba music and dance being presented to the world as Brazilian national symbols.[19]

During the Estado Novo (the New State), the populist regime inaugurated during Getúlio Vargas's presidency from 1937 to 1945, there was a movement toward the election of national symbols, including the aggregation of cultural practices such as capoeira, Candomblé, and samba as expressions of the Brazilian spirit and nationalist devotion. The aggregation of practices, until then marginalized and often criminalized, suggests that the eugenicist project defended by important figures such as Raimundo Nina Rodrigues, Arthur Ramos, and Sílvio Romero was being replaced by a new assimilationist politics. As part of these new politics, an essentialist construction of Black people, culture, and practices was adopted as part of the national culture when, in fact, it mimics and mocks the real existence of people of African descent in Brazil. The 1940s and 1950s represent the consolidation of the idea of the mixed nation, where Blacks contribute with their expressive practices but are otherwise absent from all spheres of power.[20] In the same way, this construction of a mixed nation also implied a mythical narrative of slavery, romanticized as a sad but necessary and generative episode of Brazilian history, in which the mistake of enslavement was overcome through miscegenation, a metaphor for the widespread rape of enslaved women.[21]

However, at the same time that Black cultural contributions became valuable in the discourse about the harmonious constitution of the "Brazilian race," society's structures continued to reflect the trans-generational economic effects of slavery on African descendants, as Florestan Fernandes theorizes in *A Integração do negro na sociedade de clases*.[22] Still, beyond the trans-generational effects of slavery, Blackness is devalued in itself, independently of social class or education. The processes of spatial segregation undergone by Blacks in Rio de Janeiro show that people of African descent are considered second-class citizens, asked to take the service entrance in buildings, followed in grocery stores, or have their money checked twice. Racism in Brazil is a specific anti-Black stance invested in the desire for the suppression, or at least for the submission and confinement, of these bodies.

By looking at the 7967 decree, issued in 1945 in regard to immigration control, it is easier to understand the inconsistency of the "racial democracy" narrative. According to this decree, the country had "the need to preserve and develop, in the ethnic composition of the population, the more desirable characteristics of its European ancestry."[23] Besides the influx of immigrants from Europe, the process of interbreeding, in the hopes of politicians and scientists, would make Brazilians progressively lighter skinned over the years. The interbreeding among White men and Black/mixed women constitutes the basis for Gilberto Freyre's theories of a Brazilian *race*. As a Franz Boas student, Freyre abolished race and racial difference as the primary focus of analysis in favor of a theory of nation building that romanticized slavery. His narrative is a romance in which the already mixed-race Portuguese men (and women) would indulge themselves in/ with Black flesh. From this lust, despite the sadness and the violence, the Brazilian people would emerge as a new ideal type of human, a national population that aggregates the best of each human type (race) that comes together (through sex). This population would make the Brazilian nation into a paradise free of racial tensions (such as those in the United States or South Africa), but this population, this genuine Brazilian human type, would also make the nation a non-Black nation.[24]

While cultural traits of African descent are valued in the rhetoric of *mestizaje* and racial democracy, the state representatives and the social-media discourses on security generally point the finger at the favelas, places whose majority of inhabitants are Blacks, stressing the danger, the drug trafficking, and the threat these places mean to all the good citizens. The handling of Blackness and of Blacks in the national discourse must be read as a strategy of political and social control similar to Homi Bhabha's findings regarding colonialism:

> Surely there is another scene of colonial discourse in which the native or Negro meets the demand of colonial discourse; where the subverting "split" is recuperable within a strategy of social and political control. It is recognizably true that the chain of stereotypical signification is curiously mixed and split, polymorphous and perverse, an articulation of multiple belief. The black is both savage (cannibal) and yet the most obedient and dignified servant (the bearer of the food); he is the embodiment of rampant sexuality and yet innocent as a child, he is mystical, primitive, simple-minded and yet the most worldly and accomplished liar.[25]

Afro-Brazilian cultural production was embraced in order to affirm to the international community that Brazil constituted a genuinely mixed and harmonious nation and was a potential tourist site precisely due to the sensuality, happiness, and exotic nature of its people. According to this perspective, African cultural heritage is part of the national foundation and provides definite proof that there are no racial divisions: almost all Brazilians are racially mixed, and almost all like to party at Carnival. In this context, traditional cultural practices such as samba music, Carnival, and capoeira are evoked to demonstrate the plausibility of the racial democracy narrative. However, as Brazilian cinema director Joel Zito Araújo observes: "The appropriation of Black culture, a process that entailed the participation of all types of media, took place together with the rejection and devaluation of non-hegemonic ethnic and racial groups' efforts to keep their cultural specificities. [. . .] What happened to the Black group in Brazil was a process of folklorization of its culture, as a mechanism of appropriation of Black creations and as a separation of the Black from his identity representations."[26] The folklorization of Black culture and artistic production denies artists the possibility of autonomy over their own work and runs parallel with the celebration of an assumed physical virtuosity, hypersexualized drives, and an exotic happiness that situates the Black being on the side of nature and, consequently, outside of the intellectual project of the nation-state.

Implications and Uncertainties of Heritage Tourism and Preservation Policies

There are racial, economic, and cultural implications in the tourism economy, and heritage tourism is no different. It is defined as the type of tourism that seeks to explore the past, the culture, and the history of certain sites.[27] Heritage Tourism makes it possible for people to be in touch with memory, with history, and even to reconnect with their roots. Tourism in general is supposed to promote the economic growth of communities that have some sort of tourist appeal. However, such processes could easily end up commodifying, essentializing, and forcing communities to leave their areas. Taking the example of Rio de Janeiro's remodeling of the Valongo and Gamboa area, we can see three different moments of urban hygienization and gentrification: First, in 1843, the wharf created in 1811 exclusively to receive human merchandise was buried to hide the marks of the slave trade from the sight of the nobility. In its place, a new wharf was built to welcome a princess. Second, the "Pequena África" (Little Africa)—an effervescent place of Black life in Rio de Janeiro, cradle of samba music and dance, capoeira, Candomblé religion, and Afro-Brazilian cuisine, as well as a space of sociability and employment opportunities—had its population dislodged in the early 1900s in order to facilitate the urban remodeling proposed by Mayor Pereira Passos. Third, in 2011 city authorities and entrepreneurs wanted a new process of remodeling. Bold architectural projects were elaborated, museums were built, and the population living in popular housing in Gamboa and Saúde neighborhoods and the self-declared *quilombolas* at "Pedra do Sal" faced threats of forced removal in the name of Black history and heritage preservation.

In 2012, the city municipality launched the "Porto Maravilha" plan, which presented the new ventures being built in the port and nearby areas. The project introduced this remodeling as historical preservation aligned to a bold urban development plan.[28] The magazine *Inteligência Empresarial*, a city publication related to business and commercial investment, issued an edition titled "Porto Maravilha e a Pequena África in 2011." This edition intended to introduce the "Porto Maravilha" urban plan, which, according to its coordinator, Luiz Carlos Prestes Filho, aimed to "turn two centuries of abandonment into progress."[29] In this magazine's edition, different authors, among them economists, urban development specialists, and historians, present articles on the tourism economy and the need for the preservation of the region.

The cultural segment of this entrepreneurship relied on circuits of guided tours along the "Circuito Histórico e Arqueológico da Celebração da Herança Africana," which contains museums and cultural centers.[30] In addition, the Porto Maravilha Cultural Award funded artistic proposals between 2013 and 2014, including "Histórias Afro-Brasileiras: Cenas itinerantes" (Afrobrazilian stories: Itinerant scenes), "Documentário Porto da Pequena África" (The Port of Little Africa), "Roda de Samba da Pedra do Sal de Mãos Dadas" (Pedra do Sal round dance), "Projeto Som e Samba Carioca" (Carioca Samba and Sound; samba and jongo workshops), "O Porto Importa" (The port matters; a documentary), "Ancestrais do Valongo: Centenário de Abdias Nascimento" (Valongo ancestors: The centenary of Abdias Nascimento), and the proposal discussed here, the "Herança Africana: Intervenções no caminho do Cais do Porto."[31] Notice, the awarded proposals were about Afro-Brazilian culture, history, memory, and heritage.

The disputes over the cultural proposals' authorship—in the cases of those dealing with Black memory and spatiality—bring back an initial question presented during my fieldwork among the Akoben. The dissatisfaction leading to Akoben mobilization was because of Black artists not being seen as autonomous creators of their own art but rather as employees of White cultural producers exploring and profiting from the laws created for protecting and preserving Afro-Brazilian heritage and culture. Zózimo Bulbul himself was part of Akoben, and his work on "Intervenções Urbanas" was an act of resistance against both: the commodification of Black culture and memory for touristic purposes as well as the gentrification of historically Black spaces and places. However, if on the one hand we can think of Zózimo as a work of resistance, on the other hand the logic of state sponsorship for "minorities" is evident in the case of "Herança Africana: Intervenções urbanas." The only way these artists and producers can get some funding is by justifying their artistic work by associating it with Black Awareness Week. Outside very specific moments of the year—the Slavery Abolition Anniversary in May and Black Awareness Week in November—there is no interest in sponsoring a regular tradition of Black autonomous art. Most of the Afro-Brazilian expressive practices being sponsored are the ones in accordance with the standard narrative of "traditional" Afro-Brazilian culture, i.e., samba music and Carnival, both already regulated and dominated by White producers and mass-media corporations.[32]

The archeological research that followed the discovery of Valongo Wharf was also a target of criticism, including the neglect toward archeological findings, which were kept for some time under precarious conditions in a shed near the excavations. The situation even generated newspaper coverage. On January 31, 2013, the newspaper *O Globo* presented a report on the conditions of the Valongo archeological findings and cited an e-mail sent by the administration of the Museu Nacional (National Museum) which states that the work of collecting and cataloging had been "paralyzed since the Rio de Janeiro municipality fired the team of experts engaged with this research as soon as the fieldwork stage was closed."[33] From the content of this e-mail, we notice the contradictions between the discourses of memory preservation and the economic interests being laid out by the Rio de Janeiro municipality, at that time eager to finish the urban remodeling and welcome tourists coming for the World Cup 2012 and Olympic Games 2014.

In thinking about Brazil, a country with an oscillating economy, a high level of inequality, corruption, and violence, whose public higher-education system is under attack due to the proto-fascist regime in charge, we wonder what the future of these heritage preservation initiatives will be, as well as the future of archeological, documental, and historical research on the Black experience in Brazil.[34] During a visit to Rio de Janeiro in 2019, it could be verified that the area of the wharf was surrounded by fences limiting access to the vestiges of the Valongo, and despite the small poster that is attached to the fence explaining the history of the place, there was not much happening there. Regarding the Valongo's archeological findings, the last public news was published by the *O Globo* newspaper in November 2019. The article states that the findings were being kept in precarious conditions in a barn close to the Valongo and were at risk of further deterioration or loss.[35]

Conjuring Temporalities and Territorialities in Black Performance

In the past decades a significant number of studies in the Anthropology of Music, Ethnomusicology, Performance Studies, and African Diaspora Studies have been pointing out the ways through which corporeal performance and vocal signs related to Blackness set the body and voice as sites of resistance and self-making.[36] At the same time, these performances cement practices of sociability and affective bonds among the participants of a given collective of people whose central term of identification was built upon racial lines. That said, it is my understanding that musical and performance practices are able to offer a space to contest violent processes of racialization and subjugation. I argue that the articulation between the artistic performance and the configuration of a racial discourse and consciousness helps to conform political demands and that the performance appears as a process of mediation capable of enunciating, or even formulating, the participants' multiple positioning, trajectories, and worldviews. By doing so, the event of performance offers a perspective of ontological reinvention for these racialized subjects, who through their collective artistic projects and practices can reorganize themselves.

The performances remember and remark on Black territories. Such territories, in the work analyzed here, are spatio-geographic; also, the territorialities and temporalities refer to the city, or even more, to the nation as a whole. In *Demonic Grounds: Black Women and the Cartographies of*

Struggle, Katherine McKittrick asks: "What happens to the cartographies and understanding of the world when it is continually re-imagined through and beyond the legacy of race and racism?"[37] In Rio de Janeiro cartographies of racial hierarchization are obvious and at the same time dynamic, encompassing the neoliberal ordering of the touristic spaces planned to please the foreign tourist. Spaces, places, and temporalities of Black life are constantly under the vigilance of the white-supremacist gaze and of the neo-colonial order. However, it is in those spheres that the bonds of sameness, of love, of caring, and of resistance are bred. As McKittrick continues:

> Hall's argument pivots on black representational politics, which I would suggest are also underwritten by the poetics of landscape: how black communities represent themselves, how black cinema represents black social differences, how political representation is connected to those static mis-representations Frantz Fanon finds so restrictive. I would add to these forms of representations; how black people represent the world around them, how they represent "place" in a world that has profited from black displacement, and how black geographic representation is recast through a struggle, rather than a complacency with space and place.[38]

"Intervenções" is a remembrance of the ancestors, a recognition of the centrality of the sacred in the Black experience, and a reconnection with global Blackness.[39] There was no exteriority to this project. This lack of exteriority can be thought of as a collective act of self-making that concentrates its efforts on collective participation and construction of a communality rather than in presenting or explaining something to an audience. At the same time, Hilton Cobra's speech, an explicit political stance about the exclusion faced by Blacks in Brazil, made clear that memory of ancestors, religiosity, and art are not dissociated from engagement with concrete social action.

"African Heritage: Urban Interventions" is an act of remembrance through art, through the expressive practices that are part of a very specific repertoire of human memory. It conjures the ancestors, it conjures their spiritual power while reminding us of the strength, the life, and the political trajectories of the many who came before. To recognize the sacred, or at least to not dissociate the sacred from the material or from the political, is pivotal to the Black experience through the diaspora; according to Alexander, this is what connects us to a global experience of Blackness.[40]

The event was not thought of as a presentation to an audience; it was rather a collective act of remembering, reconnecting, retelling, and re-encountering people from across the diaspora. The concurrence of this intervention with the beginning of the film festival organized by the Centro Afro Carioca de Cinema was intended to be a reunion between the descendants of those who forcibly passed through "The Door of No Return" and those who stayed and survived colonialism in Africa. On that night in November 2012, we came together in a place marked by the past, a place where our ancestors' bones, their memories, fears, and hopes, lay right beneath us.[41]

NOTES

1. João Costa Vargas, "The Black Diaspora as Genocide: Brazil and The United States. A Supranational Geography of Death and its Alternatives," in *State of White Supremacy: Racism, Governance, and the United States*, ed. M. K. Jung, J. H. Costa Vargas, and E. Bonilla-Silva (Stanford: Stanford University, 2011), 243–71. Also see Luciane O. Rocha, "Morte íntima: A gramática do genocídio antinegro na Baixada Fluminense," in *Motim: Horizontes do genocídio antinegro na diáspora*, ed. A. Flauzina and J. H. Costa Vargas (Brasília: Brado Negro, 2017), 37–66.
2. Paul Amar, "Salvando o berço do samba no Rio de Janeiro: Rebeliões do poder paralelo, infra-nacionalismos urbanos e a política racial de securitização humana," in *Antinegritude: O impossível sujeito negro na formação social brasileira*, ed. O. Pinho and J. H. Costa Vargas (Cruz das Almas, Belo Horizonte: Editora da UFRB and Fino Traço Editora, 2016), 31–58; Maria Andrea Soares, "A ontologia do tema negro: Produção artística, autonomia e posicionalidade da negritude na mobilização Akoben," in Pinho and Costa Vargas, *Antinegritude*, 217–35.
3. *Adinkras* are the iconographic symbols of the Akan people.
4. Hilton Cobra was friends to the pan-Africanist activist, playwright, theater director, and politician Abdias Nascimento and is part of the same generation of Black Brazilian activists as Lélia Gonzalez, Beatriz Nascimento, Haroldo Costa, Édson Cardoso, and the former Minister of Racial Equality Luíza Bairros. See vídeo: Hilton Cobra, "Eugenia Cultural" (Cultural Eugenics), Youtube, 2012, www.youtube.com/watch?v=dFQgFz5X1eE.
5. The adjective used to refer to people (and things) from Rio de Janeiro city.
6. "Achados arqueológicos do cais do valongo estao abandonados em terreno no porto," *O Globo Newspaper*, January 31, 2013, oglobo.globo.com/rio/achados-arqueologicos-do-cais-do-valongo-estao-abandonados-em-terreno-no-porto-7450049
7. Cherise Charleswell, "Gentrification is a Feminist Issue: A Discussion of the Intersection of Class, Race, Gender, and Housing," *Uncommon Thought* (blog), January 2017, www.uncommonthought.com/mtblog/archives/2017/01/08; Michael

Herzfeld, "Engagement, Gentrification, and the Neoliberal Hijacking of History," *Current Anthropology* 51, no.10 (2010): 259–67. See also Naum Chandler, "Of Exorbitance: The Problem of the Negro as a Problem for Thought," *Criticism* 50, no. 2 (2008): 345–410.

8. Loretta Lees, Hyung Bang Chin, and Ernesto Lopes-Morales, "Introduction," in *Global Gentrifications: Uneven Development and Displacement*, eds. Lees, Chin, and Lopes-Morales (UK: University of Bristol, 2015), 1–18.
9. Paul Amar, "Salvando o berço do Samba no Rio de Janeiro: Rebeliões do poder paralelo, infra-nacionalismos urbanos e a política racial de securitização humana," in Pinho and Costa Vargas, *Antinegritude*.
10. Scientific name: *Panicum prionitis*, Famíly: Gramineae, Genus: Gramíneas.
11. Léa Garcia is a Brazilian actress who participated in the Black Experimental Theater founded by Abdias Nascimento in 1944. She also starred in some of Bulbul's movies.
12. "Urban Interventions," Youtube, uploaded by Cultne Acervo, May 24, 2014, www.youtube.com/watch?v=zAX24_iU3q8. For further information, also see Samuca Azevedo, "Herança Africana e intervenções na zona portuária do RJ," *Enraizados, Sua revista eletrônica de cultura urbana*, November 19, 2012, www.enraizados.com.br/index.php/heranca-africana-e-intervencoes-na-zona-portuaria-do-rj.
13. The jongo is a dramatic dance and music accompanied by lyrics or verbal improvisation created by enslaved individuals in the rural area of Rio de Janeiro and Minas Gerais state. The origin of this circular dance is attributed to the Banto-Congolese cultural complex. See Edir Gandra, *Jongo da Serrinha: Dos terreiros para os palcos* (Rio de Janeiro: GGE, 1995). Also see Elizabeth Travassos, "Tradição Oral e História," *Revista de História* 157 (2007): 129–52; "Jongo da Serrinha" is an ensemble created in the 1970s in the Serrinha community (North Rio de Janeiro).
14. *Ekedis* is the title of the women assistants of the Candomblé priestesses, the *Yalorixás*.
15. The area was officially recognized as a *Quilombo* (Maroon community) in 2005 by the Palmares Foundation, a state organization related to the Ministry of Culture. See "Quilombo da Pedra do Sal é área remanescente de quilombo, afirma presidente da FCP a Rede Globo," May 24, 2007, www.palmares.gov.br/?p=2041. Last accessed on August 16, 2021.
16. M. Jacqui Alexander, *Pedagogies of Crossing: Meditations on Feminism, Sexual Politics, Memory, and the Sacred* (Durham, NC: Duke University Press, 2005), 290.
17. Raimundo Nina Rodrigues, *O animismo fetichista dos negros Baianos* (Rio de Janeiro: Fundação Biblioteca Nacional e Editora da UFRJ, [1896] 2006). See Antônio Sérgio Guimarães, "A questão racial na política brasileira—os últimos 15 anos," *Tempo Social—revista de Sociologia da USP* 13, no. 2 (2001): 121–42; Osmundo Pinho and Lívio Samsone, *Raça: Novas perspectivas antropológicas* (Salvador: EDUFBA; Associação Brasileira de Antropologia, 2008).
18. See Matthias R. Assunção, *Capoeira: A History of an Afro-Brazilian Martial Art* (London: Routledge, 2005).
19. Elisa L. Nascimento, *The Sorcery of Color: Identity, Race, and Gender in Brazil* (Philadelphia: Temple University Press, 2007). See also Michael Hanchard, *Orpheus and Power: The Movimento Negro of Rio de Janeiro and São Paulo, Brazil, 1945–1988* (Princeton, NJ:

Princeton University Press, 1999); Helena Theodoro Lopes and Beatriz Nascimento, *Negro e Cultura no Brasil* (Rio de Janeiro: UNIBRADE Centro de Cultura, 1987).
20. João H. Costa Vargas, "The Black Diaspora as Genocide: Brazil and the United States. A Supranational Geography of Death and its Alternatives," in Jung, Costa Vargas, and Bonilla-Silva, *State of White Supremacy*, 243–71. Also see Michael Hanchard, *Orpheus and Power: The Movimento Negro of Rio de Janeiro and São Paulo, Brazil, 1945–1988*; France Windance Twine, *Racism in a Racial Democracy: The Maintenance of White Supremacy in Brazil* (New Brunswick: Rutgers University, 1998); Thomas Skidmore, *The Idea of Race in Latin America* (Austin: University of Texas Press, 1990).
21. Denise Ferreira da Silva, "À Brasileira: Escrita de um desejo destrutivo," *Revista de Estudos Feministas* 14, no. 336 (2006): 61–83. Also see Kabenguele Munanga, *Rediscutindo a Mestiçagem no Brasil: Identidade nacional versus identidade negra* (Petrópolis: Vozes, 1999).
22. Florestan Fernandes, *A Integração do Negro na Sociedade de Classes* (São Paulo: Ática, 1978).
23. Decreto-lei 7967-45. Presidência da República do Brasil, 1945, presrepublica.jusbrasil.com.br/legislacao/126587/decreto-lei-7967-45.
24. Freyre asserts that the Portuguese had a long history of coexisting with different groups and amalgamating with them. He uses the example of the contact between Portugal and Morocco prior to the colonization of Brazil to justify his claim. See Gilberto Freyre, *Casa Grande e Senzala* (Madrid: Allca XX, [1933] 2002).
25. Homi K. Bhabha, *The Location of Culture* (London: Routledge, 2004), 118.
26. "A apropriação da cultura negra, um processo que contou com a participação de todos os tipos de mídia teve lugar junto com a rejeição e a desvalorização dos esforços de grupos étnico raciais não hegemônicos em manter suas especificidades culturais." See Joel Zito Araújo, *A Negação do Brasil: O negro na telenovela Brasileira* (São Paulo: SENAC editor, 2000), 35. (The translation is mine).
27. Dallen J. Timothy and Stephen W. Boyd, "Heritage Tourism in the 21st Century: Valued Traditions and New Perspectives," *Journal of Heritage Tourism* 1, no. 1 (2006): 1–16.
28. "Circuito Histórico E Arqueológico Da Celebração Da Herança Africana," CDURP-Companhia de Desenvolvimento Urbano da Região do Porto do Rio de Janeiro, accessed May 11, 2021, portomaravilha.com.br/circuito.
29. Luiz Carlos Prestes Filho, Edmundo Souto, Hans Donner, and Ephim Shluger, "Passarela Popular do Samba: Centro de Convergência Cultural e Esportiva da Zona Norte e Zona Oeste do Rio de Janeiro," in "Porto Maravilha e a Pequena África," special issue, *Inteligência Empresarial* (2011): 35.
30. The Historical and Archaeological Circuit for the Celebration of African Heritage is a region located between the neighborhoods of Gamboa and Saúde, in the Central Zone of the city of Rio de Janeiro. For further information see "Circuito Histórico e Arqueológico de Celebração da Herança Africana," Youtube, uploaded by Iphan RjNov 18, 2016, www.youtube.com/watch?v=mBcBNKjBOTM.
31. See, respectively, "Circuito Histórico de Herança Africana - Historias afro brasileiras-cenas itinerantes ano l," Youtube, uploaded by Periferia CENA Portuária, March 2,

2016, www.youtube.com/watch?v=bMMQdQc5dJU; "Porto da Pequena África," Youtube, uploaded by Casa da Tia Ciata, March 31, 2021, www.youtube.com/watch?v=HcbT172w7vo; "Roda de Samba da Pedra do Sal," Youtube, uploaded by Roda de Samba da Pedra do Sal, March 11, 2020, www.youtube.com/watch?v=yijHPxSYTiE; "Projeto Som E Samba Carioca," Prêmio Porto Maravilha Cultural, accessed May 11, 2021, portomaravilha.com.br/premiosdetalhe/cod/42; "O Porto Importa," Prêmio Porto Maravilha Cultural, accessed May 11, 2021, porto maravilha.com.br/premiosdetalhe/cod/36; "Ancestrais Do Valongo, Centenário De Abdias Nascimento," Prêmio Porto Maravilha Cultural, accessed May 11, 2021, porto maravilha.com.br/premiosdetalhe/cod/26.

32. Maria Andrea Soares, "A ontologia do tema negro," 217–35.
33. "Achados arqueológicos do cais do valongo estao abandonados em terreno no porto," *O Globo*, January 31, 2013, n.p
34. One example of the precariousness of Brazilian institutions in charge of heritage preservation is the Museu Nacional, one of the most important Brazilian museums and archeological locations, which was nearly destroyed in 2018 by a fire due to lack of maintenance of the electrical circuit. The restoration process started in 2021, but according to the staff, around 90 percent of the museum collection was lost, including artifacts of Brazilian Indigenous people and objects related to Africans and their descendants in Brazil. See "Ciência: O que o brasil perdeu com o incêndio do Museo Nacional," uol.com.br, last accessed February 22, 2022, vestibular.uol.com.br/resumo-das-disciplinas/atualidades/ciencia-o-que-o-brasil-perdeu-com-o-incendio-do-museu-nacional.htm-.
35. See "Sete anos após as escavações achados do Cais do Valongo estão em Caixas Correndo Riscos," *O Globo*, last accessed on February 22, 2022, oglobo.globo.com/rio/sete-anos-apos-escavacoes-objetos-achados-no-cais-do-valongo-estao-em-caixas-correm-risco-1-24061864-.
36. Nicole Fleetwood, *Troubling Vision: Performance, Visuality, and Blackness* (Chicago: University of Chicago Press, 2011). Also see Fred Moten, *In the Break: The Aesthetics of the Black Radical Tradition* (Minneapolis: University of Minnesota Press, 2003); E. Patrick Johnson, *Appropriating Blackness: Performance and the Politics of Authenticity* (Durham, NC: Duke University Press, 2003), 1–16; Philip Bohlmam and Ronald Radano, "Introduction," in *Music and the Racial Imagination*, ed. P. Bohlmam and R. Radano (Chicago: The University of Chicago Press, 2000), 1–56; bell hooks, "Performance Practice as a Site of Opposition," in *Let's Get It On: The Politics of Black Performance*, ed. C. Ugwu (Seattle: Bay Press, 1995), 220–21.
37. Katherine McKittrick, *Demonic Grounds: Black Women and the Cartographies of Struggle* (Minneapolis: University of Minnesota Press, 2006), 28.
38. Ibid., 29.
39. For the sacred in Black experience, see M. Jacqui Alexander, *Pedagogies of Crossing: Meditations on Feminism, Sexual Politics, Memory, and the Sacred*.
40. Ibid.
41. See *Centro Afro Carioca de Cinema*, 2013, afrocariocadecinema.org.br.

Contributors

ALBERTO ABREU is a Cuban-based narrator, essayist, curator, and cultural critic. He was the coordinator of the Virgilio Piñera Narrative Workshop, held in the city of Matanzas. His essay "Virgilio Piñera: A Man, an Island" won the UNEAC Enrique José Varona Prize in 2000. His essay "Los juegos de la escritura: O, la (re)escritura de la historia" received the Casa de las Américas 2007 prize. He is also the author of *Por una Cuba negra: Literatura, raza y modernidad en el Siglo XIX* (2017).

JEROME C. BRANCHE is a professor of Latin American literature and cultural studies, chair of the Department of Hispanic Languages and Literatures at the University of Pittsburgh, and director of publications of the *Revista Iberoamericana*. He is the author of *Colonialism and Race in Luso-Hispanic Literature* (University of Missouri Press, 2006), *The Poetics and Politics of Diaspora: Transatlantic Musings* (Routledge, 2014), and several edited books on blackness, literature, and coloniality in the Hispanic world, the most recent being *Imperial Trajectories: Transhispanic Reflections on the African Diaspora*. Branche's current book project addresses the interwoven thematic of writing, slavery, and necropolitics from a transhispanic standpoint. He will be Leverhulme Fellow and Visiting Professor at the University of London, Birkbeck College, in 2022–2023.

LÚCIA HELENA COSTIGAN is a professor of colonial Latin American, Afro-Brazilian, religious, and ethnic studies at Ohio State University. She has published *Through Cracks in the Wall: Modern Inquisitions and New Christian Letrados in the Iberian Atlantic World* (Brill Academic Publishers, 2010), and *A sátira e o intelectual criollo na colônia: Gregório de Matos e Juan del Valle y Caviedes* (Latinoamericana Editores, 1991). Her current project focuses on Latin American literary texts of the colonial period. She has edited (with Beatriz González Stephan) *Crítica y descolonización: El sujeto colonial en la cultura latinoamericana* (Academia Nacional de la Historia, 1992), has directed and edited (with Leoplodo Bernucci), the special issue of *Revista Iberoamericana*, "O Brasil, a América Hispânica e o Caribe: Abordagens comparativas" (1998), and edited *Diálogos da conversão: Missionários, índios, negros e judeus no contexto ibero-americano do período barroco* (Editora UNICAMP, 2005).

BALTASAR FRA-MOLINERO is a professor of Hispanic studies at Bates College where he is also a member of the programs in Africana and Latin American and Latinx studies. His scholarly production covers the representation of the African diaspora and Blackness in the early modern period in Spain and Latin America. He is also interested in postcolonial studies, with work on Equatorial Guinea. He is the author of *La imagen de los negros en la España del Siglo de Oro* (Verbum, 2014) as well as a double volume dedicated to Equatorial Guinea in *Afro-Hispanic Review* (28, no. 2, 2009). He has edited a double issue, "Don Quixote's Racial Other," for *Annals of Scholarship* (19, no. 2-3, 2010). With Sue E. Houchins he has co-authored the introduction, annotation, and English translation of Juan Carlos Paniagua's Life of Sor Teresa Chicaba, *Black Bride of Christ: Chicaba, an African Nun in Eighteenth-Century Spain* (Vanderbilt University Press, 2018).

ELISEO JACOB is currently a faculty member in the Department of World Languages and Cultures at Howard University. His research focuses on cultural production in Latin America's urban peripheries, including fiction, poetry, and hip hop. His current book project, *Masculinidades Marginales: Race, Masculinity, and the City in Twenty-First-Century Latin American Literature*, is an examination of writers from Brazilian and Latin American urban peripheries and how their literary representations of marginalized male youth raise urgent questions surrounding citizenship. He was recently awarded a Fulbright grant to complete a digital humanities project on the Literatura Periférica movement in São Paulo, Brazil.

AGNES LUGO-ORTIZ is an associate professor at the University of Chicago and a specialist in nineteenth-century Latin American literature, and in nineteenth- and twentieth-century Caribbean cultural history. Her work focuses on cultural production and modern socio-political identities. She has published *Identidades imaginadas: Biografía y nacionalidad en el horizonte de la guerra (Cuba 1860–1898)* (Editorial de la Universidad de Puerto Rico, 1999), and her current book-length project is *Riddles of Modern Identity: Biography and Visual Portraiture in Slaveholding Cuba (1760–1886)*. She has written various essays about the links between queer sexualities, gender, and anticolonial politics in twentieth-century Puerto Rico. Since 1994 she has been on the advisory board of the Recovering the US Hispanic Literary Heritage Project and is co-editor of *Herencia: The Anthology of Hispanic Literature of the United States, En otra voz: Antología de la literatura hispana de los Estados Unidos*, and *Recovering the US Hispanic Literary Heritage*, vol. 5.

MANUEL OLMEDO GOBANTE is an assistant professor at the University of Arkansas, where he teaches and studies early modern Spanish literature and culture. His research centers on topics such as the history of Hispanic martial arts, early modern soldierly literature, and Afro-Hispanic culture. He is currently working on a book on the social, cultural, and literary history of early modern Hispanic fencing. He is also the critical editor of the forthcoming bilingual edition of *El valiente negro en Flandes* (The Brave Black Man in Flanders), a seventeenth-century play by Andrés de Claramonte.

CASSIA ROTH is an associate professor of history and Latin American and Caribbean studies at the University of Georgia. Prior to that, she was a Marie Sklodowska-Curie Postdoctoral Research Fellow at the University of Edinburgh in Scotland and a Fulbright Postdoctoral Scholar at the Fundação Oswaldo Cruz in Rio de Janeiro, Brazil. Her book, *A Miscarriage of Justice: Women's Reproductive Lives and the Law in Early Twentieth-Century Brazil* (Stanford University Press, 2020), won the Murdo J. MacLeod Prize from the Latin American and Caribbean Section of the Southern Historical Association and Choice Outstanding Academic Title from the American Library Association. Her work, on topics as diverse as the feminist scientist Bertha Lutz to the history of cesarean sections, has appeared in numerous peer-reviewed journals, and her article "From Free Womb to Criminalized Woman: Fertility Control in Brazilian Slavery and Freedom" won the 2018 Berkshire Conference of Women Historians Best Article prize. She teaches courses on Brazilian history, gender history, slavery, and medicine and is the faculty adviser to UGA's oldest student organization, the Demosthenian Literary Society.

MARIA ANDREA DOS SANTOS SOARES is an associate professor at the UNILAB (University for Africa-Brazil Lusophone Integration). She has teaching and research experience in Afro-Brazilian culture, race relations in Brazil, Black women's thought, performance studies, and cultural studies. She has published articles and book chapters in English and Portuguese, including "Look! Blackness in Brazil: Disrupting the Grotesquerie of Racial Stereotyping in Brazilian Popular Culture" (*Cultural Dynamics* 24, no. 1, 2012), "A Ontologia do Tema Negro: Produção artística, autonomia e posicionalidade da negritude na mobilização do Akoben" (Academia.edu), and "On the Colonial Past of Anthropology: Teaching Race and Coloniality in the Global South" (*Humanities* 8, no. 2, 2019). Her research interest is in English-to-Portuguese translation of the works of African and Afro-diasporic anthropologists; the archives, monuments, and memories of transatlantic slave trade and colonization in Brazil and on the West African Coast; and Afro diasporic performance practices.

MIGUEL A. VALERIO is an assistant professor of Spanish at Washington University in St. Louis. He is a scholar of the African diaspora in the Iberian world: Latin America, Spain, Portugal, and beyond. He teaches courses in Afro-colonial culture and contemporary Afro-Latin American literature and culture. His research has focused on black Catholic brotherhoods or confraternities and Afro-creole festive practices in colonial Latin America, especially Mexico and Brazil. His research has appeared in various academic journals, including *Slavery and Abolition*, *Colonial Latin American Review*, *The Americas*, and the *Journal of Festive Studies*. He is the author of *Sovereign Joy: Afro-Mexican Kings and Queens, 1539–1640* (Cambridge University Press, 2022) and a co-editor of *Indigenous and Black Confraternities in Colonial Latin America: Negotiating Status through Religious Practices* (Amsterdam University Press, 2022). He is currently working on his second book project, *Afro-Brazilian Sovereign Spaces: The World Black Irmandades Built in Colonial Brazil*, under contract with Cambridge University Press.

ELIZABETH R. WRIGHT is a distinguished research professor of Spanish literature at the University of Georgia. Her research and teaching focus on early modern Spain in the context of imperial expansion. Her most recent book, *The Epic of Juan Latino: Dilemmas of Race and Religion in Renaissance Spain* (University of Toronto Press, 2016), traces how this one-time slave secured higher education, freedom, and social prominence. Her new book project, *Iberia's Atlantic Households: Slavery and Diaspora in the Age of Empire (1444–1640)*, asks how a new mode of slave trafficking that did not fit Mediterranean traditions of "just war" slavery became integrated into the fabric of economic life, language, and humor despite the widespread awareness of its cruelty and dubious legality. She is also the editor of the longest-running scholarly journal devoted to the study of theater in the early modern era, the *Bulletin of the Comediantes*.

Index

"À cidade da Bahia" (To the city of
  Bahia) (Matos), 167–68
Abolição (1988 film), 267
abolitionism, 103–4, 130–31, 202
abortion, 193–94
Academia Brasileira de Letras (Brazilian
  Academy of Letters), 163
Academia Imperial de Medicina (Imperial
  Academy of Medicine), 192
activism, 236–39. *See also* Akoben
  movement; *movimento negro* (Black
  Movement, Brazil)
Aeneid (Virgil), 176
Afolabi, Niyi, 247, 258–59
African American Studies, 2
Africana Studies, 2
"Afro-Brasileiro" (song), 246
Afro-Cuban, use of term, 235–36. *See also*
  Cuban national identity
Afro-descendant, use of term, 235
Afrofuturism, 142–43, 153–56
Afro-Iberian confraternities
  Alba-Medrano family and, 46–47
  cultural roles of, 34–39, *37*
  diaspora and, 39–42
  disappearance of, 42
  origins of, 29–30
  social roles of, 30–32, *33*
Afropessimism, 81, 154
Agassiz, Louis, 131–35

Aguillar, Gonzalo, 171
Aguirre, Mirta, 228
Aidoo, Lamonte, 196, 199
Akoben movement, 265–66, 276, 278–79
Alba, Luis, 46–47, 70
Alba-Medrano family, 46–47, 69–70
Alexander, M. Jacqui, 270–71, 278
Alexander VI, Pope, 85
Alfonso, María Isabel, 242–43n40
Alfonso I d'Este, 109
Algarbe, Fernando de, 54
"Algunos problemas teóricos de la
  literatura hispanoamericana"
  (Fernández Retamar), 241–42n34
Almanak das Musas (Caldas Barbosa), 174
Alte Armatur und Ringkunst (Talhoffer),
  56, *57*
Alves, Jaime, 252, 256
Amado, James, 163, 165
Amar, Paul, 268–69
American School of Ethnology, 133
Añasco, Francisco de, 51
Andrade, Oswald de, 187n4
Andrade Lima, Tânia, 267–68
Aniceto em dia de Alforria (1981 short film),
  267
Annaes de Medicina Brasiliense (Annals of
  Brazilian Medicine), 191–93
Anthony of Carthage, 32, *33*
Anti-Black City, The (Alves), 252

anti-Black racism, 81–82
"Antigamente Quilombos, Hoje Periferia" (song), 247–48, 249–51, 258
antropófagia (literary movement), 165
Aponte, José Antonio, 220–21
"Apuntes sobre el arte y la literatura" (Aguirre), 228
Aqualtune, 259
Arango y Parreño, Francisco de, 218, 225–26, 227
Araújo, Joel Zito, 274
Arbuistante y Ondeano, Melchor de, 84
Arcádia de Roma (literary academy), 173, 176
archives, 103–7. See also enslaved faces in portraiture
Argentina, 42
Armas Antárticas (Miramontes y Zuázola), 67
Arobe, Francisco de. See *Los mulatos de Esmeraldas* (Sánchez Gallque)
Articulación Regional de Afrodescendientes de América Latina y el Caribe, ARAAC (Regional Articulation of Afro-descendants of Latin America and the Caribbean), 237
asiento, 145–46
assimilationist politics, 272
Autobiografía de Juan Francisco Manzano (García Marruz), 222–24

Badu, Eryka, 153–54
Bahia (now Salvador da Bahia de Todos os Santos), 164, 166–67
Balthazar, 32
Baquero, Gastón, 215–16, 217
Barcelona, Spain, 29, 30–31
Barrio de Sepúlveda, Juan del, 143, 145–47, 148–49, 150–51
Barros, Joaõ de, 20–22, 25–26
Bastide, Roger, 181
Beaumont, Francis, 49
Benedict of Palermo, 86

Benedict the Moor, 32, *33*, 65
Benemelis, Juan Felipe, 217, 231, 233–35
Benguela, Teresa, 259
Benoist, Marie-Guillemine de DeLaville-Leroulx, Comtesse de, 122–23, *124*, 126–28
Bernal, Diego de, 54
Bestor, Jane Fair, 138n12
Beyoncé, 153–54
Bhabha, Homi, 273
Bia Doxum (Beatriz de Oliveira Ferreira), 253–54
Bindman, David, 104
Black Liberation Army (BLA), 81–82
Black Marxism (Robinson), 261n7
Black Movement (Brazil), 245, 265–66, 267. See also Akoben movement
Black Panther, 235
Black Panther (2018 film), 145, 146, 153–54
Black Panther Party, 154, 233
Black Power movement, 233, 235
Black saints, 32, *33*, 65–66. See also Chicaba (Venerable Madre Sor Teresa Juliana de Santo Domingo)
blackface, 39
Blackmore, Josiah, 14, 18
Blanco, Juan, 227–28
Blanco, Narciso, 216–17
blocos Afros, 248
blood purity (*limpieza de sangre*), 90
"Boa Esperança" (song), 247–48, 251–53
Boas, Franz, 273
Bocage, Manuel Maria Barbosa du, 173, 182
body of the enslaved, 103–4. See also enslaved faces in portraiture; enslaved women's reproductive experiences
Bolívar, Simón, 215–16
bozal, use of term, 156–57n2
Braga, Portugal, 36–38, *37*
Branagan, Thomas, 104, *106*
Branche, Jerome, 18, 145, 161, 162, 182, 186
branqueamento (racial whitening), 250

Brazil
  Afro-Iberian confraternities in, 42
  Black cultural expressions in, 271–74, 277–78. *See also* Akoben movement
  Candomblé religion in, 269–70, 271–72
  capoeira in, 70n4
  enslaved women's reproductive experiences in, 191–93, 196–206
  Portuguese language in, 161–63, 170–71, 172, 174 (*see also* Caldas Barbosa, Domingos; Matos, Gregório de)
  racial democracy in, 250, 265–66, 272–73
  tourism economy and, 265–66, 268–69, 274–77
Brazilian hip hop
  periferia as *quilombo* in, 247, 255–60
  periferia as *senzala* in, 247, 248–55
  quilombismo and, 246–48
  Zumbi dos Palmares and, 245–46
Brent, William, 242–43n40
Breu, Jörg the Younger, 56
Brevísima relación de la destruición de las Indias (Las Casas), 25
Broeck, Sabine, 80–81, 83
Bulbul, Zózimo, 266–67, 269–71, 276, 280n11
burial practices, 31–32, 40
Buscón, El (Quevedo), 62–64
Butler, Judith, 241n25
Butler, Octavia, 153–54, 156
Byron, John, 1st Lord, 116, *117*

Cabello Balboa, Miguel, 149, 151–53, 157n8
cabildos (Black societies), 42
Cadamosto, Alvise de, 111
Cadiz, Spain, 11–12
Caldas Barbosa, Antonio de, 172
Caldas Barbosa, Domingos
  discrimination and, 161–62, 163, 175–79, 182–84, 186–87
  life and works of, 172–73, 174–80, 182–85
  "racialized identity" of, 186–87
  reception of, 163–64, 173–75, 180–82, 185–86
Caldeira, Teresa, 248
Calderón de la Barca, Francisco, 91
Caldwell, Kia Lilly, 254
Camões, Luís de, 176
Campos, Augusto de, 188n18
Campos, Haroldo de, 165, 170, 188n18
Candomblé religion, 269–70, 271–72
capoeira, 70n4, 265, 272
Carbonell, Walterio, 217, 226–27, 236
Cardoso, Édson, 279n4
Carlos II, King of Spain, 89
Carmichael, Stokely, 233
Carmona, Méndez de, 51
Carneiro, Sueli, 253
Carpio, Bernardo del, 63–64
Carranza, Jerónimo Sánchez de, 49, 51, 63, 67
Carril, Lourdes, 261n8
Casa de Contratación (Seville), 13
Catholicism, 15–16, 18, 24, 251. *See also* Afro-Iberian confraternities; Black saints; Chicaba (Venerable Madre Sor Teresa Juliana de Santo Domingo)
Cavalcaselle, Giovanni Battista, *110*
Caviedes, Juan del Valle y, 164
censorship, 162–63
Centro Afro Carioca de Cinema (Afro-Carioca Cinema Center), 266, 267, 269–71, 279
Cepeda, Néstor, 216–17
Cervantes, Miguel de, 22–23, 65
Cerveira, Afonso de, 14, 23
Charleswell, Cherise, 268
Chauí, Marilene, 264n43
Chicaba (Venerable Madre Sor Teresa Juliana de Santo Domingo)
  agency and autonomy of, 89–90
  Paniagua's obituary and biography of, 82–92, 95
  poem by, 92–94
Chico-Rei, 256

Chin, Hyung Bang, 268
cholera, 61
chontas (iron spears), 145, 148, 150–51
Christianity. *See* Catholicism; evangelization
cimarrones (runaway slaves), 151
Cinco Vezes Favela (1962 film), 266–67
City of Walls (Caldeira), 248
Claramonte, Andrés de, 65
Cleaver, Eldridge, 233
Cobra, Hilton, 266, 269, 278
colorism, 253
¿Cómo surgió la cultura nacional? (Carbonel), 226–27
Compendio de la vida ejemplar de la Venerable Madre Sor Teresa Juliana de Sto. Domingo (Paniagua), 82–92, 95
conceptismo, 164–65
concrete poetry movement, 170
confesión con el demonio, La (Torres), 65
"Consejo Nacional de Cultura contesta a Alfredo Guevara, El" (Antuña), 228–29
conspiración de Aponte 1812, La (Franco), 217–18
Conspiracy of La Escalera, 220–21, 223–24
Constitution of Cádiz (1812), 12
Cooper Owens, Dierdre, 197, 203
Córdoba, Spain, 54
Cortes, Hernán, 41
Costa, Haroldo, 279n4
Council of Trent (1545–1563), 86
Covarrubias, Sebastián de, 91–92
Cowling, Camillia, 203
"Crime Bárbaro" (song), 247–48, 256–58
criminal justice system, 252–53
criollo, use of term, 187–88n6
Crónica dos feitos notáveis que se passaram na conquista de Guiné (Chronicle of the Notable Deeds that Transpired in the Conquest of Guinea) (Zurara), 14–21, 23–24, 26
Crowe, Joseph Archer, *110*

Cuba, 42. *See also* Cuban national identity
"Cuba en la sombra de Haiti" (Ferrer), 218–20
Cuba Socialista (magazine), 228–29
Cuban national identity
   activism and, 236–39
   Black and/or enslaved poets and, 216–17, 221–24
   Cuban Revolution and, 226–36
   el miedo al negro and, 215–16, 217–21, 224–26
culteranismo, 164–65
Cummins, Tom, 157n8
curros, 80
Curtis, Mary Theresa Dill, 51

dance, 35–38, *37*, 42, 79–80, 171–72. *See also jongo* (dance and musical genre); *lundu* (song and dance)
Dandara, 259
David, Jacques-Louis, 126
Davis, Angela, 55, 128
Dayan, Colin, 128
De arte athletica (Mair), 56, *58–60*
De instauranda Aethiopum salute (Sandoval), 40
Debret, Jean-Baptiste, 104, *106*
Decada primeira da Asia (The First Decade of Asia) (Barros), 20–24, 25–26
Delaney, Samuel, 156
Demonic Grounds (McKittrick), 277–78
derecho de coartación, 128
desengaño barroco (baroque disillusion), 167
des-esclavización (de-enslavement), 151
Dia da Consciência Negra (Black Consciousness Day), 245
Dianti, Laura de, 109–10, *110*, 119
DJ Hum, 246
Django Unchained (2012 film), 256–57
Dobson, William, 116, *117*
Doença, A (The Malady) (Caldas Barbosa), 174, *175*–80, 182–84, 186–87
Dominguez, Juan, 52
Domínguez Ortiz, Antonio, 25

Dominican order, 35, 39
Don Quijote (Cervantes), 22–23
Douglass, Frederick, 19–20, 130–31, *132*
Dragontea (Lope de Vega), 66–67
Duchess of Portsmouth (Mignard), 111–12, *114*
Dum Diversas (Nicolas V), 85
DuVernay, Ava, 153–54
Dyck, Anthony van, 111–12, *113*

Écija, Spain, 46–47
Elliott, Missie, 153–54
Elysio, Filinto, 173, 182
Emicida, 247–48, 251–53
emotions, history of, 193–94
Enciso, Diego Jiménez de, 64–65
Enríquez, Martín, 41
enslaved body, 103–4. See also enslaved women's reproductive experiences
enslaved faces in portraiture
  archival practices of, 104–7, 136
  in the archive of the law, 107–8, 128–31, *132*
  as courtly symbol, 107, 108–20, *110*, *113–15*, *117*, *120*
  scientific racism and, 107, 131–35, *133*, *135*
  as sign of artistic mastery, 107, 120–28, *123–24*
enslaved women's reproductive experiences
  compared to White women's experiences, 196–97, 201–2, 205–6
  history of emotions and, 193–94
  physical pain and, 194–95, 196–201, 203–5
  in Rio de Janeiro, 191–93, 196–206
  scientific racism and, 202–6
  sources on, 195–96
  training of obstetricians and, 201–2
enslavism, 81–82, 87–88
epistemicídio (epistemicide), 253
escola dos ciosos, A (Caldas Barbosa), 175
Espinosa, Alonso de, 158–59n17

Esquadrão da Morte (death squads), 249
eugenics, 271–72
evangelization, 83–86, 157n4. See also Chicaba (Venerable Madre Sor Teresa Juliana de Santo Domingo)
Extremities (Grigsby), 127

Fanon, Frantz, 55, 92, 254–55
favelas (shantytowns), 247, 265. See also Brazilian hip hop
Felicidade (enslaved woman), 197–98, 200–201, 204
femicide, 253
fencing
  in early modern Portugal, 52
  in early modern Spain, 47–51, *50*
  participation of Afro-Hispanics in, 51–55, 69
  representation of Afro-Hispanics and, 55–69, *57–60*
fencing games (*juegos de esgrima*), 48, 54
Fernandes, Florestan, 272
Fernandes, Jorge, 52
Fernández Retamar, Roberto, 241–42n34
Fernández Robaina, Tomás, 217
Fernando Simões Barbosa com ama de leite (carte de visite), 119–20, *121*
Ferreira, Justo Jansen, 203–4, 206
Ferrer, Ada, 218–20
fertility control, 194
festive practices, 34–39, *37*
Filosofía de las armas (Carranza), 51
flamenco, 79–80
Fletcher, John, 49
Flores Pavón, Sebastián, 84
Florilégio da poesia brasileira (Varnhagen), 162–63
Flory, Rae, 167
Folheto de ambas Lisboas (Pamphlet of Both Lisbons) (magazine), 35–36
Fonseca, Francisco da, 52
forró, 270
Foucault, Michel, 107, 241n26
Fracchia, Carmen, 91–92, 125

Fraginals, Manuel Moreno, 217–18
Fra-Molinero, Baltasar, 22, 55, 61–62, 68–69, 89
Francis, Gladys M., 200
Franco, José Luciano, 217–18
Frente Negra Brasileira (Black Brazilian Front), 261n1
Freyre, Gilberto, 273
Frías, Juan Antonio, 216–17
Friol, Roberto, 221–22
Fromont, Cécile, 38
Fuentes, Marisa, 195
Fulleda, Gerardo, 234

Gaceta de Cuba (newspaper), 227–28
Galanga Livre (album), 256–58
Galenic medicine, 61
Galharde, Germão, 23
Ganga Zumba, 259
Garcés, José, 84
Garcia, Léa, 269
García Canclini, Néstor, 241n33
García Marruz, Fina, 222–24
Garofalo, Leo, 30
gentrification, 268–69, 270–71
George Washington (Trumbull), 112–18, 115
Germeten, Nicole von, 39–40
Gestoso y Pérez, José de, 52
gifts, 89, 109, 150–51, 154
Giraldi, Giovan Battista, 138n12
Globo, O (newspaper), 276, 277
Godinho, Domingo Luis, 62
Gómez, Sara, 234
Góngora, Luis de, 164–65
Gonzalez, Lélia, 279n4
González, Tomás, 231–32, 233, 234, 236
Granados, Manolo, 234
Grandezas de la espada (Pacheco de Narváez), 61–62, 64–65
Grant Smith, David, 167
Grassi, Giacomo di, 62
Graubart, Karen B., 30
Gregory XV, Pope, 85

Grigsby, Darcy Grimaldo, 126, 127
Guillard Limonta, Norma, 238
Guillen Landrián, Nicolasito, 234
Gurumbé: Afro-Andalusian Memories (2016 documentary), 79–80

hagiography, 65, 82–89
hair, 254
Haitian Revolution, 215–16, 217–21, 225
Hamlet (Shakespeare), 49
Harlem Renaissance, 11
Harper's (magazine), 104, 106
Hartman, Saidiya, 128, 196, 200
Harvard University, 131–35, 132
Havana, Cuba, 96n4
Hegel, Georg Wilhelm Friedrich, 55
Henrietta of Lorraine, 111–12, 113
Henry, Prince of Portugal, 15, 17–18, 20, 21–22
"Herança Africana: Intervenções Urbanas no Caminho do Cais do Porto" (urban intervention), 266, 269–71, 276, 278–79
"herederos del oscurantismo, Los" (Blanco), 227–28
Heredia, Pedro, 62
heritage tourism, 268–69, 274–77
hermeneutics of absence, 80–81, 83
Hernández, Eugenio, 234
Hernández, Francisco, 51
Herrera, Georgina, 234
Herzfeld, Michael, 268
Herzog, Tamar, 12
hip hop music. See Brazilian hip hop
História da literatura brasileira (Romero), 170, 174
História da literatura brasileira (Veríssimo), 170, 173–74
Historia de Indias (Las Casas), 24–26
History of Rome from Its Foundations (Livy), 20
Holocausto Urbano (album), 249
Holston, James, 257
Howe, Linda S., 233

Ibáñez de Agurto, Sancho, 50
Ibero-American Studies, 2
Igareda, Ignacio de, 84
Ignacia (enslaved woman), 191–93
Illescas, Alonso de, 157n8
Imperial Academy of Medicine (Academia Imperial de Medicina), 192
Indigenous people, 85, 204, 282n34. See also *mulatos de Esmeraldas, Los* (Sánchez Gallque)
infant mortality, 192–93, 205
infanticide, 193–94
Institute of Ethnology and Folklore (Cuba), 227
Integração do negro na sociedade de clases, A (Fernandes), 272
Inteligência Empresarial (magazine), 275
intersectionality, 238
Iphigenia of Ethiopia, 32, *33*
Irving, Washington, 11

jácaras (pimp poetry), 63–64
Jaén, Spain, 46–47
Jesus, Antónia de, 172
John II of Navarre, 29, 30–31
jongo (dance and musical genre), 269–70, 271
Jonson, Ben, 49
Juan de Mérida, 65
Juan de Pareja (Velázquez), 122–26, *123*, 127–28
Juan de Valladolid ("Black Count"), 34
Juan Latino (Enciso), 64–65
Juana Inés de la Cruz, 164

Kaleb of Axum, 32

Lagos, Portugal. See slave voyage and auction in Lagos, Portugal (1444)
Lahon, Didier, 34–35
Lançarote da Ilha (Lancelot of the Isle), 13–15, 21, 23
language, 19, 161–63, 219–20, 225–26. See also Portuguese language

lanzas, Las (*The Surrender of Brede*) (Velázquez), 146
las Casas, Bartolomé de, 23–26
Latin American Studies, 2
Laura de Dianti (Titian), 109–12, *110*, 119
Le Riverend, Julio, 221
Lee, William "Billy," 112–19, *115*
Lees, Loretta, 268
Leonard, Irving A., 41
"Lesbian Afro-descendants Enrich their Identity" (Guillard Limonta), 238
LGBTI movement, 238–39
liberal arts, 50–51
liberalism, 42
Lima, Peru, 39–41
limpieza de sangre (blood purity), 90
Lisbon, Portugal, 30, 34–36
Lister, Joseph, 206n3
literacy, 82, 140–41n27
Livy, 20
Lope de Vega, 62, 65, 66–67
Lopes-Morales, Ernesto, 268
López de Úbeda, Francisco, 62, 64
los Reyes, Baltasar de, 51
Lowe, Kate, 52–53, 55, 56, 61
lundu (song and dance), 172, 173–74, 181–82, 184–85
"Lundú em louvor de uma brasileira adotiva" (Caldas Barbosa), 184–85
Lusíadas, Os (Camões), 176

Madrid, Spain, 54. See also Museo de América (Madrid)
Mair, Paulus Hector, 56, *58–60*
Malinoff, Jane, 181–82
Mandeville, John, 23
Mangache, Andrés, 152–53
Mangache, Juan, 157n4
Manifesto Antropofágico (Andrade), 187n4
Manrique Cabrera, Francisco, 64–65, 67, 68–69
Manuel I of Portugal, 31–32, 40
manumission, 151

Manzano, Juan Francisco, 216–17, 221–24
Maroon societies, 66–67, 143. See also *mulatos de Esmeraldas, Los* (Sánchez Gallque); *quilombos* (Maroon communities)
martial arts culture, 47. See also fencing
Martínez, Cristóbal, 53–54
Martínez Carmenate, Urbano, 223
Martínez Furé, Rogelio, 229–30, 234
masculinity, 154
mass incarceration, 252–53
Massinger, Philip, 49
Matos, Gregório de
  discrimination and, 161–62, 165–68, 186–87
  life and poetry of, 164–72
  posthumous publication of works by, 162–63
  "racialized identity" of, 186–87
  reception of, 164, 170–72
  Spanish baroque poetry and, 164–65, 167, 170
Mauss, Marcel, 150
mazombo, use of term, 187–88n6
McKittrick, Katherine, 277–78
medical care, 40–41. See also enslaved women's reproductive experiences
Medina Céspedes, Antonio, 216–17
Mello e Souza, Marina, 38–39
Mena Roelas, Gonzalo, 29–30
mestizaje, 272–73. See also miscegenation; mulattos
Mexico, 39–41, 42, 50
Mexico City, 39–41, 50
miedo al negro, el (fear of Blacks), 215–16, 217–21, 224–26
"miedo al negro, El" (Baquero), 215–16
Mignard, Pierre, 111–12, *114*
Miguel de Buría, 67
militante comunista, El (magazine), 229
"Miracle of the Black Leg," 98n40
Miramontes y Zuázola, Juan de, 67
"Mis treinta años" (Manzano), 223, 239n4

miscarriages, 192–93, 196–97
miscegenation, 250, 272–73. See also *mestizaje*; mulattos
modinha (song), 173–74, 185
Monáe, Janelle, 153–54
monogenesis, 132
Monte, Domingo del, 218, 222, 223–24, 227
Moore, Carlos, 233
Morato, Fernando Lima e, 181, 189n28
Morejón, Nancy, 234
Moreno, Isidro, 34
Moriscos, 46–47, 54, 69–70
motherhood, 202–3
movimento negro (Black Movement, Brazil), 245, 265–66, 267. See also Akoben movement
Movimento Negro Unificado (Unified Black Movement, MNU), 248, 260, 261n1
mulatos de Esmeraldas, Los (Sánchez Gallque)
  Afrofuturism and, 142–43, 153–56
  "discovery" of, 144–47
  history of, 142–44, *144*, 147–53
  Museo de América (Madrid) and, 142–43, *143*, 145–46
mulattos
  use of term, 149
  See also Caldas Barbosa, Domingos; *miedo al negro, el* (fear of Blacks); *mulatos de Esmeraldas, Los* (Sánchez Gallque)
Mulvey, Patricia, 32
Muñecas Marmontaño, Juan Ignacio de la, 51
Museo Arqueológico (Madrid), 144–45
Museo de América (Madrid), 142–43, *143*, 145–46
Museu Nacional (Rio de Janeiro), 282n34
music, 79–80. See also Brazilian hip hop; dance
My Bondage and My Freedom (Douglass), 19–20

Narrative of the Life of Frederick Douglass, an American Slave (Douglass), 130–31, *132*
Nascimento, Abdias, 247, 255, 260, 279n4, 280n11
Nascimento, Beatriz, 279n4
National Folk Ensemble (Cuba), 227
National Seminary of Dramaturgy (Cuba), 227
Navarro, José Gabriel, 144–45, 156n1
navios negreiros (slave ships), 251–53
necropolitics, 265
negritude, 248
"Negrofobia" (Fraginals), 217–18
Neiba, Mácsimo Hero de, 216–17
Nelson, Alondra, 154
Nicholas of Mount Calvary, 32
Nicolas V, Pope, 85
Niemeyer, Oscar, 188n18

Obras completas de Gregório de Matos (Matos), 163
Oliveira, Dory, 254–55
Olmedo Gobante, Manuel, 65
Ordóñez de Ceballos, Pedro, 49
Ortiz, Fernando, 96n4
Otovo, Okezi, 205
Our Lady of the Rosary, 35

Pacheco de Narváez, Luis, 49, 51, 53, 61–62, 64–65, 68–69
Paes, Eduardo, 268
Palomino, Antonio, 123–25
Pan-Africanism, 245–46, 247
Paniagua, Carlos Miguel de, 82–92, 95
"Pânico na Zona Sul" (song), 249
"Para una teoría de la literatura hispanoamericana" (Fernández Retamar), 241–42n34
Pardue, Derek, 245, 246–47, 248, 255–56, 257
Pareja, Juan de, 122–26, *123*, 127–28
Pasteur, Louis, 206n3
Patterson, Enrique, 217
Patterson, Orlando, 92

paturi (dance), 171–72
Pedagogies of Crossing (Alexander), 270–71
Pedro, Alberto, 234
Pedro, Master, 52
Pedro Simón, Fray, 67
Peixoto, Afrânio, 163
Penitential Tyrant, The (Branagan), 104, *106*
Pereira Passos, Francisco, 267, 275
Peres, Fernando da Rocha, 164
Pérez Sarduy, Pedro, 234, 243–44n41
periferias (working class outskirts), 247, 248–50. See also Brazilian hip hop
Perry, Imani, 154, 248
Peru, 39–41, 42, 74n47
Philip III, King of Spain, 69–70, 145, 147–48, 150, 154–55
Phillips, William, 34
photography, 105–7
physical pain, 194–95, 196–201, 203–5
pícara Justina, La (López de Úbeda?), 62, 64
picaresque novels, 62–64
Pignatary, Décio, 188n18
Pilamunga, Diego, 158n13
Plácido (Gabriel de la Concepción Valdés), 216–17, 221–24
Poemas escolhidos de Gregório de Matos (Matos), 172
Poems by a Slave in the Island of Cuba (Manzano), 239n4
Pointon, Marcia, 118
polygenesis, 132–33
Portocarrero y Meneses, Juliana Teresa, Duchess of Arcos, 82, 89–90
Portrait d'une négresse (later *Portrait d'une femme noire*; *Portrait de Madeleine*) (Benoist), 122–23, *124*, 126–28
portraiture. See enslaved faces in portraiture
Portugal
    Afro-Iberian confraternities in, 30, 34–38, *37*
    Black swordsmen in, 52
    slave voyages and, 12–13
    See also slave voyage and auction in Lagos, Portugal (1444)

Portuguese language, 161–63, 170–71, 172, 174. *See also* Caldas Barbosa, Domingos; Matos, Gregório de
Posse Mente Zulu, 245–46
post-occidentalism, 241–42n34
Prado, Caio, Jr., 166–67
Prestes Filho, Luiz Carlos, 275
Princess Henrietta of Lorraine (van Dyck), 111–12, *113*
prison system, 252–53
prodigio de Etiopia, El (Lope de Vega), 66
Prophets from the Hood (Perry), 248
"Psicopretas Vol. 1" (song), 247–48, 253–55, 258–60
Puente, El (literary group), 242–43n40

Queen of Sheba, 32
Queens, Les, 254
Quevedo, Francisco de, 62–64, 164–65, 170
Quijano, Aníbal, 149–50
Quilombhoje, 248, 260
quilombismo, 246–48, 260
"Quilombismo: An Afro-Brazilian Political Alternative" (Nascimento), 247
Quilombo (1984 film), 266–67
quilombolas, 247, 258–59
quilombos (Maroon communities), 245–46, 247, 255–60, 270

race, as social category, 149–50
racial democracy, 250, 265–66, 272–73
racial profiling, 47
Racionais MCs, 249
Radio Free Dixie, 242–43n40
Ramos, Arthur, 272
rap music. *See* Brazilian hip hop
rebated swords (*espadas negras*), 48, 54
Redondo, Augustin, 22–23
Rennó, Adriana, 175
Ribeiro dos Santos, Antonio, 185
Ribeiro Guimarães, José, 34
Ribera, Bernardo de, 92

Ribera, Manuel Bernardo de, 84
Rincon Sapiência (Danilo Albert Ambrosio), 247–48, 256–58
Rio de Janeiro, Brazil
    enslaved women's reproductive experiences in, 191–93, 196–206
    tourism economy and, 265–66, 268–69, 274–77
    Valongo Wharf in, 267–71, 274–77
Robinson, Cedric, 261n7
Roblejo, Manuel, 216–17
Rodrigues, Raimundo Nina, 250–51, 271–72
Rodríguez, Fernando, 218–20
Rodríguez, Gabriel, 84
Romani people, 79
Romeo and Juliet (Shakespeare), 49
Romero, Sílvio, 170, 174, 272
Roque, 52
Rosales, Miguel Angel, 79–80, 95
Rueda Novoa, Rocío, 151
Rufián dichoso, El (Cervantes), 65
runaway slaves, 129, 151
Russell, Peter, 22

Saco, José Antonio, 218, 227
Sagarana (1974 film), 266–67
Sagrada Congregación de Propaganda Fide (later Sagrada Congregación para la Evangelización de los Pueblos), 85
Salas, Juan de, 157n4
Saloia namorada ou o remédio a casar, A (Caldas Barbosa), 175
samba, 172, 272
Sánchez Gallque, Andrés. *See mulatos de Esmeraldas, Los* (Sánchez Gallque)
Sánchez Jiménez, Antonio, 66, 67
Sandoval, Alonso de, 40
santo negro Rosambuco, El (Lope de Vega), 65
Santos Morillo, Antonio, 62
São Paulo, 248–49

Sátiras y otras maledicencias (Matos), 171
Savage, Edward, 118–19, *120*
Sawaya, Luiza, 175, 181
Saxton, Jared, 160n36
Scarry, Elaine, 200
Schmidt-Linsenhoff, Viktoria, 126
Schomburg, Arturo, 11, 25–26
scientific racism, 107, 131–35, *133*, *135*, 202–6, 249–51
second slavery, 139–40n24
senzalas (slave quarters), 247, 248–55
Serres, Étienne-Reynaud-Augustin, 141n30
Seville, Spain
   Afro-Iberian confraternities in, 29–30, 34, 42
   curros in, 80
   fencing in, 51
   Schomburg in, 11
   as slave port, 13, 30
sexual exploitation, 94
Shakespeare, William, 49
Shakur, Assata, 81–82
Sheels, Christopher, 118–19, *120*
Sherwin, Samuel, 129
Silver, George, 49
Slave and Citizen (Tannenbaum), 139–40n24
slave narratives, 130–31, *132*. See also Douglass, Frederick
slave ships and voyages, 12–13, 104, *105*, 251–53. See also slave voyage and auction in Lagos, Portugal (1444)
slave societies, 34, 155
slave uprisings, 220–21. See also Conspiracy of La Escalera; Haitian Revolution
slave voyage and auction in Lagos, Portugal (1444)
   Barros's account of, 20–24, 25–26
   Lançarote da Ilha and, 13–15, 21, 23
   las Casas's account of, 23–26
   Zurara's account of, 14–21, 23–24, 26

Slave Voyages (database), 12
slaveness, 160n36
slavery
   disposal of corpses of, 31–32
   emotional history of, 193–94
   See also enslaved body; enslaved faces in portraiture; *senzalas* (slave quarters)
Smalls, James, 126, 127
Sociedade de Medicina do Rio de Janeiro (Society of Medicine of Rio de Janeiro), 192
sociedades de negros (Black societies), 42
Society of Medicine of Rio de Janeiro (Sociedade de Medicina do Rio de Janeiro), 192
"Sou Negrão" (song), 245–46
Sousa Viterbo, Francisco Marqués de, 52
sovereignty, 154–55
Spain
   Black and Afro-descendant population of, 11–12, 25–26, 30, 79–80
   slave voyages and, 12–13
   See also Verdadera Destreza (Spanish fencing); *specific cities*
Spivak, Gayatri, 220
Stella, Alessandro, 11–12
stillbirth, 192–93
Suite para Juan Francisco Manzano (Friol), 221–22
Surrender of Brede, The (*Las lanzas*) (Velázquez), 146
Swanenburgh, Willem, 50
syncretism, 36–39
Szászdi, A., 156n1

Talhoffer, Hans, 56, *57*
Tannenbaum, Frank, 139–40n24
Taylor, Ula, 196
Taylor, William B., 142
Teatro Experimental do Negro, 248
technology, 151, 154–55
Telles, Lorena, 201
Teresa de Bourbon, 267

Tesoro de la lengua castellana o española (Covarrubias), 91–92
Thaíde, 246
Thiesson, E., 141n30
Tinhorão, José Ramos, 175, 181
Tirant lo Blanc (chivalric romance), 22
Titian, 109–12, *110*, 119
Toledo, Antonio Sebastián de, Marquis of Mancera, 82, 89–90
Toller, Heloisa, 183
Tomich, Dale, 139–40n24
Torre, Bernabé de la, 84
Torre, Pedro, 62
Torres, Francisco de la, 65
Tortorici, Zeb, 198–99
tourism economy, 265–66, 268–69, 273–77
Trumbull, John, 112–18, *115*
Turner, Sasha, 193
Tuskegee Syphilis Experiment (1932–1972), 98n40

Úbeda, Spain, 46
umbigada (dance), 172
Unified Black Movement (Movimento Negro Unificado, MNU), 248, 260, 261n1
Urban Anthropology, 268
Urban VIII, Pope, 85
Uruguay, 42
Usillos, Gutiérrez, 151

Valencia, Spain, 30
Valerio, Miguel, 181, 189n28
valiente negro en Flandes, El (Claramonte), 65
Valongo Wharf (Rio de Janeiro), 267–71, 274–77
Vargas, Getúlio, 272
Vargas, João, 248–49
Vargas, Martín de, 54
Varnhagen, Francisco Adolfo de, 162–63
Vasari, Giorgio, 109

Vasconcelos e Sousa family, 173, 176–77, 183
Vega, Inca Garcilaso de la, 149
Velázquez, Diego, 51, 122–26, *123*, 127–28, 146
Vella, 52
Venancia (enslaved woman), 204–5
Venice, 109–11
Verdadera Destreza (Spanish fencing)
  participation of Afro-Hispanics in, 51–55, 67, 69
  as philosophical and cultural movement, 50–51
  representation of Afro-Hispanics and, 61, 63
  as style of fencing, 49–50, *50*
Vergara y Azcárate, Cayetano, 84
Veríssimo, José, 170, 173–74
Vexy Thing (Perry), 154
viajantes ditosos, Os (Caldas Barbosa), 175
Vianna, Bisa, 267
Vigée-Lebrun, Elisabeth, 126
Villaverde, Cirilo, 96n4
vingança da cigana, A (Caldas Barbosa), 175
Viola de Lereno (Caldas Barbosa), 163–64, 174, 181, 184–85
violence, 149, 152–53, 154–55
Virgil, 176
viscerality, 198–99

Wakanda, 145, 153–54, 155
Wallis, Brian, 133–34
war, 155
Washington, George, 112–19, *115*, *120*
Washington, Martha, 118–19, *120*
Washington Family, The (Savage), 118–19, *120*
Weems, Carrie Mae, 134–35, *135*
Weston, Helen, 126
Wilderson, Frank B. III, 81–82, 160n36
Williams, Robert F., 233
Wisnik, José, 172

Wolof people (*negros jolofos*), 14, 46–47, 69–70
women
  hip hop music and, 253–55, 258–60
  sexual exploitation of, 94
  See also enslaved women's reproductive experiences

Z'África Brasil, 247–48, 249–51, 258, 260
zambos de Esmeraldas, Los (Sánchez Gallque). See *mulatos de Esmeraldas, Los* (Sánchez Gallque)
Zealy, Joseph T., 131–32, *132*, 133–35
Zumbi dos Palmares, 245–46, 258–59
Zurara, Gomes Eanes de, 14–21, 23–24, 26

www.ingramcontent.com/pod-product-compliance
Lightning Source LLC
Chambersburg PA
CBHW051210300426
44116CB00006B/500